HERON DERIVATION DICTIONARY

HERON DERIVATION DICTIONARY

A Quick Reference for English Language Derivations

Published by
Heron Books, Inc.
20950 SW Rock Creek Road
Sheridan, OR 97378

heronbooks.com

Fifth Edition © 1995, 2020 Heron Books
All Rights Reserved

ISBN: 978-0-89-739206-8

No part of this publication may be produced without the permission of the copyright owner. Any unauthorized copying, translation, duplication or distribution, in whole or in part, by any means, including electronic copying, storage or transmission, is a violation of applicable laws.

The Heron Books name and the heron bird symbol are registered trademarks of Delphi Schools, Inc.

Printed in the USA

14 December 2020

Contents

Introduction to the 5th Edition

This dictionary was originally created for middle and high school students learning the value of derivations in understanding words. Its 11,447 entries came from a comprehensive list of recommended books for teen readers, from *Old Yeller, A Wrinkle in Time* and *The Yearling* all the way up to Dickens' *David Copperfield,* Voltaire's *Candide* and Plato's *Republic.* As dictionaries for younger readers did not always include derivations or had overly sophisticated derivations, the *Heron Derivation Dictionary* filled a need.

Within a few years, the book's popularity was found to extend beyond teens, and this has remained true since the first edition was published in 1995.

This new edition retains all the original entries with some minor adjustments, while getting an overhaul in design and readability. The intention has always been to provide uncomplicated, easily assimilated derivations. That remains unchanged.

Whether you are a teen or a reader of any age, we hope you find this new edition useful. Our wish is simple: to enhance the pleasures available to those who enjoy a good read.

Why This Dictionary?

This dictionary is all about beginnings.

A *derivation* is where something came from, its beginning. The wheelbarrow, we think, was created by a Chinese general almost 2000 years ago to carry military supplies. That's its derivation. Every object or idea has some kind of derivation. Words do too.

The word *muscle*, for example, has a derivation. Flex your upper arm and look at your bicep. What does it look like? Some Roman did this and gave birth to the word we now know as *muscle*, which meant "little mouse" in Latin, the language of the Ancient Romans.

More recently, the creators of Instagram needed a name for their photo-sharing app. They took the words "instant camera" and "telegram" and came up with the name: Instagram. Some word derivations are centuries old. Some are quite new.

Exploring the meanings of words is one of the great joys of learning. When learning about a word, you might also wonder:

> Why do we say this word for that idea?
>
> Where was it first used this way?
>
> Why is it pronounced or spelled this way?
>
> Does this word come from some other language?
>
> Is it really old?
>
> What was the word back then and what did it mean in that time and place?

Virus, for example, is another word that comes to us from Latin. From ancient records, one discovers the word was first used by some Roman roughly 2500 years ago. It meant "poison" or "slimy liquid." It was useful in describing certain things, so others started using it and soon it was part of the language. Over the centuries, the word *virus* has moved forward in time, making its way into English as we speak and write it today—which we call Modern English.

Here's another word story.

The English word *vinegar* began as the Latin words *vinum aigre,* "wine that is soured." *Vinum* meant "wine," *aigre* meant "sour." Later the French combined these into *vinaigre* to describe "sour wine." English speakers borrowed that word and changed it to *vinegar.* There are many types of vinegar today but making a red wine vinegar isn't hard: just open a bottle of red wine and leave it for several days. You might not like the taste, but you will have made vinegar.

This simple derivation can help you understand the word vinegar better. And that's why this dictionary was created:

To help you explore the beginnings of words,
their derivations.

Reading Derivations

Every word listed in a dictionary is called an entry. This book has 11,480 entries, each with a derivation.

As you look at these derivations, you will find them short and to the point. Many derivations have fun and fascinating stories behind them, and there are books and websites that share these well. This dictionary just gives derivations, as simply as possible.

To help you understand how to read the derivations, let's look at a few sample entries.

> **bold** OLD ENGLISH *beald* brave.

Old English was the earliest form of English. The Old English word *beald* meant "brave." Over time, this word changed to become our Modern English word *bold.*

> **virus** LATIN poison, slimy liquid.

In this derivation, no Latin word is given. This is because the Latin word is the same as the modern English word. Compare this with the previous example, where the Old English word *beald*, being different from the modern word, is given.

> **grin** OLD ENGLISH *grennian.*

In this example, no meaning is given for the original Old English word. This is because the meaning hasn't changed.

> **peel** FRENCH *peler* take off, from LATIN *pilare* make bald, from *pilus* hair.

When a word has traveled through different languages, the derivation will often show this. In this case, the word came from Latin to French, then into English. First was the Latin word *pilus,* meaning "*hair.*" Later someone used this to create the Latin word *pilare,* meaning "making something bald." The French changed the spelling and meaning a bit. From there it arrived to English as *peel.*

active See **act**.

This means the derivation of the word "active" is essentially the same as the derivation of the word "act." By going to the entry "act," you will find a derivation that applies to both words.

act Latin *agere* to do.

At the back of the book is a list of the languages included in the word derivations in this dictionary. Below some of these is a sub-list of related languages you may run into in other dictionaries. Whereas another dictionary might say "from French, from Old French," for simplicity this dictionary will just say "from French."

You will also find a world map. Noted on it, for the sake of orientation, are the locations where all the languages included in the derivations in this dictionary have been or are used. It shows locations only; it doesn't differentiate relative time periods.

Lastly, a full glossary is given in the back. It provides explanations of many different languages, including all of those referenced in this dictionary, as well as many often found in other dictionaries. This can help if you find yourself in a larger dictionary running into languages or other derivation-related terminology you aren't familiar with.

A quick glance at the map or glossary will usually provide you with all the information you need.

A Brief History of English

BEFORE ENGLISH WAS BORN

Though English is spoken today by millions of people around the world, it was born on an island called Britannia, later Britain.

Today Britain is the home of England, Scotland and Wales.

For hundreds of years this island was the home of a people called the Britons. Around 43 CE, however, as part of expanding their empire, the Romans invaded and took control of the island.

They introduced many changes, including the development of organized towns and proper roads for travelling between them. For nearly four hundred years they protected the island from further invasions, until the Roman Empire began to fall apart. By 410 CE, Britain was no longer protected by the power of the Roman army and its soldiers.

Soon invading tribes began arriving on Britain's shores. The largest of these were two tribes called the Angles and the Saxons, from parts of what we now call Denmark and Germany.

Marauding warriors and pirates, they seized land and wealth, making the island theirs.

The Britons retreated to Ireland and Wales and with them went the language that had been used in Britain for hundreds of years.

Scotland
Denmark
Angles
Saxons
England
Wales
Germany

THE BIRTH OF OLD ENGLISH
Anglo-Saxon, 450 - 1100 CE

The Angles and Saxons spoke a completely different language than the Britons. They were a rougher people and their language sounded that way. Sometimes we refer to their language as *Anglo-Saxon*. They called it *Englisc,* and gradually it became the language spoken throughout Britain by both peasants and kings.

This was how English was born.

Old English (*old* meaning the first English spoken) is another name used for Anglo-Saxon. In this dictionary, all Anglo-Saxon words will simply be called *Old English.*

Many of the words we use today come directly from Old English, even simple words like *I, he, she, you, we, where, who* and *when.* Even the word *England* comes from "Angle-land."

It was a fairly simple but lively and descriptive language. It had a lot of short, punchy words, thousands of which we still use.

MOON
north
GLOW
cat
pig
arrow
friend
break
jump
OWL
kiss
RED
queen
laugh
year
raven
GHOST
NAME
BLOOD
CHILD
dog
FIGHT
ACORN
free
hook
SCAB
MOTHER
bruise
EARTH
hand
heaven

THE VIKING INFLUENCE
Old Norse, 800 CE

About four hundred years after the Anglo-Saxon invasion, from the northernmost parts of Europe came new seafaring pirates and traders called Vikings. These new invaders, also called Norsemen, landed in the north of England.

They spoke a language we call *Old Norse.*

For the next 200 years there were continuous battles between the Anglo-Saxons and the Vikings. Naturally some Old Norse words got picked up and added into Old English.

Here are a few words that originally came from Old Norse.

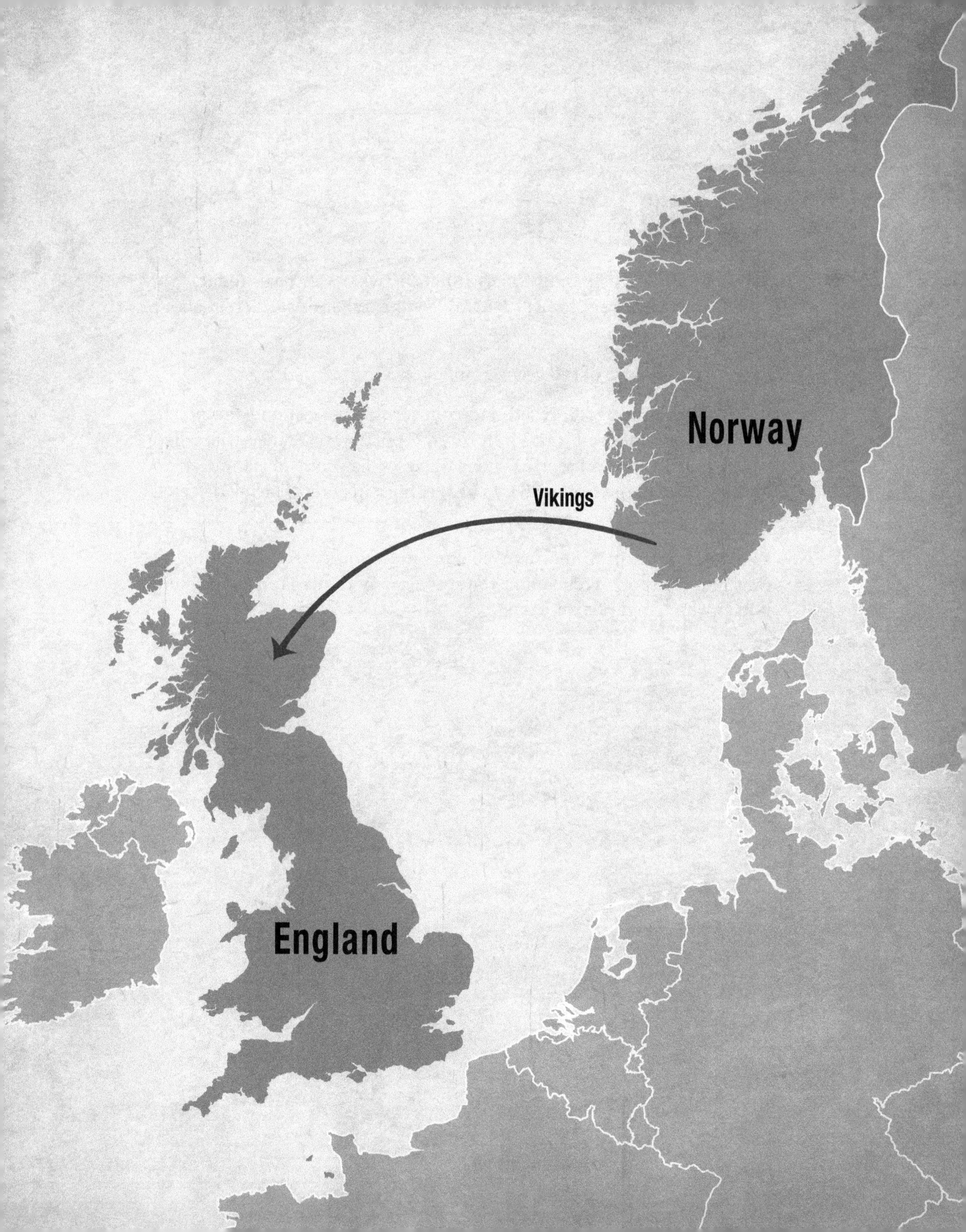
Norway
Vikings
England

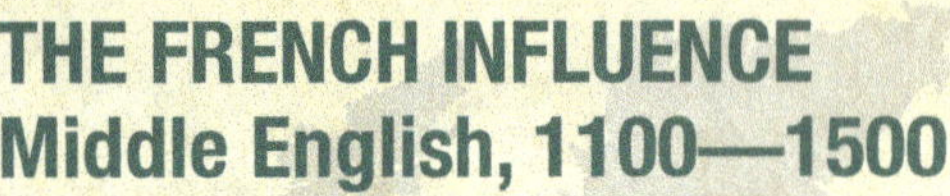

THE FRENCH INFLUENCE
Middle English, 1100—1500

Between Old English and Modern English (what we speak today) is a period of the language we call *Middle English*. What was different about Middle English?

It was the influence of the French language.

Previous invasions of England had come from the east and the north. This time it came from the south, from a portion of France still called Normandy. In 1066 a French Duke named William of Normandy led an invasion, and in the famous Battle of Hastings, his French army defeated the Anglo-Saxons.

William, known in history as William the Conqueror, became King of England. He spoke French and rewarded many of his French-speaking nobles with Anglo-Saxon land.

The Anglo-Saxon peasants resented William and his French-speaking aristocrats and never stopped speaking their own tongue. As a result, there came to be two words in use for many things, an English word and a French one: for examples, *cow* and *beef, ask* and *question, hide* and *conceal.*

Over time, the language became a mixture of Anglo-Saxon and French, what we now call Middle English.

Here are some of the words that came from French, all as a result of the Norman invasion and William taking over the throne.

THE GREEK AND LATIN INFLUENCE
Modern English, 1500 – present day

The next major development of the English language came with the invention of the printing press in 1440. With increasing numbers of printed books available and being shared, many people in Europe began to discover the writings of the great Ancient Greek and Roman civilizations. Knowledge started to spread like wildfire. This time came to be known as the Renaissance, or "rebirth" (see derivation in this dictionary) of the ideas of Ancient Greece and Rome, ideas which had largely been lost in Europe for centuries.

With this dramatic change came new words. People learning to read and write ancient Greek and Latin found words they liked and brought them directly into English. Then they created even more new words by combining parts of Greek and Latin words.

Here are just a few examples of words that entered English at this time:

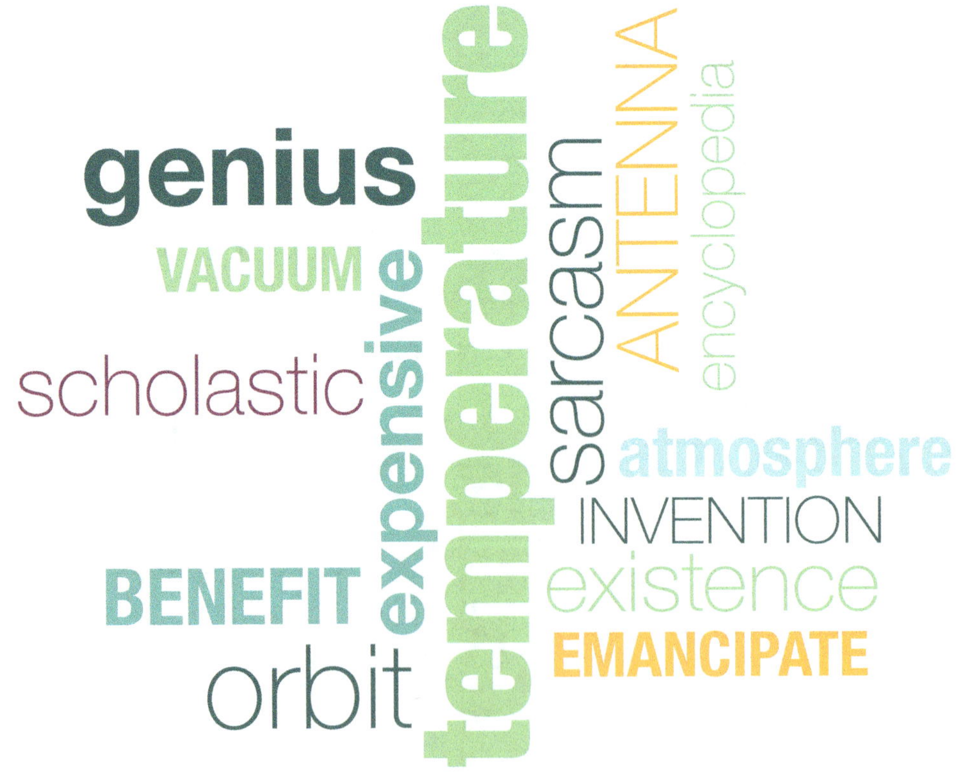

THE INFLUENCE OF LITERATURE
Modern English

With the addition of so many new words during the Renaissance, English became more expressive and literature flowered. William Shakespeare (1564 – 1616) liked to invent colorful and expressive words, and through his plays and poems added over 200 of these to English. Believe it or not, this one man added the following words to the language, not to mention many others.

Amazingly, other writers added even more!

Here are a few more common words that came from literature:

fragrance .... from the poem *Paradise Lost* by John Milton in 1667
(scent, usually pleasant)

butterfinger .... from *The Pickwick Papers* by Charles Dickens in 1836
(person who drops things)

MUNCHKIN .... from *The Wonderful Wizard of Oz* by L. Frank Baum in 1900
(small, likable child)

nerd .... from *If I Ran the Zoo* by Dr Seuss in 1950
(person who studies too much and lacks social skills)

grok .... from *Stranger in a Strange Land* by Robert Heinlein in 1961
(to understand deeply)

There are thousands of words that settled into the language because a writer made them up. Readers liked the word, used it and it became part of English.

THE INFLUENCE OF EXPLORATION AND TRADE
Modern English

As English exploration and trade grew, merchants brought back not only goods but new words as well. Words like *cigar, tomato, chocolate, rodeo* and *tornado* came from Spain. Musical terms came from Italy along with words like *pizza, spaghetti, broccoli* and *balloon.* From Germany came words like *hamburger, pretzel* and *kindergarten.*

As English moved to America, Native American words found their way into the language. Many were names of places and geographical features, but also everyday words.

With the world becoming more and more connected, English has acquired words from all over, like *burrito, igloo, leprechaun, boomerang, zombie, robot, mosquito, limousine, cashew* and *coconut,* to name just a few. And with the growth of technology and social media, more English words are being created all the time, words like *selfie, blog, screen time, smartphone, hashtag, e-bike*, and so many more.

TODAY AND TOMORROW
Modern English

English is now spoken by more than 25% of the world's population and is the language of international business and the internet. The development of Modern English will continue to be a fascinating story of growth and change—always reflecting the interests, activities, ideas and experiences of the people who speak it.

So, thanks to Native Americans, Shakespeare and Spaniards, you can now go find a *hammock*, relax and enjoy a *zany* book—with a delicious piece of dark *chocolate.*

A SIMPLIFIED TIMELINE
of the English Language

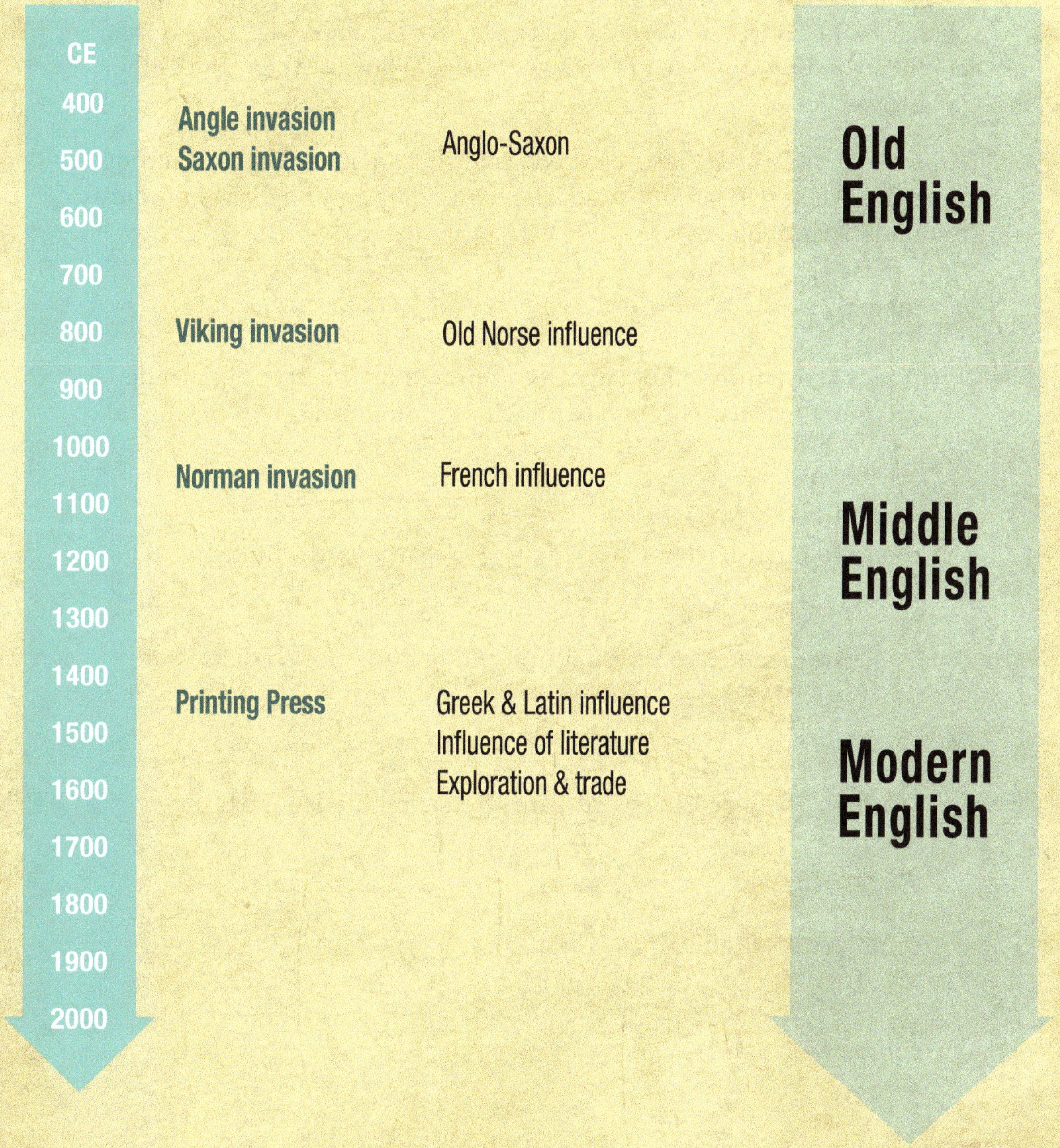

CE	Event	Influence	Period
400	Angle invasion		
500	Saxon invasion	Anglo-Saxon	Old English
600			
700			
800	Viking invasion	Old Norse influence	
900			
1000	Norman invasion	French influence	
1100			Middle English
1200			
1300			
1400	Printing Press	Greek & Latin influence	
1500		Influence of literature	Modern English
1600		Exploration & trade	
1700			
1800			
1900			
2000			

How English Builds Its Vocabulary

The more you explore derivations, the more you realize how languages change over time.

English, like any other language, is a living, growing thing. As a culture changes and grows, so does its language. People make up new words, combine existing words to create new ones, and borrow them from other languages.

Knowing how words have entered English can make understanding words and their derivations easier. Here are eight ways English continues to build its vocabulary.

1. BORROWED

Words arrive from other languages through invasions, travel, trade, and more recently, through worldwide communication in the digital age.

ketchup
comes to English from Chinese *ke-tsiap,* sauce used with fish

roster
comes from Dutch *rooster*, a list or grid of duties for soldiers

2. COMBINED

Words, or even parts of words, are often combined to make a new word.

applesauce
combines *apple* and *sauce*

livestream
combines *live* and *stream*

3. EXPANDED

A prefix or suffix can be added to an existing word, expanding it and making a new word. English has thousands of words like this.

rethink

adds the prefix *re-* (again) to the word *think*

merrily

adds the suffix *-ly* (in a _____ way) to the word *merry*

4. SHORTENED

Words can be shortened, abbreviated or turned into acronyms (words formed from the first letters of a phrase).

fridge

is now a word for *refrigerator*

vs

is an abbreviation for *versus* and is now often used without a period

BFF

(best friends forever) is now a word found in most dictionaries

5. NEW DEFINITIONS

Often new words aren't new, they just have new definitions or find use as a different part of speech.

surf

is now something you can do on the internet as well as on ocean waves

Google

was the name of a company that then became a verb ("google it")

6. SOUND IMITATION

Many words are made by imitating a sound.

hiss
is a word describing a sound like that of a snake

boom
is a word describing the sound of an explosion

7. NAME STEALING

The most famous example of a word coming directly from a name is *sandwich*, from the name of its inventor, the Earl of Sandwich.

diesel
comes from the name of a German inventor, Rudolf Diesel

granola
was a brand name over a hundred years ago

8. INVENTION

Lastly, many words are just made up. Sometimes they become popular and part of the language. Sometimes they just die away. Often it's nearly impossible to find out who used it first.

nifty, puzzle and **gimmick**
are words invented by unknown people in history

Want to make up a word? Maybe you already have. If you can popularize it, it just might end up in a dictionary. And that's a word you will already know the derivation for!

DERIVATIONS

a Old English *an* one, an.

a-[1] Old English *an, on* in, on, at, out of.

a-[2] Greek *a-, an-* not.

aardvark Afrikaans earth pig, from *aard* earth + *vark* pig.

ab- Latin *ab-*, from, away, down.

aback Old English *onbæc.*

abacus Latin counting board, from Greek *abax*, probably from Hebrew *abaq* dust. The early abacus was a board covered with dust or sand, on which figures could be drawn and then brushed away.

abalone Native American *aulun.*

abandon French *mettre a bandon* put under someone else's power.

abase French *abaisser* to lower, from Latin *ad-* to + *bassus* low.

abash French *abaiss*, from *esbahir*, from Latin *ex-* out + *bahir* open wide.

abate French *abattre* beat down, from Latin *ad-* to + *battuere* strike.

abatis French *abateis,* from Latin *abateticius* throwing down.

abattoir See **abate**.

abbey French *abbaie* monastery (place where monks live), from Latin *abbatissa*, office of an abbot.

abbot Old English *abbod*, from Latin *abbas*, from Greek, from Semitic *abba* father.

abbreviate Latin *abbreviatus, ab-* from + *brevis* short.

abdicate Latin *abdicare,* from *ab-* off + *dicare* to announce.

abdomen Latin belly.

abduct Latin *abductus*, from *ab-* away + *ducere* lead.

aberrant Latin *aberrare*, from *ab-* from + *errare* wander.

abet French *abeter* to excite, from *a-* to + *beter* bait (tease).

abeyance French *abeance,* from *abauer,* from *a-* at + *bayer* gape (stare at with the mouth open).

abhor Latin *abhorrere* shrink back from, from *ab-* away + *horrere* have the hair stand on end.

abide Old English *abidan*, from *a-* completely + *bidan* remain.

ability French *ablete*, from Latin *habilis* easy to handle, from *habere* have.

abject Latin *abjicere,* from *ab-* away + *jacere* throw.

abjure LATIN *abjurare,* from *ab-* away + *jurare* swear.

ablative LATIN *ablatus,* from *auferre ab-* away + *ferre* bring.

able FRENCH *ablete,* from LATIN *habilis* easy to handle, from *habere* have.

-able FRENCH, from LATIN *-abilis.*

ablution LATIN *abluere,* from *ab-* off + *luere* lave (wash away).

abnegate LATIN *abnegare,* from *ab-* away + *negare* deny.

abnormal FRENCH *anormal,* from LATIN *abnormis,* from *ab-* away + *norma* carpenter's square, rule.

abode See **abide**.

abolish FRENCH, from LATIN *abolotio,* from *abolere* destroy.

abominate LATIN *abominari* think of as a bad omen.

aborigine LATIN *ab-* from + *origine* the beginning.

abort LATIN *aboriri* miscarry.

abound FRENCH *abonder,* from LATIN *abundare* overflow, from *ab-* from + *unda* wave.

about OLD ENGLISH *abutan,* from *a-* to + *butan* outside.

above OLD ENGLISH *abufan,* from *a-* to + *bufan* above.

abracadabra LATIN.

abrade LATIN, from *abradere,* from *ab-* away + *radere* scrape.

abreast See **a-**[1] + **breast**.

abridge FRENCH *abregie,* from LATIN *abbreviare,* from *ab-* to + *errare* wander.

abrogate LATIN *abrogare* repeal, from *ab-* away + *rogare* propose.

abrupt LATIN *abrumpere,* from *ab-* away + *rumpere* break.

abscess LATIN *abscidere,* from *ab(s)-* from + *cedere* go.

abscond LATIN *abscondere,* from *ab(s)-* from + *condere* hide.

absent LATIN *abasense,* from *ab-* away + *esse* be.

absolute MIDDLE ENGLISH *absolut* from LATIN *absolutus,* freed, acquitted, finished, from *absolvere,* set free, acquit. See **absolve**.

absolution MIDDLE ENGLISH from LATIN *absolutio,* from *absolvere.* See **absolve**.

absolve LATIN *absolvere* set free, acquit, from *ab-* from + *solvere* loosen.

absorb LATIN *absorbere,* from *ab-* from + *sorbere* drink.

abstain FRENCH *abstenir* refrain from, from LATIN *abstinere* withhold, from *ab-* from + *tenere* hold.

abstinence See **abstain**.

abstract LATIN *abstrahere* draw away from, from *ab-* away from + *trahere* draw.

abstruse LATIN *abstrudere,* from *ab-* away + *trudere* thrust.

absurd LATIN *absurdus* not to be heard of, from *ab-* away + *surdus* dull, deaf.

abundance FRENCH plenty, from LATIN *abundare* overflow, from *ab-* from + *unda* wave.

abuse FRENCH *abuser* misuse, from LATIN *abuti,* from *ab-* away + *uti* use.

abut FRENCH *aboter,* from LATIN *a-* to + *bout* end.

abutment See **abut** + **-ment**.

abyss LATIN *abyssus* bottomless pit, from GREEK *abussos*, from *a-* without + *byssos* bottom.

acacia LATIN, from GREEK *akakia* thorny tree.

academy FRENCH *academie*, from GREEK *akademia* a grove near Athens which became the place for Plato's (a famous Greek philosopher) Academy.

acappella ITALIAN singing in a chapel style, from LATIN *ad-* to + *capella* chapel.

accede LATIN *accedere,* from *ad-* to + *cedere* go.

accelerate LATIN *accelerare*, from *ad-* to + *celerare* hasten, from *celer* quick.

accent FRENCH proper speaking manner, from LATIN *ad-* to + *cantus* song added to speech.

accept LATIN *acceptare* receive, from *ad-* to + *capere* take.

access LATIN *accedere*, from *ad-* to + *cedere* go.

accessory LATIN *accedere,* from *ad-* to + *cedere* go.

accident LATIN *accidens* chance, from *ad-* to + *cadere* fall.

acclaim LATIN *acclamare* shout applause.

accolade FRENCH, from ITALIAN *accollare* to embrace, from LATIN *ad-* to + *collum* neck.

accommodate LATIN *accommodare* to fit with, from *ad-* to + *commodus* convenient.

accompany FRENCH *a-* to + *compaignon* comrade. See **companion**.

accomplish FRENCH *accomplier* to complete, from LATIN *ad-* to + *complere* complete.

accord FRENCH *accorder* to agree, from LATIN *ad-* to + *cor* heart.

accordion ITALIAN *accordare* be in tune.

accost FRENCH, from ITALIAN, from LATIN *accoster,* from *ad-* to + *costa* rib, side.

account FRENCH *acompter* to count up, from *a-* to + *conter* tell, from LATIN *computare.* See **compute**.

accouter FRENCH *acostrer*, from LATIN *ad-* to + *consuere* sew together.

accretion LATIN *accrescere,* from *ad-* to + *crescere* grow.

accrue FRENCH increase, from *accreistre,* from LATIN *accrescere*, from *ad-* to + *crescere* grow.

accumulate LATIN *accumulare*, from *ad-* to + *cumulare* pile up.

accurate LATIN *accurare*, from *ad-* to + *cura* care.

accurse OLD ENGLISH *cursian* curse.

accuse FRENCH *acuser*, from LATIN *accusare,* from *ad-* to + *causa* a cause.

accustom FRENCH *acostumer* become used to, from *à-* to + *costume* habit.

ace FRENCH *as,* from LATIN unit.

acerbate LATIN *acerbare* make harsh or bitter.

acetonaemia **acetone** + GREEK *(h)aimia* blood.

acetone LATIN *acetum* vinegar.

acetylene See **acetone** + **-ene**.

ache OLD ENGLISH *acan.*

achieve FRENCH *achever* complete, succeed, accomplish, from *à chef* at an end.

acid LATIN *acidus* sour.

acknowledge See **knowledge**.

acme GREEK *akme* a point, top.

acne LATIN, from GREEK *akme* point, top.

acolyte LATIN, from GREEK *akolouthos* follower.

aconite FRENCH *aconit*, from LATIN *aconitum*, from GREEK *akoniton.*

acorn OLD ENGLISH *æcern.*

acoustic FRENCH *acuostique,* from GREEK *akoustikos,* from *akouein* hear.

acquaint FRENCH *acointier,* from LATIN *adcognitare* to make known, from *ad-* to + *cognoscere* know.

acquiesce FRENCH, from LATIN *acquiescere,* from *ad-* to + *quiescere* to keep quiet, from *quies* rest.

acquire LATIN *acquirere* to get in addition, from *ad-* to + *quaere* seek.

acquit FRENCH *aqujiter* to set free, from LATIN *acquitare* to settle a claim, from *ad-* to + *quietare* quiet.

acre OLD ENGLISH *æcer* field.

acrid LATIN *acris* bitter.

acriflavine LATIN *acris* bitter + *flavis* yellow.

acrimony LATIN *acer* sharp.

acrobat FRENCH *acrobate,* from GREEK *akrobatos* walking on tiptoe, from *akros* high point + *bainen* go.

acronym GREEK *akros* at the end or top + *onyma* name.

acropolis GREEK *akropolis,* from *aktos* top + *polis* city.

across FRENCH *à croix* in the form of a cross.

acrostic FRENCH *acrostiche,* from GREEK *akrostichis,* from *akros* at the end + *stichos* line of poetry.

act LATIN *agere* do.

actinobacillosis LATIN *actinobacillus* a bacterium.

action FRENCH, from LATIN *agere* do.

active See **act**.

actual See **act**.

actuary LATIN *actuarius* clerk, from *actus.* See **act**.

actuate LATIN *actuatus*, from LATIN *actus.* See **act**.

acumen LATIN a point, from *acuere* sharpen.

acupuncture LATIN *acur* needle + *pungere* pierce.

acute LATIN *acuere* sharpen, from *acus* needle.

-acy FRENCH, from LATIN, from GREEK *-ateia* quality, condition.

ad- LATIN *ad-* to, at, toward.

adage FRENCH, from LATIN *adagium,* from *ad-* to + *aio* I say.

adagio ITALIAN *ad agio* at ease.

adamant FRENCH diamond, hardest metal, from GREEK *adamas,* from *a-* not + *daman* tame.

adapt FRENCH *adapter* to fit, from LATIN *adaptare,* from *ad-* to + *aptare* fit.

add LATIN *addere* add to, join, attach, from *ad-* to + *dare* give.

addendum LATIN that which is to be added, from *addere* add to. See **add**.

adder MIDDLE ENGLISH *nadder,* from OLD ENGLISH *nædre* snake.

addict LATIN *addicere,* from *ad-* to + *dicere* say.

addle OLD ENGLISH *adela* mud.

address FRENCH *a-* to + *dresser* direct, from LATIN *dirigere.* See **direct**.

adduce LATIN *adducere,* from *ad-* to + *ducere* lead.

-ade LATIN *-ata.*

Adelphi GREEK brothers.

adenoids GREEK *aden* gland + *eidos* form, shape.

adept LATIN *adeptus* a person skilled in alchemy, from having attained, from *adipisci* attain, from *ad-* to + *apisci* grasp.

adequate LATIN *adaequare,* from *ad-* to + *aequare* make equal.

adhere LATIN *adhaerere,* from *ad-* to + *haerere* stick.

adieu FRENCH, from LATIN *ad-* to + *Deus* God.

adjacent LATIN *adjacere* to be near, from *ad-* to + *jacere* lie still.

adjective LATIN *adjectivum* added word, from *ad-* to + *jacere* throw.

adjourn FRENCH *a* at + *jorn* day, from LATIN *diurnum* daily, from *dies* day.

adjudge LATIN *adjudicare,* from *ad-* to + *judicare* judge.

adjudicate See **adjudge**.

adjust LATIN *ad-* to + *justus* lawful, from *jus* law.

adjutant LATIN *adjuvare,* from *ad-* to + *juvare* help.

administer FRENCH *aministrer* to manage, from LATIN *administrare,* from *ad-* to + *ministrare* serve.

admiral FRENCH *amiral* officer of high rank, from ARABIC *amir-al-* commander of.

admire LATIN *admirari,* from *ad-* to + *mirari* wonder.

admit LATIN *admittere,* from *ad-* to + *mittere* send.

admonish FRENCH *amonester* to warn, from LATIN *admonere,* from *ad-* to + *monere* warn.

ado MIDDLE ENGLISH *at do* to do.

adobe SPANISH *adobe* brick that is dried by the sun instead of a fire, from ARABIC *at-tob* brick.

adolescent LATIN *adolescere,* from *ad-* to + *alecere* grow up, from *alere* feed.

adopt LATIN *adoptare,* from *ad-* to + *optare* choose.

adore FRENCH *adorare,* from *ad-* to + *orare* speak.

adorn FRENCH *adorner* to provide, from LATIN *adornare,* from *ad-* to + *ornare* decorate.

adrenal LATIN *ad-* + *renalis* of the kidneys, from *renes* kidneys.

adroit FRENCH *à droit* properly, from LATIN *ad-* to + *directus* straight.

adult LATIN *adultus.*

advance FRENCH *avancier* leave before someone, from LATIN *abante,* from *ad-* away + *ante* before.

advantage FRENCH *avant* before, from LATIN *ab ante* away before.

advent LATIN *adventus* arrival, from *advenire,* from *ad-* to + *venire* happen.

adventure FRENCH *aventure* chance, from LATIN *advenire.* See **advent**.

adverb LATIN *adverbium,* from *ad-* to + *verbum* word.

adversary FRENCH *aversier,* from LATIN *adversus,* from *ad-* to + *vertere* turn.

adverse FRENCH *advers* opposite, from LATIN *advertere,* from *ad-* to + *vertere* turn.

advert See **advertise**.

advertise FRENCH *advertir,* from LATIN *advertere,* from *ad-* to + *vertere* turn.

advice FRENCH *avis* opinion, from LATIN *ad-* to + *videre* look.

advocate FRENCH *avocat,* from LATIN *advocatus,* from *ad-* to + *vocare* call, from *vox* voice.

adze (adz) OLD ENGLISH *adesa.*

aer- GREEK *aer* air.

aerator See **aer-** + **-ate** + **-or.**

aerial LATIN *aerius* relating to air, from GREEK *aerios.*

aerie LATIN *aerea* nest of a bird, from FRENCH *aire,* from LATIN *area* open space.

aero- GREEK *aer* air.

aerobic FRENCH *aérobie,* coined 1863 by Louis Pasteur, from GREEK *aero-* air + *bios* life.

aeronautics GREEK *aer* air + *nautes* sailor.

aesthetic GREEK *aisthanesthai* perceive.

affable LATIN *affabilis,* from *ad-* to + *fari* speak.

affair FRENCH *afaire* concern, from *à faire* to be done, from LATIN *ad-* to + *facere* do, make.

affect LATIN *affectare* produce an effect upon, from *ad-* to + *facere* do, make.

affiliate LATIN *affiliare* to adopt, from *ad-* to + *filius* son.

affinity FRENCH *afinite,* from LATIN *affinis* near, from *ad-* to + *finis* end.

affirm FRENCH *afemer,* from LATIN *affirmare,* from *ad-* to + *firmare* make firm.

affix LATIN *affixare,* from *ad-* to + *figere* fasten.

afflatus LATIN *afflare* to blow on, from *ad-* to + *flare* blow.

afflict LATIN *affligere,* from *ad-* to + *flugere* strike.

affluence FRENCH, from LATIN *affluere,* from *ad-* to + *fluere* flow.

afford OLD ENGLISH *geforthian* accomplish.

affray FRENCH *esfraer* frighten, from LATIN *ex-* out of + GERMAN *frith* peace.

affright OLD ENGLISH *afyrht.*

affront FRENCH *afronter* hit in the face, from LATIN *ad frontem* to the face.

Afghan PASHTO *afghānī,* the people of Afghanistan.

aficionado SPANISH *aficionar,* from LATIN *affectio* warm feeling.

afoot See **a-**[1] + **foot.**

afore OLD ENGLISH *on foran.*

afraid MIDDLE ENGLISH *affraied,* from FRENCH *afrayer* frighten.

afreet ARABIC *'ifrit* evil demon or monster of Muslim mythology.

aft OLD ENGLISH *æftan.*

after OLD ENGLISH *æfter* behind in place or time.

again OLD ENGLISH *ongegn,* from *on-* toward + *gegn* direct.

against See **again.**

agalactia LATIN *agalaxia,* from GREEK *agalacia* not milk.

agape See **gape.**

agate FRENCH, from LATIN, from GREEK *achates.*

agave LATIN *Agave,* from GREEK *Agaue,* from *agauos* noble.

age FRENCH lifetime, from LATIN *aetas* time period.

-age FRENCH, from LATIN *aticum* belonging to.

agent LATIN *agere* do.

agglomerate LATIN *agglomerare,* from *ad-* to + *glomerare* form into a ball.

aggrandize FRENCH *agrandir,* from LATIN *ad-* to + *grandire* increase.

aggravate LATIN *aggravare,* from *ad-* to + *gravis* heavy.

aggregate LATIN *aggregare,* from *ad-* to + *gregare* herd.

aggression LATIN *aggressio* attack, from *aggredi* attack, from *ad-* to + *gradi* step.

aggrieve LATIN *aggravare.* See **aggravate**.

aghast MIDDLE ENGLISH *agasten* terrify, from OLD ENGLISH *gast* ghost.

agile FRENCH, from LATIN *agere* act.

agitate LATIN *agitare* move back and forth.

aglet FRENCH *aiguille,* from LATIN *acucula,* from *acus* needle.

agnostic GREEK *a-* not + *gignoskein* know.

ago MIDDLE ENGLISH *agon* go away, from OLD ENGLISH *agan,* from *a-* away + *gan* go.

agog FRENCH *a-* to + *gogue* joyful.

agony LATIN *agonia* great suffering, from GREEK *agonia* contest.

agree FRENCH *agreer* to please, from LATIN *ad-* to + *gratus* pleasing.

agriculture LATIN *agricultura*, from *ager* field, acre + *cultura* cultivate (farming of the land).

ague FRENCH sharp fever, from LATIN *acuta febris* sharp or severe fever.

aid FRENCH *aïder* to help, from LATIN *adjuvare,* from *ad-* to + *juvare* help.

aide FRENCH. See **aid**.

ail OLD ENGLISH *egle* harmful.

aileron FRENCH *aile,* from LATIN *ala* wing.

aim FRENCH *aesmer* to value, from LATIN *ad-* to + *aestimare* estimate.

air FRENCH, from LATIN *aer*, from GREEK *aer.*

Airedale the district of *Airedale* in West Riding, Yorkshire, England.

aisle FRENCH *ele* wing (of a building), from LATIN *ala* wing.

akimbo MIDDLE ENGLISH *in kenebowe*, in keen bow (at a sharp angle).

-al FRENCH, from LATIN *alis.*

alabaster FRENCH, from LATIN, perfume box made of alabaster, from GREEK *alabastos* vase of alabaster.

alack MIDDLE ENGLISH *ah, lack*, from *lack* loss, shame.

alacrity LATIN *alacritas* liveliness.

alarm FRENCH *alarme* warning of danger, from Italian *all'arme!* to arms! going back to LATIN *ad-* to + *ille* that + *arma* weapons.

alas FRENCH *a las* ah weary.

albatross SPANISH, from ARABIC *al qadus* water container, from GREEK *kados,* probably from HEBREW *kad* water jug.

albino SPANISH *albo* snow white, from LATIN *albus* white.

album LATIN blank tablet on which notices were written.

albumen LATIN *albumen* white of an egg, from *albus* white.

alcalde SPANISH, from ARABIC *al-qadi* the judge.

alchemy FRENCH *alcquimie,* from LATIN *alchimia,* from ARABIC *al-kimiya,* from GREEK *cheein* pour.

alcohol LATIN powder for decorating the eyelids, from ARABIC *al kuhl.*

alcove FRENCH, from SPANISH *alcoba,* from ARABIC *al* the + *qobbah* area that has an arched ceiling.

alderman OLD ENGLISH *eald* old + *man* man.

ale OLD ENGLISH *ealu.*

alert FRENCH *alerte* to arms, from ITALIAN *all'erta* on the watch.

alfalfa SPANISH, from ARABIC *al-fastasah.*

algae LATIN *alga* seaweed.

algebra Italian, from Arabic *al-jabr* put broken parts back together.

alias Latin another.

alibi Latin *allus ibi* elsewhere.

alidade French, from Spanish *alidada,* from Arabic *alʿidadah* a ruler, index of an astrolabe.

alien French, from Latin *alienus,* from *allus* other.

alight[1] (step down) Middle English *a-* out, off + *lihtan* get down.

alight[2] (having light) Old English *leoht* light.

align French *aligner,* from Latin *ad-* to + *linea* line.

alike Old English *gelic.*

aliment Latin *alimentum,* from *alere* nourish.

alimentary See **aliment** + **-ary**.

alimony Latin *alimonia* support, from *alere* feed.

alive Old English *on life* having life.

alkali Middle English *alkaly,* from Arabic *alqili* ashes, from *qalai* cook with fire.

all Old English *eall.*

allay Old English *alecgan,* from *a-* down + *lecgan* keep back.

allege Latin *allegare,* from *ex-* out of + *litigare* sue.

allegiance French *a-* to + *ligeance,* from *liege,* from German *ledig* free.

allegory Latin *allegoria,* from Greek *allegoria,* from *allos* other + *agoreuelin* speak.

allergy Greek *allos* other + *ergon* work.

alleviate Latin *alleviare,* from *ad-* to + *levis* light.

alley[1] (walkway) French *alee* passage, from *aler* go, from Latin *ambulare* walk.

alley[2] (marble) See **alabaster**.

alliance French *aliance* connection, from *alier.* See **ally**.

alligator Spanish *el lagarto* the lizard.

allocate Latin *allocatus* to allot, from *ad-* to + *locare* place.

allot French *aloter,* from *à* to + *loter* divide by lot (share).

allow French *alouer* grant, from Latin *allocare* to allot, from *ad-* to + *locus* a place.

alloy French *aloi* standard, from *aloier* join, from Latin *alligare.* See **ally**.

allude Latin *alludere* to joke, from *ad-* to + *ludere* play.

allure French *alurer* attract, from *à* to + *lure* bait.

ally French *alier* bind to, from Latin *alligare* join together, from *ad-* to + *ligare* bind.

almanac Latin *almanach* diary, from Greek *almenichiaka* calendar.

almighty Old English *eal* all + *mihtig* mighty.

almond French *almande,* from Latin *amygdala,* from Greek *amygdale.*

almost Old English *eallmæst.*

alms Old English *æmesse,* from Latin *eleemosyna,* from Greek *eleemosyne* pity.

aloe Latin, from Greek *alie.*

aloft Old Norse *a lopt* in the air.

alone Middle English *al one* all one.

along Old English *andlang,* from *and-* over against + *lang* long.

aloof probably from Dutch *te leof* to windward (direction from which the wind is blowing).

aloud Old English *a-* on + *hlud.*

alpaca SPANISH *allpaca.*

alphabet LATIN *alphabetum* the letters of a language, from GREEK *alphabeto,* from *alpha* A + *beta* B, the first two letters of the Greek alphabet.

alpine LATIN *alpinus.*

also OLD ENGLISH *ealswa* wholly so.

altar OLD ENGLISH, from LATIN *altaria* part of a holy table used to hold burnt offerings.

altazimuth See **altitude** + **azimuth**.

alter FRENCH *alterer* change, from LATIN *alterare*, from *alter* other.

alternate LATIN *alternare* do a thing by turns, from *alturnus* one after the other, from *alter* other.

although MIDDLE ENGLISH *al thogh.* See **all** + **though**.

altimeter See **altitude** + **-meter**.

altitude LATIN *altus* high.

altogether See **all** + **together**.

altruism FRENCH *altruisme,* from ITALIAN *altrul* for or to others, from LATIN *alter* other.

alulate LATIN *ala* wing.

alum FRENCH, from LATIN *alumen.*

aluminum LATIN *aluminum,* from *alumen* alum (a special kind of salt).

always See **all** + **way**.

amass FRENCH, from LATIN *a-* to + *massare* pile up, from LATIN *massa* mass. See **mass**.

amateur FRENCH lover of something, from LATIN *amare* love.

amaze OLD ENGLISH *amasian* confuse completely.

ambassador FRENCH *ambassaduer,* from LATIN *ambactia* mission (special job), from *ambactus* servant.

amber FRENCH, from ARABIC *anbar* ambergris (gray amber).

ambient LATIN *ambire,* from *ambi-* around + *ire* go.

ambiguous LATIN *ambigere*, from *ambi-* around + *agere* act.

ambition LATIN *ambitio* going around (to get votes).

amble FRENCH *ambler* amble, from LATIN *ambulare* walk.

ambrosia LATIN *ambrosia* food of the gods, from GREEK *ambrotos,* from *a-* not + *brotos* mortal (can live forever).

ambulance FRENCH *hôpital ambulant* hospital on wheels.

ambulate LATIN *ambulare* walk.

ambuscade FRENCH *embuschier.* See **ambush**.

ambush FRENCH *embuschier* place in ambush, from LATIN *in-* in + *boscus* wood.

ameliorate FRENCH *améliorer,* from *a-* to + *meillor,* from LATIN *melior* better.

amen OLD ENGLISH, from LATIN, from GREEK, from HEBREW truth.

amenable FRENCH *a-* to + *mener* lead, from LATIN *minare* make animals move.

amend FRENCH *amender* make better, from LATIN *emendae* correct, from *ex-* out of + *menda* fault.

America *Amerigo* Vespucci (1454–1512), Italian explorer of South America.

amethyst LATIN *amethystus,* from GREEK *a-* not + *methystos* drunken, because it was believed that the stone could prevent drunkenness.

amiable FRENCH *amiable*, from LATIN *amicabilis*, from *amicus* friend.

amicable LATIN *amicabilis,* from *amicus* friend.

amid Middle English *on* at + *middan* middle.

amigo Spanish friend, from Latin *amicus.*

amino- *am-* in. See **ammonia** + **-ine**.

amiss Old English *an-* to + *missan* fail to hit.

amity French *amitié,* from Latin *amicus* friend.

ammonia Greek *ammoniac,* from *ammoniakon* temple of Ammon (near which it grew).

amnesia Greek *amnesia,* from *a-* not + *mnasthai* remember.

amnesty Latin, from Greek *amnestia* forgetful. See **amnesia.**

amoeba Latin, from Greek *ameibein* change.

amok Malay *amuk.*

among Old English *on gemang,* from *on-* in + *gemang* crowd.

amorous French, from Latin *amorosus,* from *amor* love.

amount French *amonter* to amount to, from Latin *ad-* to + *mons* mountain.

ampersand Latin *and per se and* literally, "(the sign) & by itself is (the word) and."

amphibian Greek *amphibios* living a double life, from *amphi* both + *bios* life.

amphitheatre Latin, from Greek *amphi-* both sides + *theatre* from French, from Latin *theatrum* stage, from Greek *theatron* place for seeing plays.

ample French full, from Latin *amplus* large.

amplify French *amplifer* enlarge, from Latin *amplificare,* from *amplus* ample + *facere* do, make.

amplitude Latin *amplitudo,* from *amplus* large.

amulet French, from Latin.

amuse French *amuser,* from *à* to + *muser* stare at.

an Old English *an.*

-an Latin *–anus* belonging to.

anachronism French *anachronisme,* from Latin *anachronismus,* from Greek *anachronismos* a wrong time reference.

anagram French *anagramme,* from Greek *ana* backwards + *gramma* letter, from *graphein* write.

anal Latin *anus* a ring.

analogy Greek *ana* according to + *logos* word.

analysis Latin, from Greek solution, from *ana-* up + *lyein* loose.

anarchy Latin *anarchia,* from Greek *an-* without + *archos* leader.

anathema Latin, from Greek thing devoted to evil, from *anatithenai* dedicate, from *ana-* up + *titheai* set.

anatomy French *anatomie* science of dissecting (learning about something by cutting it carefully into parts), from Latin *anatomia* dissection, from Greek *anatome,* from *ana-* up + *temnein* cut.

-ance French, from Latin *-antia.*

ancestor French *ancestre* forefather, from Latin *antecessor,* from *ante-* before + *cedere* go.

anchor Old English *ancor,* from Latin *anchora,* from Greek *ankyra* hook.

anchovy Greek *aphye* small fish.

ancient French *ancien* old, from Latin *ante* before.

and Old English *and.*

andiron French *andier.*

anecdote FRENCH, from GREEK *anekdota* things not published (such as gossip), from *an-* not + *ek-* out + *didonai* give.

anemia LATIN, from GREEK *an-* without + *haima* blood.

anemometer GREEK *anemos* wind + FRENCH *mètre,* from GREEK *metron* measure.

anemone LATIN, from GREEK *anemone* wind flower.

anesthesia GREEK *an-* without + *aisthesis* feeling.

anew OLD ENGLISH *of niowe* over again.

angel FRENCH *angele* holy messenger, from LATIN *angelus,* from GREEK *angelos* messenger.

anger OLD NORSE *angr* grief.

angle FRENCH *angle,* from LATIN *angulus* corner, from GREEK *ankylos* bent.

Anglo- LATIN *Anglus.*

anguish FRENCH *anguisse,* from LATIN *angustia* narrow.

animal LATIN living creature, from *anima* breath, life.

animate LATIN *animare* give life to, from *anima* breath, life.

animosity LATIN *animositas* spirit.

anise FRENCH *anis,* from LATIN *anesum,* from GREEK *aneson.*

ankh EGYPTIAN soul, life.

ankle OLD ENGLISH *ancleow.*

anna HINDI *ana.*

annals LATIN *annales libri* yearly books, from *annus* year.

anneal OLD ENGLISH *onælan* burn.

annex FRENCH, from LATIN *annectere,* from *ad-* to + *nectere* bind.

annihilate LATIN *annihilare,* from *ad-* to + *nihil* nothing.

anniversary LATIN *anniversarius,* from *annus* year + *vertere* turn.

announce FRENCH *anoncier,* from LATIN *ad-* to + *nuntiare* report, from *nuntius* messenger.

annoy FRENCH *anoier,* from LATIN *in odio habere* have in hate.

annual FRENCH *annuel,* from LATIN *annualis,* from LATIN *annus* year.

annular LATIN *anularis,* from *anulus,* from *anus* a ring.

annulet LATIN, from *anulus* a ring + FRENCH *-el,* from LATIN *-ellus.*

anode GREEK *ana-* up + *hodos* way.

anodyne LATIN, from GREEK *an-* without + *odyne* pain.

anoint FRENCH *enoindre,* from LATIN *inunguere,* from *in-* on + *ungere* smear with something greasy.

anomalous LATIN, from GREEK *an-* not + *homos* same.

anonymous GREEK *anonymos,* from *an-* without + *onyma* name.

anorak ESKIMO *anorak* heavy jacket.

answer OLD ENGLISH *andswaru* formal (sworn) statement in reply (to being accused of something), from *and-* in reply + *swerian* swear.

ant MIDDLE ENGLISH *amete,* from OLD ENGLISH *æmete.*

-ant LATIN *-antem* or *-entem.*

antagonize GREEK *antagonizesthai* struggle against, from *anti-* opposite + *agon* struggle.

Antarctic LATIN *antarcticus,* from GREEK *antarktikós,* from *ant-* against + *arktikos.* See **arctic**.

ante- LATIN before.

antecedent LATIN *antecedere* go before, from *ante-* before + *cedere* go.

antediluvian LATIN *ante-* before + *diluvium* flood.

antelope FRENCH, from LATIN, from GREEK *antholops* deer.

antenna LATIN horn, from long pole for a sail.

anthem OLD ENGLISH *antefn* verse of a song sung in response, from LATIN *antiphona,* from GREEK *antiphonos*, from *anti-* against + *phone* voice.

anther FRENCH *anthère*, from LATIN *anthera* medicine extracted from a flower, from GREEK *anthera*, from *antheros* flowery, from *anthos* flower.

anthology GREEK *anthologia* a gathering of flowers, from *anthos* flower + *legein* gather.

anthracite GREEK *anthrax.*

anthrax LATIN, from GREEK burning coal.

anthropo- GREEK *anthropos* man.

anthropomorphism GREEK *anthropos* man + *morphe* form, shape.

anti- GREEK against.

antibiotic LATIN *antibiosis,* from *anti-* against + GREEK *biosis* way of life, from *bios* life.

antic ITALIAN *antico* old, from LATIN *antiquus*. See **antique**.

anticipate LATIN *anticipare*, from *anti-* before + *capere* take.

anticline GREEK *anti-* against + *kleinen* incline.

antidote FRENCH, from LATIN *antidotum*, from GREEK *antidoton*, from *anti-* against + *didonai* give.

antimony LATIN *antimonium.*

antipathy LATIN, from GREEK *anti-* against + *pathein* feel.

antique FRENCH, from LATIN *antiquus* old, from *ante* before.

antiseptic GREEK *anti-* against + *sepein* make rotten or decayed.

antithesis GREEK *anti-* against + *tithenai* place.

anus LATIN *anus* a ring.

anvil OLD ENGLISH *anfilt,* from *an-* on + possible *filtan* beat.

anxious LATIN *anxius*, from *angere* choke.

any OLD ENGLISH *ænig* no matter which, at all.

aorta LATIN *aorta*, from GREEK *aorte,* from *aeirein* raise.

apart FRENCH *à part* aside, from LATIN *ad-* to + *pars* part.

apartment FRENCH *appartement,* from ITALIAN *appartamento* separation, from *parte* part.

apathy FRENCH *apathie,* from LATIN *apathia,* from GREEK *apatheia,* from *a-* without + *pathos* emotion.

aperitif FRENCH, from LATIN *apertus* open.

aperture LATIN *apertus* open.

apex LATIN a point.

aphelion LATIN, from GREEK, from *apo* away from + *helios* sun.

aphesis GREEK *apo-* from + *hienai* send, letting go.

aphid LATIN *aphides*, plural of **aphis**.

aphis Coined by Linnaeus, probably from GREEK *apheides* unsparing, lavishly bestowed.

aphorism FRENCH, from GREEK *aphorizein* divide, from *apo-* away + *horizein* go around.

apiary LATIN *apiarium,* from *apis* bee

aplomb FRENCH perpendicular, from *a*- to + *plomb* according to the plummet (weight).

apocalypse LATIN, from GREEK *apokalyptein* make known.

apogee FRENCH, from LATIN, from GREEK *apo*- from + *ge* earth.

apology LATIN *apologia* defense, from GREEK *apologia* speech in defense, from *apo*- from + *logos* speech.

apophthegm GREEK *apophthegma*, from *apo*- from + *phthengesthai* utter.

apoplexy FRENCH *apoplexie,* from LATIN *apoplexia,* from GREEK, from *apo*- down + *plessein* hit.

apostle OLD ENGLISH *apostol,* from LATIN *apostolus,* from GREEK *apostolos*, from *apo*- from + *stellein* send.

apostrophe FRENCH, from LATIN *apostrophus*, from GREEK *apostrophos*, from *apo*- from + *strephein* turn.

apothecary LATIN *apothecarius*, from *apotheca,* from GREEK *apotheke* storehouse, from *apo*- from + *tithenai* put.

apothegm See **apophthegm**.

Appalachian SPANISH *apalachen,* from NATIVE AMERICAN name for a particular village.

appall FRENCH *apallir*, from *a*- to + *palir* become pale, from LATIN *pallidus* pale.

appaloosa NATIVE AMERICAN *a palouse* after an American Indian tribe called the *Palouse.*

apparatus LATIN *ad*- to + *parare* prepare.

apparel FRENCH *apareiller* to clothe, from *a*- to + *pareiller* put like with like, from LATIN *ad*- to + *par* equal.

apparent LATIN *apparere.* See **appear**.

apparition FRENCH, from LATIN *apparere*, from *ad*- to + *parere* come into sight.

appeal FRENCH *apeler* to call, from LATIN *appellare* to call upon, from *ad*- to + *pellere* push.

appear FRENCH *aparoir* to show oneself, from LATIN *apparere*, from *ad*- to + *parere* come into sight.

appease FRENCH *apaiser* to pacify (calm), from *a* to + *pais* peace, from LATIN *pax.*

appellation LATIN *appellare.* See **appeal**.

append LATIN *appendere* to hang on, from *ad*- to + *pendere* hang.

appendix See **append**.

appertain FRENCH, from LATIN *appertinere,* from *ad*- to + *pertinere,* from *per*- hold thorougly + *tenere.*

appetite FRENCH *apetit* desire, from LATIN *appetitus*, from *ad*- to + *petere* look for.

applaud LATIN *applaudere*, from *ad*- to + *plaudere* clap the hands.

apple OLD ENGLISH *æppel.*

application See **apply**.

applique See **apply**.

apply FRENCH *aplier,* from LATIN *applicare* to attach to, from *ad*- to + *plicare* fold.

appoint FRENCH *apointier* to arrange, from LATIN *ad*- to + *punctum* point.

appose FRENCH *aposer* set beside, from LATIN *apponere,* from *ad*- near + *ponere* put.

appositive LATIN *appositus,* from *ad*- near + *ponere* place.

appraise See **praise**.

appreciate LATIN *appretiare* to value at a price, from LATIN *ad*- to + *pretium* value, reward.

apprehend LATIN *apprehendere* to understand, from *ad*- to + *prehendere* take.

apprentice FRENCH *aprentis*, from LATIN *apprehendere* to understand, from *ad-* to + *prehendere* take.

approach FRENCH *aprochier* to come near to, from LATIN *a-* to + *prope* near.

appropriate LATIN *appropriare*, from *ad-* to + *proprius* one's own.

approve FRENCH *aprover*, from LATIN *approbare*, from *ad-* to + *probare* test, prove.

approximate LATIN *approximatus* to come near to, from *ad-* to + *proximare* approach.

apricot FRENCH, from ARABIC, from LATIN *precoquere*, from *prae-* before + *coquere* cook.

April MIDDLE ENGLISH *Avril*, from FRENCH *avrill*, from LATIN *aprilis*, possibly from GREEK *Aphrodite*, goddess of love and beauty.

apron MIDDLE ENGLISH *a napron*, from FRENCH *naperon*, from *nape* a cloth, from LATIN *mappa* napkin.

apropos FRENCH *à propos*, from LATIN *ad-* to + *propositum* plan.

apse LATIN *apsis*, from GREEK *hapsis* loop, arch, from *haptein* fasten together (joining arcs to form a circle, especially in making a wheel).

apsidiole FRENCH *apsidiole* a small apse.

apt LATIN *aptus* fitted.

aptitude LATIN *aptitudo* fitness, from *aptus* fit, suited.

apyrexia LATIN, from GREEK *a-* not + *pyrexis* feverishness.

aquarium LATIN *aqua* water.

aquastat LATIN *aqua* water + *stata* still.

aquatint FRENCH *aquatinte*, from LATIN *aqua tincta* dyed water, from *tingere* dye.

aqueduct LATIN *aqua* water + *ducere* lead.

arabesque FRENCH, from ITALIAN *Arabo* Arab, from ARABIC *arab*, with reference to a particular Arabic design.

Arabic FRENCH, from LATIN *Arabicus*.

araneidan LATIN *aranea* spider.

arbiter LATIN witness, from *ad-* to + *baetere* go.

arbitrary LATIN *arbitrarius* uncertain, from *arbiter* judge (showing the uncertainty of judges' decisions).

arbor FRENCH *erber* place where grass or herbs are grown, from LATIN *herba* grass, herb.

arboreal LATIN *arboreus*. See **arbor**.

arc FRENCH, from LATIN *arcus* a bow, arch.

arcade FRENCH arch, from LATIN *arcus* bow, arch.

arcane LATIN *arcanus* secret.

arch FRENCH *arche* chest, from LATIN *arcus* bow, arch.

-arch GREEK *archos* ruler.

arch- LATIN *arch(i)-*, from GREEK *arch(i)-*, from *archos* ruler.

archaeology GREEK *archaios* ancient, from *arche* the beginning + *logos* word.

archaic GREEK *archaikos* ancient.

archetype LATIN *archetypum* original pattern, from GREEK *archetypon*, from *archos* first + *typos* type.

archie the name *Archibald*.

archipelago ITALIAN, from GREEK *archi* chief + *pelagos* sea.

architect LATIN, from GREEK *archi-* chief + *tekton* carpenter.

architrave ITALIAN *archi-* beginning, origin + *trave* beam, from LATIN *trabem*.

archive FRENCH *archif*, from LATIN *archivum*, from GREEK *archeion* public building, from *arche* the beginning.

arctic FRENCH *artique*, from LATIN *articus*, from GREEK *arktos* northern.

ardent FRENCH *ardant* burning, from LATIN *ardens* burn.

ardor FRENCH, from LATIN *ardere* burn.

arduous LATIN *arduus* difficult.

are OLD ENGLISH *aron*.

area LATIN *area* open space.

arecoline PORTUGUESE *areca* palm tree + *-ine* like.

arena LATIN *arena* sandy place. Sand was used to cover the ground of large areas for sporting events in ancient Rome.

areola LATIN *areola* small area.

argon GREEK *a-* without + *ergon* work.

argue FRENCH *arguer* reason, from LATIN *arguere* prove, make clear.

arid LATIN *arere* be dry.

arise OLD ENGLISH *arisan*.

aristocracy FRENCH *aristocratie* rule of the nobly born, from GREEK *aristokaratia* rule of the best, from *aristos* best + *kratos* power.

arithmetic FRENCH *arismetrique*, from LATIN *arithmetica* science of numbers, from GREEK *arithmos* number.

ark OLD ENGLISH *earc*, from LATIN *arcere* enclose.

armada SPANISH *armar* provide with weapons, from LATIN *armare*, from *arma* weapons.

armature LATIN *armare* provide with weapons, from *arma* weapons.

armistice LATIN *arma* arms + *-stitium*, from *stare* stand.

armor See **armature**.

army FRENCH *armer* arm, from LATIN *armare*. See **armature**.

arnica LATIN.

aroma FRENCH *aromat*, from LATIN *aromata*, from GREEK sweet spice.

around See **a-**[1] + **round**.

arouse See **a-**[1] + **rise**.

arrange FRENCH *arengier* to put into order, from *à-* to + *rengier* put in order, from *renge* line, row.

array MIDDLE ENGLISH *arrayan* prepare, equip, from French *arreyer* arrange, equip, from *arredare* put in order.

arrears FRENCH *ariere* backward, from LATIN *ad-* to + *retro* behind.

arrest FRENCH *arester* to stay, from LATIN *ad-* to + *restare* stop.

arrive FRENCH *ariver* come to land, from LATIN *ad-* to + *ripa* shore.

arrogant LATIN *arrogare* claim for oneself, from *ad-* to + *rogare* ask.

arrow OLD ENGLISH *arwe*.

arsenal ITALIAN *arsenale* a dock, from ARABIC *dar sina a* wharf, workshop.

arsenic FRENCH, from LATIN, from GREEK *arsenikon* a yellow type of arsenic, from PERSIAN *zar* gold.

arsenicum LATIN *arsenicum* arsenic.

arson FRENCH, from LATIN *ardere* burn.

art MIDDLE ENGLISH, from FRENCH, from LATIN *ars*.

artery LATIN *arteria* this blood vessel, probably from GREEK *aeirein* raise.

arthropod LATIN *arthropoda*, from GREEK *arthron* joint + *podos* foot.

artichoke ITALIAN *articiocco*, from SPANISH *alcarchofa*, from ARABIC *al-harsuf.*

article FRENCH, from LATIN *articulus* division, from *artus* joint.

articulate LATIN *articulare* divide into joints, from *articulus* division, from *artus* joint.

artifact LATIN *ars* art + *factum* thing made.

artificial LATIN *artificium* work that requires great skill with the hands, from *ars* skill, art + *facere* do, make.

artillery FRENCH *artillerie,* from *artiller* protect from attack.

artisan FRENCH, from LATIN *ars* art.

-ary LATIN *-arius, -aria, -arium.*

as[1] (like, etc.) OLD ENGLISH *ealswa.*

as[2] (coin) LATIN *as* unit of weight

ascend LATIN *ascendere*, from *ad-* to + *scandere* climb.

ascertain FRENCH *acertener,* from LATIN *ad-* to + *certain* sure.

ascetic GREEK *askein* train the body.

ascites LATIN, from GREEK *askites* dropsy.

ascot a race course called Ascot Heath in Berkshire, England where such ties were fashionable.

ascribe LATIN *ascribere,* from *ad-* to + *scribere* write.

asepsis GREEK *a-* not + *sepein* make rotten.

ash[1] (grayish powder) OLD ENGLISH *æsce.*

ash[2] (tree) OLD ENGLISH *æsc.*

ashamed OLD ENGLISH *ascamian* feel shame.

asinine LATIN *asinus* ass.

ask OLD ENGLISH *ascian* to question.

askance MIDDLE ENGLISH *askoin,* from *a-* on + *skwyn,* from DUTCH *schuin* sideways.

askew See **a-**[1] + **skew**.

asleep FRENCH *on slaepe* in sleep.

asp LATIN *aspis*, from GREEK.

asparagus OLD ENGLISH *sparage,* from LATIN *sparagus,* from *asparagus,* from GREEK *asparagus.*

aspect LATIN *aspectus* look, from *ad-* to + *specere* look, behold.

aspen OLD ENGLISH *æspe.*

asperity LATIN *asper* rough, uneven.

asphalt LATIN *asphaltus,* from GREEK *asphaltos,* probably from *a-* not + *sphallein* cause to fall.

asphodel LATIN *asphodel*, from GREEK *asphodelos.*

asphyxia GREEK a stopping of the pulse, from *a-* not + *sphyzein* pulse.

aspirant See **aspirate**.

aspirate LATIN *aspirare,* from *ad-* to + *spirare* breathe.

aspire See **aspirate**.

ass OLD ENGLISH *assa,* from LATIN *asinus.*

assail FRENCH, from LATIN *assilire,* from *ad-* to + *salire* leap.

assassin FRENCH, from ARABIC *hashishiyyin* eaters of (the drug) hashish, Muslim suicide killers active at the time of the Christian Crusades.

assault FRENCH *asaut* attack, from LATIN *ad-* to + *saltus* leap.

assay FRENCH *essai* test, from LATIN *exagium,* from *ex-* out + *agere* act.

assemble FRENCH *assembler* to gather, from LATIN *ad-* to + *simul* together.

assent FRENCH *assetir,* from LATIN *assentire,* from *ad-* to + *sentire* feel.

assert LATIN *asserere*, from *ad-* to + *serere* join.

assess FRENCH *assesser* determine, tax, from LATIN *assessare*, from *assidere* to sit beside and help a judge, from *ad-* to + *sedere* sit.

asset FRENCH *assets*, from LATIN *ad-* toward + *satis* enough (to pay debts).

assign FRENCH, from LATIN *assignare* to give a share to, from *ad-* to + *signare* sign.

assimilate LATIN *assimilare*, from *ad-* to + *similare* make like.

assist FRENCH *assister* to help, from LATIN *assistere*, from *ad-* to + *stare* stand.

associate LATIN *associare* to join, from *ad-* to + *socius* companion.

associative See **associate**.

assonance FRENCH *assonance*, from LATIN *assonare* respond to, from *ad-* to + *sonare* sound.

assort FRENCH *assorter* to match, from LATIN *ad-* to + *sors* sort.

assuage FRENCH, from LATIN *ad-* to + *suavis* sweet.

assume LATIN *assumere*, from *ad-* to + *sumere* take.

assure FRENCH *aseürer* to make sure, from LATIN *assecurare*, from *ad-* to + *securus* sure.

aster LATIN, from GREEK *aster* star.

asterisk LATIN, from GREEK *aster* star.

asteroid GREEK *asteroeides* star-like, from *aster* star + *-eidos* form, shape.

asthma GREEK breathing hard.

astigmatism GREEK *a-* without + *stigma* a mark + *-ismos*.

astonish MIDDLE ENGLISH *astonen* stun, from FRENCH *estoner*, from LATIN *ex-* out + *tonare* thunder.

astound See **astonish**.

astral LATIN *astralis* relating to stars, from *astrum* star, from GREEK *astron*.

astride See **a-**[1] + **stride**.

astro- GREEK *aster* star.

astrolabe FRENCH, from LATIN, from GREEK *astron* star + *lambanein* take.

astrology FRENCH *astrologie*, from LATIN *astrologia* astronomy, from GREEK *astrologia*, from *astron* star + *-logia*, from *logos* word.

astronaut GREEK *astron* star + *nautes* sailor, from *naus* ship.

astronomy FRENCH *astronomie*, from LATIN *astronomia*, from GREEK *astron* star + *nomos* law.

astute LATIN *astus* craft.

asylum LATIN safe place, from GREEK *asylon*, from *a-* not, without + *style* right to take.

at OLD ENGLISH *æt*.

atavism FRENCH *atavisme*, from LATIN *atavus*, from *at-* beyond + *avus* grandfather.

-ate LATIN *-atus*.

atheism FRENCH *athéisme*, from GREEK *atheos*, from *a-* without + *theos* god.

athlete LATIN, from GREEK *athlos* contest + *athlon* prize.

athwart See **a-**[1] + **thwart**.

-atic FRENCH, from LATIN, from GREEK *atikos*.

-ation FRENCH, from LATIN *-tionis*.

atlas *Atlas*, one of the giants of Greek mythology, who was believed responsible for holding up the sky.

atmosphere LATIN *atmosphaera*, from GREEK *atmos* vapor + *sphaira* sphere.

atoll Maldive Islands, in the Indian Ocean.

atom LATIN *atomus* smallest bit, from GREEK *atomos* cannot be divided, from *a-* not + *temnein* divide, from the early belief that atoms could not be split.

atone MIDDLE ENGLISH *at-onen at one* as in "to be at one with", or in agreement with.

atrium LATIN.

atrocious LATIN *atrox* fierce, from *ater* black.

atrophy LATIN *atrophia* lack of food, from GREEK *a-* not + *trephein* feed.

attach FRENCH *attachier* to fasten, from *a-* to + GERMAN *takk* pointed thing.

attack FRENCH *attaquer,* from ITALIAN *attaccare* to join battle, from LATIN *ad-* to + GERMAN *takk* pointed thing.

attain FRENCH *ataindre* to reach, from LATIN *attingere*, from *ad-* to + *tangere* touch.

attainder See **attain.**

attaint See **attain.**

attempt FRENCH *atempter* to try, from LATIN *attemptare*, from *ad-* to + *temptare* try.

attend FRENCH *atendre* to wait, from LATIN *attendere,* from *ad-* to + *tendere* stretch.

attenuate LATIN *attenuare* to make thin, from *ad-* to + *tenuare,* from *tenuis* thin.

attercop OLD ENGLISH *attorcoppa* poison-head, from *ator* poison.

attest LATIN *attestari*, from *ad-* to + *testari* be a witness to.

attic FRENCH *attique* small, well-decorated room at the top of the house, following the style of Athens in ancient Greece, from LATIN *Atticus* having to do with Athens, from GREEK *Attikos.*

attire FRENCH *atirier* arrange, dress, from *a tire* in order.

attitude ITALIAN *attitudine* posture, from LATIN *aptitudo* fitness, from *aptus* fit, suited.

attorney FRENCH *atorné* one appointed, from *atorner,* from LATIN *ad-* to + *tornare* turn.

attract LATIN *attrahere*, from *ad-* to + *trahere* draw.

attribute LATIN *attribuere*, from *ad-* to + *tribuere* assign.

attrition LATIN *attritio,* from *ad-* to + *terere* rub.

auburn FRENCH *auborne,* from LATIN *alburnus,* from *albus* white, changed by MIDDLE ENGLISH *brun* brown.

auction LATIN *auctio* increase, from *augere.*

audacity LATIN *audax* bold.

audience FRENCH hearing, from LATIN *audire* hear.

audit LATIN *auditus* a hearing. In earlier times audits were done orally rather than in writing.

audition LATIN *auditio* hearing.

auger OLD ENGLISH *nafogar* drill for the nave (hub) of a wheel, from *nafu* nave or hub of a wheel + *gar* piercer.

aught MIDDLE ENGLISH, from OLD ENGLISH *awiht.*

augment LATIN *augmentare* grow.

augur LATIN priest at a fertility rite, from *augere* increase, enlarge, enrich.

august LATIN *augustus* majestic, magnificent, from *augere* increase, enlarge, enrich.

August OLD ENGLISH *August,* from LATIN *Augustus* title of the first Roman emperor, from *augustus* worthy of respect.

aunt LATIN *amita.*

aura LATIN, from GREEK *aer* air.

aureole LATIN *aureus* golden.

auricle LATIN *auris* ear.

aurora Latin dawn.

auroscope Latin *aurum* gold + Greek *-skopion,* from *skopein* view, examine.

auscultation Latin *auscultatio* listening + *-tion,* from French, from Latin *-tionis.*

auspicious Latin *auspicium* omen (sign of something to come).

austere Latin *austerus* harsh, from Greek *austeros*, from *avos* dry.

Australia Latin *terra australis* southern land.

author French *autor* writer, creator, from Latin *auctor* creator.

authority French *autorite* power, from Latin *auctor* author, one in charge.

auto- Greek *autos* self.

autocrat French *autocrate,* from Greek *autokrates,* from *autos* self + *kratos* power.

autograph French *autographe* one's own signature, from Latin *autographus* written with one's own hand, from Greek *autographos,* from *autos* self + *graphein* write.

automatic Greek *automatos* self acting.

automaton See **automatic**.

automobile See **auto-** + **mobile**.

autonomous Greek *autonomia,* from *autos* self + *nomos* law.

autopsy Latin *autopsia*, from Greek seeing with one's own eyes, from *autos* self + *opsis* a sight.

autumn Latin *autumnus.*

auxiliary Latin *auxiliarius,* from *auxilium* aid.

avail French *valoir* be of value, from Latin *valere* be strong.

avalanche French *avaler* descend, from *lavanche,* from Latin, *labi* slip.

avant-garde French advance guard.

avarice French, from Latin *avarus* greedy, from *avere* want.

avenge Latin *a-* to + *vindicare* claim.

avenue French, from Latin *advenire.* See **advent**.

aver French *averrer,* from Latin *ad-* to + *verus* true.

average French *avarie*, from Italian, from Arabic *'awar* damaged goods. From the way payment for damage to goods on ships was figured out in the Middle Ages.

averse Latin *avertere*, from *a-* from + *vertere* turn.

avert French *avertir,* from Latin *avertere.* See **averse**.

aviary Latin *avis* bird.

aviation French, from Latin *avis* bird.

avid Latin *avidus* greedy.

avocado Spanish *aguacate.*

avoid French *esvuidier*, from *es-* out + *vuide* empty.

avouch French *avochier,* from Latin *advocare,* from *ad-* to + *vocare* call, from *vox* voice.

avow French *avouer,* from Latin *advocare,* from *ad-* to + *vocare* call.

await French, from Latin *a-* to + *waitier* wait.

awake Old English *awacian* waken.

award French *eswarder* observe, from Latin *ex-* from + *wardare* observe.

aware Old English *genær.*

away Old English *aweg.*

awe Old Norse *agi* be afraid.

awful Middle English *agheful*, from *aghe.* See **awe**.

awkward Old Norse *öfugr* turned the wrong way.

awl Old Norse *alr.*

awning nautical usage, perhaps from French *auvans*, from *auvent* a sloping roof.

awry See **wry**.

ax (axe) Old English *eax.*

axial Latin *axis* axle, pivot + *-al* French, from Latin *alis.*

axillary Latin *axilla* armpit.

axiom Latin *axioma* principle, from Greek *axioma.*

axis Latin *axis* axle, pivot.

axle Old Norse *oxull.*

ayah Portuguese *aia* governess.

aye Old Norse *ei.*

ayont See **beyond**.

azimuth French *azimut*, from Arabic *as-sumut* the ways.

azure French *azur*, from Arabic *lazhuward* lapis lazuli, a deep blue color or stone.

B

baa imitative.

babble imitative.

babe Middle English *baban*, probably a nursery word.

babel Hebrew *Babel* Babylon, an ancient city in SW Asia. According to an ancient story, the people there tried to build a tower to the sky and were stopped by God, who caused them to speak in different languages so they couldn't finish the tower.

baboon French *babuin* ape, fool, from *baboue* lip (of animals), from *bab* imitative.

baby Middle English *babi*. See **babe**.

bachelor French *bacheler* young man, from Latin *baccalarius* young nobleman wishing to become a knight.

back Old English *bæc*.

bacon Middle English, from French *bacun* ham, lard strips.

bacteria Latin, from Greek *bakterion* stick. When bacteria were first seen under the microscope they looked like little sticks.

bad Middle English *badde* wicked.

badge Middle English *bage* the emblem.

badger origin uncertain.

badinage French *badiner* joke, from *badin* silly, from Latin *badare* stare at with the mouth open.

baffle probably from Scottish *bauchle* dishonor.

bag Old Norse *baggi* pack, bundle.

bagatelle French, from Italian *bagatella,* from Latin *baca* berry.

bagel Greek *beugen* bend.

baggage French *bagage,* from Latin *baga* chest.

baguette French, from Italian *bacchetta,* from Latin *baculum* a staff.

bail[1] (deposit) French *bail* custody, from *baillier* have in charge, from Latin *bajulare* one who takes care of things.

bail[2] (remove water) French *baille* bucket, from Latin *baca* trough (container for animals to drink from).

baile Middle English call to combat, from French *bailler* deliver blows.

bailey Middle English *baylle*, from French *baile*, from Latin *bajulus* porter.

bailiff French *baillif*, from *bail* custody. See **bail**[1].

bailiwick FRENCH *bailiff*, from *bail* custody + MIDDLE ENGLISH *wik*, from OLD ENGLISH *wic* village.

bairn OLD ENGLISH *bearn.*

bait OLD NORSE *beita* cause to bite.

baize FRENCH *baie*, from LATIN *badius* brown.

Bajan *Barbadian*, a person who lives on the Caribbean island of Barbados.

bake OLD ENGLISH *bacan.*

bakelite L. H. *Baekeland* (1863-1944), its inventor + LATIN, from GREEK *ites.*

balaclava a Russian village. The cap was worn by soldiers in a 19th century battle there.

balalaika RUSSIAN.

balance FRENCH instrument used for weighing, from LATIN *bilanx* having two scales, from *bi-* two + *lanx* plate.

balcony ITALIAN *balcone*, from GERMAN *balcho* beam.

baldric MIDDLE ENGLISH *bauderik*, from FRENCH *baudrei*, from LATIN *balteus* belt.

bale FRENCH *balu.*

baleful OLD ENGLISH *bealu* evil + *-ful* complete.

balk OLD ENGLISH *balca* ridge.

ball[1] (sphere) OLD NORSE *böillr* globe.

ball[2] (dance) FRENCH *bal*, from *baler* dance, from LATIN *ballare*, from GREEK *ballizein.*

ballad FRENCH *balade* dancing song, from LATIN *ballare.*

ballast GERMAN, from DANISH *balrast*, from *bar* bare + *last* a load.

ballet FRENCH *ballet* little dance, from ITALIAN *balletto*, from *ballare* dance.

balletomane FRENCH. See **ballet** + **mania**.

ballistic LATIN, from GREEK *ballein* throw.

balloon ITALIAN *pallone* large ball, from *palla* ball.

ballot ITALIAN *ballotta* little ball, from the ancient Greek method of voting by using different colored balls to vote yes and no.

ballotade FRENCH *ballotte* small ball.

bally BRITISH, slang for *bloody.*

ballybonkers origin uncertain.

balm FRENCH *basme*, from LATIN *basamum* balsam (something that heals), from GREEK *balsamon.*

balsam OLD ENGLISH, from LATIN *basamum.* See **balm**.

baluster FRENCH *balustre*, from ITALIAN *balaustro* pillar. See **balustrade**.

balustrade FRENCH, from ITALIAN *balaustrata* provided with balusters, from *balaustro* pillar, from *balausta* flower of the wild pomegranate, from GREEK *balaustion.* Staircase uprights had double curves, like parts of the pomegranate flower.

bambas SPANISH sneakers.

bamboo PORTUGUESE *bambu*, probably from MALAY *samambu.*

bamboozle probably from an earlier beggar term invented in England about the 1700s.

ban OLD ENGLISH *bannan* summon, from FRENCH *ban* a public order.

banal FRENCH, belonging to common people. See **ban**.

banco SPANISH bank.

band[1] (group) FRENCH *bande* band, group.

band[2] (flat strip) FRENCH *bande* bond, tie.

bandage See **band**[2].

bandana HINDI *bandhnu* method of dyeing.

bandit Italian *bandire* outlaw.

bandoleer French *bandoulière,* from Spanish *bandolera,* from *banda* scarf.

bane Old English *bana* murderer.

bang Old Norse *banga* pound.

bangle Hindi *bangri* glass bracelet.

banish French *banir.* See **ban**.

banister alteration of **baluster**.

bank[1] (place to keep money) Italian *banca* bench (of a banker).

bank[2] (shallow place) Old Norse *bakki.*

bankrupt Italian *banca rotta* broken bench, from the Medieval custom of breaking the bench of a moneychanger (person who changes money for foreigners) who can't pay his bills, from Latin *banca* bench + *rotta* broken, from *rumpere* break.

banner French *baniere* flag, from Latin *bandum.*

bannister alteration of **baluster**.

bannock Old English *bannuc.*

banquet French, from Italian *banchetto* little bench.

banquette French, from Norman *banque,* from Dutch *bank* bench.

bantam *Bantam,* a place in South Asia, where the birds are thought to originate.

banter origin uncertain.

baobab Latin *bahobab,* possibly from Arabic *'abū hibāb* source of seeds.

baptism French *baptiser,* from Latin *baptizare,* from Greek *baptein* dip in water.

bar[1] (long narrow thing) French *barre,* from Latin *barra* barrier.

bar[2] (unit of pressure) Greek *baros* weight.

bar mitzvah Hebrew *bar* son of + *mitsva* commandment, from *tsiva* command.

barb French *barbe* beard, from Latin *barba.*

barbarous Latin *barbaricus* foreign, from Greek *barbaros.*

barbecue Spanish *barbacoa* used to describe a Native American style of cooking on a rack of wood, from Native American *barbakoa* wooden rack.

barbel French, from Latin *barbus* the fish, from *barba* beard.

barber French *barbour,* from *barbe* beard, from Latin *barba.*

barberry Latin *barbers,* from Arabic *barbaris.*

barbican French *barbicane,* from Latin *barbacana,* from Persian *barbar-kanah* house on a wall.

bard Middle English, from Scottish *bard,* Welsh *bard* and Irish *bardd.*

bare Old English *bær* without covering.

bargain French *bargaignier* haggle (argue about price or terms).

barge French flat boat, from Latin *barca.*

bark[1] (tree covering) Old Norse *borkr.*

bark[2] (dog sound) Old English *beorcan.*

barley Old English *bere.*

barlow (knife) name of maker.

barnacle Middle English *barnakille* barnacle goose (a type of bird believed to hatch from barnacles), from Latin *bernacula,* origin unknown.

barometer Greek *baros* weight + *metron* measure.

baron French man, warrior.

baroque French, from Portuguese *barroco* a pearl that is not perfect.

barouche German, from Italian, from Latin *birotus,* from *bi-* two + *rota* wheel.

barrack French *baraque* hut, from Spanish *barraca* mud hut, from *barro* clay, from Latin *barrum* clay.

barracuda Spanish.

barrage French *tir de barrage* curtain of fire, from *barrage* barrier, from *barrer* bar, from French *barre.* See **bar**[1].

barranca Spanish.

barre French bar.

barrel French *baril* cask.

barren French *baraigne* sterile (not able to reproduce).

barrette French *barre* bar.

barricade French barrier, from *barrique* barrel, from Spanish *baril* cask.

barrier French, from *barre* rod. See **bar**[1].

barrister See **bar**[1].

barrow[1] (wheelbarrow) Old English *bearwe.*

barrow[2] (mound) Old English *beorg* hill.

barter French *barater,* from Old Norse *baratta* quarrel.

bartizan altered form of *brattice*, from Middle English *bretice*, from French *bretesche* wooden tower.

basalt Latin *basaltes.*

base[1] (stand) Latin *basis* foundation, from Greek pedestal, base.

base[2] (low) French *base*, from Latin *bassus* low, short.

basement Latin *basis* foundation, from Greek pedestal, base + French, from Latin *-mentum.*

bash possibly from Danish *baske* strike.

basidium Latin *basis* foundation, from Greek pedestal, base.

basil French *basile*, from Latin *basilicum*, from Greek *basilikon*, from *basileus* king.

basin French *bacin* bowl, from Latin *bacca* water container.

basis Latin *basis* foundation, from Greek pedestal, base.

basket origin uncertain.

Basque French *basquine,* from Spanish *vascon* the Basque region between Spain and France, from Latin *Vasconia.*

bass[1] (low voice) Middle English *bas,* from Latin *bassus* low.

bass[2] (fish) Old English *bærs.*

bassinet French *berceau* cradle.

bassoon French *basson*, from Italian *bassone*, from *basso* low.

bastard French *fils de bast* child of the packsaddle and not from the marriage bed, meaning the child's parents were not married, from Latin *bastum.*

baste French *bassiner* moisten, from *bassin* basin.

bastille French guarded fort, from *bastir* build.

bastion See **bastille**.

bat[1] (club) Old English *batt* club.

bat[2] (mammal) Middle English *bakke,* of Scandinavian origin.

bat[3] (blink) French *batire* beat.

batch Middle English *bacche* a baking.

bate See **abate**.

bateau French *batel*, from Old English *bat* boat.

bath Old English *bæth* liquid for bathing.

bathetic See **bathos.**

bathos Greek depth.

batiste French *baptiste*, possibly from the use of similar cloths to wipe the heads of children after baptism.

batling See **bat**[1] + **-ling.**

baton French small stick, from *baston*, from Latin *bastum* stick.

battalion French *battaillon,* from Italian *battaglione,* from Latin *battalia* battle, from *battuere* beat.

batten French *baton* small stick, from Latin *bastum* stick.

battenburg the name of a town in Germany.

batter French *battre,* from Latin *battuere* beat.

battery French *batterie* beat, from Latin *battuere.*

battle French *bataille* a fight, from Latin *battualia* exercises to help in fighting, from *battuere* beat.

battledore origin unknown, possibly from French *batedor* beater, from *batre* beat.

bauble Middle English *babel*, from French *baubel, belbel* toy, probably from Latin *bellus* pretty.

bauxite French *Les Baux* a town in southeast France, where it is found.

bavin origin uncertain.

bawdkin French *baudekin,* from Latin *baldakinus,* from *Bagdad* the city in Asia where the fabric was made.

bawl Latin *baulare* bark, and possibly from Old Norse *baula* moo like a cow.

bay[1] (water) French *baie,* from Latin.

bay[2] (color) French *bai,* from Latin *badius.*

bay[3] (dog bark) French *abaiier.*

bayonet French *Bayonne* city in France where it was first made.

bayou French, from Native American *bayuk* river, creek.

bazaar Persian *bazar* market.

bazooka a resemblance to a musical instrument invented and named that by an American comedian in the 1930s.

be Old English *beon.*

be- Old English *be-* about, near, by.

beach a dialect in Sussex, England, referring to pebbles made smooth by the waves, from Old English *bæce, bece* stream.

beacon Old English *beacen.*

bead Middle English *bede*, from Old English *gebed* prayer. In some religions beads are strung together and for each one a prayer is said.

beadle Old English *bydel*, from *beodan* bid, order.

beagle Middle English *begle*, possibly from French *beguele* noisy person.

beak French *bec* bird's bill, from Latin *beccus.*

beaker Old Norse *bikarr,* from Latin *bacar* wine glass.

beam Old English *bæm* piece of wood.

bean Old English.

bear[1] (carry) Old English *beran* carry, support.

bear[2] (mammal) Old English *bera.*

beard Old English.

beat Old English *beatan.*

beatitude French, from Latin *beatitudo*, from *beatus* happy, blessed.

beau FRENCH fine, handsome, from LATIN *bellus* pretty.

beauty FRENCH *beaute,* from LATIN *bellus* beautiful.

beaver[1] (animal) MIDDLE ENGLISH *bever*, from OLD ENGLISH, from *beofor.*

beaver[2] (armor) MIDDLE ENGLISH *bavier*, from FRENCH *baviere* bib.

because MIDDLE ENGLISH *bi* by + FRENCH reason, from LATIN *causa.*

beck[1] (gesture) See **beckon.**

beck[2] (brook) MIDDLE ENGLISH *bek*, from OLD NORSE *bekkr* brook.

beck[3] (tool) OLD ENGLISH *becca* hook.

beck[4] (tub) possibly from DUTCH *bekken,* from German *becken* basin.

beckon MIDDLE ENGLISH *beknen*, from OLD ENGLISH *beacnian* make signs, from *beacen* beacon.

become OLD ENGLISH *becuman* happen.

bed OLD ENGLISH *bed* couch to sleep on.

bedaub See **be-** + **daub.**

beech OLD ENGLISH *bece.*

beef FRENCH *boef,* from LATIN *bovis* ox.

been See **be.**

beep imitative.

beetle MIDDLE ENGLISH *bital*, from OLD ENGLISH *bitela*, from *bitan* bite.

befall OLD ENGLISH *befeallan* fall.

before OLD ENGLISH *be-* by + *foran* before.

beg FRENCH *begger,* from *begard,* from DUTCH *beggaert.*

beget OLD ENGLISH *begitan* get.

begin OLD ENGLISH *beginnan* start.

beguile See **be-** + **guile.**

behalf OLD ENGLISH *be* by + *healf* half, side.

behave See **be-** + **have.**

behemoth LATIN *Behemoth* mythical animal, from HEBREW *b'hemoth* beast.

behest OLD ENGLISH *behæs.*

behind OLD ENGLISH *behindan.*

beholden OLD ENGLISH *bihealdan* hold.

behoove OLD ENGLISH *behofian* need.

beige FRENCH.

bejabbers AMERICAN slang, from *by Jesus.*

belabor See **be-** + **labor.**

belabour See **be-** + **labor.**

belay OLD ENGLISH *beleagan.*

belch OLD ENGLISH *bealcan.*

beleaguer DUTCH *belegeren* camp beside, from *be-* by + *leger* camp.

belfry FRENCH *berfrei,* from GERMAN *bercfrit* protecting tower, from *bergen* protect + *frid* peace. Originally a moveable tower used in attacks. It was later used as a watchtower (where one could keep a watch out for fire or enemies) which had an alarm bell to ring when something dangerous was sighted.

belie OLD ENGLISH *beleogan* deceive by lies.

belief MIDDLE ENGLISH *bileafe* faith, from OLD ENGLISH *geleafa* faith.

bell OLD ENGLISH *belle.*

belladonna ITALIAN *bella donna* fair lady, from the use of its juice in cosmetics.

belle FRENCH feminine of *beau* fine, handsome, from LATIN *bellus* pretty.

belligerent LATIN *belligerare* make war.

bellow OLD ENGLISH *bylgian* roar like a bull.

bellows See **belly**.

belly Old English *belig* bag.

belong Middle English *belongen* concern, from Old English *langian* want.

below See **be-** + **low**.

belt Old English, from Latin *balteus.*

bench Old English *benc* long seat.

bend Old English *bendan* stretch a bow.

beneath Old English *be-* near + *neothan* down.

benediction Latin *benedictionem*, from *benedicere* praise, from *bene* well + *dicere* speak.

benefactor Latin *bene* well + *facere* do, make.

benefit Middle English *benfet,* from French, from Latin *benefactum,* from *ben facere* do well.

benevolence French goodwill, from Latin *benevolentia*, from *bene* well + *velle* wish.

benign French *benigne* kind, from Latin *benignus*, from *bene* well + *genus* birth.

benignant See **benign**.

benne African *bene* the sesame plant.

benzene See **benzoin**.

benzoin French, from Italian *benzoino,* from Arabic *lubqan jawi* incense from Java, an island in South Asia.

bequest Middle English *biqueste*, from Old English *be-* by + *cwiss* saying.

berate Old English *be-* about, near, by + Middle English *raten* scold.

bereave Old English *befeafian,* from *be-* by + *reafian* rob.

beret French *beret* cap worn by Basque peasants, from *berret,* from Latin *birrus* a hooded cloak.

bergere French shepherdess.

berry Old English *berie.*

berserk See **berserker**.

berserker Old Norse *berserkr* warrior clothed in bearskin, from *ber* bear + *serkr* coat.

berth probably from **bear**[1].

bertha feminine name, from German *berahta* bright one.

beseech Old English *besecan.*

beset Old English *besettan* set near.

beside Old English *besidan.*

best Old English *betst.*

bestial Latin *bestia* beast.

bestride Old English *bestridan.*

bet probably from **abet**.

bete noir French black beast.

betel Middle English, from Malay *vetilla.*

betray Middle English, from French *trair* hand over, from Latin *tradere.*

betroth Middle English *be-* about + *treuthe*, from Old English *treowth* truth.

better Old English *betera* improved in health.

between Old English *betweonum*, from *be-* by + *tweon(um)* in pairs.

betwixt Old English *betwix.*

bevel probably from French *baivel.*

beverage French *bevre,* from Latin *bibere* imbibe (drink).

bevy possibly from French *bevee* drink, as a gathering for that purpose.

bewilder Old English *be-* about, near, by + Middle English *wilder* get lost, probably from **wilderness**.

bewuther Old English *be-* about, near, by + Old Norse *kvidra* go back and forth.

beyond Old English *begeondan* farther on than.

bezel French *bisel* sloping edge.

bezoar Spanish, from Arabic *bazahr*, from Persian *padzahr*, from *pad* expelling + *zahr* poison.

bi- Latin *bi-* twice, doubly, two.

bias French *biais* slant.

bib Latin *bibere* imbibe (drink).

bibble See **bib** + **-le**.

Bible Latin, from Greek *biblia* collection of writings, from *biblos* papyrus.

bibliography Greek *bibliographia* the writing of books, from *biblion* little book + *graphein* write.

biceps Latin *bi-* two + *caput* head.

bicker Middle English *bikeren*.

bicorn Latin *bicornis,* from *bis* twice + *cornu* horn.

bicycle Latin *bi-* two + Greek *kyklos* wheel.

bid Old English *beodan* offer.

biddy[1] (hen) imitative.

biddy[2] (fussy old woman) form of *Bridget,* a female name. Figuratively related to **biddy**[1].

bide Old English *bidan* wait.

bier Old English *bær* a bed.

bifurcate Latin *bi-* two + *furca* fork.

big Middle English *bigg,* origin uncertain.

bigamy Latin *bigamus* twice married, from *bi-* two + Greek *gamos* marriage.

bigot French, supposedly used to insult the Normans.

bijou French, from Breton *bizou* ring, from *biz* finger.

bijouterie See **bijou**.

bilberry Old Norse *bollr* ball + *ber* berry.

bile French, from Latin *bilis.*

bilge See **bulge**.

bilious French *bilieux*, from Latin *biliosus*, from *bilis* bile.

bilk first used in the game of Cribbage, possibly from **balk**.

bill French *bille*, from Latin *billa* important paper with official stamp, from *bulla* knob (rounded part that sticks out).

billet French *bullete,* from Latin *bulla* knob.

billingsgate *Billings,* the name of a gate in London. In the 17th century a fish market was located near the gate, and the speech there was abusive and foul.

billion See **bi-** + **million**.

billow Old Norse *bylgia* a wave.

billycock See **bully** + **cock**[2].

bin Old English manger, crib.

binary Latin *bini* two together.

bind Old English *bindan* tie together.

binge British *binge* soak.

binnacle Spanish *bitácula,* from Latin *habitaculum* place to live.

binocular Latin *bini* two together + *oculus* eye.

bio- Greek *bios* life.

biography Greek *biographia* a writing of lives, from *bios* life + *graphein* write.

biology See **bio-** + **-logy**.

biome Greek *bios* life + *-oma* group.

biped LATIN *bipes* two-footer.

bird MIDDLE ENGLISH *brid*, from OLD ENGLISH *bridd* young bird.

birth OLD NORSE *byrth.*

biscuit FRENCH *pain bescoit* twice-baked bread (which stays preserved longer than single-baked bread), from *bis* twice + *cuit* cooked, from LATIN *coquere.*

bisect LATIN *bi-* two + *secare* cut.

bishop OLD ENGLISH *bisceop* church bishop, from LATIN *episcopus,* from GREEK *episkopos,* from *epi* on + *skopos* watcher.

bismuth GERMAN *wismut.*

bisque See **biscuit**.

bit[1] (bridle part) OLD ENGLISH *bite* bite.

bit[2] (small piece) OLD ENGLISH *bita* small piece bitten off.

bit[3] (for a drill) OLD ENGLISH *bite* bite.

bite OLD ENGLISH *bitan* cut into with the teeth.

bitt nautical, origin uncertain.

bitter OLD ENGLISH *biter* not sweet.

bittern FRENCH *butor,* probably from LATIN *butio.*

bitts See **bit**[1].

bivouac FRENCH, from GERMAN *biwacht,* from *bi-* by + *wacht* guard.

bizarre FRENCH, from ITALIAN *bizzaro* lively.

black OLD ENGLISH *blæc.*

blackamoor See **black** + **moor**[1].

blackmail OLD ENGLISH *blæc* black + SCOTTISH *male* rent, from OLD ENGLISH *mal* payment, from OLD NORSE agreement. Originally payment taken by dishonest clan chieftains from Scottish and English farmers who paid to not have their crops destroyed.

bladder OLD ENGLISH *blædre* sac in the body.

blade OLD ENGLISH *blæd* broad flat part of a tool.

blame FRENCH *blasmer* accuse, from LATIN *blasphemare* speak badly of.

blanch FRENCH *blanchir* whiten, from *blanc* white.

blancmange FRENCH *blanc* white + *manger* eat.

bland LATIN *blandus* soft.

blank FRENCH *blanc* white.

blanket FRENCH *blankete* white wool cloth, from *blanc* white.

blare MIDDLE ENGLISH *bleren* bellow (yell loudly).

blasé FRENCH *blaser.*

blaspheme FRENCH, from LATIN, from GREEK *blasphemein* speak evil of.

blast OLD ENGLISH *blæst* gust of wind.

blatant LATIN *baltier* babble (say quickly or foolishly).

blather OLD NORSE *blathra* talk in a foolish way.

blaze OLD ENGLISH *blæse* flame.

bleach OLD ENGLISH *blæcan,* from *blac* pale.

bleak OLD NORSE *bleikr* white.

blear OLD ENGLISH *blere* watery.

bleat OLD ENGLISH *blætan.*

bleed OLD ENGLISH *bledan* lose blood.

blemish FRENCH *blesmir* injure, origin uncertain.

blend OLD NORSE *blanda* mix.

bless OLD ENGLISH *bletsian* make holy with blood.

blight possibly from Old Norse *blikja* turn pale.

blimp perhaps from **limp,** not having a rigid frame.

blind Old English.

blink Middle English *blenchen.*

blip imitative.

bliss Old English *blithe.*

blister French *blestre* a swelling, from Old Norse *blastr.*

blithe Old English.

blitzkrieg German *blitz* lightning + *krieg* war.

blizzard a newspaper in Iowa that was the first to use the word to describe a heavy snowstorm in the late 1800s.

bloat Middle English *blote* soft, from Old Norse *blautr* soft.

blob imitative.

block French *bloc* log, from Dutch *blok* a mass.

blond French fair, origin uncertain.

blood Old English *blod.*

bloom Old Norse *blom* flower.

bloomers Amelia J. *Bloomer* (1818–1894) who promoted them.

blossom Old English *blostma.*

blot perhaps from blend of **blemish** and **spot.**

blotch perhaps from blend of **blot** and **botch.**

blouse French the shirt, origin uncertain.

blow[1] (hit) Middle English *blaw.*

blow[2] (push air out) Old English *blawan* send air out.

blubber Middle English *blober* a bubble, probably imitative.

blucher name of a Prussian military officer.

bludgeon perhaps from French *bougeon,* from *bouge* a club.

blue Middle English *blewe,* from French *bleu,* related to German *blão,* blue.

bluestocking mid-18th century London parties featuring intellectual discussions. Instead of full dress many who came wore simpler clothing, notably Benjamin Stillingfleet who wore blue-gray tradesman's stockings.

bluff possibly from Dutch *bluffen* brag.

blunder Old Norse *blunda* shut the eyes.

blunt perhaps from Old Norse *blundra.* See **blunder.**

blur See **blear.**

blush Old English *blyscan* make red.

bluster German *blusteren* blow with strength.

boa Latin.

boar Old English *bar.*

board Old English *bord* table.

boast French *bost* brag.

boat Old English *bat* small ship.

boatswain Old English *batswegan,* from *bat* small ship + *swegan,* from Old Norse *sveinn* boy.

bob Middle English *bobben* move up and down.

bobbin French *bobine.*

bobbish See **bob.**

bobble See **bob.**

bobeche French.

bobolink imitative of the bird's song.

bode Old English *bodian* announce.

bodice See **body**.

bodkin Old English *boydekin.*

body Old English *bodig* physical form of man or animal.

bog Irish *bogach,* from *bog* soft.

boggle Scottish *bogle* ghost.

bog-spavin See **bog** + **spavin**.

bogus 1827 name for a machine that copied money, possibly from Welsh *bwg* ghost.

bogy possibly from Welsh *bwg* ghost.

boil French *boillir* make bubbles, from Latin *bulla* bubble.

boisterous French *boisteus* rough.

bold Old English *beald* brave.

bole Old Norse *bolr.*

boll Old English *bolla* bowl.

bollard probably from **bole**.

Bolshevik Russian *bolshevik* member of the majority, from *bolshe* greater.

bolster Old English bed.

bolt Old English arrow.

bomb French *bombe,* from Latin *bombus* a booming, from Greek *bombos* deep hollow sound.

bombard French *bombarder,* from *bombarde* cannon, from Latin *bombarda* weapon for throwing stones, from *bombus.* See **bomb**.

bombast French, from Latin *bombax* cotton, from Greek *bombyx* silk.

bombazine French, from Latin *bambax.* See **bombast**.

bona fide Latin *bona fides* good faith.

bonanza Spanish fair weather, from Latin *bonus* good.

bond[1] (fasten) Middle English. See **band**[2].

bond[2] (slave) Middle English. See **bondage**.

bondage Old English *bonda,* from Old Norse *bonde,* from *bua* live in a place.

bone Old English *ban.*

bonfire Middle English *bone fire* fires built outside for burning bones.

bong imitative.

bongo[1] (antelope) African name.

bongo[2] (drum) Spanish.

bonhomie French *bonhomie,* from *bonhomme* good-natured man, from *bon* good + *homme* man.

bonnet French *bonet* material used for hats.

bonny Scottish, probably ultimately from French *bon,* from Latin *bonus* good.

bonsai Japanese *bon* basin + *sai* plant.

bonus Latin good.

boo imitative.

booby probably from Spanish *bobo* stupid.

book Old English *boc* writing tablet.

boom imitative.

boon Old Norse *bon* a petition.

boor Dutch *boer,* from *gheboer* fellow traveler.

boost American, origin uncertain.

boot French *bote.*

booth Old Norse *buth* temporary place to be, from *bua* live in a place.

booty French *butin,* from German *bute* share.

booze Dutch *buizen.*

borage French, from Latin *borrago* rough hair.

border French *bordeüre* an edge.

bore[1] (hole) OLD ENGLISH *borian* make a hole.

bore[2] (wave) MIDDLE ENGLISH *bare*, from OLD NORSE *bara* a billow.

bore[3] (tiresome) possibly figurative, from **bore**[1] (on the idea of moving forward slowly, as in boring a hole).

boreal LATIN *borealis,* from GREEK mythological figure *Boreas*, god of the north wind.

boreen IRISH *bothar* a road + diminutive *-een.*

born See **bear**[1].

borough OLD ENGLISH *burg* town.

borrow OLD ENGLISH *borg* pledge.

bosh TURKISH *bosh* empty, worthless.

bosom OLD ENGLISH *bosm* breast.

boss[1] (in charge) DUTCH *baas* person in charge, master.

boss[2] (knob) MIDDLE ENGLISH & FRENCH *boce* hump, swelling.

botanical FRENCH *botanique* botany, from GREEK *botane* plant, herb.

botch MIDDLE ENGLISH *bocchen* mend.

both OLD NORSE *nathir* the two.

bother probably from IRISH *pother.*

bottle FRENCH *boteille* container having a neck, from LATIN *butticula,* from *buttis* wooden barrel for holding liquids.

bottom OLD ENGLISH *botm* lowest part.

boudoir FRENCH lady's private room, from *bouder* sulk, from a lady going to her boudoir when she was angry.

bough OLD ENGLISH *bog.*

boulder MIDDLE ENGLISH *bulder*, from *bulderstan* noisy stone (in a stream water roars around it).

boulevard FRENCH defensive wall, from DUTCH *bolwerc* bulwark (defensive wall).

bounce MIDDLE ENGLISH *bunsen* beat.

bound FRENCH *bodne* boundary, from LATIN *bodina* limit.

boundary LATIN *bunnarium.*

bounty FRENCH *bonte* goodness, from LATIN *bonitas.*

bouquet FRENCH bunch (as of flowers), from *bosc* forest.

bourbon *Bourbon* County, Kentucky, where it was first made.

bourgeois FRENCH, from LATIN *burgus* castle.

bourne FRENCH *boune.* See **bound.**

bout OLD ENGLISH *byht.*

boutique FRENCH, from GREEK *apotheke* place for storing things.

bovine LATIN *bovis* OX.

bow[1] (bend) OLD ENGLISH *bugan.*

bow[2] (weapon) OLD ENGLISH *boga.*

bow[3] (of a boat) probably from GERMAN *boog.*

bowel FRENCH *boel* intestine, from LATIN *botellus* sausage.

bower OLD ENGLISH *bur* a place to live.

bowl OLD ENGLISH *bolla* hollow container.

bowsprit probably GERMAN *bochspret*, from *boch* bow of a boat + *spret* pole.

box OLD ENGLISH container made of wood, from the box tree, from LATIN *buxus* box tree.

boy MIDDLE ENGLISH *boi.*

boycott Captain Charles *Boycott* (1832–1897) who was harassed by Irish farmers for his bad treatment of them.

brace FRENCH the two arms, from LATIN *bracchium* arm, from GREEK *brachion.*

bracelet French little arm, from Latin *bracchium.* See **brace**.

brachet Middle English *braches,* from German *bracco.*

brachiocephalic Latin *brachiocephalicus,* from Greek *brachion* arm + *kephale* head.

bracken Middle English *bracken,* related to Swedish *broekne* fern.

bracket French *brague* the front flap of knee pants, from Latin *braca.*

brackish Dutch *brak* salt.

bract Latin *bractea* thin metal plate.

brad Old Norse *broddr* a spike.

brae Old Norse *bra.*

brag Middle English *braggen*, origin unknown.

braggadocio brag (by adding an Italian ending). Invented by 16th century English writer Edmund Spenser.

braid Old English *bregdan* weave.

brail French *bracale* belt.

Braille Louis *Braille* (1809–1852) French teacher who invented it.

brain Old English *brægen* main part of the nervous system.

brake[1] (fern) Middle English. See **bracken**.

brake[2] (slow down) Middle English, from German, from *breken* break.

brake[3] (brushwood) German *brake* stumps.

bramble Old English *bræmel,* from *brom* broom.

bran French *bren.*

branch French *branche* bough, from Latin *branca* paw, claw.

brand Old English *biernan* burn.

brandish French *brand* sword.

brandy Dutch *brandewign,* from *branden* burn + *wign* wine, from Latin *vinum.*

brant See **brand**.

brass Old English *bræs* melting together of copper and tin.

brassiere French, originally arm guard, from *bras* arm.

bravado Spanish *bravada,* from *bravo* brave.

brave French, from Italian *bravo* bold, wild, possibly from Latin *rabidus* fierce.

brawl Dutch *brallen* boast.

brawn French *braon* fleshy part.

braxy Scottish, origin uncertain.

bray Middle English *braien*, from French *braire*, from Latin *bragire* cry out.

brazen Old English *bræsen,* from *bræs* brass.

brazier French *braise* hot coals.

breach Old English *bryce* breaking.

bread Old English *bread* crumb.

breadth Middle English *bræde,* from Old English *brædu,* from *brad* broad.

break Old English *brecan* shatter.

breakfast See **break** + **fast**[2].

breast Old English *breost.*

breath Old English *bræth* air breathed out.

breeches Old English *brec* covering for the buttocks.

breed Old English *bredan* feed.

breeze Spanish *briza* cold northeast wind.

brethren See **brother**.

breviary Latin *brevairum,* from *brevis* brief.

brevity Latin *brevis* brief.

brew Old English *breowan* make beer.

bribe French bit of bread given to a beggar, from *briber* beg.

bric-à-brac French *à bric et à brac* at random, any old way.

brick Dutch *bricke.*

bride Old English *bryd.*

bridegroom Old English *brydguma* bride man.

bridge Old English *brycg* something built over a river or other waterway.

bridle Old English *bridel.*

brief French *bref,* from Latin *brevis.*

brier Old English *brer.*

brig See **brigade**.

brigade French troop, from Italian *brigare* fight.

brigalow Australian Aboriginal *buriagalah.*

brigand See **brigade**.

brigantine French *brigantin,* from Italian *brigantino* pirate ship, from *brigante* robber. See **brigade**.

bright Old English *beorht* shining.

brilliant French *briller* shine, from Latin *beryllus* beryl (a mineral).

brim Middle English *brimme* rim.

brimstone Middle English *brinston,* from *brinn* burn + *ston* stone.

brindled probably from Middle English *brended,* from *brinn* burn.

brine Old English *bryne* salt water.

bring Old English *bringan* cause to come.

brink Middle English *brink,* from German shore.

briolette French sparkle.

briquette French. See **brick**.

brisk French *brusque.*

bristle Old English *byrst* hog's hair.

brittle Middle English *britel* easily broken.

broach French *broche* stick used in roasting, from Latin *brocca* pointed stick, from *broccus.*

broad Old English *brad* wide.

brocade Italian *broccato* the material, from Latin *broccus* sticking out like teeth.

broccoli Italian *brocco* plant stalk.

brochure French a stitched work, from *brocher* stitch, from *broche* pointed tool, from Latin *broccus* pointed teeth.

brogue[1] (dialect) probably from Irish *barrog* hold (on the tongue).

brogue[2] (shoe) Irish *brog* shoe.

broil[1] (cook) French *broiller* roast.

broil[2] (quarrel) French *brouiller* confuse.

broker French *brocour* seller of wine.

bronchitis Greek *bronchos* windpipe.

bronco Spanish rough.

bronze French, from Italian *bronzo.*

brooch See **broach**.

brood Old English *brod* the young of an animal.

brook Old English *broc.*

broom Old English *brom.*

brothel Middle English miserable person, from Old English *breothan* go to ruin.

brother Old English *brothor.*

brougham British aristocrat Lord *Brougham* (1778–1868).

brow Old English *bru.*

browse French *broust* bud.

bruise Old English *brysan* crush.

brumal Latin *brevima* shortest winter day.

brunch combination of **breakfast** + **lunch**.

brunet(te) French *brun,* from German brown.

brunt Middle English *bront* a hit or blow, of Scandinavian origin.

brush French *broce* bush, from Latin *bruscia.*

brusque French harsh, from Italian *brusco* sour, from Latin *brucas* heather (a flower).

brute French *brut* rude, from Latin *brutus* heavy, stupid.

bryony Latin *bryonia*, from Greek *bryein* swell.

bubbe probably from German *bube* boy or lad.

bubble Dutch *bobble.*

buccal Latin *bucca* cheek.

buccaneer French *boucanier* pirate, hunter, from *boucan,* a rack for cooking meat, from Native American *mukem* rack.

buck Old English *bucca* male goat.

buckboard See **buck** + **board**, probably from the bouncy ride.

bucket French *buket* pail, from Old English *buc* pitcher.

buckle French *boucle* metal ring, from Latin *buccula* cheek strap of a helmet, from *bucca* cheek.

buckram French *boucassin* course, sticky linen, from *boquerant* a costly and delicate fabric, from Latin *bucaranus.*

buckwheat Dutch *boecweite* from *boec* beech (tree) + *weit* wheat, as the grains of buckwheat resemble beech tree nuts.

bucolic Latin, from Greek *boukolos* herdsman, from *bous* ox.

bud Middle English *budde.*

Buddha Hindi enlightened, from *budh* awake, know, related to Sanskrit *bodhati* is awake, understands.

buddy possibly from British *butty* friend.

budge French *bouger* stir, from Latin *bullire* boil.

budget French *bougette* little bag, from Latin *bulga*. Originally meant a pouch or wallet.

buff Middle English *buffe leather*, from French *buffle* buffalo.

buffalo Portuguese *bufalo* water buffalo, from Latin *bufalus*, from *bubalus* wild ox, from Greek *boubalos* buffalo.

buffer French *buffe* a blow.

buffet French bench.

buffoon Italian *buffare* joke, puff (from medieval clowns making noise by puffing their cheeks and blowing out).

bug possibly from Middle English *bugge* something frightening, scarecrow.

bugle French *bugle* wild buffalo (the bugle horn is a musical instrument that had been made from the horn of an ox or buffalo), from Latin *buculus* steer.

build Old English *bold* dwelling or house.

bulb Latin *bulbus* root, onion, from Greek *bolbos.*

bulbul Arabic.

bulge French *boulge* leather bag, swelling, from *bougette* little bag, from Latin *bulga.*

bulk Old Norse *bulki* heap.

bull Old English *bula* male of the cattle family.

bullet FRENCH *boule* ball, from LATIN *bulla* bubble or knob.

bulletin FRENCH *bulletin* ticket, from LATIN *bulla.*

bullion DUTCH, from FRENCH *billon* small coin, from *bille* stick.

bullock OLD ENGLISH *bullue,* from *bula* a steer.

bully DUTCH *boel* friend, later changed by the influence of the word *bull.* See **bull.**

bullyrag See **bully** + **rag**[2].

bulrush probably from OLD ENGLISH *bulla* + *rise* a small, grasslike plant.

bulwark DUTCH *bolwerc* bulwark (defensive wall), from *bole* flat piece of wood + *were* work.

bum GERMAN *bummler* tramp.

bumbershoot Slang combination of **umbrella** and **parachute.**

bump imitative.

bumpkin DUTCH *bommekijn* small cask (barrel for holding liquid).

bumptious possibly from **bump.**

bun probably from FRENCH *buigne* a swelling.

bundle MIDDLE ENGLISH *bundel* sheaf.

bungalow HINDI *bangla* low thatched house, from the *Bengal* region of India.

bungle imitative.

bunker SCOTTISH *bonkar* box.

bunt FRENCH *buter* strike.

bunting possibly from MIDDLE ENGLISH *bonting* cloth for sifting flour.

buoy FRENCH *boise* anchored floating marker.

bur MIDDLE ENGLISH *burre,* from SCANDINAVIAN.

burble imitative.

burden OLD ENGLISH *byrthen* load.

bureau FRENCH desk, from LATIN *burra* cloth.

bureaucracy FRENCH *bureaucratie,* from *bureau* desk, office + GREEK *-kratia* power, rule.

burg See **borough.**

burgeon FRENCH *burjon* bud.

burgher MIDDLE ENGLISH *burgh.* See **borough.**

burglar FRENCH *burgler* thief, from LATIN *burglator,* from *burgus.*

burial OLD ENGLISH *byrgels* tomb.

burlap probably from MIDDLE ENGLISH *borel* coarse cloth, from FRENCH *burel.*

burlesque FRENCH, from ITALIAN *burlesco* comical, from *burla* joke.

burly OLD ENGLISH *borlice* excellent.

burn OLD ENGLISH *bærnan.*

burnish FRENCH *burnir* polish, from *brun* brown.

burr[1] (prickle) See **bur.**

burr[2] (sound) imitative.

burro SPANISH, from LATIN *burricus* small horse.

burrow OLD ENGLISH *burg* town.

burst OLD ENGLISH *berstan* break.

bury OLD ENGLISH *byrgan.*

bus short for *omnibus,* from FRENCH, from LATIN bus for all.

bush MIDDLE ENGLISH.

bushel FRENCH *boissel* the measurement, from *boisse* one sixth of a bushel.

business OLD ENGLISH *bisignes.* See **busy.**

buskin probably from DUTCH *brosekin* small leather boot.

bust[1] (sculpture) FRENCH *buste,* from LATIN *bustum* tomb, which was often decorated with a bust of the dead.

bust[2] (break) See **burst**.

bustard LATIN *avis tarda* slow bird.

buster SPANISH *busté,* dialect form of *usted* you.

bustle OLD NORSE *buask* get ready.

busy OLD ENGLISH *bisig* be active.

but OLD ENGLISH *butan.*

butane butyl, from LATIN *butyrum* butter + *-ane* chemical suffix.

butcher FRENCH *bochier* seller of goat meat, from *boc* male goat.

butt[1] (end) possibly from FRENCH *bout* end, from OLD NORSE *butr* block of wood.

butt[2] (hit against) MIDDLE ENGLISH *buter,* from FRENCH *boter* push, shove.

butte FRENCH rising ground, from *but* goal.

butter OLD ENGLISH, from LATIN *butyrum,* from GREEK *boutyron,* from *bous* ox, cow + *tyros* cheese.

buttock OLD ENGLISH *buttuc* rump.

button FRENCH *boton* knob sewn to clothing, from *boter* bud.

buttress FRENCH *bouterez* supports.

buy OLD ENGLISH *byegan* purchase.

buzz imitative.

by OLD ENGLISH *be, bi.*

bylaw MIDDLE ENGLISH *bilage,* from OLD NORSE *bi-lagu* town law, from *bua* dwell + *lagu* law.

byre OLD ENGLISH *bur* hut.

C

cab French *cabriolet* one-horse carriage, from Italian *capriola* leap like a goat, from Latin *caper* goat, because the carriage bounced like a goat leaping.

cabal French *cabale* plot, from Latin *cabbala,* from Hebrew *qabbalah* lore, tradition, from *qibbel* receive.

cabana Spanish *cabaña,* from Latin *capanna* hut.

cabane earlier form of **cabin.**

cabaret French tavern, from Latin *camera.* See **chamber.**

cabbage French *cabouche,* possibly from Latin *caput* head.

cabin French *cabane* hut, from Latin *capanna.*

cabinet French small room, from *cabine* gambling house.

cable French, from Latin *capulum,* from *capere* take hold.

cabochon French *caboche* the head, from Latin *caput* head.

caboose Dutch *kabuys* ship's kitchen.

cabriole French *cabriole* a leap.

cabriolet See **cab.**

cache French *cacher* hiding place, from Latin *coactare* force.

cachet French *cacher.* See **cache.**

cackle imitative.

cacophony Latin, from Greek *kakos* bad + *phone* voice.

cactus Latin, from Greek *kaktos* plant with prickly leaves.

cad probably from short for **cadet.**

cadaver Latin probably from *cadere* fall.

caddie Scottish for **cadet.**

caddy Malay *catty,* a unit of weight (equal to a little more than a pound.)

cadence French, from Latin *cadentia* falling (of dice), from Latin *cadere* fall.

cadet French chief, from Latin *caput* head.

cadge Middle English variation of **catch.**

cadre French, from Italian *quadro* square, from Latin *quadrus.*

Caesar Latin *caedere* cut.

café French coffeehouse, from Italian *caffé.* See **coffee.**

cafeteria Spanish coffeehouse.

caffeine German, from Italian *caffé.* See **coffee.**

cag[1] (keg) Old Norse *kaggi* keg, cask.

cag[2] (stump) Old English.

cag[3] (argument) nautical slang.

cage French, from Latin *cavea.*

cagged (insulted) See **cag**[3].

cahoots French *cahute* hut.

cairn early Scottish *carn* heap of stones.

caisson French ammunition wagon, from *caisse* chest, from Latin *capsa* box.

caitiff French *caitif* a captive, from Latin *captivus.*

cajole French *cajoler* chatter like a bird in a cage, from French *gaiole* cage, from Latin *cavea.*

cake Old Norse *kaka* small amount of baked dough.

calabash Spanish *calabaza,* possibly from Arabic *aqr'ah yabisah* dry gourd (dried, hollowed out shell of some fruits, used for drinking from).

calabozo Spanish underground prison.

calamity Latin *calamitas* bad fortune.

calandria Spanish lark (bird).

calcify Latin *calx* lime + French *-fier,* from Latin *ficare,* from *facere* do, make.

calcine French, from Latin *calcinare* heat.

calcium Latin *calx* lime, because it is found in lime.

calculate Latin *calculare* compute, from *calculus* small stone, as counting was done in ancient times with stones used as counters.

calculus Latin. See **calculate**.

caldron French, from Latin *caldaria* warm bath, from *calidus* warm.

calendar Latin *kalendorium*, from *calendarium* account book, from *calendae* calends, the first day of the month in the ancient Roman calendar, when accounts were due for payment in ancient Rome.

calender French *calendre*, from Latin *calendar*, from *cylindrus.* See **cylinder**.

calf Old English *cealf* and Old Norse *kalfr.*

caliber Greek *calibre* bore (inside tube) of a gun, from Arabic *qalib* mold, from Greek *kalopous* a form used by shoemakers to make shoes.

calico *Calicut,* city in India where the cloth first came from.

caliper See **caliber**.

caliph French *calife*, from Arabic *khalifa* successor.

caliphate See **caliph** + **-ate**.

calisthenics Greek *kallos* beauty + *sthenos* strength.

call Old English *ceallian* shout, from Old Norse *kalla.*

calligraphy Greek *kalligraphia* beautiful writing, from *kallos* beauty + *graphein* write.

calliope Latin, from Greek *kallos* beauty + *ops* voice.

callous Latin *callosus* hard skinned.

callow Old English *calu* bald.

calm French *calme* quiet, from Italian *calma* rest, from Greek *kauma* heat of the sun when everyone rests.

calomel French, from Greek *kalos* beautiful + *melas* black.

calorie French, from Latin *calor* heat.

calumny French *calomnie*, from Latin *calumnia* accuse falsely.

Calvary Latin *calvaria* skull.

calyx LATIN, from GREEK *kalyx.*

cambium LATIN *cambiare* exchange.

camboose variation of **caboose**.

cambric *Cambrai* in France where the material was first made.

camel FRENCH, from LATIN *cameilus,* from GREEK *kamelos,* from HEBREW *gamal.*

camellia G. J. *Kamel* (1661–1706) Jesuit missionary to the Far East.

cameo ITALIAN *cammeo,* from LATIN *camaeus.*

camera shortened form of *camera obscura* (a darkened room with a small opening, an early means of replicating an image from the environment), literally dark chamber, from LATIN *camera* vault, room.

camisole from FRENCH woman's jacket, from LATIN *camisa* shirt.

camouflage FRENCH disguise.

camp FRENCH field of battle, from ITALIAN *campo* field, from LATIN *campus.*

campaign FRENCH *campagne* open country, military campaign, from LATIN *campania* open country, from *campus* field. Early armies didn't like fighting in the cold of winter so they waited for warmer weather and open country.

camphor FRENCH *camphre*, from LATIN *camfora*, from ARABIC *kafur*, from MALAY *kapur* camphor tree.

campus LATIN field.

can[1] (able) OLD ENGLISH *cunnan* know.

can[2] (container) OLD ENGLISH *canne* a cup.

canal LATIN *canalis* pipe, channel, from *canna* reed.

canapé FRENCH for covered sofa, from the idea of covering toast or bread with something, from LATIN *canapeum* mosquito net, from GREEK *konops* mosquito.

canard FRENCH hoax, from *vendre des canards a moitié* sell ducks by halves (a joke), deceive, from *caner* cackle (make a sound like a hen).

canary *Canary* Islands, where the birds are native.

can-can FRENCH *cancan,* from *canard* duck, because the dance looks somewhat like the walk of a duck.

cancel MIDDLE ENGLISH *cancellen*, from FRENCH *cancellare* mark out by using a pattern of crossed strips, from LATIN erase, from *carcer* prison, because of the pattern of the bars.

cancer LATIN, from GREEK *karkinos* crab, because the swollen blood vessels around some tumors look like the legs of a crab.

candelabrum LATIN candlestick, from *candela* candle.

candescent LATIN *candescere,* from *candere* glow.

candid LATIN *candidus* white, shining.

candidate LATIN *candidatus* person dressed in white, from *candidus* white. In ancient Rome people seeking political office wore white togas, which stood for integrity.

candle OLD ENGLISH *candel,* from LATIN *candela.*

candor LATIN brightness, purity.

candy FRENCH *sucre candi*, sugar that has been crystallized, from ARABIC *sukkar* sugar + *qandi* candied (coated with crystallized sugar).

cane FRENCH *can(n)e* reed, from LATIN *canna,* from GREEK *kanna.*

canikin diminutive of **can**[2].

canine LATIN *canis* dog.

canister LATIN *capistrum* basket made of reeds, from GREEK *kanna* reed.

canker FRENCH *cancre*, from LATIN *cancer.* See **cancer**.

cannibal Spanish *canibal* a savage, from *galibi* strong men.

cannikin See **canikin**.

cannon French *canon* gun barrel, from Latin *canna* reed. See **cane**.

cannula Latin small reed or pipe.

canny Old English *cunnan* know.

canoe Spanish *canoa,* from Native American *canaoua.*

canon Old English, from Latin *canon*, from Greek *kanon* rule.

canopic Latin *Canopus* a town in ancient Egypt.

canopy Latin *canapeum* mosquito net, from Greek *konops* mosquito.

cant[1] (talk) Latin *cantus* song, chant.

cant[2] (slant) Middle English *cant* corner, from Latin *canthus* tire of a wheel.

cantabile Italian, from Latin *cantare* sing.

cantaloupe French, from Italian *Cantalugo* town near Rome where the fruit was first grown in Europe.

cantankerous probably from Middle English *contek* argument.

canteen French *cantine,* from Italian *cantina* cellar, from Latin *cantus* corner.

canter short for Canterbury, a city in England that was a religious center in the 1300s. People rode their horses in the "Canterbury gallop" to get there.

cantilever See **cant**[2] + **lever**.

cantilly See **cant**[1].

cantle Middle English *cantel* corner, from French, from Latin *cantellus,* from *canthus* tire of a wheel.

canton French, from Italian, from Latin *cantus* corner.

cantor Latin singer.

cantrev Welsh *cant* hundred + *tref* town.

cantrip Scottish.

canula See **cannula**.

canvas French *canevas* made of hemp (a plant that has a strong stem), from Latin *cannabis* hemp, from Greek *kannabis.*

canvass See **canvas**.

canyon Spanish *cañón,* from Latin *canna,* from Greek *kanna* reed.

cap Old English *cæppe* hood, from Latin *cappa* hood.

capable Latin *capabilis* able, from *capere* take.

capacious Latin *capere* take.

capacity Latin *capacitas*, from *capere* take.

caparison French *caparasso* large hooded cloak, from Latin *capa* hood.

cape[1] (garment) French, from Spanish *capa*, from Latin *cappa* mantle, cloak.

cape[2] (land) Latin *caput* headland, from *caput* head.

caper French *capriole* leap, from Italian *capriola* leap (like a goat), from Latin *caper* goat.

capillary Latin *capillus* hair.

capital[1] (head) Middle English, from Latin *capitalis* of the head, from *caput* head.

capital[2] (money) Latin *capitale* stock, property, from *capitalis*. See **capital**[1].

capitol French *capitolie*, from Latin *Capitolium* the religous house (temple) for the god Jupiter in ancient Rome.

capitulate Latin *capitulatus* arrange under separate headings, from *caput* head.

capo short for ITALIAN *capotasto* chief key.

capon OLD ENGLISH, from LATIN *capo.*

capote FRENCH diminutive of **cape**[1].

caprice FRENCH, from ITALIAN *capriccio* whim (a sudden wish to do something without a reason).

Capricorn FRENCH *capricorne,* from LATIN *caper* goat + *cornu* horn.

capriole FRENCH leap, from ITALIAN *capriola* leap (like a goat), from LATIN *caper* goat.

capsize perhaps from SPANISH *capuzar* sink by the head, from *cabo* head.

capstan FRENCH *cabestan* something used for winding rope, from LATIN *capistrum.*

capsule FRENCH small container, from LATIN *capsa* box.

captain FRENCH *capitaine* commander of troops, from LATIN *capitaneus* chief, from *caput* head.

caption FRENCH, from LATIN *capere* take.

captivate LATIN *captivus* prisoner.

captive LATIN *captivus* prisoner.

capture FRENCH, from LATIN *capere* take.

car MIDDLE ENGLISH *carre* cart, from LATIN *carra,* a type of wheeled cart.

carabineer FRENCH *carabinier.*

caracol FRENCH *caracol, caracole,* from ITALIAN *caracollo* wheeling of a horse, from SPANISH *caracol* snail, spiral shell.

carafe FRENCH, from ITALIAN *caraffa,* from ARABIC *gharraf* drinking cup.

carambola PORTUGUESE, from HINDI *karanbal* a fruit tree.

caramel FRENCH *calamele,* from LATIN *calamella* sugar cane, from *canna* cane + *mellis* honey.

carat FRENCH, from GREEK *keration* the small seed of the carob tree, used as a weight in ancient times because the seeds are usually the same size and weight.

caravan FRENCH *caravoane,* from PERSIAN *karwan* company of travelers.

carbine FRENCH *carabin* mounted rifleman, possibly from LATIN *chadabula* engine for throwing stones, from GREEK *katabolh* destruction.

carbohydrate See **carbon** + **hydrate**.

carbon FRENCH, from LATIN *carbo* coal.

carbuncle MIDDLE ENGLISH, from FRENCH, from LATIN *carbunculus* a little coal.

carcanet FRENCH *carcan* iron collar on pillories, from LATIN *carcannum.*

carcass FRENCH *carcasse.*

carcinoma LATIN, from GREEK *karkinoma* cancer, from *karkinos* crab.

card FRENCH *carte* piece of stiff paper, from LATIN *charta* leaf of papyrus, from GREEK *chartes.*

cardiac FRENCH *cardiaque,* from LATIN *cardiacus* relating to the heart, from GREEK *kardia* heart.

cardigan the Earl of *Cardigan* (1797–1868), English general.

cardinal LATIN *cardinalis* chief, from *cardo* hinge (place where two things are joined), from the idea that when something is important other things hinge, or depend on it.

cardio- GREEK *kardia* heart.

care OLD ENGLISH *caru* trouble.

careen FRENCH *carener,* from ITALIAN *carenare,* from LATIN *carina* keel (steel or wood piece along the bottom of a boat).

career FRENCH *carrière* racecourse, from LATIN *carriara* street, from *carrus* wagon.

caress FRENCH *carasse,* from ITALIAN *carezza,* from LATIN *carus* dear.

caret LATIN something lacking.

cargo SPANISH load, from LATIN *carricare,* from *carrus* a wheeled cart.

caricature FRENCH picture that makes fun, from ITALIAN *caricare* load, from LATIN *carrus* wheeled cart. The picture was of a very overloaded wagon, and therefore making fun.

caries LATIN decay, from GREEK *ker* death.

carillon FRENCH chime, from LATIN *quaternio* group of four, from *quarter* four times, a group of four bells.

carnage FRENCH, from LATIN *caro* flesh.

carnation ITALIAN *carrigione* the color of one's skin.

carnelian LATIN *carneolus,* from *carnem* flesh, because of the flesh color.

carnival ITALIAN *carnevale* church holy day, from LATIN *carnelevarium* time during the religious year (Lent) when no meat is eaten, from *caro* meat + *levare* take away.

carnivorous LATIN *carnivorus,* from *caro* flesh + *vorare* devour, eat.

carol FRENCH *carole* dance, from GREEK *choraules* flute player playing with the chorus.

carotene LATIN *carota* carrot + *-enus,* from GREEK *-enos.*

carouse FRENCH *carous* all out, from GERMAN *garaus* drink.

carp[1] (fish) FRENCH *carpe,* from GERMAN *carpa.*

carp[2] (nag) OLD NORSE *karpa* brag.

carpal LATIN *carpalis,* from *carpus* wrist.

carpenter FRENCH *carpentier* worker in wood, from LATIN *carpentum* carriage.

carpet FRENCH *carpite,* from LATIN *carpita* woolen cloth, from *carpere* card (use a metal comb on cloth).

carrack MIDDLE ENGLISH, from FRENCH *carague,* from SPANISH *carraca,* from ARABIC *qurqur* merchant ship.

carragheen *Carragheen* near Waterford, Ireland.

carriage FRENCH *carier.* See **carry**.

carrion FRENCH, from LATIN *caro* flesh.

carronade *Carron,* Scotland, where it was first made.

carrot FRENCH *carotte,* from LATIN *carota,* from GREEK *karoton.*

carry FRENCH *carier* take in a vehicle, from LATIN *carricare* load, from *carrus* two-wheeled wagon.

cart OLD ENGLISH *cræt* chariot and OLD NORSE *kartr* a two-wheeled vehicle.

cartage See **cart** + **-age**.

cartel FRENCH, from ITALIAN *cartello* written challenge, from LATIN *c(h)arta* paper. See **card**.

carter See **cart** + **-er**.

cartilage FRENCH, from LATIN *cartilago.*

carton FRENCH board, from ITALIAN *cartone,* from *carta* paper, from LATIN *charta.*

cartoon FRENCH *carton,* from ITALIAN *cartone* sketch.

cartridge FRENCH *cartouche,* from ITALIAN *carta.* See **card**.

carve OLD ENGLISH *ceorfan* cut.

carven See **carve**.

cascade FRENCH waterfall, from LATIN *casus* a falling.

case[1] (event) FRENCH *cas* event, from LATIN *casus* chance, from *cadere* fall.

case[2] (box) LATIN *capsa* box, from *capere* take.

cash FRENCH *casse* money, from LATIN *capsa* box.

cashew FRENCH *acajou,* from NATIVE AMERICAN *acajoba.*

casino ITALIAN *case* house, from LATIN *casino* hut.

cask LATIN *quassare* shake hard.

casserole FRENCH *casse* bowl, from GREEK *kyathos.*

cassette FRENCH *casse* case. See **case**[2].

cassia MIDDLE ENGLISH, from LATIN, from GREEK *kasia* kind of cinnamon, from HEBREW *qesi'ah.*

cassock FRENCH *kazhaghand* jacket, from *kazh* silk.

cast OLD NORSE *kasta* throw.

caste FRENCH *casta* breed, from LATIN *castus* pure.

caster See **cast** + **-er**.

castigate LATIN *castigare* make clean, from *castus* pure.

castle FRENCH *castel*, from LATIN *castellum* fortress.

castor[1] (oil) FRENCH, from LATIN, from GREEK *kastor* beaver.

castor[2] (caster) See **cast**.

castrate LATIN *castrare* cut.

casual LATIN *casualis* chance, from *casus.*

casualty LATIN *casualitas.* See **casual**.

cat OLD ENGLISH.

cataclysm LATIN, from GREEK *kata-* down + *klyzein* wash.

catacomb LATIN *catacumba,* from *cata,* from GREEK *kata* by + *tumba* tomb.

catalog FRENCH *catalogue* list, from LATIN *catalogus*, from GREEK *katalogos* register.

catalyst GREEK *katalysis* breaking up into parts, from *kata-* down + *lyein* loose.

catamaran TAMIL *kattumaram*, wood tied together.

catamount MIDDLE ENGLISH *cat of the mountain.*

catapult LATIN, from GREEK *katapeltes,* from *kata-* down + *pallein* throw with force.

cataract LATIN *cataracta,* from GREEK *kataraktes,* from *kata-* down + *rhegnynai* break.

catastrophe GREEK *katastrophe* overturn, from *kata-* down + *strephein* turn.

catch FRENCH *cachier* hunt, from LATIN *captare* chase.

catechism LATIN *catechizare*, from GREEK *katechizein* teach, from *kata-* completely + *ecein* sound.

category LATIN class in logic, from GREEK *kategoria.*

cater FRENCH *acatour* buyer.

caterpillar OLD NORSE *catepilose,* from LATIN *catta pilosa* hairy cat.

caterwaul MIDDLE ENGLISH *caterwawen,* probably from DUTCH *kater* tomcat + *w(r)awlen* howl like a cat.

cathedral LATIN *ecclesia cathedralis* church having a bishop's (high official in the Catholic Church) seat, from *cathedra* chair.

catholic LATIN *catholicus* universal, from GREEK *katholikos.*

catling See **cat** + **-ling**.

cattle FRENCH *catel,* from LATIN *captale* property, from *caput* head.

caucus possibly from an 18th century political club called the *Caucus* club, from LATIN *caucus* drinking cup, from GREEK *kaukos.*

caudal LATIN *cauda* tail + FRENCH, from LATIN *alis.*

cauldron FRENCH *caudron,* from LATIN *caldaria,* from *cal(i)dus* hot.

cauliflower ITALIAN *cavolfiore,* from LATIN *caulis* cabbage.

caulk MIDDLE ENGLISH *cauken* walk, from FRENCH *cauguer,* from LATIN *calcare,* from *calx* a heel.

cause FRENCH reason, from LATIN *causa.*

causeway BRITISH *causey,* from LATIN *calx* limestone + OLD ENGLISH *weg* path.

caustic LATIN *causticus* eat or wear away, from GREEK *kastikos.*

caution LATIN *cautio* careful.

cavalcade FRENCH riding on a horse, from ITALIAN *cavalcata,* from LATIN *caballus* regular horse (not of particular quality or breeding).

cavalier FRENCH knight who rides a horse, from LATIN *caballarius* horseman, from *caballus* regular horse (not of particular quality or breeding).

cavalry FRENCH *cavalerie,* from ITALIAN *cavalieria.* See **cavalier**.

cave FRENCH den, from LATIN *cavare* make hollow.

caveat LATIN let him beware.

cavil FRENCH *caviller* make fun of, from LATIN *cavillari.*

cavort AMERICAN, originally *cauvaut,* probably from *ca-* + *vault* jump, leap.

cay SPANISH *cayo* barrier reef, from FRENCH *cay* sand bank, from LATIN *caium.*

cease FRENCH *cessar* stop, from LATIN *cessare.*

cedar FRENCH *cedre,* from LATIN *cedrus,* from GREEK *kedros.*

cede FRENCH, from LATIN *cedere* go.

ceil MIDDLE ENGLISH *celen,* from FRENCH *celer* conceal, from LATIN *celare,* probably influenced by *caelum* heaven.

ceiling See **ceil**.

celandine MIDDLE ENGLISH *celidoine,* from LATIN *celidonia,* from *chelidonia,* from GREEK *chelidon* a swallow, from an ancient story that swallows appeared at the time the flowers blossomed.

celebrate LATIN *celebrare* honor.

celerity FRENCH, from LATIN *celeritas,* from *celer* swift.

celery FRENCH *céleri,* from ITALIAN, from LATIN, from GREEK *selinon* parsley (green leafy edible plant).

celestial FRENCH *celestiel* heavenly, from LATIN *caelestis.*

celibate LATIN *caelebs* unmarried.

cell LATIN *cella* small room.

cellar MIDDLE ENGLISH *celer,* from FRENCH *celier,* from LATIN *cellarium* set of cells, food containers, from *cella* small room.

cellophane LATIN *cella* small room + GREEK *phainein* show.

cellulose FRENCH, from LATIN *cellula* small room for storing things, from *cella* small room.

cement FRENCH *ciment* mixture of stone and crushed bricks, from LATIN *caementum.*

cemetery LATIN *coemeterium,* from GREEK *koimeterion* burial ground.

censor LATIN critic.

censure LATIN *censura* opinion.

cent LATIN *centum* hundred.

centaur LATIN *Centaurus,* from GREEK *Kentauros.*

centennial LATIN *centum* a hundred + *annus* year.

center LATIN *centrum* middle point of a circle, from GREEK *kentron.*

centrifugal LATIN *centrifugus* fleeing from the center, from LATIN *centrum* middle point + *fugere* flee. See **center**.

centurion See **century**.

century LATIN *centuria,* from *centum* hundred.

ceramic GREEK *keramos* potter's clay.

cereal LATIN *cerealis* grain, from the Roman goddess of grain and agriculture, Ceres.

cerebellum LATIN *cerebrum* the brain.

ceremony FRENCH *ceremonie* formal or holy procedure, from LATIN *cerimonia.*

cerise FRENCH cherry.

certain FRENCH, from LATIN *certus* sure.

certificate See **certify**.

certify FRENCH *certifier* make sure, from LATIN *certificare,* from *certus* sure + *facere* do, make.

certitude FRENCH, from LATIN *certitudo.*

cerulean LATIN *caeruleus,* probably from *caelulum* like the sky, from *caelum* heaven.

cession FRENCH, from LATIN *cedere* go.

cestus LATIN *caestus,* from *caedere* strike, beat.

chafe FRENCH *chaufer* warm, from LATIN *calefacere,* from *calere* be warm + *facere* do, make.

chaff OLD ENGLISH *ceaf.*

chaffer OLD NORSE *kapfor* trading journey.

chagrin FRENCH grief.

chain FRENCH *chaeine,* from LATIN *catena.*

chair FRENCH *chaiere* seat, from LATIN *cathedra,* from GREEK *kathedra.*

chaise FRENCH seat. See **chair**.

chalcedony FRENCH *calcedoine,* from LATIN *calcedonius,* from GREEK *chalkedon* precious stone.

chalet FRENCH *chalé* herder's mountain hut, from *chaslet,* small farmhouse, from *chasel* farmhouse, from LATIN *casa* house.

chalice FRENCH, from LATIN *calix* a cup.

chalk OLD ENGLISH *cealc,* from LATIN *calyx* kind of soft stone.

challenge FRENCH *chalenge* accusation, from LATIN *calumnia* false accusation.

challis possibly from the English last name *Challis.*

chamber FRENCH *chambre* bedroom, from LATIN *camera* arched ceiling, from GREEK *kamara,* having an arched covering.

chamberlain MIDDLE ENGLISH *chaumberlein,* from FRENCH *chamberlenc,* from GERMAN *chamarling,* from LATIN *camera* arched ceiling.

chameleon LATIN *chamaeleon,* from GREEK *chamai* dwarf + *leon* lion.

chamois FRENCH, from LATIN *camox.*

champ imitative.

champagne the town of *Champagne* in northeast France, where the wine is made.

champion MIDDLE ENGLISH *champiun* person in combat, from FRENCH, from LATIN *campio* fighter in the field, from *campus* field.

chance FRENCH *cheance* fall of the dice, from LATIN *cadentia,* from *cadere* fall.

chancellor MIDDLE ENGLISH, from FRENCH *cancelier,* from LATIN *cancellarius* an officer in a court of the Roman Empire.

chancery FRENCH *chancellerie,* from FRENCH *cancelier.* See **chancellor**.

chandelier French *chandelabre*, from Latin *candelabrum*, from *candela* candle.

chandler French *chandelier* maker and seller of candles, from Latin *candela* candle.

change French *changier* make different, from Latin *cambiare* exchange.

channel French *chanel* canal, from Latin *canalis.*

chant French *chanter* sing, from Latin *cantare.*

chanteuse French.

chanty French *chanter* sing.

chaos Latin empty space, from Greek.

chaparral Spanish *chaparro* evergreen oak.

chapati Hindi *chapati* unleavened bread.

chapel French *chapele*, from Latin *cappella* cloak, from the cloak of a saint which was kept in a holy place for people to see.

chaperone French *chaperon* protector, from *chape* hood, from Latin *cappa.*

chaplain French *chapelain,* from Latin *cappella.* See **chapel**.

chaps Mexican *chaparejos.*

chapter French *chapitre* section of a book, from Latin *capitulum.*

char Old English *cierr* time of working.

charabanc French car with bench.

character Latin mark of quality, from Greek *charakter* sharpen.

charade French a game, from *charra* chatter (speak quickly and foolishly).

charcoal Middle English *char cole,* probably from *charren* turn + *cole* coal.

chard French *carde*, from Latin *carduus* thistle, artichoke.

charge French *charger* load, from Latin *carricare* load a wagon, from *carrus* two-wheeled wagon.

charisma Greek favor, gift of talent from the gods.

charity French *charité,* from Latin *caritas* Christian love, from *carus* beloved.

charlatan French, from Italian *ciarlatano*, from *ciarla* chat, prattle.

charm French *charme* magical song, from Latin *carmen* song.

chart French *charte* map, from Latin *charta* paper, from Greek *chartes* sheets of papyrus.

charter French *chartre,* from Latin *charta.* See **card**.

chartreuse French.

chary Old English *cearig* careful.

chase French *chacier* hunt, from Latin *captare* try to catch.

chasm Latin *chasma* opening, from Greek.

chassee French *chassé* dance step.

chassis French frame, from Latin *capsa* box.

chaste French, from Latin *castus.*

chasten Latin *castigare* punish.

chat[1] (talk) Middle English shortened form of **chatter**.

chat[2] (firewood) French *chats* cats, because of the soft roundness of the flowers of walnuts and willow.

chateau French, from Latin *castellum* castle.

chatelaine French, from Latin *castellum.* See **castle**.

chattel French *chatel.* See **cattle**.

chatter Middle English *chateren* twitter, gossip; of echoic origin.

chauffeur French *chauffer* one who stokes a fire, from Latin *calefacere* make warm. (The first cars got their power from steam, so the French called the drivers chauffeurs.)

chauvinism French *chauvinisme,* from Nicolas *Chauvin,* a French soldier who was overly loyal to the emperor Napoleon I (1769–1821).

chaw See **chew**.

cheap Old English *ceap* bargain, from Latin *caupo* one who trades.

cheat[1] (be unfair) Middle English *eschete,* from French *escheoir* get (fall to) one's share, from Latin ex- out + *cadere* fall.

cheat[2] (low quality bread) possibly from **cheat**[1].

check French *eschec* loss (in the game of chess), from Persian *shah* king (the most important chess piece).

cheek Old English *ceoke* jaw.

cheer French *chere* face, from Latin *cara,* from Greek *kara* face.

chef French *chef de cuisine* head (chief) cook, from Latin *caput* head.

chemise Middle English, from French, from Latin *camisia* shirt.

chemist French *chimiste,* from Latin *chemista.*

cherish French *cher,* from Latin *carus.*

cheroot French *cheroute,* from Tamil *churuttu* roll of tobacco.

cherry French *cherise,* from Latin, from Greek *kerasos* cherry tree.

cherub (cherubim) Hebrew *k'rub* winged angel.

chest Old English *cest* box, from Latin *cista,* from Greek *kiste.*

chestnut Middle English *chesteine,* from French *chastaigne,* from Latin *castanea,* from Greek *kastaneia.*

chevet French *chevet* pillow.

chevron Middle English *cheveroun,* from French *chevron,* from Latin *capra* goat.

chew Middle English *chewan,* from Old English *ceowan* bite.

chic French, from German *Schick* having good taste.

chicory Middle English *cicory,* from French *cicoree,* from Latin *cichorium,* from Greek *kichoreia.*

chide (chidden) Old English *cidan* quarrel.

chief French *chief, chef* leader, from Latin *caput* head.

chiffonier French *chiffon,* from *chiffe* rag.

chilblain See **chill** + *blain,* from Old English *blegen* a sore.

child Old English *cild.*

chili Spanish *chile* from Native American *chilli.*

chill Middle English *ciele* coldness, from *kal* be cold.

chime French *chimbe* cymbal, from Latin *cymbalum,* from Greek *kymbalon.*

chimera Latin *chimaera,* from Greek *chimaira* monster, originally a goat that has lived through one winter, from *cheima* winter.

chimney French *cheminee* fireplace, from Latin *caminata,* from *caminus,* from Greek *kaminos.*

chin Old English *cin.*

chine Middle English, from Old English *eschine,* from German *skina* small bone, shin bone.

chink Middle English *chine.*

chinook early NATIVE AMERICAN name *Tsinuk.*

chinosol GERMAN, from *china*, a variant spelling of *kina* or *quina*. See **quinine**.

chip OLD ENGLISH *cipp* log.

chipmunk NATIVE AMERICAN *atchitamon* squirrel.

chirk MIDDLE ENGLISH *chirken* creak, from OLD ENGLISH *circian* roar.

chiropractic GREEK *cheir* hand + *praktikos* practical.

chirp MIDDLE ENGLISH *chirpen*, from *chirken* twitter.

chirrup imitative.

chisel FRENCH, from LATIN *cisellus* cutting tool, from *caedere* cut.

chiton GREEK.

chitterling MIDDLE ENGLISH *chiterling* intestines, from GERMAN *kut* soft parts of the body.

chivalry FRENCH *chevalier* knight, from LATIN *caballarius* horseman, from *caballus* regular horse (not of particular quality or breeding).

chloride See **chloro-** + **-ide**.

chlorine See **chloro-** + **-ine**[1].

chloro- GREEK *chloros* pale green.

chlorodyne See **chloro-** + **anodyne**.

chloroform See **chloro-** + **formic**.

chlorophyll FRENCH *chlorophylle,* from GREEK *chloros* green + *phyllon* a leaf.

chloroplast GREEK *chloros* pale green + *-plast*, from GREEK *plastos* formed.

chock FRENCH *chouque* log.

chocolate FRENCH, from SPANISH, from NATIVE AMERICAN *chocolatl.*

choice FRENCH *choisir* choose.

choir FRENCH *cuer,* from LATIN *chorus* singers and dancers, from GREEK *choros.*

choke OLD ENGLISH *aceocian.*

choler FRENCH *colere,* from GREEK, from *chole* bile (stomach fluids that cause a bad taste in the mouth). The ancient Greeks thought bile caused anger.

cholesterol FRENCH *colere,* from GREEK, from *chole* bile (stomach fluids that cause a bad taste in the mouth) + GREEK *stereos* stiff.

choline See **choler** + **-ine**[1].

choose OLD ENGLISH *ceosan.*

chop MIDDLE ENGLISH *choppen,* probably from FRENCH *choper, coper* cut.

chord LATIN *chorda.* See **accord**.

choreography GREEK *choreia* dance + *-graphia* description, from *graphein* write.

choriamb LATIN *choriambus*, from GREEK *choriambos*, from *choreios* chorus + *iambos* forceful speech.

choriambus See **choriamb**.

chorister MIDDLE ENGLISH *querister*, from FRENCH *cuerister*, from LATIN *chorus* choir, from GREEK *choros.* See **chorus**.

chorizo SPANISH pork sausage.

chortle blend of **chuckle** and **snort**, invented by the English writer Lewis Carroll (1832–1898).

chorus LATIN, from GREEK *choros* a dance, chorus.

chow CHINESE *kaú* dog.

Christ OLD ENGLISH *Crist,* from LATIN *Christus,* from GREEK *Cristos,* translation of HEBREW *mashiah* Messiah (Jesus).

chromatic LATIN *chromaticus,* from GREEK *chroma* color.

chrome GREEK *chroma* color.

chronic Latin *chronicus* time, from Greek *chronos.*

chronicle Middle English *cronicle,* from French *chronique,* from Latin *chronica,* from Greek *chronos* time.

chrono- Greek *chronos* time.

chronology See **chrono-** + **-logy**.

chronoscope See **chrono-** + **-scope**.

chrysalis Latin *chrysallis*, from Greek gold colored, from *chrysos* gold.

chrysanthemum Latin, from Greek *chrysos* gold + *anthemon* flower.

chrysoprase French *crisopace,* from Latin *chrysoprasus,* from Greek *chrysoprasos,* from *chrysos* gold + *prason* leek (a green vegetable).

chuck French *choquer* knock.

chuckle imitative.

chug imitative.

chukka Hindi *chakkar* circle.

chum[1] (bait) perhaps from Scottish *chum* food.

chum[2] (friend) British slang for roommate.

chunk variant of **chuck**.

chunter imitative.

chuppah Hebrew *huppah* cover.

church Old English *circe* building for Christians to pray in, from Greek *kyriakon* house of the Lord, from *kyrios* master, lord.

churl Old English *ceorl* peasant.

churn Old English *cyrin* container for making butter.

chute French fall, from Latin *cadere.*

cicada Latin.

-cide Latin *caedere* kill.

cider French *cidre,* from Latin *sicera,* from Greek *sikera,* from Hebrew *shekar* strong drink.

cigar Spanish *cigarro.*

cigarette diminutive of **cigar**.

cilia Latin *cilia*, plural of *cilium*, an eyelid, eyelid-edge, eyelash.

cinch Spanish *cincha* strap on a saddle, from Latin *cingula* belt.

cinder Old English *sinder.*

cinema Greek *kinema* motion.

cinnamon French *cinnamom,* from Latin, from Greek, from Hebrew *qinnamon.*

cipher French *cifre* zero, from Arabic *çifr* empty.

circle Latin *circulus,* from *circus* ring.

circuit Middle English, from French, from Latin *circuitus* a going round, from *circumire,* from *circum* around + *ire* go.

circulate Latin *circulari* form a circle.

circum- Latin around.

circumference Middle English, from Latin *circumferentia,* from *circum-* around + *ferre* carry.

circumspect Middle English, from Latin *circumspectus,* from *circum-* around + *specere* look.

circumstance Latin *circumstantia* surrounding condition, from *circum-* around + *stare* stand.

circus Latin circle, from Greek *kirkos.*

cirque French, from Latin *circus* circle, from Greek *kirkos.*

cirrus Latin *cirrus* curl.

cistern French *cisterne,* from Latin *cisterna* reservoir.

citadel ITALIAN *cittade* city, from LATIN *civitas* city, state.

cite FRENCH, from LATIN *citare* order to appear (before a judge), from *ciere* wake up.

cithara LATIN, from GREEK *kithara.*

citizen FRENCH *citeain* person in town, from *cite* city, from LATIN *civitas* city, state.

citrate See **citrus** + **-ate**.

citrus LATIN, from GREEK *kitron.*

city FRENCH *cité* large town, from LATIN *civis* citizen.

civilize FRENCH, from LATIN *civilis,* from *civis* citizen.

clabber IRISH *clabar.*

claim FRENCH *cla(i)mer* call out, from LATIN *clamare* call.

clairvoyant FRENCH *clairvoyance* having clear sight.

clam MIDDLE ENGLISH *clamp,* from OLD ENGLISH *clamm* grasp, bond.

clamber MIDDLE ENGLISH *clambren.*

clammy probably from OLD ENGLISH *clam* clay.

clamor FRENCH *clamour*, from LATIN *clamor* loud cry.

clamp[1] (hold together) DUTCH *klampe.*

clamp[2] (a pile or mound) DUTCH *klamp* heap.

clan MIDDLE ENGLISH, from SCOTTISH *clann* family, from IRISH *cland* offspring, from LATIN *planta* sprout.

clandestine LATIN *clandestinus.*

clang LATIN *clangere* sound again.

clangor LATIN *clangor* sound, noise.

clank See **clang**.

clap OLD ENGLISH *clæppan* beat.

clapboard GERMAN *klappholt* wood, from *klappen* fit together + *holt* wood.

clapper See **clap**.

clapperdudgeon See **clapper** + **dudgeon**.

claret MIDDLE ENGLISH, from FRENCH *vin claret* clear wine, from LATIN *clarus* clear.

clarify FRENCH *clarifier* make clear, from LATIN *clarificare,* from *carus* clear + *facere* do, make.

clarinet FRENCH *clarine* bell, from LATIN *clarus* clear.

clarion FRENCH *clairon*, from LATIN *clarlo,* from *clarus* clear.

clash imitative.

clasp MIDDLE ENGLISH *claspe.*

class FRENCH *classe,* from LATIN *classis* one of the six divisions of the Roman people, based on ownership of land and wealth.

classic LATIN *classicus* of the highest class, from *classis.* See **class**.

classify LATIN *classis.* See **class**.

clatter possibly from OLD ENGLISH *clatere* a rattle.

clause FRENCH, from LATIN *clausa* end of a sentence, from *claudere* close.

clavicle FRENCH *clavicule,* from LATIN *clavicula,* from *clavis* a key.

clavier FRENCH, from LATIN *claviarius* keyboard.

claw MIDDLE ENGLISH *claue,* from OLD ENGLISH *clawu.*

claymore SCOTTISH *claidheamhmor,* from *claidheamh* sword + *mor* great.

clean OLD ENGLISH *clæne* clear.

clear FRENCH *cler* pure, from LATIN *clarus* bright.

cleat OLD ENGLISH lump.

cleave[1] (divide) OLD ENGLISH *cleofan.*

cleave[2] (cling to) OLD ENGLISH *cleofian.*

cleft MIDDLE ENGLISH *clift,* from OLD ENGLISH *clyft.*

clemency MIDDLE ENGLISH *clemencie,* from LATIN *clemens* merciful.

clement LATIN *clemens* merciful.

clench OLD ENGLISH *(be)clencan* hold.

clergy FRENCH *clergie,* from LATIN *clericus.*

clerk OLD ENGLISH *clerc,* from LATIN *clericus* priest. During the Middle Ages, those who could read and write were mostly church people.

clever probably from NORWEGIAN *klöver* skillful.

clew OLD ENGLISH *cleowen* ball of thread. See **clue.**

cliché FRENCH, thin metal sheet used in 18th century printing, from the sound of a printing block dropped onto the still hot metal sheet. Later the word came to stand for something repeated in an identical way.

click imitative.

client LATIN *cliens* person dependent.

cliff OLD ENGLISH *clif.*

climate LATIN *clima* region, from GREEK *klima.*

climax LATIN, from GREEK *klimax* ladder.

clinch OLD ENGLISH *(be)clencan* hold.

cling OLD ENGLISH *clingan* shrink.

clinic LATIN *clinicus* treating patients who are in bed, from GREEK *kline* bed.

clink DUTCH *klinken,* imitative.

clip OLD NORSE *klippa* cut short.

clipper MIDDLE ENGLISH *clippen.* See **clip.**

clipt See **clip.**

clique FRENCH *cliquer* make a noise.

cloak FRENCH *cloche* bell, from LATIN *clocca.* The shape of a cloak is like a bell.

cloche FRENCH bell.

clock FRENCH *cloke,* from LATIN *clocca* bell. Many clocks had bells that rang when the hour came.

clod OLD ENGLISH.

clodpole See **clod** + GERMAN *poll* head.

clog MIDDLE ENGLISH *clogge* lump of wood.

cloister FRENCH *clostre* religious place to go for quiet, from LATIN *claustrum* enclosed place.

close FRENCH *clore* shut, from LATIN *claudere.*

closet FRENCH *clos,* from LATIN *claudere* close.

closure FRENCH, from LATIN *clausura,* from *claudere* close.

clot OLD ENGLISH *clott.*

clothes OLD ENGLISH *clathas,* from *clath* cloth.

cloud OLD ENGLISH *clud* mass of rock.

clout MIDDLE ENGLISH *cloule,* from OLD ENGLISH *clut* lump.

clove[1] (spice) MIDDLE ENGLISH *clowe,* from FRENCH *clou de girofle* nail of clove, from LATIN *clavus* nail, because of the shape.

clove[2] (slice of garlic) OLD ENGLISH *clufu* thing cloven.

cloven See **cleave**[1].

clown OLD NORSE *klunni* awkward person.

club OLD NORSE *clubba* thick stick.

cluck OLD ENGLISH *cloccian.*

clue OLD ENGLISH *cleowen* ball of thread. In an early legend a ball of thread was used to mark the way through a maze.

clump GERMAN *klumpe* shoe made from a piece of wood.

clumsy MIDDLE ENGLISH *clumsid* numb with cold, from OLD NORSE *klumsa* lockjaw (disease which causes the jaw to become stiff or tight).

cluster OLD ENGLISH *clyster* bunch.

clutch[1] MIDDLE ENGLISH *clucchan*, from OLD ENGLISH *clyccan*, bend the fingers, clench.

clutch[2]**:** (of eggs) MIDDLE ENGLISH *clucchen*, from OLD ENGLISH *clekken* create, from OLD NORSE *klekja* hatch.

co- LATIN *co-, com-* with.

coach FRENCH *coche*, from Hungarian *kocsi* the town of Kocs, where the coaches were made.

coagulate LATIN *coagulare*, from *co-* together + *agere* drive, make.

coal OLD ENGLISH *col* charcoal.

coalesce LATIN *coalescere*, from *co-* together + *alescere* grow up.

coalition LATIN *coalitio* meeting, from *coalescere*, from *co-* together + *alescere* grow up.

coarse See **course**.

coast FRENCH *coste* shore, from LATIN *costa* side.

coat MIDDLE ENGLISH, from French *cote*, origin unknown.

coax obsolete *coax, cokes* a fool.

cob OLD ENGLISH, used in several senses, most meaning "big," "rounded" or "head," but possibly of different origins.

cobalt GERMAN *kobold* goblin, from the belief that goblins put it in place of valuable silver in the mines.

cobble (paving stone) MIDDLE ENGLISH *cob* a rounded lump.

cobbler MIDDLE ENGLISH *cobelere.*

cobra PORTUGUESE *cobra (de capello)* serpent (with hood), from LATIN *colubra* a snake.

cocciliana LATIN *coccineus* scarlet + MODERN ENGLISH, from FRENCH *liana* twining plant.

coccus LATIN, from GREEK *kokkus* grain, seed, berry.

coccyx LATIN, from GREEK *kokkyx* cuckoo.

cochlea LATIN, from GREEK *kokhlias* snail, screw.

cock[1] (rooster) OLD ENGLISH *cocc* male bird.

cock[2] (tilt) OLD ENGLISH *cocc* male bird, from the way the bird tilts its head when it crows.

cockatoo DUTCH *kaketoe*, from MALAY *kakatua.*

cockle MIDDLE ENGLISH *cokel*, from FRENCH *coquille* shell, from LATIN *conchylium*, from GREEK *konchylion* shellfish.

cockney MIDDLE ENGLISH *cokenei* spoiled child, from *coken-ey* cock's egg.

cocktail[1] (shape) See **cock**[1] + **tail**.

cocktail[2] (drink) AMERICAN *cocktay*, from FRENCH *coquetier* egg-cup (first served in New Orleans in such cups).

cocoa SPANISH *cacao.*

cod OLD ENGLISH *codd* bag.

coddle LATIN *cal(i)dus* warm.

code FRENCH list of laws, from LATIN *codex* wooden tablet for writing.

codger probably from BRITISH *cadger* beggar.

codicil FRENCH *codicille*, from LATIN *codicillus* short writing.

coefficient See **co-** + **efficient**.

coerce LATIN *coercerce* shut in.

coffee ITALIAN *caffé,* from ARABIC *qahwah,* from an area in Africa called *Kaffa* where the coffee plant came from originally.

coffer MIDDLE ENGLISH, from FRENCH *cofre* a chest, from LATIN *cophinus* basket, from GREEK *kophinos.*

coffin FRENCH *cofin* chest, from LATIN *cophinus* basket, from GREEK *kophinos.*

cog[1] (tooth on a wheel) MIDDLE ENGLISH *cogge,* of SCANDINAVIAN origin.

cog[2] (ship) MIDDLE ENGLISH *cogge,* from FRENCH *cogue.*

cogent LATIN *cogere* force together.

cognition LATIN *cognoscere* knowledge, from *co-* together + *(g)noscere* know.

cohere LATIN *cohaerere,* from *co-* together + *haerere* stick.

cohort FRENCH *cohorte,* from LATIN *cohors* enclosed space or crowd.

coigne (coynye) IRISH *coinnemh.*

coil FRENCH *collir* collect, from LATIN *colligere.*

coin FRENCH, from LATIN *cuneus.*

coincide LATIN *coincidere* fall upon together, from *co-* together + *incidere* fall upon.

colander LATIN *colatorium,* from *colare* drain.

cold OLD ENGLISH *cald.*

colic MIDDLE ENGLISH *colik,* from FRENCH *colique,* from LATIN *colicus,* from GREEK *kolon* colon, from the area in the body that is affected.

collaborate LATIN *collaborare,* from *com-* with + *laborare* work.

collage FRENCH *colle* glue, from GREEK *kolla.*

collapse LATIN *collabi* fall in ruins.

collar FRENCH *colier* necklace, from LATIN *collum* neck.

collaret See **collar**.

collate LATIN *conferre,* from *com-* together + *ferre* bring.

collateral LATIN *collateralis,* from *com-* together + *lateralis* lateral (at the side).

colleague FRENCH *collègue,* from LATIN *collega,* from *com-* with + *legare* have help.

collect LATIN *colligere,* from *com-* together + *legere* gather.

college LATIN *collegium* association of persons.

collet FRENCH, from *col* neck, from LATIN *collum.*

colloquy LATIN *colloquium,* from *com-* together + *loqui* speak.

collude LATIN *com-* with + *ludere* play.

collusion See **collude**.

cologne FRENCH *Cologne,* from GERMAN *Köln,* city in Germany.

colon GREEK *kolon* clause.

colonel FRENCH *coronel,* from ITALIAN *colonna* military column, from LATIN *columna* column.

colonnade FRENCH, from ITALIAN, from LATIN *colomna* pillar.

colony LATIN *colonia* farm.

color MIDDLE ENGLISH, from FRENCH, from LATIN *colos* covering.

colossus LATIN huge statue, from GREEK *kolossos.*

colter See **coulter**.

columbine FRENCH *colombin,* from LATIN *columbina,* from *columbinus* like a dove.

columel LATIN *columella* small pillar.

column LATIN *columna* pillar.

com- LATIN *com-, cum-* with, together, very much.

coma LATIN, from GREEK *koma* deep sleep.

comanche SPANISH, from NATIVE AMERICAN *kimachi* stranger, other.

comb MIDDLE ENGLISH, from OLD ENGLISH *camb* toothed object.

combat FRENCH *combatre* fight, from LATIN *com-* with + *battuere* beat.

combine LATIN *combinare* unite, from *com-* with + *bini* two each.

combustion FRENCH, from LATIN *combusto,* from *comburere* burn up.

come OLD ENGLISH *cuman.*

comedy FRENCH *comedie* funny play, from LATIN *comoedia,* from GREEK *komoidia,* from *komos* party + *aeidein* sing. Ancient Greek comedies were festivals with singing.

comet OLD ENGLISH *cometa,* from LATIN, from GREEK *kome* hair.

comfort FRENCH *comforter* urge, from LATIN *comfortare* make stronger, from *com-* together + *fortis* strong.

comic MIDDLE ENGLISH *comice,* from LATIN *comicus* , from GREEK *komikos.*

comma LATIN, from GREEK *komma* that which is cut off, from *koptein* cut off.

command FRENCH *comander* order, from LATIN *commandare,* from *com-* together + *mandare* order.

commemorate LATIN *commemorare,* from *com-* much + *memorare* remind.

commence FRENCH, from LATIN *com-* together + *initiare* initiate (start).

commend LATIN *commendare,* from *com-* with + *mandare* command.

commensurate LATIN *com-* together + *mensura* a measure.

comment LATIN *commentum* invention, from *com-* together + *meminisse* remember.

commerce LATIN *commercium,* from *com-* together + *merx* merchandise.

commiserate LATIN *commiserari,* from *com-* with + *miserare* pity.

commissar See **commissary**.

commissary LATIN *commissarius,* from *commissus* entrusted.

commission FRENCH charge, from LATIN *commissio* contest. See **commit.**

commissure LATIN *commissura* joining.

commit LATIN *committere,* from *com-* together + *mittere* send.

committee FRENCH. See **commit.**

commode FRENCH, from LATIN *commodus* suitable, from *com-* together + *modus* measure.

commodity FRENCH *commodité* benefit, from LATIN *commoditatem* fitness, from *commodus.* See **commode.**

common FRENCH *comun* general, from LATIN *communis* shared by all, from *com-* together + *munia* public duties.

commotion LATIN *commotio,* from *com-* together + *movere* move.

commune[1] (talk with) FRENCH *comuner* share, from *comun.* See **common.**

commune[2] (place) FRENCH *commune,* from LATIN *communia* group sharing a common life, from *communis.* See **common.**

communicate LATIN *communicare* share.

communion FRENCH, from LATIN *communis.* See **common.**

communism FRENCH *communisme,* from *commun* general, from LATIN *communis.* See **common.**

community FRENCH *com(m)unete,* from LATIN *communitas,* from *communis.* See **common.**

commutation See **commute** + **-ation**.

commute LATIN *commutare* change, from *com-* with + *mutare* change.

compact MIDDLE ENGLISH, from LATIN *compactus,* from *compingere,* from *com-* together + *pangere* fasten, fix.

companion FRENCH, from LATIN *companio* friend who eats with one, from *com-* with + *panis* bread.

company FRENCH *compagnie* group of soldiers, from LATIN *companes* group of soldiers living and eating together, from *com-* with + *panis* bread.

compare FRENCH *comparer,* from LATIN *comparare,* from *com-* with + *par* equal.

compartment FRENCH *compartir,* from ITALIAN *compartimento,* from *compartire,* from *com-* very much + *partire* divide.

compass FRENCH *compas* measure, from LATIN *com-* together + *passus* step.

compassion FRENCH, from LATIN *compassio,* from *com-* with + *pati* suffer.

compatible FRENCH, from LATIN *compati* suffer with. See **compassion**.

compel LATIN *compellere,* from *com-* together + *pellere* drive.

compendium LATIN *compendium* a shortening, from *com-* together + *pendere* weigh.

compensate LATIN *compensare,* from *com-* with + *pensare* weigh.

compete LATIN *competere,* from *com-* together + *petere* seek.

competent See **compete**.

compile FRENCH, from LATIN *compilare,* from *com-* together + *pilare* make smaller.

complacent LATIN *complacere* be pleasing, from *com-* very much + *placere* please.

complain FRENCH *complaindre,* from LATIN *complangere,* from *com-* very much + *plangere* hit the chest.

complaisance See **complacent**.

complement LATIN *complementus,* from *complere.* See **complete**.

complete FRENCH, from LATIN *complere,* from *com-* very much + *plere* fill.

complex LATIN *complecti,* from *com-* with + *plectere* weave.

compliment FRENCH, from ITALIAN *complimento,* from LATIN *complere.* See **complete**.

comply FRENCH, from LATIN *complere.* See **complete**.

component LATIN *componere.* See **compose**.

compose FRENCH *composer,* from LATIN *componere,* from *com-* with + *poser* place.

composite See **compose**.

compost FRENCH, from LATIN *compositum.* See **compose**.

compote FRENCH. See **compose**.

compound FRENCH, from LATIN *componere.* See **compose**.

comprehend LATIN *comprehendere,* from *com-* with + *prehendere* take, seize.

compulsion MIDDLE ENGLISH, from LATIN *compulsio,* from *compellere.* See **compel**.

compunction LATIN *compunctio* pricking of the conscience, from *compungere,* from *com-* with + *pungere* prick.

compute LATIN *computare,* from *com-* with + *putare* figure out.

comrade FRENCH *comarade* roommate, from SPANISH *camarada,* from *camara* room, from LATIN *camera.*

con[1] (negation) LATIN *contra* against.

con[2] (study) OLD ENGLISH *cunnan* know, know how. See **can**[1].

con[3] (swindle) AMERICAN *confidence man*, from scams in which the victim is persuaded to hand over money as a token of confidence.

con[4] (guide ships) FRENCH *conduire*, from LATIN *conducere*. See **conduct**.

con- See **com-**.

concatenate LATIN *concatenare* link together, from *com-* together + *catenare*, from *catena* a chain.

concave FRENCH, from LATIN *concavus* hollow, from *com-* very much + *cavus* hollow.

conceal FRENCH *conceler* hide, from LATIN *concelare*.

concede LATIN *concedere* yield.

conceit MIDDLE ENGLISH *conceite*. See **conceive**.

conceive LATIN *concipere* receive, from *com-* together + *capere* take.

concentrate FRENCH, from LATIN *com-* together + *centrum* center.

concentric FRENCH *concentrique*, from LATIN, from *com-* together + *centrum* center.

conception See **conceive**.

concern LATIN *concernere* relate to, from *com-* together + *cernere* find out about.

concert FRENCH, from ITALIAN, from LATIN *concertare*, from *com-* with + *certare* strive (work for).

concertina See **concert** + **-ina**.

conch MIDDLE ENGLISH *conke*, from LATIN *concha*, from GREEK *konche*.

conciliate LATIN *conciliare*, from *com-* with + *calare* call.

concise LATIN *concidere*, from *com-* very much + *cadere* cut.

conclave FRENCH, from LATIN a room that could be locked, from *com-* with + *clavis* a key.

conclude LATIN *concludere*, from *com-* together + *claudere* shut.

concoct LATIN *concoquere*, from *com-* together + *coquere* cook.

concord FRENCH *concorde*, from LATIN *concordia*, from *concors* of the same mind, from *com-* together + *cors* heart.

concrete LATIN *concrescere*, from *com-* together + *crescere* grow.

concur LATIN *concurrere*, from *com-* together + *currere* run.

concussion LATIN *concutere*, from *com-* together + *quatere* shake.

condemn LATIN *condemnare*, from *com-* very much + *damnare* harm, condemn.

condense LATIN *condensare*, from *com-* together + *densus* dense.

condescend LATIN *condescendere*, from *com-* together + *descendere* descend.

condiment LATIN *condimentum* a spice, from *condire* pickle (using something like vinegar to preserve food).

condition FRENCH *condicion*, from LATIN *conditio* agreement, from *com-* together + *dicere* speak.

condole LATIN *condolere*, from *com-* with + *dolere* be sad about.

condone LATIN *condonare*, from *com-* very much + *donare* give.

condor SPANISH, from NATIVE AMERICAN *cuntur* name for the bird.

conduce See **conduct**.

conduct LATIN *conducere*, from *com-* together + *ducere* lead.

conduit See **conduct**.

condyle French, from Latin *condylus,* from Greek *kondylos* knuckle.

cone French *cône,* from Latin *conus,* from Greek *konos.*

confabulate Latin *confabulare,* from *com-* together + *fabulari* converse.

confection Latin *conficere,* from *com-* with + *facere* do, make.

confederate Latin *confoederare* unite in a league (group), from *foedus* league.

confer Latin *conferre,* from *com-* together + *ferre* bring.

confess Latin *confiteri,* from *com-* together + *fateri* acknowledge.

confetti Italian *confetto,* from Latin *confectum,* small candy.

confide Latin *confidere,* from *com-* very much + *fidere* trust.

configure Latin *configurare,* from *con-* together + *figurare* shape.

confine French, from Latin *confinum,* from *com-* with + *finis* end.

confirm French, from Latin *confirmare,* from *com-* very much + *furmare* strengthen, from *firmus* firm.

confiscate Latin *confiscare* put in a chest, from *com-* together + *fiscus* money chest, treasury.

conflagation Latin *conflagrationem,* from *com-* very much + *flagrare* burn.

conflict Latin *confligere,* from *com-* very much + *fligere* strike.

conform French *conformir,* from Latin *conformare,* from *com-* together + *formare* form.

confound French *confondre* destroy, from Latin *confundere,* from *com-* together + *fundere* pour.

confront Latin *confrontare,* from *com-* together + *frons* forehead.

confuse Middle English *confusen,* from Latin *confundere,* from *com-* together + *fundere* pour.

confusticate alteration of **confuse** or **confound**.

conga Spanish *Congo* (a dance).

congeal French, from Latin *congelare,* from *com-* together + *gelare* freeze.

congenial See **com-** + **genial**.

conger Latin *conger* sea-eel, from Greek *gongros.*

congest Latin *congerere* pile up, from *com-* together + *gerere* carry.

conglomerate Latin *conglomerare,* from *com-* together + *glomerare* gather into a ball, from *glomus* a ball.

congratulate Latin *congratulari,* from *com-* together + *gratulari* wish joy, from *gratus* agree.

congregate Latin *congregare* assemble, from *com-* together + *gregare* gather, from *congrex* flock.

congress Latin *congredi,* from *com-* together + *gradi* walk, from *gradus* a step.

congruent Latin *congruere* agree.

congruous See **congruent**.

conifer Latin *conus* cone + *ferre* bring.

conjecture Latin *conjectura,* from *com-* together + *jacere* throw.

conjugate Latin *conjugare,* from *com-* together + *jugare* join, from *jugum* yoke.

conjunction French, from Latin *conjungere,* from *com-* together + *jungere* join.

conjure French, from Latin *conjurare,* from *com-* together + *jurare* swear.

conker See **conquer**.

connect LATIN *connectere,* from *com-* together + *nectere* tie together.

connive LATIN *conivere* wink.

connoisseur FRENCH, from LATIN *cognoscere,* from *co-* together + *(g)noscere* know.

connote LATIN *connotare,* from *com-* together + *notare* mark.

conquer FRENCH *conquerre* win, from LATIN *conquaerere,* from *com-* very much + *quaerere* look for.

conquest FRENCH *conqueste,* from LATIN *conquestus,* from *conquistus.*

conscience FRENCH awareness of good and evil, from LATIN *conscire,* from *com-* with + *scire* know.

conscious LATIN *conscius* aware. See **conscience**.

consecrate LATIN *consecrare,* from *com-* together + *sacrare* make holy, from *sacer* sacred.

consecutive FRENCH *consécutif,* from LATIN *consecutivus,* from *consequi.* See **consequence**.

consensus LATIN. See **consent**.

consent FRENCH *consentir* agree, from LATIN *com-* together + *sentire* feel.

consequence FRENCH, from LATIN *consequi,* from *com-* with + *sequi* follow.

conservatory See **conserve**.

conserve FRENCH *conserver* preserve, from LATIN *conservare,* from *com-* with + *servare* keep.

consider FRENCH *considerer* observe closely, from LATIN *considerare,* from *com-* with + *sidus* star.

consign LATIN *consignare* seal, from *com-* together + *signare,* from *signum* sign.

consist LATIN *consistere,* from *com-* together + *sistere* cause to stand, from *stare* stand.

console FRENCH *consoler* comfort, from LATIN *consolari,* from *com-* with + *solari* solace (comfort).

consolidate LATIN *consolidare,* from *com-* together + *solidare,* from *solidus* solid.

consonance LATIN *consonans* sound or letter, from *consonare,* from *com-* with + *sonare* sound.

consort FRENCH colleague, partner, wife, from LATIN *consortem* partner, neighbor, from *com-* with + *sors* a share.

conspicuous LATIN *conspicere* look at, from *com-* very much + *specere* see.

conspire FRENCH, from LATIN *conspirare,* from *com-* together + *spirare* breathe.

constable FRENCH *conestable* officer in charge of the stable, from LATIN *cones stabuli* "officer of the stable". The care of a king's horses was a very important matter.

constant FRENCH, from LATIN *constare,* from *com-* together + *stare* stand.

constellation MIDDLE ENGLISH *constellacion,* from FRENCH *constellation,* from LATIN *constellatus,* from *com-* with + *stellare* shine, from *stella* star.

consternation LATIN *consternare* make afraid.

constituent LATIN *constituere.* See **constitute**.

constitute LATIN *constituere,* from *com-* together + *statuere* cause to stand.

constrain MIDDLE ENGLISH *constreinen,* from FRENCH *constreindre,* from LATIN *constringere* bind together, from *com-* together + *stringere* pull tight.

constrict LATIN *constrictus,* from *constringere.* See **constrain**.

construct LATIN *constructus,* from *com-* with + *struere* pile up.

construe LATIN *construere.* See **construct.**

consul LATIN *consulere,* from *con-* together + *salire* leap.

consult LATIN *consultare.*

consume LATIN *consumere,* from *com-* together + *sumere* take.

consummate LATIN *consummare,* from *com-* together + *summa* sum.

contact LATIN *contingere,* from *com-* together + *tangere* touch.

contagion LATIN *contagio* a touching, from *contingere.* See **contact.**

contain FRENCH *contenir,* from LATIN *continere,* from *com-* together + *tenere* hold.

contaminate LATIN *contaminare* make unclean, from *contamen* contact, from *com-* together + *tangere* touch.

contemplate LATIN *contemplari* observe, from *com-* together + *templum* temple (religious building). The ancient Roman priests watched in their temples for signs from the heavens.

contemporary LATIN *com-* with + *temporarius,* from *tempus* time.

contempt LATIN *contemnere,* from *com-* together + *temnere* scorn.

contend LATIN *contendere,* from *com-* together + *tendere* stretch.

content See **contain.**

contest LATIN *contestari,* from *com-* together + *testari* be a witness to, from *testis* witness.

context MIDDLE ENGLISH, from LATIN *contexere* weave together, from *com-* together + *texere* weave.

contiguous LATIN *contingere.* See **contact.**

continent[1] (land) FRENCH, from LATIN *terra continens* continuous land, from *com-* with + *tenere* hold.

continent[2] (self-restraining) LATIN *continentem,* from *continere* hold together. See **contain.**

contingent LATIN *contingere.* See **contact.**

continue FRENCH *continuer* proceed, from LATIN *continuare* connect. See **contain.**

contort LATIN *contorquere,* from *com-* very much + *torquere* twist.

contour FRENCH, from ITALIAN, from LATIN *contornare,* from *com-* very much + *tornare* turn.

contra- LATIN *contra-* against.

contraband SPANISH *contrabanda,* from ITALIAN *contrabando,* from LATIN *contra-* against + *bannum* law.

contract LATIN *contrahere,* from *com-* together + *trahere* draw.

contradict LATIN *contradicere* speak against, from *contra-* against + *dicere* say.

contraption origin unclear, perhaps based on **contrive.**

contrary FRENCH, from LATIN *contrarius,* from *contra-* against.

contrast FRENCH *constraster,* from LATIN *contra-* against + *stare* stand.

contribute LATIN *contribuere,* from *com-* with + *tribuere* pay out.

contrite FRENCH, from LATIN *conterere* grind, from *com-* together + *terere* wear out.

contrive FRENCH *controver* invent, from LATIN *con-* with + *tropus* manner of speech.

control FRENCH *contrerolle* copy kept of something to check it, from LATIN *contra-* against + *rotulus* little wheel.

controversy MIDDLE ENGLISH *controversie,* from LATIN *controversia,* from *contra-* against + *vertere* turn.

contumely FRENCH, from LATIN *contumelia,* from *com-* very much + *tumere* swell up.

contuse MIDDLE ENGLISH *contusan,* from LATIN *contundere,* from *com-* very much + *tundere* beat.

conundrum origin unknown.

convalesce LATIN *convalescere,* from *com-* very + *valescere* grow strong.

convection LATIN *convehere,* from *com-* together + *vehere* carry.

convene FRENCH, from LATIN *convenire,* from *com-* together + *venire* come.

convenient MIDDLE ENGLISH, from LATIN *convenire.* See **convene.**

convent FRENCH, from LATIN *convenire.* See **convene.**

convention LATIN *conventio* meeting. See **convene.**

converge LATIN *convergere,* from *com-* together + *vergere* turn.

converse FRENCH, from LATIN *convertere,* from *com-* with + *vertere* turn.

convert FRENCH *convertir* turn. See **converse.**

convex LATIN *convehere,* from *com-* together + *vehere* bring.

convey FRENCH *conveier,* from LATIN *com-* together + *via* way.

convict LATIN *convincere* prove. See **convince.**

convince LATIN *convincere,* from *com-* very + *vincere* conquer.

convolute LATIN *convolvere,* from *com-* together + *volvere* roll.

convolve See **convolute.**

convolvulus See **convolute.**

convoy FRENCH *convoier,* from LATIN *com-* with + *via* road.

convulse LATIN *convellere,* from *com-* together + *vellere* pluck (to pull).

cony FRENCH *conis,* from LATIN *cuniculus* rabbit.

coo imitative.

cook MIDDLE ENGLISH *cok,* from FRENCH *coc,* from LATIN *coquere* cook.

cookie probably from DUTCH *koekje,* from *coek* cake.

cool OLD ENGLISH *col.*

coolie HINDI *quli* hired servant.

coop MIDDLE ENGLISH coupe, from OLD ENGLISH *cype, cypa* basket, cask, probably from LATIN *cupa* tub, cask.

cooper MIDDLE ENGLISH, from LATIN *cuparius,* from *cupa* tub, cask.

cooperate LATIN *cooperari* work together, from *co-* together + *operari* work.

coordinate LATIN *coordinare,* from *co-* with + *ordinare* arrange, from *ordo* order.

cope FRENCH *couper* strike, from *colper,* from LATIN *colaphus,* from GREEK *kolaphos.*

copious LATIN *copiosus,* from *copia* abundant (more than enough).

copper OLD ENGLISH *copor,* from LATIN *cuprum,* from *aes Cyprium* metal of Cyprus, from GREEK *Kypros* Cyprus, place where copper was found in ancient times.

copperas MIDDLE ENGLISH and FRENCH *coperose,* from LATIN *aqua cuprosa* copper water.

copse MIDDLE ENGLISH *coppice,* from FRENCH *coupeiz* cut wood, from LATIN *colpare* strike, from *colpus* a blow. See **cope.**

copy FRENCH *copie,* from LATIN *copia* plenty.

coquet FRENCH *coqueter* flirt, from *coq* rooster.

coquette See **coquet.**

coquina SPANISH *coquina* shell-fish, from LATIN *concha* conch.

coracle WELSH *corwg* leather-covered boat.

coral FRENCH, from LATIN *coralium,* from GREEK *korallion.*

coraline LATIN *corallina*, from *corallinus* coral-red. See **coral.**

corbel FRENCH *corb,* from LATIN *corvus* raven, from beaked shape.

corchorus GREEK.

cord FRENCH *corde,* from LATIN *chorda,* from GREEK *chorde* intestine.

cordeling FRENCH *cordeler* twist.

cordial LATIN *cordialis* relating to the heart, from *cor* heart.

cordon FRENCH ribbon, from *corde.* See **cord.**

cordovan SPANISH *Cordoba* the city in Spain where the leather is manufactured.

corduroy See **cord** + *duroy* a woolen fabric originating in England. The French term *corde du roi* "cord of the king" referred to fabric used for king's hunting clothes.

core FRENCH, probably from LATIN *cor* heart.

coriander MIDDLE ENGLISH, from FRENCH, from LATIN *conriandrum,* from GREEK *koriandron.*

cork SPANISH *alcorque,* from ARABIC *qurk,* from LATIN *cortex* bark of the cork oak tree.

cormorant MIDDLE ENGLISH, from FRENCH *cormareng,* from *corp marenc,* from LATIN *corvus marinus,* from *corvus* raven + *marinus* marine.

corn OLD ENGLISH grain with the seed still in.

cornea MIDDLE ENGLISH, from LATIN *cornia tela* horny web, from the way the eye looks when it has a certain eye disease.

corner FRENCH *cornere* angle, from LATIN *corneria,* from *cornu* point.

cornet FRENCH little horn, from LATIN *cornu.*

cornice FRENCH part of a wall, from ITALIAN *cornice,* from GREEK *koronis* something curved.

cornpone See **corn** + NATIVE AMERICAN *pone* baked bread.

cornucopia LATIN *cornu copia* horn of plenty, from Greek mythology.

corolla LATIN crown, from GREEK *korone* wreath.

corollary LATIN *corollarium* wreath of flowers given as a gift, from *corolla* little wreath. See **crown.**

corona See **crown.**

coronary See **crown.**

coronation See **crown.**

coronet FRENCH *coronete*, from *corone*, from LATIN *corona* crown.

corporal[1] (soldier) FRENCH, from LATIN *caporale,* from *capo* head.

corporal[2] (body) LATIN *caporalis,* from *corpus* body.

corporate LATIN *corporare* make into a body or group, from *corpus* body.

corps See **corpse.**

corpse FRENCH *corps* body, from LATIN *corpus.*

corpulence FRENCH, from LATIN *corpulentia,* from *corpus* body.

Corpus Christi LATIN body of Christ.

corpuscle LATIN *corpuscuium,* from *corpus* body.

corral SPANISH something closed or fenced in, from *corro* ring, from *correr,* from LATIN *currere* run.

correct LATIN *corrigere,* from *com-* together + *regere* lead straight.

correlate LATIN *correlatio,* from *com-* with + *referre,* from *re-* back + *ferre* bring.

correspond LATIN *correspondere* answer each other, from *com-* together + *respondere* answer.

corridor FRENCH passage, from ITALIAN *corridore* runner, from LATIN *currere* run.

corrigible FRENCH, from LATIN *corrigere.* See **correct.**

corroborate LATIN *corroborare* strengthen, from *com-* very much + *robur* oak, strength.

corrode LATIN *corrodere,* from *com-* very much + *rodere* gnaw.

corrugate LATIN *corrugare* wrinkle.

corrupt LATIN *corrumpere* ruin, from *com-* together + *rumpere* break to pieces.

corsage FRENCH chest, from *cors* body, from LATIN *corpus.*

corsair FRENCH *corsaire,* from ITALIAN *corsao,* from LATIN *cursus* course.

corse See **corpse.**

corselet See **corset.**

corselette See **corset.**

corset FRENCH little body, from *cors* body, from LATIN *corpus.*

cortege FRENCH, from ITALIAN *corteggio,* from LATIN *cohors* crowd.

cortex LATIN bark of a tree.

cortisone GREEK *cortiscosteron,* from *cortico* cortex (gray matter covering the brain).

coruscate LATIN *coruscus* shimmer.

corvette FRENCH, from LATIN *corbita navis* slow sailing ship, from *corbis* basket.

corynebacterium GREEK *koryne* club + LATIN, from GREEK *bakterion* stick. When bacteria were first seen under the microscope they looked like little sticks.

cosmetic GREEK *kosmetikos* skilled in arranging, from *kosmos* order, the world.

cosmic GREEK *kosmikos,* from *kosmos* order, the world.

cosmography See **cosmos** + **-graphy.**

cosmonaut RUSSIAN *kosmonaut,* from GREEK *kosmos* order, the world + *nautes* sailor.

cosmopolitan GREEK *kosmopolites* citizen of the world, from *kosmos* order, the world + *polites* citizen, from *polis* city.

cosmos GREEK *kosmos* order, the world.

cossack RUSSIAN *kozak.*

cossus LATIN the larvae of a moth found under tree bark.

cost FRENCH *co(u)ster,* from LATIN *constare,* from *com-* together + *stare* stand.

coster (hanging) FRENCH *costier* side, from LATIN *costera* is found.

costume FRENCH style of dress, from ITALIAN dress, from LATIN *consuetudo* custom, from *com-* very much + *sue* be used to.

cot[1] (bed) HINDI *khat.*

cot[2] (house) See **cottage.**

cote OLD ENGLISH, from OLD NORSE *kot.* See **cottage.**

cotehardie FRENCH *cote-hardie.*

coterie FRENCH organization of peasants, from *cotier* tenant of a cote. See **cottage.**

cottage FRENCH *cotage,* from *cote* hut, probably from OLD NORSE *kot* hut.

cottier FRENCH *cotier,* from *cota* cot. See **cottage.**

cotton French *coton,* from Arabic *qutn.*

couch French *couche* place for lying down, from Latin *collocare* place together, from *com-* together + *locare* place.

couchant French.

cough Middle English *coughen,* from Greek *keuchen* grasp.

coulter Old English *culter*, from Latin *culter* knife.

council French *concile* assembly, from Latin *concilium,* from *com-* with + *calere* call.

counsel French *conseil* advice, from Latin *consilium.*

count[1] (add up) French, from Latin *computare,* from *com-* with + *putare* think.

count[2] (nobleman) French, from Latin *comitis* companion, from *com-* with +*ire* go.

countenance French, from Latin *continentia* bearing, from *continere* contain.

counter- Latin *contra-* against.

counter[1] (opposite) French *contre* against, from Latin *contra-*.

counter[2] (long table) French *counteour* counting table, from Latin *computatorium* place for counting, from *computare,* from *com-* with + *putare* think.

counterfeit French *contrefaire* copy, from Latin *contra-* against + *facere* do, make.

countermand French, from Latin *contra-* against + *mandare* command.

counterpoint[1] (music) French *contrepoint,* from Latin *cantus contrapunctus* song pointed against, from *contra-* against + *puncta* prick.

counterpoint[2] (stitching) French *cuilte contrepointe* quilt stitched through and through, from *coute pointe*, from Latin *culcita puncta* quilted mattress, from *culcita* cushion + *puncta* prick.

country French *contree* area, from Latin *contrata* landscape, from *contra-* against, that which is opposite one's view, or the landscape in front of you.

county French *conte* land ruled by a count, from Latin *comes.*

coup French blow (hit), from Latin *colpus,* from *colaphus*, from Greek *kolaphos.*

couple French *co(u)ple* pair, from Latin *copula* connection.

coupon French piece cut off, from *couper* cut, from *coup.*

courage French *corage* feelings, from Latin *cor* heart.

course French *cours* a running, from Latin *cursus* place for running.

courser See **course**.

court French *cort* royal court, from Latin *cohors* company of soldiers.

courteous French *corteis,* from *cort.* See **court** + **-eous**.

courtesan French, from Italian *cortigana* court lady, from *corte* court.

courtesy French *curteisie,* from *court.*

courtier possibly from French *cortoyer* be at court. See **court**.

couscous French, from Arabic *kuskus,* from *kuskasa* hit or pound into small parts.

cousin French, from Latin *consobrinus* child of a mother's sister.

couture French sewing, from Latin *consuere,* from *com-* together + *suere* sew.

cove[1] (small bay) Old English *cofa* cave, cell.

cove[2] (person) British slang, possibly from Gypsy *cova* person, thing.

covenant French promise, from *covenir* agree, from Latin *convenire.* See **convene**.

cover French *covir* hide, from Latin *cooperire* cover entirely.

covert French *covrir* cover. See **cover**.

covet French *coveitier,* from Latin *cupiditas* desire.

covey French *covee* flock of birds, from *cover* hatch, from Latin *cubare* lie down.

cow Old English *cu.*

coward Middle English, from French *coart,* from *cove* tail, from Latin *cauda.* A frightened animal puts its tail between its legs.

cower Scandinavian.

cowl Old English *cug(e)le* monk's hood, from Latin *cucullus* hood.

cowlick See **cow** + **lick**, probably from the idea that the hair looks as if it had been licked by a cow.

cowslip Old English *cuslyppe,* from *cu* cow + *slyppe* slimy stuff.

coxa Latin *coxa* hip.

coxcomb See **cock**[1] + **comb**.

coxswain Middle English *cok* ship's boat + Old Norse *sveinn* boy.

coy French, from Latin *quietus* quiet.

cozy possibly from Norwegian *koselig* snug.

crab Old English *crabba.*

crack Old English *cracian* make a sharp breaking sound.

crackle See **crack**.

-cracy French, from Latin, from Greek *-kratia,* from *kratos* rule.

cradle Old English *cradol.*

craft Old English skill.

crag Middle English, related to Welsh *craig* rock.

crakow *Crakow,* in Poland, from where the shoes originally came.

cram Old English *crammian* stuff.

cramp French *crampe.*

crampon French *crampoun* brace.

crane Old English *cran* the bird, from the way the machine looks like the long neck of a bird.

cranium Latin, from Greek *kranion.*

crank Middle English, from Old English *cranc* bent.

cranny French *cran,* from Latin *crena* a notch (a V-shaped cut).

crape See **crepe**.

crash Middle English *crashen* smash, from French *crasir.*

crass Latin *crassus* gross.

cratch Middle English *crecche,* from French *creche* manger.

crate Latin *cratis* something made from wicker (wood strips woven together).

crater Greek *krater.*

cravat French *cravate* necktie, from *Cravate* (French for "Croatian"). Croatians in the 17th century French army wore linen scarves.

crave Old English *crafian* demand.

craven French, from Latin *crepare* creak.

craw Middle English *craue.*

crawl Old Norse *krafla.*

crawfish See **crayfish**.

crayfish Middle English *crevise*, from French *crevice*, from German *krebiz* crab.

crayon French pencil, from *craie* chalk, from Latin *creta.*

craze Middle English *crasen* crack.

creak Middle English *creken.*

cream French *cresme* fatty part of milk, from Latin *cramum,* from *chrisma* holy oil, from Greek *chrisma* ointment (medicine for healing the skin).

crease Middle English *creste* crest, from French, from Latin *crista.*

create Latin *creare* make.

creature French animal, from Latin *creature* thing created, from *creare* make.

creche French, from German *kiprra* crib.

credence French, from Latin *credere.* See **creed.**

credenza Italian, from Latin *credentia* credence (originally a sideboard holding food to be tasted before serving).

credible Latin *credere.* See **creed.**

credit French trust, from Latin *creditum* loan, from *credere.* See **creed.**

creed Old English *creda* belief, from Latin *credo* I believe, from *credere* trust.

creek Middle English *creke,* from Old Norse *kriki* a winding.

creel Middle English, originally Scottish.

creep Old English *creopan.*

creepie See **creep.**

cremate Latin *cremare.*

crenel French *crenel,* from *cren* notch.

crenelate See **crenel** + **-ate.**

creosote Greek *kreas* flesh + *sozein* save.

crepe French *crépe,* from Latin *crispus.*

crepuscular Latin *crepusculum* twilight.

crescendo Italian increase, from Latin *crescere* grow.

crescent French *creissant* crescent of the moon, from Latin *crescere* grow.

crest French, from Latin *crista.*

crevasse French *crevace.* See **crevice.**

crevice French *crevace,* from *crever* split, from Latin *crepare* crack.

crew French *creistre* grow, from Latin *crescere.*

crib Old English *cribb* basket.

cribbage See **crib** + **-age.**

cricket[1] (insect) French *criquer* creak.

cricket[2] (game) French, probably from Dutch *cricke* a stick.

crime French fault, from Latin *crimen* offense.

criminently colloquial expression. See **crime.**

crimp German *krimpen* shrink.

crimson Latin, from Arabic *qirmiz.*

cringe Old English *cringan* fall in battle.

crinkle Old English *crincan.*

crinoline French hair cloth, from Italian *crinolino,* from *crino* horsehair + *lino* thread, from Latin *crinis* hair + *linum* flax.

cripple Old English *crypel* lame person.

crisis Latin, from Greek *krinein* separate.

crisp Old English curly, from Latin *crispus.*

criss-cross Middle English *crist-crosse* Christ's cross.

criterion Greek *krites* judge.

critic Latin *criticus* able to judge, from Greek *kritikos,* from *krites* judge.

croak Old English *crœcettan.*

crochet French little hook, of Scandinavian origin.

crock Old English *crocca* clay pot.

crocodile FRENCH, from LATIN, from GREEK *kiokodillos.*

crocus LATIN, from GREEK *krokos.*

croissant FRENCH crescent.

croker See **crocus.**

crone DUTCH *croonje* old sheep, from FRENCH *carogne* dead body of an animal, from LATIN *caro* flesh.

crony long-time friend, perhaps from GREEK *khronios* long-lasting, from *khronos* time.

crook OLD NORSE *krokr* hook.

croon DUTCH *cronen* growl.

crop OLD ENGLISH *cropp* ear of corn.

croquet FRENCH *crochet,* from *croc* hook.

cross OLD ENGLISH *cros,* from OLD NORSE *kross,* from LATIN *crux.*

crotch MIDDLE ENGLISH *crucche.* See **crutch.**

crotchet FRENCH *crochet,* from *croc* hook.

crouch FRENCH *crochir* become bent, from *croc* hook, of SCANDINAVIAN origin.

croup[1] (ill) imitative.

croup[2] (rump) FRENCH *croupe.*

crow OLD ENGLISH *crawa.*

crowd OLD ENGLISH *cruden* press.

crown FRENCH *corone* crown, from LATIN *corona* wreath, from GREEK *korone* curved object.

crucial FRENCH cross-shaped, from LATIN *crux* cross, from choosing a road at a crossroad.

crucible LATIN *crucibilum* night lamp used to light a holy cross, from *crux* cross.

crucify FRENCH *crucifier* nail to a cross, from LATIN *crucifigere,* from *crux* cross + *figere* fix.

crude LATIN *crudus* raw.

cruel FRENCH harsh, from LATIN *crudelis.*

cruet FRENCH, from LATIN *crudus* rough.

cruise DUTCH *kruisen* cross, from LATIN *crux* cross.

cruller DUTCH *krullen* curl.

crumb OLD ENGLISH *cruma* piece.

crumpet MIDDLE ENGLISH *crumplen,* from *crimplen* wrinkle.

crumple OLD ENGLISH *crump* bent, crooked.

crunch imitative.

crupper FRENCH *cropiere,* from *crope* rump.

crusade LATIN *cruciata,* from *cruciare* mark with the sign of a cross, from *crux* cross.

crush FRENCH *cruis(s)ir* break.

crust FRENCH *crouste,* from LATIN *crusta* shell.

crustacean LATIN *crusta* shell.

crutch OLD ENGLISH *crycc* staff.

crux LATIN cross.

cry FRENCH *crier* shout, from LATIN *quiritare* call for help from the *Quirites* (Roman citizens).

crypt LATIN *crypta* cave, from GREEK *kryptos* hidden.

crystal FRENCH *cristal,* from LATIN *crystallum* ice, from GREEK *krystallos.*

cub MIDDLE ENGLISH *cubbe* young fox.

cube LATIN *cubus* solid square, from GREEK *kybos.*

cubicle LATIN *cubiculum,* from *cubare* lie down.

cubit OLD ENGLISH, from LATIN *cubitum* the elbow.

cuckoo FRENCH *coucou cucu.* Imitative.

cucumber FRENCH, from LATIN *cucumis.*

cuddle possibly from MIDDLE ENGLISH *couthelen,* from *couth* someone known.

cudgel Old English *cycgel* club.

cue[1] (signal) possibly from the letter Q, for Latin *quando* meaning "when". The mark was found in the text of 16th century plays to show when the actor is to enter.

cue[2] (stick) French *queue,* from *coue,* from Latin *cauda* tail.

cuff Middle English *cuffe* glove, from Latin *cuphia* covering for the head.

cuisine French, from Latin *coquina* kitchen, from *coquere* cook.

cul-de-sac French bottom of a sac, from Latin *saccus* bag. See **sack**[1].

culet[1] (dues) French *cuillete,* from Latin *collecta* collection of dues.

culet[2] (bottom) French *cul,* from Latin *culus* anus.

culinary Latin *culina* kitchen.

cull French *coillir* collect, from Latin *colligere.*

cullet French *collet,* from *col* neck, from Latin *collum.*

culminate Latin *culminare,* from *culmen* peak.

culotte French *cul* rear end, from Latin *culus.*

culprit French *culpable prit* guilty, ready, from Latin *praesto* ready. From medieval law courts where the prosecutor said "Guilty—ready", which meant that he thought the accused was guilty and he was ready to prove it.

cult French *culte,* from Latin *cultus* cultivation, worship, from *culere.* See **cultivate.**

culter See **coulter.**

cultivate Latin *cultivare* prepare land for crops, from *culere* work land by plowing, etc.

cultivator See **cultivate.**

culture Latin farming.

culverin French *couleuvre,* from Latin *colubra* snake. Names of reptiles were frequently applied to early cannon.

culvert origin uncertain.

cum Latin.

cum laude Latin.

cumber French *encomber,* from *en-* in + *combre* something in the way.

cumbrous See **cumber** + **-ous.**

cummerbund Hindi *kamarband* male covering cloth for the lower abdomen.

cumulate Latin *cumulare* heap up.

cumulus Latin a heap.

cuneiform Latin *cuneus* a wedge + French *forme* shape, from Latin *forma.*

cunning Middle English knowing, from Old English *cunnan* know.

cup Old English *cuppa,* from Latin *cupa* tub.

cupola Italian dome (rounded roof), from Latin *cupula* little cask (barrel for holding liquid), from *cupa* tub.

cur Old Norse *kurra* growl.

curb Middle English *courbe* bend, from French *courber,* from Latin *curvare.*

curd Middle English *crud* any thickened liquid, probably from Old English *crudan* press.

cure French *curer* heal, from Latin *curare.*

curfew French *coeverfu* cover fire, putting fires out at night, from *covrir* cover + *feu* fire. See **cover.**

curiosity Latin *curiositas* desire for knowledge.

curl Middle English *curlen,* from *crulle* curly.

curlew French *corlieu.* Imitative.

curlicue See **curl** + **cue**[2].

currant FRENCH *raisins de Corauntz* raisins of Corinth.

current FRENCH *courre* run, from LATIN *currere.*

curriculum LATIN course of study.

curry[1] (brush) MIDDLE ENGLISH *curraien,* from FRENCH *correier* put in order.

curry[2] (sauce) TAMIL *kari.*

curse OLD ENGLISH *curs.*

cursive LATIN *cursivus* running, from *currere* run.

cursory LATIN *cursorius* quick in motion, from *cursor* runner.

curt LATIN *curius.*

curtail FRENCH *court* short, from LATIN *curtus* cut short.

curtain FRENCH, from LATIN *cortina* something (like a cloth) that is hanging around an enclosed place, from *cors* enclosed place.

curtsy See **courtesy**.

curve LATIN *curvus* bent.

cushion FRENCH *coissin,* from LATIN *coxa* hip.

cusp LATIN *cuspis* a point.

custard LATIN *crusta* crust.

custody LATIN *custodia* guard.

custom FRENCH *custume,* from LATIN *consuetudo* habit, from *com-* very much + *suere* be used to.

cut MIDDLE ENGLISH *cutten,* of SCANDINAVIAN origin.

cute See **acute**.

cutlass FRENCH *coutelas,* from LATIN *cultellus* little knife, from *culter* knife.

cutler FRENCH, from LATIN *culter* knife.

cutlery See **cutler** + **-y**[3].

cutlet See **cut** + **-let**.

cwm WELSH.

-cy FRENCH *–cie,* from LATIN *–cia,* from GREEK *-kia.*

cyanide GREEK *kyanos* blue + *-ide* use in names of simple chemical compounds.

cycle LATIN *cyclus,* from GREEK *kyklos* circle.

cyclo- GREEK *kyklos* circle.

cyclone GREEK *kyklon* moving in a circle, whirling around, from *kyklos* circle.

cyclops LATIN, from GREEK *kyklops* round-eyed.

cyclorama GREEK *kyklos* circle + *horama* sight, from *horan* see.

cygnet FRENCH *cynge,* from LATIN *cygnus* swan, from GREEK *kyknos.*

cygnus LATIN, from GREEK *kyknos.*

cylinder LATIN *cylindrus,* from GREEK *kylin dein* roll.

cymbal FRENCH, from LATIN *cymbalum,* from GREEK *kymble* hollow part of something used for eating or drinking.

cynic LATIN *cynicus* name for a group of Greek thinkers called the *Cynics,* from GREEK *kynikos* doglike, describing the bad temper thought to be shown by those thinkers.

cypress FRENCH, from LATIN *cupressus,* from GREEK *kyparissos.*

cyst LATIN *cystis,* from GREEK *kystis* pouch.

cythara See **cithara**.

cytoplasm GREEK *kytos* hollow, basket + *plasma* something molded.

czar RUSSIAN *tsar* emperor, from LATIN *Caesar* title used by Roman emperors.

D

dab Middle English *dabben* strike.

dabble See **dab**.

dad child's word *dada*.

dadder See **dodder**.

daddle See **dodder**.

daffodowndilly See **daffodil**.

daffodil Middle English *affodill* asphodel, from Latin *affodillus*, from *asphodelus*, from Greek *asphodelos*.

daft Middle English *daffte* foolish, from Old English *gedæfte*.

dagger Latin *daggarius*.

dahlia Anders *Dahl,* 18th century Swedish botanist.

daily Old English *dælic*, from *dæg* day.

dainty French *daintie* pleasure, from Latin *dignitas* worth, from *dignus*.

dairy Middle English *deierie*, from Old English *dæge* female maker of bread.

dais French *deis* high table, from Latin *discus* table, dish, from Greek *diskos* round plate.

daisy Old English *dæges eage* day's eye.

dale Old English *dæl*.

dally French *dalier* talk.

dam[1] (hold water) German something built to hold back water.

dam[2] (lady) French *dame* lady.

damage French harm, from Latin *damnum* loss.

damask Middle English *damaske*, from Latin *Damascus,* city in the Middle East where the cloth, steel, etc. came, from, from Greek *Damaskos*, from Arabic *Dimashq*.

dame French lady, from Latin *domina*.

damn French *damner* harm, from Latin *damnare*.

damosel archaic or poetic for **damsel**.

damp German steam.

damsel French *dameisele,* from Latin *domina* lady.

damson Middle English *damascene*, from Latin *Prunum Damascenus* plum of Damascus. See **damask**.

dance French *danser*.

dancette Latin *denticatus,* from *dens* tooth.

dandelion French *dent de lion* tooth of lion, from the pointed leaves, from Latin *dens leonis*.

dander perhaps from Spanish *redundar* overflow, from Latin *redundare*.

dandiprat perhaps from SCOTTISH, from *dandy* nickname for *Andrew* + *prat* prank, frolic.

dandruff MIDDLE ENGLISH *dandruffe*, origin unknown, second part, from *huff, hurf* scab.

dandy SCOTTISH nickname for *Andrew.*

danger FRENCH *dangier* power, from LATIN *dominium* ownership, from *dominus* master.

dangle SCANDINAVIAN.

dapper possibly from DUTCH *dapper* moving lightly.

dapple OLD NORSE *depill* a spot.

dare OLD ENGLISH *durran.*

dark OLD ENGLISH *deorc.*

darling OLD ENGLISH *deorling* one dearly loved, from *deore* dear.

darn FRENCH *darner* mend.

dart FRENCH *dars* javelin, from LATIN *dardus.*

dash SWEDISH *daska* slap.

dastard MIDDLE ENGLISH, probably of SCANDINAVIAN origin.

data LATIN things given, from *dare* give.

date MIDDLE ENGLISH, from LATIN *dare* give. In ancient Rome, the first words of a letter were "I give this letter at Rome on (whatever the date was)".

dative LATIN *dativus,* from *dare* give.

dato SPANISH, from MALAY *datu* ruler.

datum LATIN something given, from *dare* give.

datura HINDI *dhatura* native name of the plant.

daub FRENCH, from LATIN *dealbare* wash walls white, from *de-* entirely + *albus* white.

daughter OLD ENGLISH *dohtor.*

daunt FRENCH *danter* tame, from LATIN *domitare.*

dauphin FRENCH the name *Dolphin.*

davenport variously a couch, a desk or china, all from names of the makers.

davit FRENCH diminutive of *David.*

dawdle perhaps from early MODERN ENGLISH *daddle* walk unsteadily.

dawn OLD ENGLISH *dagian* become day, from *dæg* day.

day OLD ENGLISH *dæg.*

daze OLD NORSE *dasast* become weary, from *dasi* tired.

dazzle See **daze**.

de- either LATIN *de-* from, away, down, entirely, or *dis-* apart, away.

deacon OLD ENGLISH minister of the Christian Church, from LATIN *diaconus,* from GREEK *diadonos* servant.

dead OLD ENGLISH *dead.*

deaf OLD ENGLISH *deaf.*

deal OLD ENGLISH *dælan* divide.

dean FRENCH *deien* head of a church, from LATIN *decanus* leader of ten persons, from *decem* ten.

dear OLD ENGLISH *deore* beloved.

debase See **de-** + **abase**.

debate FRENCH *debatre* argue, from LATIN *de-* down + *battuere* beat.

debauch FRENCH *desbaucher* persuade to do something bad.

debilitate LATIN *debilitare* weaken, from *debilis* weak.

debit FRENCH, from LATIN *debitum* what is owing, from *debere.* See **debt**.

debonair French *de bon aire* "of good breed".

debouch French *de-* away + *bouche* the mouth.

debris French *debrisier* break into pieces, from *de-* down + *brisier* break.

debt French, from Latin *debere* owe, from *de-* from + *havere* have.

debut French *débuter* lead off, from *jouer de but* a first play, as in a game.

decade French, from Latin *decas,* from Greek *dekas* group of ten, from *deka* ten.

decadence French, from Latin *decadentia,* from *de-* away + *cadere* fall (from what is good).

decal French *decalcomania,* from *de-* away + *calquer* copy + *manie* mania, fad.

decanter French, from Latin *de-* from + *canthus* edge + Old English *-ere.*

decapitate French, from Latin *decapitare,* from *de-* off + *caput* head.

decay French *decair* fall off, from Latin *de-* away + *cadere* fall.

decease French, from Latin *decedere,* from *de-* from + *cedere* go.

deceit French *deceite,* from *deceveir.* See **deceive**.

deceive French *deceveir,* from Latin *decipere* capture, from *de-* from + *capere* take.

December French *Decembre,* from Latin *December* name of the tenth month of the Roman calendar which started with March as the first month, from *decem* ten.

decent Latin *decere* suitable.

decibel Latin *decem* ten + *bel* after Alexander Graham *Bell.*

decide Latin *decidere,* from *de-* off, from *caedere* cut.

deciduous Latin *deciduus,* from *decidere* fall off, from *de-* down + *cadere* fall.

decimal Latin *decimus* tenth.

decimate Latin *decimare,* from *decem* ten. In ancient Rome, armies who revolted were punished by killing every tenth soldier in that army.

decipher See **de-** + **cipher**.

decision See **decide**.

deck Dutch *dec* roof.

declaim Latin *declamare,* from *de-* very much + *clamare* shout.

declare Latin *declarare* make clear, from *de-* completely + *clarus* clear.

declension French, from Latin *declinare.* See **decline**.

decline French *decliner* turn aside, from Latin *declinare,* from *de-* from + *clinare* bend.

declivity Latin *de-* down + *clivus* a slope.

décor French, from Latin *decere* befit (be proper).

decorate Latin *decorare,* from *decus* ornament.

decorum Latin *decorus* proper.

decoupage French, from *decouper,* from *de-* out + *couper* cut.

decoy Dutch *de kooi* the cage, from Latin *cavea.*

decrease French *decreistre,* from Latin *decrescere,* from *de-* from + *crescere* grow.

decree French, from Latin *decretum,* from *de-* from + *cernere* decide.

decrepit French, from Latin *de-* very much + *crepare* creak.

decry French *descrier* cry down, from Latin *disquiritare.* See **de-** + **cry**.

dedicate LATIN *dedicare* declare, from *dicere* speak.

deduce LATIN *deducere,* from *de-* down + *ducere* lead.

deed OLD ENGLISH *dæd* act.

deem OLD ENGLISH *deman* judge.

deep OLD ENGLISH *deop.*

deer OLD ENGLISH *deor* animal, beast.

deface FRENCH *desfacier,* from LATIN *dis-* away + *facies* face.

defame FRENCH *diffamer,* from LATIN *diffamare,* from *dis-* away + *fama* reputation.

default FRENCH *defaute* lack, from LATIN *de-* from + *fallere* fail.

defeat FRENCH *desfaire,* from *dis-* from + *facere* do, make.

defect LATIN *deficere* failure, from *de-* from + *facere* do, make.

defend FRENCH *defendre* protect, from LATIN *defendere,* from *de-* away + *fendere* strike.

defense FRENCH, from LATIN *defendere.* See **defend.**

defer MIDDLE ENGLISH *differen,* from FRENCH *differer,* from LATIN *differre,* from *dis-* apart + *ferre* bring.

defiant FRENCH. See **defy.**

deficit FRENCH *déficit* shortage, from LATIN *deficere* be wanting. See **defect.**

defile FRENCH *defouler* walk on and make dirty, from OLD ENGLISH *fylan* dirty.

define MIDDLE ENGLISH *deffinen* state, explain the meaning of, from FRENCH *definer,* from LATIN *definire* limit, determine, define, from *de-* fully, completely + *finire* limit, mark the boundary of.

definite MIDDLE ENGLISH precise, established, from LATIN *definitus,* from *definire* mark the limits of.

deflate LATIN *de-* down + *in-* in + *flare* blow.

deflect LATIN *deflecter,* from *de-* from + *flectere* bend.

deform LATIN *deformare,* from *de-* from + *forme* form.

defraud FRENCH, from LATIN *defraudare,* from *de-* from + *fraus* fraud.

defray FRENCH, from LATIN *de-* entirely + *fraier* spend.

deft OLD ENGLISH *gedæfte* gentle.

defunct LATIN *defungi* finish, from *de-* from + *fungi* perform.

defy MIDDLE ENGLISH *defien,* from FRENCH *derier* lose faith in God, from LATIN *dis-* apart + *fidus* faithful.

degenerate LATIN *degenerare,* from *de-* down + *genus* race.

degrade FRENCH *degrader* take away the rank of, from LATIN *de-* down + *gradus* grade or rank.

degree FRENCH *defré* step, from LATIN *degradare,* from *de-* down + *gradus* grade or rank.

deify FRENCH *deifier* make a god of, from LATIN *deus* a god + *facere* make.

deign FRENCH *deignier* think worthy, from LATIN *dignari.*

deism FRENCH, from LATIN *deus* god.

déjà vu FRENCH already seen.

deject LATIN *dejicere,* from *de-* from + *jacere* throw.

delaine MODERN ENGLISH *muslin delaine,* from FRENCH *mousseline de laine* woolen muslin.

delay French *delaier,* from *de-* entirely + *laier* leave, from Latin *laxare.*

delectable French, from Latin *delectare.* See **delight**.

delegate Latin *delegare,* from *de-* from + *legare* send.

delete Latin *delere,* from *de-* from + *linere* smear.

deliberate Latin *deliberare* weigh well, from *de-* completely + *libare* weigh, from *libra* scales.

delicate Latin *delicatus* dainty. See **delight**.

delicatessen German *Delikatesse* very good food, from French, from Latin *delicatus* very nice.

delicious French *delicieus* fine, from Latin *deliciosus* pleasant, from *delicia.*

delight French *delitier* please, from Latin *delectare,* from *de-* from + *lacere* cause to want.

delineate Latin *delineare* sketch out, from *de-* down + *linea* line.

delinquent Latin *delinquere,* from *de-* from + *linquere* leave.

delirium Latin *delirum* madness, from going outside of the furrow (groove made during plowing), from *de-* from + *lira* line.

deliver French *delivrer* set free, from Latin *deliberare,* from *de-* from + *liber* free.

dell Old English *del.*

delphi Greek *delphis,* from *delphinos* dolphin, related to *delphys* womb.

delude Latin *deludere,* from *de-* from + *ludere* play.

deluge French flood, from Latin *diluvium,* from *dis-* off + *lavere* wash.

deluxe French *de luxe* of luxury, from Latin *de-* of + *luxus* luxury.

delve Old English *delfan* dig.

demagogue Greek *demagogos* popular leader, from *demos* people + *agogos* leader.

demand French *demander* ask, from Latin *demandare,* from *de-* from + *mandare* trust.

demarcation Spanish *linea de demarcacion,* from *de-* from + *marcar* mark. Originally the Line of Demarcation laid down by the Pope, dividing the New World between Spain and Portugal.

demeanor French, from Latin *de-* from + *minari* threaten.

dementia Latin madness, from *de-* down + *mens* mind.

demerit French, from Latin *demereri* merit, from *de-* from + *mereri* deserve.

demesne French *demeine* belonging to a lord, from Latin *dominum.*

demi- French, from Latin *dimedius,* from *dimidus,* from *dis-* apart + *medius* middle.

demiculverin See **demi-** + **culverin**.

demijohn French *damejeanne* Lady Jane.

demise French *demettre* send away, from Latin *dimittere,* from *de-* down + *mittere* send.

demitasse French *demi-* half + *tasse* a cup.

democracy French *democratie* popular government, from Latin *democratia,* from Greek *demokratia,* from *demos* people + *kratein* rule.

demoiselle French, from earlier *damoiselle.* See **damsel**.

demolish French *demolir,* from Latin *demoliri,* from *de-* down + *moliri* build, from *moles* a mass.

demon Latin *daemon* evil spirit, from spirit, from Greek *daimon* fate.

demonstrate Latin *demonstrare,* from *de-* from + *monstrare* show.

demur FRENCH *demourer* delay, from LATIN *demorari,* from *de-* from + *mora* delay.

demure MIDDLE ENGLISH *de-* entirely + FRENCH *mëur* ripe, from LATIN *maturus.*

den OLD ENGLISH *denn* home of a wild animal.

denigrate LATIN *denigrare* blacken, from *de-* entirely + *nigrare* make black, from *niger* black.

denizen FRENCH *deinzein* one living within, from *dein* within, from LATIN *de-* from + *intus* within.

denominate LATIN *denominare,* from *de-* entirely + *nominare,* from *nomen* name.

denominator See **denominate.**

denote LATIN *denotare,* from *de-* down + *notare* mark, from *nota* note.

denouement FRENCH *dé-* out + *nouer* tie, from LATIN **dis-** + *nodus* a knot.

denounce FRENCH *denouncier* announce, from LATIN *denuntiare,* from *de-* entirely + *nuntiare* announce.

dense LATIN *densus* thick.

dent MIDDLE ENGLISH. See **dint.**

denticle LATIN *denticulus,* from *dentem, dens* tooth.

dentil FRENCH *dentille,* from *dent* tooth, from LATIN *dens.*

dentist FRENCH *dentiste,* from *dent* tooth, from LATIN *dens.*

denude LATIN *denudare,* from *de-* off + *nudare* strip.

deny FRENCH *denoier* oppose, from LATIN *denegare,* from *de-* entirely + *negare* reject.

deodorant LATIN *de-* from + *odor* smell.

depart FRENCH *departir* divide, from LATIN *dis-* apart + *partire* divide.

depend FRENCH *dependre,* from LATIN *dependere,* from *de-* down + *pendere* hang.

depict LATIN *depingere,* from *de-* from + *pintere* paint.

deplete LATIN *deplere,* from *de-* from + *plere* fill.

deplore LATIN *deplorare,* from *de-* entirely + *plorare* cry.

deploy FRENCH *déployer* unfold, from LATIN *displicare,* from *dis-* apart + *plicare* fold.

deport FRENCH *deporter* send away, from LATIN *deportare,* from *de-* from + *portare* carry.

depose FRENCH *deposer* put down, from LATIN *de-* from + *pausare* halt.

deposit LATIN *deponer* put aside, from *de-* down + *ponere* put.

depot FRENCH warehouse, from LATIN *depositum* deposit (something put down). See **deposit.**

deprave LATIN *depravare,* from *de-* down + *pravus* wicked.

deprecate LATIN *deprecare,* from *de-* off + *precari* pray.

depreciate LATIN *depretiare,* from *de-* down + *pretium* price.

depredation LATIN *depraedari,* from *de-* entirely + *praedari* waste.

depress LATIN *deprimere,* from *de-* down + *premere* press.

deprive FRENCH *depriver,* from LATIN *de-* down + *privare* separate.

depth OLD ENGLISH *depthe,* from *deop.*

depute FRENCH *deputer,* from LATIN *deputare,* from *de-* down + *putare* make clean.

deputy See **depute.**

derail FRENCH *dérailler.* See **rail.**

derailleur FRENCH *dérailleur*. See **rail**.

derange FRENCH *deranger* change the arrangement of, from *des-* apart + *rengier* put in a row.

derby *Derby*, the name of a town in England, which is the site of an annual horse race.

derelict LATIN *derelinquere*, from *de-* entirely + *relinquere* relinquish (give up or abandon).

deride LATIN *deridere*, from *de-* down + *ridere* laugh.

derive FRENCH *deriver*, from LATIN *derivare*, from *de-* from + *rivus* stream.

derrick *Derrick*, the name of an early 17th century London hangman. First applied to the gallows, later to the crane.

dervish Middle East *darvesh* beggar.

descant FRENCH, from LATIN *dis-* apart + *cantus* song.

descend FRENCH *descendre*, from LATIN *de-* down + *scindere* climb.

describe LATIN *describere*, from *de-* from + *scribere* write.

descry FRENCH *descrier* announce, from *des-* from + *crier* cry, from LATIN *quiritare*.

desecrate MODERN ENGLISH *de-* do the opposite of + *(con)secrate*.

desert FRENCH, from LATIN *deserere*, from *de-* from + *serere* join.

deserve FRENCH *deservir*, from LATIN *deservire*, from *de-* entirely + *servire* serve.

design FRENCH *désigner* mark out, from LATIN *designare*, from *de-* out + *signum* a mark.

desire FRENCH *desirer*, from LATIN *desiderare* miss.

desist FRENCH, from LATIN *de-* from + *sistere* cause to stand, from *stare* stand.

desk LATIN *desca*, from LATIN *diskos* table, from LATIN *discus* dish, from GREEK *diskos* round plate.

desolate LATIN *desolare* abandon, from *de-* entirely + *solare* make lonely, from *solus* alone.

despair FRENCH *desperer* lose hope, from LATIN *desperare*, from *de-* away + *spes* hope.

desperado Old Spanish, from LATIN *desperare*. See **despair**.

desperate LATIN *desperare* lose hope. See **despair**.

despise FRENCH *despire* insult, from LATIN *despicere*, from *de-* down + *spicere* look.

despite FRENCH *despit* anger, from LATIN *despicere*, from *de-* down + *spicere* look.

despoil FRENCH, from LATIN *de-* entirely + *spoilare* spoil.

despond LATIN *despondere* give up, from *de-* from + *spondere* promise.

despot FRENCH chief lord, from GREEK *despotes* master.

dessert FRENCH *desservir* clear the table, from *des-* from + *servir*, from LATIN *servire* serve.

destiny FRENCH *destiner* fix, from LATIN *destinare* establish, from *de-* entirely + *stare* stand.

destroy FRENCH *destruire* ruin, from LATIN *destruere*, from *de* down + *struere* build.

desultory LATIN *desultor* one who jumps, from *desiltre*, from *de-* from + *salire* leap.

detail FRENCH *detailler* cut in pieces, from LATIN *de-* entirely + *talea* cutting.

detain LATIN *detinere*, from *de-* from + *tenere* hold.

detect LATIN *detegere*, from *de-* from + *tegere* cover.

deter LATIN *deterrere*, from *de-* from + *terrere* frighten.

detergent LATIN *detergere,* from *de-* off + *tergere* wipe.

deteriorate LATIN *deterior* worse.

determine FRENCH *determiner* make a decision about, from LATIN *determinare* limit, from *de-* entirely + *terminare* set bounds, from *terminus* an end.

detest FRENCH *detester,* from LATIN *detestari* curse somebody while calling a god to observe (witness) it, from *de-* entirely + *testis* witness.

detonate LATIN *detonare,* from *de-* from + *tonare* thunder.

detour FRENCH *détour,* from *détourner* turn away, from LATIN *dis-* apart + *tornare* turn. See **turn.**

detract LATIN *detrahere,* from *de-* from + *trahere* draw.

detriment LATIN *detrimentum,* from *deterere* damage, from *de-* off + *terere* rub.

deuce MIDDLE ENGLISH *dewes* two, from FRENCH *deus,* from LATIN *duo* two.

deuterium LATIN, from GREEK *deuteros* second.

devastate LATIN *devastare,* from *de-* entirely + *vastare* make empty, from *vastus* empty.

develop FRENCH *développer* unfold, from LATIN *dis-* apart + FRENCH *voloper* wrap.

deviate LATIN *deviare* go aside, from *de-* away + *via* way.

device FRENCH *devise* invention, from *deviser* divide. See **devise.**

devil OLD ENGLISH *deofol,* from LATIN *diabolus,* from GREEK *diabolos,* from *diaballein* make false statements about someone, from *dia-* across + *ballein* throw.

devious LATIN *devius,* from *de-* from + *via* road.

devise FRENCH *derviser* divide, from LATIN *dividere.*

devoid FRENCH *desvoidier,* from LATIN *dis-* apart + *vacare* be empty.

devolve LATIN *devolvere,* from *de-* down + *volvere* roll.

devote LATIN *devovere,* from *de-* from + *vovere* vow.

devour FRENCH *devorer* tear to pieces, from LATIN *devorare,* from *de-* entirely + *vorare* swallow.

devout FRENCH *devot,* from LATIN *devovere,* from *de-* from + *vovere* vow.

dew OLD ENGLISH *deaw.*

dexter LATIN on the right side, skillful.

dextrose See **dexter** + **-ose.**

dharma HINDI moral law, from SANSKRIT justice.

dia- GREEK *dia-* through, apart, across, around.

diabetes LATIN, from GREEK *diabainein* pass through (having to do with getting rid of body fluids), from *dia-* through + *bainein* go.

diabolic FRENCH *diabolique,* from LATIN *diabolicus,* from GREEK *diabolikos* devilish, from *diabolos.*

diabolo ITALIAN, from GREEK *diabolos* accuser, slanderer.

diacritic GREEK *diakritkios,* from *dia-* across + *krinein* separate.

diadem LATIN *diadema* royal wear for the head, from GREEK *diadema* band, from *dia-* around + *dien* bind.

diagnosis LATIN, from GREEK *diagnosis* see differences, from *dia-* between + *gignoskein* know.

diagon See **diagonal.**

diagonal Latin *diagonalis* from one angle across to another angle, from Greek *diagonios,* from *dia-* across + *gonia* angle, corner.

diagram Latin *diagramma* scale, from Greek figure that is marked with lines, from *dia-* across + *graphein* write.

dial Latin *dialis* having to do with the day, from *dies* day.

dialect Latin *dialectus,* from Greek *dialektos* speech, from *dia-* between + *legein* talk.

dialogue French *dialoge,* from Greek *dialogos,* from *dia-* between + *legein* talk.

diameter French *diametre* diameter of a circle, from Greek *diametros,* from *dia-* through + *metron* measure.

diamond French *diamant,* from Latin *diamas,* from *adamas,* from Greek *a-* not + *daman* tame.

diaper French *dia(s)pre* fine cloth, from Latin *diasprus,* from Greek *diaspros* pure white.

diaphanous Greek *diaphanes,* from *dia-* through + *phainein* show.

diaphragm Latin *diaphragma,* from Greek *dia-* through + *phragma* a fence.

diary Latin *diarium* daily record, from *dies* day.

diastolic Greek *diastole,* from *dia-* apart + *stellien* put.

diatom Greek *diatomos* cut in two, from *diatemnein,* from *dia-* through + *temnein* cut.

diatonic French *diatonique,* from Latin, from Greek *diatonikos* stretched through, from *dia-* through + *teinein* stretch.

diatribe Latin *diatriba,* from Greek *diatribe* wearing away, from *dia-* through + *tribein* rub.

dibble Middle English *dibbel,* probably from *dibben* dip.

dibs *dibstone* part of a child's game.

dice Middle English *dis.* See **die**[2].

dickcissel imitative.

dickens probably from the name *Dick.*

dicker Latin *dicker* set of ten pelts (skin and fur of animals). These were used for trading purposes.

dictate Latin *dictare,* from *dicere* say.

diction Latin *dicere* say.

dictionary Latin *dictionarium* book of sayings, from *dicere* say.

dictum See **diction**.

didactic Greek *didaktikos,* from *didaskein* teach.

dido (prank, caper) American slang, origin uncertain.

die[1] (dead) Old Norse *deyja* cease to live.

die[2] (one dice) Middle English *de* one of a pair of dice, from French *de,* from Latin *datum* something given, from *dare* give.

diesel Rudolf *Diesel* (1858–1913), German inventor.

diet Middle English *diete,* from French, from Latin *diaeta,* from Greek *diaita* way of living.

differ Middle English *differren* see differences, from French *different,* from Latin *differe,* from *dis-* apart + *ferre* bring.

difficulty Latin *difficultas* trouble, from *dis-* apart + *facilis* easy.

diffident Latin *diffidere,* from *dis-* not + *fidere* trust.

diffuse Latin *diffundere,* from *dis-* apart + *fundere* pour.

dig French *diguer,* from *digue* ditch, from Dutch *dij.*

digest LATIN *digerere* separate, from *di-* apart + *gerere* carry on.

digit LATIN *digitus* finger, toe.

dignify FRENCH *dignifier* make worthy, from LATIN *dignificare*, from *dignus* worthy + *facere* do, make.

dignitary LATIN *dignitas* dignity.

dignity FRENCH *dignete,* from LATIN *dignus* worthy.

digress LATIN *digredi,* from *dis-* apart + *gradi* go.

dike OLD ENGLISH *diki.*

dilapidated LATIN *dilapidare* throw away, from *dis-* apart + *lapis* stone.

dilate LATIN *dilatare,* from *dis-* apart + *latus* wide.

dilemma LATIN, from GREEK *di-* two + *lemma* suggestion.

dilettante ITALIAN *dilettare,* from LATIN *delectare* delight.

diligence FRENCH speed, from LATIN *diligentia* carefulness, from *di-* apart + *legere* choose.

dill OLD ENGLISH *dile* dill, anise.

dilute LATIN *diluere* wash away, from *dis-* off + *luere,* from *lavare* wash.

dim OLD ENGLISH *dimm* dark.

dime FRENCH *disme,* from LATIN *decima* tenth part, from *decimus* tenth, from *decem* ten.

dimension FRENCH measure, from LATIN *dimensio,* from *dis-* off + *metiri* measure.

diminish LATIN *diminuere* make smaller.

diminution MIDDLE ENGLISH, from FRENCH, from LATIN *deminutio.*

diminutive FRENCH *diminutif* smallness, from LATIN *deminutivus,* from *deminuere* lessen.

dimity ITALIAN *dimito* coarse cotton, from LATIN *dimitum,* from GREEK *dimiton* double threaded.

dimples MIDDLE ENGLISH *dimpel.*

din OLD ENGLISH *dyne* noise.

dine FRENCH *disner* have dinner, from LATIN *dis-* away + *jejunium* fast (eating little or no food) or breaking a fast.

ding probably from OLD NORSE *dengja* hammer.

dinghy HINDI *dingi* small boat.

dingy BRITISH of unknown origin, possibly from OLD ENGLISH *dyncgig* dirty, dung-covered.

dinner FRENCH *dîner* dine. See **dine**.

dinosaur GREEK *deinos* terrible + *sauros* lizard.

dint OLD ENGLISH *dynt* a blow.

diopter FRENCH *dioptre,* from LATIN *dioptra,* from GREEK *dioptra* instrument for leveling, from *dia* through + *opsis* sight.

dioptric GREEK *dioptricos* having to do with the **diopter**.

dip OLD ENGLISH *dyppan.*

diphtheria LATIN, from FRENCH, from GREEK *diphthera* leather, from *dephein* tan hides, named so because of the hardness of the layer of tissue that develops in the air passages due to the disease.

diploma LATIN, from GREEK folded letter, from *diploos* double.

dire LATIN *dirus* terrible.

direct LATIN *directus* straight, from *dirigere* lay straight, from *dis-* apart + *regere* guide.

directrix LATIN *directrix,* from *director.* See **direct**.

dirge LATIN *dirige* direct, which happened to be the first word in a funeral song. Later came to mean any funeral song. See **direct**.

dirk SCOTTISH, origin uncertain, probably from the proper name.

dirt OLD NORSE *drit* waste, from the body.

dis- LATIN *dis-* apart, away, not, entirely.

disaster FRENCH *désastre,* from LATIN *dis-* apart + *astrum* star, from GREEK *astron,* from the ancient belief that the stars could cause bad fortune.

disburse FRENCH *desbourser* take money from a purse, from LATIN *dis-* apart + *bursa* purse. See **purse**.

discard FRENCH. See **dis-** + **card**[1].

discern FRENCH *discerner,* from LATIN *discernere,* from *dis-* apart + *cernere* separate.

discharge FRENCH *descharger* unload, from LATIN *dis-* from + *carrus* wagon.

disciple OLD ENGLISH *discipul*, from LATIN *discipulus*, from *discere* learn.

discipline FRENCH, from LATIN *discipulus.* See **disciple**.

discombobulate AMERICAN made up word, originally *discombobricate.*

discomfit FRENCH *desconfire* defeat, from LATIN *dis-* apart + *conficere* make happen.

disconsolate See **dis-** + **console**.

discord FRENCH *descorde* a quarrel, from LATIN *discordare,* from *dis-* apart + *cor* heart.

discount FRENCH *desconter,* from LATIN *dis-* apart + *computare* count.

discourage FRENCH *descourager,* from LATIN *dis-* apart + *cor* heart.

discourse FRENCH, from LATIN *dis-* from + *currere* run.

discover FRENCH *descovrir* uncover, from LATIN *discooperire,* from *dis-* apart + *cooperire* cover.

discreet MIDDLE ENGLISH *discret,* from LATIN *discretus.*

discrepancy FRENCH, from LATIN *discrepare* sound differently, from *dis-* from + *crepare* rattle.

discriminate LATIN *discriminare* divide, from *discernere.* See **discern**.

discuss LATIN *discutere,* from *dis-* apart + *quatere* shake.

disdain FRENCH *desdeignier* scorn, from LATIN *dis-* not + *dignari* think worthy.

disease FRENCH *desaise* sickness, from LATIN *dis-* apart + *aise* comfort.

disgorge FRENCH *desgorger,* from **dis-** + **gorge**.

disgrace FRENCH bad favor, from LATIN *dis-* apart + *gratia* favor.

disgruntle LATIN *dis-* apart + ancient *gruntle* grumble.

disguise FRENCH *desguisier,* from LATIN *dis-* apart + *guise* fashion.

disgust FRENCH *dis-* not + LATIN *gustus* taste.

dish OLD ENGLISH *disk.*

dishabille FRENCH *des-* not + *habiller* dress.

dishevel FRENCH *des-* apart + *cheval* hair, from LATIN *capillus.*

dismal MIDDLE ENGLISH, from FRENCH *dis mal* evil days (in the Middle Ages certain days were thought to be unlucky), from *dis mal,* from LATIN *dies mali,* from *dies* day + *malus* bad, evil.

dismay FRENCH *des-* entirely + *esmayer* take away the power.

dismiss LATIN *dimittere,* from *dis-* away + *mittere* send.

disparage FRENCH *desparagies* cause to marry beneath one's rank, from LATIN *dis-* apart + *parage* being equal in rank, from *par* equal.

disparate LATIN *disparare,* from *dis-* apart, not + *parare* make equal, from *par* equal.

dispatch SPANISH *despachar* send, from FRENCH *despeechier* set free, from LATIN *dis-* not + *impedicare* tangle up, from *pes* foot.

dispel LATIN *dispellere,* from *dis-* away + *pellere* drive.

dispense FRENCH *dispenser* give out, from LATIN *dispensare,* from *dis-* apart + *pendere* weigh.

disperse LATIN *dispergere,* from *dis-* out + *spargere* scatter.

display FRENCH *despleier* show, from LATIN *displicare,* from *displicare,* from *dis-* apart + *plicare* fold.

disport FRENCH *des-* not + *porter,* from LATIN *portare* carry.

dispose FRENCH *disposer* arrange, from LATIN *disponere,* from *dis-* apart + *ponere* place.

dispute FRENCH *desputer* quarrel, from LATIN *disputare,* from *dis-* apart + *putare* think.

disrupt LATIN *disrumpere,* from *dis-* apart + *rumpere* break.

dissect LATIN *dissecare,* from *dis-* apart + *secare* cut.

dissemble FRENCH *des-* not + *semble,* from LATIN *simulare* pretend.

disseminate LATIN *disseminare,* from *dis-* apart + *seminare* sow, from *semen* seed.

dissent LATIN *dissentire,* from *dis-* apart + *sentire* feel.

dissipate LATIN *dissipare,* from *dis-* apart + *supare* throw.

dissociate LATIN *dissoclare,* from *dis-* apart + *sociare* join, from *soclus* companion.

dissolve LATIN *dissolvere,* from *dis-* apart + *solvere* loosen.

dissonance LATIN *dissonare,* from *dis-* apart + *sonare* sound.

dissuade LATIN *dissuadere,* from *dis-* away + *suadere* get to do something.

distaff OLD ENGLISH *distæf,* from *dis-* flax (fiber) + *stæf* a staff.

distance LATIN *distare,* from *dis-* apart + *stare* stand.

distemper FRENCH, from LATIN *distemperare* disorder, from *dis-* apart + *temperare* mix in proportion.

distill FRENCH, from LATIN *destillare,* from *de-* down + *stillare* drip, from *stilla* a drop.

distinct LATIN *distinguere,* from *dis-* apart + *stinguere* prick.

distinguish LATIN *distinguere.*

distort LATIN *distorquere,* from *dis-* completely + *torquere* twist.

distract LATIN *distrahere,* from *dis-* apart + *trahere* draw.

distress FRENCH *distrece* bad fortune, from LATIN *distringuere,* from *dis-* apart + *stringere* pull tight.

distribute LATIN *distribuere,* from *dis-* apart + *tribuere* give shares.

distributive See **distribute** + **-ive.**

district FRENCH, from LATIN *districtus,* from *distringere,* from *dis-* apart + *stringere* stretch.

disturb LATIN *disturbare,* from *dis-* entirely + *turbare* put out of order, from *turba* a mob.

ditch OLD ENGLISH *dic.*

divan TURKISH *diwan.*

dive OLD ENGLISH *dyfan* dip.

diverge LATIN *divergere,* from *dis-* apart + *vergere* bend.

diverse LATIN *divertere,* from *dis-* apart + *vertere* turn.

divert FRENCH, from LATIN *divertere.* See **diverse**.

divide LATIN *dividere* separate.

divine FRENCH, from LATIN *divinus,* from *divus* a god.

divorce FRENCH, from LATIN *divortium,* from *divitere,* from *dis-* apart + *vertere* turn.

divulge LATIN *divulgare,* from *dis-* apart + *vulgare* make public, from *vulgus* the common people.

dizzy OLD ENGLISH *dysig* foolish.

do OLD ENGLISH *don.*

docile FRENCH, from LATIN *docilis,* from *docere* teach.

dock DUTCH *dicke* pier.

doctor LATIN teacher, from *docere* teach.

doctrine FRENCH teaching, from LATIN *doctrina,* from *doctor.* See **doctor**.

document FRENCH, from LATIN *documentum* example, lesson, from *docere* teach.

dodder MIDDLE ENGLISH *daderen.*

dodge possibly from SCOTTISH *did* jog.

dodger See **dodge**.

dodo PORTUGUESE *doudo* foolish.

doff MIDDLE ENGLISH *do off.*

dog OLD ENGLISH *docga.*

doggerel OLD ENGLISH.

doggery See **dog** + **-ery**.

dogma LATIN, from GREEK *dokein* think.

doily the name of a 17th century London shopkeeper.

doit DUTCH *duit* small coin.

doldrums OLD ENGLISH *dol* dull.

dole OLD ENGLISH *dal* portion.

dolerite FRENCH, from GREEK *doloros* deceitful.

doll nickname for Dorothy.

dollar GERMAN *daler,* from *thaler,* German silver coin, first made in the city of Joachims*thal* in the 16th century.

dollop MIDDLE ENGLISH *dallop* patch, tuft or clump of grass.

dolorous FRENCH *doloros,* from LATIN *dolorosus,* from *dolor* pain, grief.

dolphin FRENCH, from LATIN, from GREEK *delphis.*

dolt MIDDLE ENGLISH *dult,* from *dul* dull, from OLD ENGLISH *dol* stupid.

-dom OLD ENGLISH *dom.*

domain FRENCH *domaine* estate, from LATIN *dominus* master.

dome FRENCH, from LATIN, from GREEK *doma* housetop.

domestic LATIN *domesticus* having to do with a household, from *domus* house.

domicile FRENCH, from LATIN *domus* house.

dominant FRENCH ruling, from LATIN *dominari* rule.

domineer DUTCH *domineren* rule, from FRENCH *dominer,* from LATIN *dominari* rule.

dominion FRENCH rule, from LATIN *dominium* ownership.

don[1] (nobleman) SPANISH, from LATIN *dominus* master.

don[2] (put on) MIDDLE ENGLISH *do* on.

donation French, from Latin *donum* gift.

donjon See **dungeon.**

donkey possibly from the man's name *Duncan.*

donne See **don**[1].

donut See **dough** + **nut.**

doom Old English *dom.*

door Old English *dor* gate.

dope Dutch *doop* sauce, from *doopen* mix.

dormant French *dormir* sleep, from Latin *dormire.*

dormer French, from Latin *dormitorium,* from *dormire* sleep.

dormitory Latin *dormitorius,* from *dormire* sleep.

dormouse Middle English, possibly from French *dormir* sleep + Old English *mus.* The rodent is inactive in winter.

dorsal Latin *dorsum* the back.

dory Central America *dori* a type of canoe.

dose French quantity, from Latin *dosis,* from Greek giving.

doss French *dos*, from Latin *dossum*, from *dorsum* back.

dossier French 'bundle of papers', from *dos* back, because the shape of the bundle is somewhat like the shape of a back. See **doss.**

dot Old English *dotte* head of a boil.

dotage See **dote.**

dotard See **dote.**

dote Middle English *doten.*

dottle Middle English *dosel* a plug.

double French, from Latin *duplus* having two parts.

doublet French something folded.

doubt French, from Latin *dubitare* hesitate.

dough Old English *dag.*

doughty Old English *dohtig* competent, good, valiant, from *dyhtig* strong.

dour Latin *durus* hard.

douse Middle English strike, punch.

dove Middle English *douve* pigeon, probably from Old English *dufe.*

dovecote See **dove** + **cote.**

dowager French *douagere,* from Latin *dos* dowry, from *dare* give.

dowdy Middle English *doude* unattractive woman.

dowel Middle English *doule.*

down[1] (direction) Old English *ofdune* downwards, from *dun* hill.

down[2] (feathers) Old Norse *dunn.*

down[3] (grassy land) Old English *dun* hill.

dowry French *doaire,* from Latin *dotarium,* from *dotare,* from *dos,* from *dare* give.

doxology Latin *doxologia,* from Greek *doxa* praise + *-logia,* from *logos* word.

doze Middle English *dosen,* from Old Norse *dusa* be quiet, rest, doze.

drab French *drap* cloth, from the way undyed cloth looked, from Latin *drappus.*

drabble Middle English, from German *drabbeln* walk or splash in mud.

drachm Middle English *dragme*, from French *dragme*, from Latin *drachma*, from Greek. See **dram.**

drachma Latin, from Greek *drachme* handful. See **dram.**

draft Old Norse *drattr* act of pulling.

drag Old Norse *draga.*

dragon French, from Latin *draco* reptile monster, from Greek *drakon,* from *derkesthai* see.

drain Old English *dreahnian.*

drake Middle English, from German *antrahho.*

dram French, from Latin, from Greek *drachme* handful, from *drassesthai* grab.

drama Latin, from Greek a deed, from *dran* do.

drape French *draper,* from *drap* cloth, from Latin *drappus.*

draw Old English *dragan* drag.

drawer See **draw**.

drawl Dutch *dralen* wait.

dray Middle English *dreye*, from Old English *dræge* something pulled.

dread Middle English *dreden* fear, from Old English *adrædon.*

dream Old English joy, music, from Old Norse *draumr* dream.

dreary Old English *dreorig* sad.

dredge probably from Dutch *dregge* drag.

dregs Old Norse *dregg.*

drench Old English *drencan* make drink, from *drinken* drink.

dress French *drecier* arrange, from Latin *dirigere.* See **direct**.

dressage French training.

drey See **dray**.

dribbet Middle English *driblet.* See **drip** + **-let**.

drift Old Norse snowdrift.

drill Dutch *drillen* make a hole.

drink Old English *drincan.*

drip Old English *dryppan.*

drive Old English *drifan* push.

drivel Old English *dreflian* slobber.

drizzle Middle English *dresen* fall, from *dreosan.*

drogue possibly from Scandinavian.

droll French *drôle* funny, odd, from *drolle* merry man, from Dutch funny little person.

dromedary French, from Latin, from Greek *dramein* run.

dromond French *dromon,* from Latin *dromonen,* from Greek *dromon* runner.

drone[1] (bee) Old English *dran* male bee.

drone[2] (sound) imitative.

drool Old English *dreflian* slobber.

droop Old Norse *drupa* hang the head.

drop Old English *dropa.*

dropsical See **dropsy**.

dropsy French, from Latin, from Greek *hydrops,* from *hydro* water.

droshky Russian *drogi* wagon.

dross Old English *dros.*

drought Old English *drugoth* dryness.

drove Old English *draf.*

drown Old English *druncnian* sink.

drowse Old English *drusan, drusian* sink.

drowsy See **drowse**.

drudge Middle English, from Old English *dreogan* work, suffer, endure.

drug French *drogue* medicine, from Dutch *droog* dry.

drugget French *droguet.*

druid LATIN *druides,* related to IRISH *draiodh* sorcerer, magician.

drum DUTCH *tromme.*

druthers combination of *I'd* and *rather.*

dry OLD ENGLISH *dryge.*

dryad LATIN *dryas,* from GREEK *drys* tree.

dual LATIN *dualis* containing two, from *duo* two.

dub OLD ENGLISH *dubbian* strike.

dubbin See **dub** + **-ing**.

dubious LATIN *dubiosus* doubtful, from *dubium* doubt.

ducat FRENCH, from ITALIAN *ducato* coin with the image of a duke on it.

duchess FRENCH *duchesse* wife of a duke, from LATIN *dux* leader.

duct LATIN *ducere* lead.

dudgeon probably from FRENCH *en digeon* at the top of the dagger.

due FRENCH *devoir* owe, from LATIN *debere.*

duel LATIN *duellum,* from *bellum* war.

duet ITALIAN, from LATIN *duo* two.

duff See **dough**.

duffel DUTCH the cloth, from *Duffel,* the town in Belgium where it was first made.

duke FRENCH *duc* lord, from LATIN *dux* leader.

dulce LATIN *dulcis* sweet.

dulcet FRENCH *doucet,* from LATIN *dulcis* sweet.

dulcimer (dulcimore) FRENCH *doulce mer, doulcemele*, from LATIN *dulce* sweet + *melos* song, from GREEK *melos* melody.

dull OLD ENGLISH *dol* stupid.

dumb OLD ENGLISH *dumb* unable to speak.

dumbfound See **dumb** + **confound.**

dump OLD NORSE *dumpa* strike.

dumpling BRITISH *dump* damp, doughy + **-ling**.

dun OLD ENGLISH brownish black.

dunce John *Duns* Scotus, a 14th century religious scholar whose writings were at first popular but in the 16th century were made fun of.

dune OLD ENGLISH *dun.*

dung OLD ENGLISH *dung.*

dungeon FRENCH *donjon,* from LATIN *dominio* tower, from *dominus* master.

dunk GERMAN *tunken* dip.

dunlin See **dun** + **-ling.**

duo ITALIAN *duo* duet, from LATIN *duo* two.

dupe FRENCH, from LATIN *upupa* hoopoe (a stupid bird).

duplicate LATIN *duplicare* double.

durable FRENCH, from LATIN *durare* last, from *duras* hard.

duration LATIN *duratio* hardness, from *durare* last, from *duras* hard.

duress FRENCH *duresce* hardness, from LATIN *duritia.*

dusk OLD ENGLISH *dox* dark.

dust[1] (dirt) OLD ENGLISH.

dust[2] (form of do) MIDDLE ENGLISH *doest.*

duty FRENCH *duete* what is due, from *devoir* owe. See **due.**

dwarf OLD ENGLISH *dweorg.*

dwell OLD NORSE *dvelja* delay.

dwindle OLD ENGLISH *dwinan* dry up.

dye OLD ENGLISH *deag.*

dyke See **dike**.

dynamic French *dynamique* having energy, from Greek *dynamikos* powerful, from *dynamis* power.

dynamite Greek *dynamis* power.

dynamo *dynamoelectric machine,* from Greek *dynamis* power + Latin *electricus,* from *electrum* amber (a hard yellowish or brown material used to make jewelry), from Greek *electron* because amber attracts other things to it when rubbed.

dynasty Latin *dynastia* rule, from Greek *dynasthai* be strong.

dysentery Latin *dysenteria,* from Greek *dysenteria,* from *dys* bad + *entera* intestines.

dyspepsia Latin, from Greek *dys-* bad + *pepsis* cooking, from *peptein* digest.

E coli LATIN *E(scherichia) coli,* from T. *Escherich,* the German physician who discovered it in 1886 + *coli* of the colon.

each OLD ENGLISH *ælc.*

eager FRENCH *egre* keen, from LATIN *acer* sharp.

eagle FRENCH *aigle,* from LATIN *aquila.*

ear OLD ENGLISH *eare.*

earl OLD ENGLISH *eorl* warrior.

early OLD ENGLISH *ælice.*

earn OLD ENGLISH *earnian.*

earnest OLD ENGLISH *eornoste* serious.

earth OLD ENGLISH *eorthe* ground.

ease FRENCH *aise* comfort, from LATIN *adjacere* lie near.

easel DUTCH *ezel* little donkey, from LATIN *asinus,* because a donkey is used to support something.

east OLD ENGLISH.

easy FRENCH *aisier* put at ease, from *aise* comfort. See **ease.**

eat OLD ENGLISH *etan.*

eaves OLD ENGLISH *efes.*

eavesdrop OLD ENGLISH *efesdrypa* water that drips from the eaves (lower edge of a sloping roof), referring to someone standing under the eaves where rain could drip on them while trying to hear people talking inside the house.

ebb OLD ENGLISH *ebba.*

ebony LATIN *ebenus,* from GREEK *ebenos* from EGYPTIAN *hbny.*

ebullient LATIN *ebullire,* from *ex-* out + *bullire* boil.

eccentric MIDDLE ENGLISH *eccentrik,* from LATIN *eccentricus,* from *eccentros* out of the center, from GREEK *ekkentros,* from *ek-* out of + *kentron* center.

Eccles Name of a town in Lancashire, England.

echelon FRENCH rung of a ladder, from *échelle* ladder, from *eschelle,* from LATIN *scala.*

echo MIDDLE ENGLISH *ecco,* from LATIN *echo,* from GREEK.

eclair FRENCH lightning.

eclectic GREEK *eklegein,* from *ex-* out + *legein* pick.

eclipse FRENCH, from LATIN, from GREEK *ekleipsis* leaving out, from *ek-* out + *leipein* leave.

eco- GREEK *oikos* house, dwelling place.

ecology GERMAN *Ökologie,* from GREEK *oikos* house + *-logia* study of.

economy LATIN *oeconomia* management of a household, from GREEK *oikonomos* manager, from *oikos* house + *nemein* manage.

ecosystem See **eco-** + **system**.

ecstasy FRENCH *extasie,* from LATIN *ecstasis,* from GREEK *ekstasis,* from *ek-* out + *histanai* place.

eddy OLD NORSE *itha* whirlpool.

edelweiss GERMAN *edel* noble + *weiss* white.

edema MIDDLE ENGLISH, from GREEK *oidema,* from *oidein* swell, from *oidos* tumor, swelling.

edge OLD ENGLISH *ecg* sword.

edifice FRENCH, from LATIN *aedificium* a building.

edify FRENCH *edifier* build, from LATIN *aedificare.*

edit LATIN *editio* bringing forth, from *ex-* out + *dare* give.

edition See **edit**.

editor See **edit**.

educate LATIN *educare* train, from *ex-* out + *ducere* lead.

-ee FRENCH *-é.*

eerie OLD ENGLISH *earg* timid.

efface FRENCH *effacer* erase, from *esfacier,* from *es-* out + *face* appearance, from LATIN *facies* face.

effect FRENCH, from LATIN *effectus,* from *efficere* accomplish, from *ex-* out + *facere* do.

effeminate LATIN *effeminare,* from *ex-* out + *femina* woman.

efficacious LATIN *efficax,* from *efficere.* See **effect**.

efficient See **effect**.

effigy LATIN *effigies* image.

effloresce LATIN *efflorescere,* from *ex-* out + *florescere* blossom.

effluent LATIN *effluentia,* from *effluere,* from *ex-* out + *fluere* flow.

effort FRENCH *esforcier* force, from LATIN *ex-* out + *fortis* strong.

effrontery FRENCH, from LATIN *effrons* shameless, from *ex-* from + *frons* forehead.

effulgence LATIN *effulgentia,* from *effulgere,* from *ex-* out + *fulgere* shine.

effuse LATIN *effundere,* from *ex-* out + *fundere* pour.

efreet ARABIC *'ifrit* evil demon or monster of Muslim mythology.

egg OLD NORSE.

eglantine FRENCH *aigient,* from LATIN *aculeus,* from *acus* a point.

ego LATIN *ego* I.

egregious LATIN *egregius* chosen from the herd, from *ex-* out of + *grex* herd.

egress LATIN *egressus* a going out, from *ex-* out + *gradi* step.

egret FRENCH *aigrette,* from *aigron* a heron.

eider OLD NORSE *æthr.*

either OLD ENGLISH *æther* each of two.

ejaculate LATIN *ejaculatus,* from *ejaculari,* from *ex-* out + *jaculari* throw, from *jaculum* javelin.

eject LATIN *ejicere* throw out.

eke OLD ENGLISH *ecan* increase.

ekename See **eke** + **name**.

elaborate LATIN *elaborare,* from *ex-* out + *laborare,* from *labor* labor.

élan FRENCH *élancer* dart.

elapse LATIN *elabi,* from *ex-* out + *labi* glide.

elastic LATIN *elasticus,* from GREEK *elaunein* drive.

elastoplast BRITISH Trademark name for a band-aid, probably a combination of **elastic** + **plaster**.

elate LATIN *elatus,* from *effere,* from *ex-* out + *ferre* bring.

elbow OLD ENGLISH *elboga.*

elder OLD ENGLISH *eldra* older.

elect LATIN *eligere,* from *ex-* out + *legere* choose.

electric LATIN *electricus,* from *electrum* amber (a hard yellowish or brown material used to make jewelry), from GREEK *electron* because amber attracts other things to it when rubbed.

electroplate See **electric** + **plate**.

electuary LATIN *electuarium* lick out.

elegant LATIN *elegans,* from *ex-* out + *legare* choose.

element LATIN *elementum* first principle.

elementary See **element**.

elephant FRENCH *oligant* ivory, from LATIN *elephantus,* from GREEK *elephas.*

elevate LATIN *elevare,* from *ex-* out + *levare* lift.

elevon See **elevate** + **aileron**.

elicit LATIN *elicere,* from *ex-* out + *laedere* strike.

eligible FRENCH qualified, from LATIN *eligibilis* preferred, from *eligere* choose.

Elijah HEBREW *eliyahu* Jehovah is God.

eliminate LATIN *eliminare* push out, from *ex-* out + *limen* threshold (bottom frame of a door).

elite FRENCH select few, from *élire* choose, from LATIN *eligere.*

elixir LATIN, from ARABIC *al-iksir* probably from GREEK *xerion* powder for drying out wounds, from *xeros* dry.

ellipse LATIN *ellipsis,* from GREEK *elleipsis* fall short (of a perfect circle).

ellipsis LATIN, from GREEK *elleipein.* See **ellipse**.

elocution LATIN *elocutionem, elocutio,* from LATIN *eloqui* speak out.

elongate LATIN *elongare* make last longer, from *ex-* out + *longus* long.

elope FRENCH *aloper,* from OLD ENGLISH *a-* away + *hleapan* run.

eloquent FRENCH, from LATIN *eloqui,* from *ex-* out + *loqui* speak.

else OLD ENGLISH *elles.*

elucidate LATIN *elucidare* give understanding to, from *ex-* out + *lucidus* clear, from *lux* light.

elude LATIN *eludere* deceive, from *ex-* out + *ludere* play.

em- See **en-**.

emaciate LATIN *emaciare* make thin, from *ex-* out + *macies* thin.

emanate LATIN *emanare,* from *ex-* out + *menare* flow.

emancipate LATIN *emancipare* set free, from *ex-* away + *manus* hand + *capere* take, from the ancient Roman custom of the father taking the hand of his son and then letting go, which meant that the boy was released from the control of his parents.

embalm FRENCH *embaumer.* See **en-** + **balm**.

embarcadero SPANISH *embarcar,* from FRENCH *embarquer* put on a boat, from LATIN *in-* in + *barca* small boat.

embargo SPANISH, from LATIN *in-* in + *barra* barrier.

embark FRENCH *embarquer* put on a boat, from LATIN *in-* in + *barca* small boat.

embarrass FRENCH *embarrasser* get in the way of, from LATIN *in-* in + *barra* bar. See **bar**.

embassy FRENCH *ambassee* errand, from LATIN *ambactus* servant.

embellish FRENCH *embellir* make beautiful, from LATIN *in-* in + *bellus* handsome.

ember OLD ENGLISH *æmerge.*

embezzle FRENCH *enbeseiller* destroy, from *en-* in + *besiler* destroy.

emblem LATIN *emblema* ornament, from *en-* in + *ballein* throw.

embonpoint FRENCH *en bon point* in good condition.

emboucheur FRENCH, from LATIN *in-* in + *bucca* the cheek.

embrace FRENCH *embracer* hug, from LATIN *in-* in + *brachium* arm, from GREEK *brachion* arm.

embrasure FRENCH opening of a window, from *embraser* widen.

embrocate LATIN, from GREEK *en-* in + *brechein* wet.

embroider FRENCH *en-* in + *brosder* design with needlework.

embroil FRENCH *embrouiller* confuse, from *en-* in + *brouillier* dirty.

embryo LATIN, from GREEK *embryon,* from *en-* in + *bryein* make larger.

embryotomy See **embryo** + *-tomy* cutting.

emend LATIN *emendare* correct, from *ex-* out + *mendum* a fault.

emerge LATIN *emergere* rise up, from *ex-* out of + *mergere* dip.

emergency See **emerge**.

emeritus LATIN *emereri,* from *ex-* out + *mereri* serve.

emery FRENCH *emeri,* from FRENCH *emmery,* from ITALIAN *smeriglo,* from GREEK *smyris* abrasive powder.

-emia GREEK *haima* blood.

emigrate LATIN *emigrare,* from *ex-* out + *migrare* move away from.

eminence LATIN *eminere* stand out.

emir FRENCH, from ARABIC *amir* commander.

emissary LATIN. See **emit**.

emit LATIN *emittere,* from *ex-* out + *mittere* send.

emotion FRENCH, from LATIN *emovere,* from *ex-* out + *movere* move.

empathy GREEK *empatheia,* from *en-* in + *pathos* feeling.

emperor FRENCH *emperere,* from LATIN *imperiator,* from *imperare* command, from *im-* in + *parare* put in order.

emphasis LATIN, from GREEK *en-* in + *phainein* show.

empire FRENCH, from LATIN *imperare.* See **emperor**.

employ FRENCH *employer* use, from LATIN *implicare,* from *in-* in + *plicare* fold.

emporium LATIN trading place, from GREEK *emporos* traveler + *poros* way.

empty OLD ENGLISH *æmtig.*

emulate LATIN *aemulari* try to equal.

emulsion LATIN *emulsio,* from *emulgere,* from *ex-* out + *mulgere* milk.

-en OLD ENGLISH.

en- GREEK in.

enamel FRENCH *enameler* decorate with enamel.

enamor French *en-* in + *amour,* from Latin *amor* love.

-ence French, from Latin *-entia.*

enchant French *enchanter,* from Latin *incantare,* from *in-* in + *cantare* chant.

enchilada Spanish *enchilar,* seasoned with chili.

enclave French piece of land closed in on all sides, from Latin *inclavare* lock in, from *in-* in + *clavis* key.

encore French again.

encounter French, from Latin *in-* in + *contra* against.

encourage French *encoragier* give courage to, from *en-* in + *corage* feelings.

encroach French *encrochier* take, from *en-* in + *croc* hook.

encumber French *encombrer* block up, from Latin *in-* in + *cumbrus* barrier.

encyclopedia Latin *encyclopaedia* a course of general education, from Greek *enkyklios paideia* general education.

end Old English *ende.*

endeavor Middle English *endeveren* work at a duty, from *en-* in + *dever* duty, from French *devoir* owe, from Latin *debere.*

endemic Greek *endemos* native, from *en-* in + *demos* people.

endive French *endive,* from Greek *entybon,* perhaps from Egyptian *tybi* January, which is when the plant grows in Egypt.

endo- Greek *endon* within, from *en-* in + *domos* house.

endocardium See **endo-** + Greek *cardia* heart.

endocrine See **endo-** + Greek *krinein* separate.

endorse Middle English *endossen* write on the back of, from French *endosser,* from Latin *in-* in, on + *dorsum* back.

endow See **en-** + French *douer,* from Latin *dotare* dowry.

endure French *endrer* make hard or strong, from Latin *indurare,* from *in-* in + *durare* harden, from *duras* hard.

-ene Latin *-enus,* from Greek *-enos.*

enema Latin, from Greek *en-* in + *hienai* send.

enemy French *enemi* one who has hatred for another, from Latin *inimicus* not friendly, from *in-* not + *amicus* friend.

energy Latin *energia,* from Greek *energeia,* from *en-* in + *ergon* work.

enforce French *enforcier* make stronger, from Latin *in-* in + *fortis* strong.

engage French *engager* pledge, from *en-* in + *gage* pledge.

engender French *engendrer,* from Latin *ingenerare,* from *in-* in + *generare* generate (produce).

engine French *engin* skill, from Latin *ingenium* genius, from *in-* in + *gignere* produce.

England Old English *Engla land* the land of the Angles.

engrail Middle English *engrele,* from French *engresler,* from *en-* in + *gresle* hail shower, as though cut by hail in a shower.

engrave French *en-* in + *graver* cut into, from Greek *graphien* write.

engross French *engrosser* write in large letters, from Latin *in-* in + *grossus* thick.

enhance French *enhancer,* from *enhaucier* raise, from Latin *in-* in + *altus* high.

enigma Latin *aenigma* riddle, from Greek *ainigma,* from *ainos* fable, riddle.

enjoin French *enjoindre* direct, from Latin *injungere,* from *in-* in + *jungere* join.

enjoy French *enjoier* give joy to, from *en-* in + *joie* joy, from Latin *gaudium* be glad.

enmity French *enemistie,* from Latin *inimicus* unfriendly.

ennui French, from Latin *in odio* in hatred.

enormous Latin *enormis* huge, from *ex-* out of + *norma* pattern.

enough Old English *genog.*

enrich See **en-** + **rich.**

enroll French *enroller,* from *en-* make, put in + *rolle.* See **roll.**

ensconce Latin *in-* in + probably French *sconce* hiding place.

ensemble French together, from Latin *in-* in + *simul* at the same time.

ensign French *enseigne* sign, from Latin *insigne* mark.

ensue French, from Latin *insequi,* from *in-* in + *sequi* follow.

ensure French *enseurer* make sure.

-ent French *-ent,* Latin *-ens.*

entablature Italian *intavolatura,* from *intavolare,* from *in* in + *tavola* table.

entail Middle English *en-* in + *taile* agreement, from French *taillier* cut, from Latin *talea.*

enter French *entrer,* from Latin *intrare,* from *intra* within.

enterprise French *entreprise,* from Latin *entreprendre,* from *inter-* among + *prehendere* take.

entertain French *entretenir* amuse, from Latin *inter-* among + *tenere* hold.

enthusiasm Greek *enthousiasmos,* from *enthous* inspired by a god, from *en-* in + *theos* god.

entice French *enticier* set on fire, excite, probably from Latin *in-* in + *titio* firebrand (someone who stirs up trouble).

entire French *entier,* from Latin *integer* whole.

entitle See **en-** + **title.**

entity Latin *entitas* existence, from *ens* a thing, from *esse* be.

entomology Greek *entoma* notched animals + *-logia,* from *logos* word.

entourage French *entourer* surround.

entrails French, from Latin *intralia,* from *interaneus* internal, from *inter-* between.

entrance French *entirer* go into.

entreat French, from *en-* in + *traiter* treat.

entrechat French.

entrecote Latin *inter-* between + *costa* rib.

entree French *entrer* enter.

entrepreneur French *entreprendre.* See **enterprise.**

entry French *entrer* enter.

enumerate Latin *enumerare,* from *ex-* out + *numerare* count, from *numerus* a number.

enunciate Latin *enuntiare,* from *ex-* out + *nuntius* messenger.

envelop French *enveloper* cover with something, from Latin *in-* in + *volvere* roll.

envelope See **envelop.**

environment French *environner* surround, from *en-* in + *virer* turn around.

envoy French *envoyé* person sent, from Latin *in viam* on the way.

envy French *envi,* from Latin *invidere,* from *in-* upon + *videre* look.

enzyme Greek *enzymos,* from *en-* in + *zyme* cause bread to rise.

eon Greek *aion* an age.

-eous Latin *-eus.*

epaulet French *épaule* shoulder, from Latin *spatula* blade.

épeé French *espe,* from Latin *spatha*, from Greek *spathe* a broad flat sword.

epergne perhaps from French *épargne* saving, economy.

epic Latin *epicus,* from Greek *epilos,* from *epos* song, story.

epi- Greek *epi-* upon, at, close upon (in space or time), on the occasion of, in addition.

epicenter See **epi-** + **center.**

epidemic French *épidemique* happening over a large area, from Greek *epidemios,* from *epi-* among + *demos* people.

epidermis See **epi-** + Greek *derma* skin.

epidural See **epi-** + Latin *dural*, from *dura mater* + French, from Latin *alis.*

epiglottis See **epi-** + Greek *glottis.*

epigram French, from Latin, from Greek *epigramma,* from *epi-* upon + *graphein* write.

epilogue French, from Greek *epilogos* conclusion, from *epi-* upon + *logos* word.

episode Greek *epeisodios* following after the entrance, from *epi-* upon + *eis-* into + *hodos* a way.

epistle French letter, from Latin *epitsola,* from Greek *epistole* letter, from *epi-* to + *stellein* send.

epitaph Latin *epitaphium,* from Greek *epitaphion,* from *epi-* on + *taphos* tomb.

epithet Latin *epitheton,* from Greek *epitheton,* from *epi-* on + *tithenai* put.

epitome Latin make shorter, from Greek *epi-* upon + *tennein* cut.

epoch Latin *epocha* measure of time, from Greek *epoche,* from *epi-* upon + *eschein* have.

equable Latin *aequare* make equal, from *aequus* equal.

equal Latin *aequalis* even.

equanimity Latin *aequanimitas,* from *aequus* even + *animus* mind.

equator Latin *aequator,* from *aequare* make equal, from *aequus* even.

equerry French *ècurie* stable, from *escuerie* office of a squire (country gentleman who owns land), from Latin *equus* horse.

equilateral Latin *aequus* equal + *latus* side.

equilibrium Latin *aequilibrium* level position, from *aequus* even + *libra* balance.

equinox French *equinoxe,* from Latin *equinoxium,* from *aequinoctium* time of equal days and nights, from *aequus* even + *nox* night.

equip Old Norse *skipa* put enough men on a ship, from *skip* ship.

equitation Latin *equitatio* riding, from *equus* horse.

equity French, from Latin *aequitas* equality, from *aequus* equal.

equivalent Latin *aequivalere* have equal power, from *aequus* even + *valere* be strong.

equivocal Latin *aequus* even + *vocare* call.

equivocate Latin *aequivocus* of a similar sound, from *adquus* equal + *vox* voice.

-er Old English *-ere.*

era LATIN *aera* counters (things used for counting), from *aes* brass (used for counters).

erase LATIN *eradere* scrape off, from *ex-* out + *radere* scrape, from the way the ancient Romans erased words written on a wax tablet by scraping off the wax.

erect LATIN *erigere* set up.

ermine FRENCH, probably from GERMAN *harmo* weasel.

erode LATIN *erodere* eat away at.

err FRENCH *errer* wander, from LATIN *errare.*

errand OLD ENGLISH *ærende* message.

errant FRENCH *errer* travel, from LATIN *iter* journey.

erratic LATIN *errare* wander.

error FRENCH *errour,* from LATIN *error,* from *errare* wander.

erst OLD ENGLISH *ærest.*

erupt LATIN *erumpere,* from *ex-* out + *rumpere* break.

-ery FRENCH *-erie,* from LATIN *-aria.*

erysipelas LATIN, from GREEK *erythros* red, from *pelas* skin.

escape FRENCH *escaper* get away, from LATIN *ex cappa* out of one's cape, from someone getting away by slipping out of his cape when it was grabbed.

escarpment FRENCH.

escort FRENCH *escorte* guide, from ITALIAN *scorgere* guide, from LATIN *ex-* out + *corrigere* make straight.

escutcheon FRENCH *escuchon,* from *escusson,* from LATIN *scutum* shield.

esophagus GREEK *oisophagos,* from *oisein* carry + *-phagos* eat.

esoteric GREEK *esoterikos* inner, from *eso* within.

espadrille FRENCH, from SPANISH *esparto* rope-soled shoe, from LATIN *spartum,* from GREEK *sparton* rope made of a fiber called *spartos.*

espionage FRENCH *espionnage* spying, from *espier* spy.

espouse FRENCH, from LATIN *sponsare,* from *sponsus.* See **spouse.**

espresso ITALIAN *caffè espresso* pressed-out coffee.

-esque ITALIAN *-esco.*

esquicitos SPANISH.

esquire FRENCH *escuier* squire (a knight's attendant), from LATIN *scutarius* one who holds a shield, from *scutum* shield.

-ess FRENCH, from LATIN *-issa,* from GREEK.

essay FRENCH *essai* trial, from LATIN *exagium,* from *exigere* weigh.

essence FRENCH being, from LATIN *essentia,* from *esse* be.

establish FRENCH *establir* decide, from LATIN *stabilire* make firm.

estate FRENCH *estat* condition, from LATIN *status.*

esteem FRENCH *estimer* figure the value of, from LATIN *aestimare* value.

estimate LATIN *aestimare* value.

estrange FRENCH *estrangier,* from LATIN *extraneare* treat as a stranger, from *extraneus* strange.

estre FRENCH being, condition.

estrus LATIN *oestrus,* from GREEK *oistros* strong emotion.

estuary LATIN *aestus* tide.

-et French.

etch Dutch, from German *etzen* cause to eat.

eternal Latin *aeternalis* everlasting, from *aeternus.*

ether Latin, from Greek *aithein* burn.

ethereal Latin *aetherius.*

ethical Latin *ethicus* moral, from Greek *ethikos,* from *ethos* character.

ethnic Latin, from Greek *ethnikos* national, from *ethnos* nation.

ethnology See **ethnic** + **-logy**.

ethylene See **ether** + **-ene**.

etiquette French a ticket.

-ette French.

ettin Old English *eoten.*

ettle Old Norse *ætla* (also *etla, atla*) purpose.

etude French study.

etymology Latin *etymologia* study of the origins of words, from Greek *etymos* true + *-logia,* from *logos* word.

eucalyptus Latin *eu-* good + Greek *kalyptos* covered (from the covering of the buds), from *kalyptein* cover.

eukaryote Latin *eukaryota,* from Greek *eu-* good + *karyon* nut.

eulogy Latin, from Greek *eulogia* praise, from *eu-* well + *logia* speaking, from *legein* speak.

eunuch Latin, from Greek *eunouchos* bed guardian, from *eune* bed + *echein* keep.

euphemism Greek *euphemismos,* from *eu* well + *pheme* speech.

euphony Latin, from Greek *eu-* well + *phone* voice.

euthanasia Greek *eu-* well + *thanatos* death.

evacuate Latin *evacuare* empty out, from *ex-* out + *vacuus* empty.

evade Latin *evadere,* from *ex-* out + *vadere* go.

evaluation French *évaluer* estimate, from Latin *ex-* out + *valere* be worth.

evanesce Latin *evanescere,* from *ex-* out + *vanescere* disappear.

evangel French *evangile,* from Latin *evangelium,* from Greek *euangelion* good news, from *eu* well + *angelos* messenger.

evaporate Latin *evaporature,* from *ex-* out + *vapor* steam.

even Old English *efen.*

evening Old English *æfnian.*

event Latin *eventus,* from *ex-* out + *venir* come.

eventual Latin *eventu(s)* event.

ever Old English *æfre.*

every Old English *æfreælc.*

evict Latin *evincere,* from *ex-* totally + *vincere* conquer.

evident French, from Latin *evidens* clear, from *ex-* out + *videre* see.

evil Old English *yfel* bad.

evince Latin *evincere,* from *ex-* totally + *vincere* conquer.

eviscerate Latin *eviscerare,* from *ex-* out + *viscera* internal organs.

evoke French, from Latin *ex-* out + *vocare* call, from *vox* voice.

evolution See **evolve**.

evolve Latin *evolvere,* from *ex-* out + *volvere* roll.

ewe Old English *eowu.*

ewer FRENCH *aiguier,* from LATIN *aquarius* having to do with water, from *aqua* water.

ex- LATIN *ex-* out, out of, away, upward, from, totally, without.

exacerbate LATIN *exacerbare* irritate, from *ex-* totally + *acerbus* harsh.

exact LATIN *exigere,* from *ex-* out + *agere* do, act.

exaggerate LATIN *exaggerare* pile or heap up, from *ex-* out + *agger* heap.

exalt FRENCH, from LATIN *exaltare,* from *ex-* out + *altus* high.

examine FRENCH *examiner* question, from LATIN *examin* weigh accurately.

example FRENCH *essample* pattern, from LATIN *exemplum,* from *ex-* out + *emere* buy.

exasperate LATIN *exasperare* make rough, from *ex-* totally + *asper* rough.

excavate LATIN *excavare* hollow out, from *ex-* out + *cavus* hollow.

exceed FRENCH *exceder,* from LATIN *excedere,* from *ex-* out + *cedere* go.

excel FRENCH, from LATIN *excellere,* from *ex-* out + *cellere* rise.

excelsior LATIN *excelsus* high, from *excellere* excel.

except FRENCH, from LATIN *exipere,* from *ex-* out + *capere* take.

excerpt LATIN *excerpere,* from *ex-* out + *carpere* pick.

excess FRENCH, from LATIN *excedere,* from *ex-* out + *cedere* go.

exchange FRENCH, from LATIN *excambiare.* See **ex-** + **change**.

exchequer FRENCH *eschekier* chessboard, from LATIN *scaccus.*

excite LATIN *excitare,* from *ex-* out + *ciere* call.

exclaim FRENCH, from LATIN *exclamare,* from *ex-* out + *clamare* shout.

exclude LATIN *excludere,* from *ex-* out + *claudere* close.

excoriate LATIN *excoriare,* from *ex-* off + *corium* skin.

excrete LATIN *excernere,* from *ex-* out + *cernere* separate.

excruciate LATIN *excruciare,* from *ex-* totally + *cruciare* crucify, from *crucis,* from *crux* cross.

excursion LATIN *excurrere,* from *ex-* out + *currere* run.

excuse FRENCH *excuser* cancel, from *ex-* from + *causa* cause.

execute FRENCH *execute* carry out, from LATIN *ex(s)ecutor,* from *ex(s)equi,* from *ex-* totally + *sequi* follow.

executive LATIN *ex(s)equi.* See **execute**.

exemplary FRENCH, from LATIN *exemplus* example.

exemplify LATIN *exemplificare* copy out, from *exemplum* an example + *facere* do, make.

exempt LATIN *eximere.* See **example**.

exercise FRENCH *exercice* practice, from LATIN *exercitium,* from *ex-* out + *arcere* enclose. Originally to turn a farm animal out of its pen.

exert LATIN *exserere* stretch out, from *ex-* out + *serere* join.

exhale FRENCH, from LATIN *exhalare,* from *ex-* out + *halare* breathe.

exhaust LATIN *exhaurire,* from *ex-* out + *haurire* draw.

exhibit LATIN *exhabere,* from *ex-* out + *habere* hold.

exhilarate LATIN *exhilarare* make glad, from *ex-* totally + GREEK *hilaros* happy.

exhort LATIN *exhortari,* from *ex-* out + *hortari* urge.

exhume LATIN *exhumare,* from *ex-* out + *humus* the ground.

exile FRENCH *exil* send away, from LATIN *ex(s) ilium.*

exist FRENCH, from LATIN *existere,* from *ex-* from + *sistere* make stand.

exit LATIN *exitus* going out.

exo- GREEK *exo* outside.

exodus LATIN, from GREEK *ex-* out + *hodos* way.

exoduster See **exodus.**

exonerate LATIN free from a burden, from *ex-* from + *onus* burden.

exorbitant LATIN *exorbitare,* from *ex-* out + *orbita* track, orbit.

exosphere See **exo-** + **sphere.**

exotic LATIN *exoticus* foreign, from GREEK *exotikos,* from *exo* outside.

expand LATIN *expandere,* from *ex-* out + *pandere* spread.

expatiate LATIN *ex-* out + *spatiari* walk about, from *spatium* space.

expect LATIN *ex(s)pectare,* from *ex-* out + *spectare* look.

expectorate LATIN *expectorare* force out of the breast, from *ex-* out + *pectus* breast.

expedient LATIN *expedire* free the feet, from *ex-* out + *pes* foot.

expedite See **expedient.**

expedition FRENCH, from LATIN *expedire* free the feet, from *ex-* out + *pes* foot.

expel LATIN *expellere,* from *ex-* out + *pellere* push.

expend LATIN *expendere,* from *ex-* out + *pendere* weigh.

expense LATIN *expensa* money to reduce costs, from *expendere* pay, from *ex-* out + *pendere* weigh.

experience FRENCH testing, from LATIN *experientia,* from *ex-* out of + *periculum* danger.

experiment FRENCH, from LATIN *experimentum,* from *experiri.* See **experience.**

expert FRENCH able, from LATIN *experiri* prove. See **experience.**

expire LATIN *ex(s)pirare,* from *ex-* out + *spirare* breathe.

explain LATIN *explanare,* from *ex-* out + *planare* make level, from *planus* level.

explicate LATIN *explicare,* from *ex-* out + *plicare* fold.

explicit LATIN *explicare.* See **explicate.**

explode LATIN *explodere* drive off the stage by clapping and making noise, from *ex-* out + *plaudere* applaud.

exploit FRENCH, from LATIN *explicare,* from *ex-* out + *plicare* fold.

explore LATIN *explorare* search out, from *ex-* out + *plorare* cry out.

exponent LATIN *exponere,* from *ex-* out + *ponere* put.

export LATIN *ex-* out + *portare* carry.

expose FRENCH *exposer* place in view, from LATIN *exponere,* from *ex-* out + *ponere* put.

exposition See **expose.**

expostulate LATIN *expostulare,* from *ex-* very much + *postulare* demand.

expound MIDDLE ENGLISH, from FRENCH *espondre,* from LATIN *exponere,* from *ex-* out + *ponere* put.

express Latin *exprimere* press out, from *ex-* out + *premere* press.

expulsion See **expel**.

expunge Latin *expungere,* from *ex-* out + *pungere* prick.

exquisite Latin *exquirere* search out, from *ex-* out + *quaerere* ask.

extant Latin *ex(s)tare* exist, from *ex-* out + *stare* stand.

extend Latin *extendere,* from *ex-* out + *tendere* stretch.

extensor Latin, from *extendere.* See **extend**.

extenuate Latin *extenuare,* from *ex-* out + *tenuare* make thin, from *tenuis* thin.

exterior Latin outward.

exterminate Latin *exterminare* drive out, from *ex-* out + *terminus* boundary.

external Latin *externus* on the outside.

extinct Latin *extinguere,* from *ex-* out + *stinguere* extinguish (kill).

extinguish Latin *extinguere,* from *ex-* out + *stinguere* extinguish.

extirpate Latin *ex(s)tirpare,* from *ex-* out + *stirps* root.

extol Latin *extollere,* from *ex-* upward + *tollere* raise.

extra Latin more than.

extra- Latin *exter(us)* beyond, outside, besides.

extract Latin *extrahere* draw out, from *ex-* out + *trahere* draw.

extradition French, from Latin *ex-* out + *traditio* surrender.

extraneous Latin *extraneus,* from *extra* more than.

extraordinary Latin *extra ordinem* out of the usual order.

extrapolate Latin *extra* more than + *inter* between + *polire* polish.

extravagant Latin *extravagari* wander outside the boundary, from *extra* beyond + *vagari* wander.

extreme French, from Latin *exterus* outward.

extricate Latin *extricare,* from *ex-* out + *tricae* difficulties.

extroversion Latin *extra-* more than + *versio* a turning.

exuberence Latin *exuberare,* from *ex-* totally + *uber* growing easily.

exude Latin *ex(s)udare,* from *ex-* out + *sudare* sweat.

exult Latin *ex(s)ultare,* from *ex-* out + *salire* leap.

eye Old English *eage.*

eyot Middle English *eyt* river island, from Old English *igeoo.*

eyrie See **aerie**.

fable FRENCH story, from LATIN *fabula.*

fabric FRENCH, from LATIN *fabrica* workshop, from *faber* a workman.

fabulous LATIN *fabulosus,* from *fabula* story.

facade FRENCH, from ITALIAN, from LATIN *facia* face.

face FRENCH, from LATIN *facies.*

facet FRENCH *facette,* from *face.* See **face**.

facetious FRENCH *facétie* joke, from LATIN *facetia.*

facile LATIN *facilis,* from *facere* do, make.

facility FRENCH, from LATIN *facilis.* See **facile**.

facsimile LATIN *fac simile* make similar.

fact LATIN *factum* something done, from *facere* do, make.

factor LATIN one who does, from *facere* do, make.

factory LATIN *factoria* place where things are made, from *factor* one who does, from *facere* do, make.

factotum LATIN *fac totum* do everything.

faculty FRENCH *faculte* ability, from LATIN *facultas,* from *facere* do, make.

fade FRENCH *fader,* from *fade* pale.

fag origin uncertain, probably from **flag**[4].

fagot FRENCH bundle of sticks, probably from GREEK *phakelos* bundle.

Fahrenheit G.D. *Fahrenheit,* 18th century German scientist.

fail FRENCH *faillir* be wanting, from LATIN *fallere* deceive.

fain OLD ENGLISH *fægen* glad.

faint FRENCH *feindre* copy, from LATIN *fingere* shape.

fair OLD ENGLISH *fæger* beautiful.

faith FRENCH *feit* trust, from LATIN *fides.*

fake[1] (pretend) probably from earlier *feague, feake,* from GERMAN *fegen* clean, sweep.

fake[2] (rope coil) nautical, origin uncertain.

falcon FRENCH, from LATIN *falconis,* from *falx* shaped like a sickle.

fall OLD ENGLISH *feallan* drop.

fallacy LATIN *fallacia,* from *fallere* deceive.

fallible LATIN *fallibilis* not honest, from *fallere* deceive.

fallow OLD ENGLISH *fealh.*

false FRENCH, from LATIN *fallere* deceive.

falsetto LATIN. See **false**.

falter MIDDLE ENGLISH *faltren,* probably from OLD NORSE *fultra(sk).*

fame French, from Latin *fama.*

familiar French *familier* closely acquainted, from Latin *familia* household.

family Latin *familia* household, from *famulus* servant.

famish French, from Latin *fames* hunger.

famous Latin *fama* fame.

fan Old English *fann.*

fanatic Latin *fanaticus* encouraged by a god, from *fanum* temple.

fancy See **fantasy**.

fandango Spanish.

fang Old English *fon.*

fantasy French, from Latin, from Greek *phantasia* appearance, from *phainein* show.

fantoccini Italian, plural of *fantoccino,* diminutive of *fantoccio* puppet, from *fante* boy, servant.

fantod origin uncertain.

far Old English *feor(r).*

farandole French, from Italian *farandola.*

farce French humorous cause, from Latin *facire* stuff, from comic routines "stuffed" between the acts of medieval religious plays.

fardel[1] (bundle) Middle English, from French, from Italian *fardello,* from *fardo,* from Arabic *fardah,* a camel's load.

fardel[2] (a fourth) Middle English, from Old English *feortha dæl* fourth part.

fare Old English *faran* go.

farl See **fardel**[2].

farm French *ferme,* from Latin *firma* fixed payment, from *firmare* fix, from the original use of the word to mean a tax fixed on farmland, and later meaning the land itself.

faro French *pharaon* pharaoh, possibly because one of the cards used in the game formerly bore the picture of Pharaoh. See **pharaoh**.

farrago Latin *farrago* medley, mix of grains for animal feed, from *far* corn.

farrier French, from Latin *ferrum* iron.

farrow Old English *fearh* young pig.

farther Middle English *ferther.*

farthing Old English *foerthing.*

farthingale French *vergugalie,* from Spanish *verdugo* tree shoot, from Latin *viridis* green.

fasces Latin *fascis* a bundle.

fascia Latin a band, a sash.

fascinate Latin *fascinare* charm.

fascism Italian *Fascismo* Italian fascism, from *fascio* bundle, from *fasces* bundle of rounded sticks with an ax, the symbol in ancient Rome of authority.

fashion French *façon* appearance, from Latin *factio* party.

fast[1] (swift) Old English *fæst* firm.

fast[2] (not eat) Old English *fæstan.*

fastidious Latin *fastidiosus* full of disgust, from *fastidium* extreme dislike.

fat Old English *fætt.*

fatal Latin *fatalis* deadly, from *fatum* destiny.

fate Latin *fatum* destiny, what is spoken, from *fari* speak.

father Old English *fæder* male parent, God.

fathom Old English *fæthm* length of the arms when stretched out.

fatigue French *fatiguer* make tired, from Latin *fatigare.*

fatuous Latin *fatuus* foolish.

faucet MIDDLE ENGLISH, from FRENCH *fausset* stopper, perhaps from LATIN *faux* throat. A faucet was originally a screw which controlled the flow of liquid from a spigot.

faugh (exclamation) imitative.

fault FRENCH *faute* gap, from LATIN *fallere* lie to.

faun LATIN *Faunus* a Roman nature god.

favor FRENCH kindness, from LATIN goodwill.

fealty FRENCH *feauté,* from LATIN *fidelitas,* from *fides* faith.

fear OLD ENGLISH *fær* danger.

feasible FRENCH *faisible* can be done, from LATIN *facere* do, make.

feast FRENCH *feste* festival, from LATIN *festa.*

feat FRENCH, from LATIN *factum* something done. See **fact**.

feather OLD ENGLISH *fether.*

feature FRENCH *feture* form, from LATIN *factura.*

February LATIN *Februarius,* from *februarius mens* Roman month of purification, from *februm* way to purify (make clean).

feces LATIN *faeces.*

feckless SCOTTISH *feck* effect + OLD ENGLISH *-leas.*

fecund LATIN *fecundus* fruitful.

federal LATIN *foedus* a league.

fedora the name of a play and the title character, played by Sarah Bernhardt in 1882, in which she wore such a hat.

fee MIDDLE ENGLISH, from OLD ENGLISH *feoh* cattle, property, from OLD NORSE, from LATIN *pecus,* from GREEK *pokos.* In early days a person's wealth was based on the number of cattle owned.

feeble FRENCH *feble* lacking strength, from LATIN *flere* cry.

feed OLD ENGLISH *fedan.*

feel OLD ENGLISH *felan* touch.

feign FRENCH *feindre* copy, from LATIN *fingere* make.

feint FRENCH *feindre.* See **feign**.

feisty MIDDLE ENGLISH *fist* bodily gas escaping.

felicity FRENCH *felicite* happiness, from LATIN *felicitas.*

feline LATIN *felinus* having to do with a cat, from *felis* cat.

fell[1] (make fall) OLD ENGLISH *feallan.* See **fall**.

fell[2] (bad) FRENCH *fel* cruel, fierce, from LATIN *fello* villain. See **felon**[1].

fellow OLD ENGLISH *feolaga* partner, from OLD NORSE *felagi,* from *fe* cattle + *lag* putting property together for a common purpose.

felon[1] (criminal) FRENCH wicked person, from LATIN *fello.*

felon[2] (boil) LATIN *fel* gall, poison.

felt OLD ENGLISH.

female FRENCH *femelle,* from LATIN *femilla* young woman.

feminine FRENCH, from LATIN *femina.* See **female**.

femur LATIN.

fence MIDDLE ENGLISH *fens* defense.

fend See **defend**.

fennel OLD ENGLISH, from LATIN *feniculum,* from *femum* hay.

ferment FRENCH, from LATIN *fervere* boil.

fern OLD ENGLISH *fearn.*

ferocious LATIN *ferox* wild.

ferret FRENCH, from LATIN *fuor,* from *fur* thief.

ferrule FRENCH *virelle,* from LATIN *viriola* bracelet, spelling influenced by *ferrum* iron.

ferry OLD ENGLISH *ferian* carry.

fertile FRENCH, from LATIN *fertilis* have children.

ferule LATIN *ferula* rounded stick.

fervent LATIN *fervere* boil.

fervid LATIN *fervidus* burning.

fervor FRENCH, from LATIN *fervere* boil.

fess FRENCH, from LATIN *fascia* a band.

fester FRENCH *festre,* from LATIN *fistula* tube.

festival FRENCH *festival,* from LATIN *festum* feast.

festoon FRENCH *feston* wreath, from LATIN *festum* feast.

fet OLD ENGLISH *fetian* fetch.

fetch OLD ENGLISH *feccan* bring.

fete FRENCH *feste* festival.

fetid LATIN *f(o)etidus* stink.

fetish FRENCH *fétiche* something that has magical power, from PORTUGUESE *fetiço* charm, from LATIN *facticus* art.

fetlock MIDDLE ENGLISH *fitlok,* from DUTCH.

fetter OLD ENGLISH *fot* foot.

fettle MIDDLE ENGLISH *fetlen* make ready, probably from OLD ENGLISH *fetel* belt.

feud[1] (quarrel) FRENCH *faide,* from GERMAN *gahida* quarrel.

feud[2] (feudal land) LATIN *feodum,* from GERMAN *feho* cattle + *od* wealth.

fever OLD ENGLISH *fefor,* from LATIN *febris.*

few OLD ENGLISH *feawe.*

fewter FRENCH *feutre,* from LATIN *filtrum* felt lining.

fey OLD ENGLISH *fæge* fated.

fiancé FRENCH *fiancer,* from *fidus* faithful.

fiasco ITALIAN bottle. "Make a bottle" was a saying that carried the meaning "fail in a performance," or "pull off a complete flop." The reason for the saying is unknown.

fib MIDDLE ENGLISH, origin uncertain, perhaps from fable.

fiber FRENCH, from LATIN *fibra.*

fibula LATIN a clasp.

-fic FRENCH *fique,* from LATIN *ficus,* from *facere* do, make.

fichu FRENCH.

fickle OLD ENGLISH *ficol.*

fiction FRENCH, from LATIN *fictio* a making.

fiddle OLD ENGLISH *fithele.*

fidelity FRENCH, from LATIN *fidelitas* faithfulness, from *fides* faith.

fidget MIDDLE ENGLISH *fiken* fidget, hasten, from OLD NORSE *fikjask* desire eagerly.

fie imitative.

fief FRENCH *fief,* from *fieu* fee.

field OLD ENGLISH *feld* open land.

fiend OLD ENGLISH *feond* enemy, devil.

fierce FRENCH *f(i)ers* wild, from LATIN *ferus.*

fiesta SPANISH.

fife GERMAN *Pfeife* pipe, from LATIN *pipare* sound like a bird.

fig FRENCH, from LATIN *ficus.*

fight OLD ENGLISH *feohtan* struggle.

figment LATIN *figmentum* something made.

figure FRENCH form, from LATIN *figura* thing made.

filament LATIN *filamentum,* from *filum* thread.

filbert the feast day of Saint *Philbert,* which occurred during the harvest of the nuts.

filch MIDDLE ENGLISH *filchen.*

file MIDDLE ENGLISH *filen,* from FRENCH *filer* to string papers on a thread, from LATIN *filum* thread.

filial LATIN *fillus* son, *filla* daughter.

filibuster SPANISH *filibustero,* from DUTCH *vrijbulter* pirate. See **freebooter**. In the middle of the 19th century bands of adventurers were organized in the U.S. to go to Central America (where they were called *filibusteros*) to create problems for governments. The word came to be in use in American politics to give the idea that a filibuster created problems for the government.

filigree FRENCH, from ITALIAN, from LATIN *filum* a thread + *granum* grain.

fill OLD ENGLISH *fyllan.*

fillet FRENCH *fil,* from LATIN *filum.*

fillip imitative.

film OLD ENGLISH *filmen* thin layer.

filter FRENCH, from LATIN *filtrum* strainer.

filth OLD ENGLISH *fylth* rotten.

filtration See **filter**.

fin OLD ENGLISH *finn.*

final LATIN *finalis,* from *finis* end.

finale ITALIAN.

finance FRENCH payment, from *finer* pay, from LATIN *finire* end.

finca SPANISH *fincar* ranch.

finch OLD ENGLISH *finc.*

find OLD ENGLISH *findan.*

fine[1] (superior) FRENCH, from LATIN *finis* end.

fine[2] (payment) FRENCH *fin* exact, from LATIN *finis* end.

finesse FRENCH delicate, from *fin.* See **fine**[1].

finger OLD ENGLISH.

finish FRENCH *finir,* from LATIN *finire* end.

finite LATIN *finire* end.

fiord OLD NORSE *fjörthr.*

fir OLD ENGLISH *fyrh.*

fire OLD ENGLISH *fyr.*

firk OLD ENGLISH *fercian.*

firkin DUTCH *vierdel* a fourth.

firm FRENCH *ferme* strong, from LATIN *firmus.*

firmament LATIN *firmamentum,* from *firmare* make strong, from *firmus* firm.

first OLD ENGLISH *fyrst.*

fiscal FRENCH, from LATIN *fiscalis,* from *fiscus* money basket.

fish OLD ENGLISH *fisc.*

fission LATIN *fissio* split by force.

fit MIDDLE ENGLISH *fitten,* from OLD NORSE *fitja* knit.

fix LATIN *figere* fasten.

fixture LATIN *fixtura,* from *fixus,* from *figere* fasten.

fizz imitative.

fjord See **fiord**.

flabbergast probably from **flabby** + **aghast**.

flabby See **flap**.

flaccid LATIN *flaccus* flabby.

flag[1] (banner) MIDDLE ENGLISH *flagge,* probably from OLD NORSE *flogra* wave or flap quickly.

flag[2] (paving) OLD NORSE *flaga* stone slab.

flag[3] (wild iris) MIDDLE ENGLISH *flagge.* See **flag**[1].

flag[4] (droop) MIDDLE ENGLISH *flakken, flacken* flap, flutter, probably from OLD NORSE *flakka* flicker, flutter.

flagellum LATIN *flagellum* whip, scourge.

flagon FRENCH *flascon* bottle, from LATIN *flasco.*

flagrant LATIN *flagrare* burn.

flail FRENCH *flaiel,* from LATIN *flagellum* whip.

flair FRENCH sense of smell, from LATIN *fragrare* smell sweet.

flake OLD NORSE *flackna* flake off.

flamboyant FRENCH *flamboyer* flame, from LATIN *flamma.*

flame FRENCH *flam(m)e* blaze, from LATIN *flamma.*

flamenco SPANISH gypsy-like.

flamingo SPANISH *flamengo* flame-colored.

flange perhaps from FRENCH *flanche* flank, side.

flank FRENCH *flanc* side.

flannel WELSH *gwlanen,* from *gwlan* wool.

flap MIDDLE ENGLISH *flappe,* probably imitative.

flare MIDDLE ENGLISH spread out hair, origin uncertain.

flash MIDDLE ENGLISH *flaschen* splash.

flask FRENCH *flasque* container for gunpowder, from LATIN *flasca* wine bottle.

flat OLD NORSE *flatr* level.

flatter FRENCH *flater* calm.

flaunt possibly from NORWEGIAN *flanta* show off.

flautist ITALIAN *flautista,* from *flauto* flute.

flavor FRENCH *flaur* odor, from LATIN *flare* blow.

flaw See **flake.**

flax OLD ENGLISH *fleax.*

flay OLD ENGLISH *flean.*

fleam MIDDLE ENGLISH *fleme,* from LATIN *phlebotomus,* from GREEK *phlebotomon,* from *phlebos* vein + *tomos* piece cut off.

fleck OLD NORSE *flekkr.*

flection See **flexion.**

fledge OLD ENGLISH *flycge* having feathers.

flee OLD ENGLISH *fleon.*

fleece OLD ENGLISH *fleos.*

fleet OLD ENGLISH *fleotan* float.

flesh OLD ENGLISH *flæsc.*

flet OLD ENGLISH *flett* flat.

fleur-de-lis FRENCH *fleur* flower + *de* of + *lis* lily.

flewsey MODERN ENGLISH *flue* fluff.

flex LATIN *flectere* bend.

flexion LATIN *flexionem* bend.

flicker MIDDLE ENGLISH *flikeren,* from OLD ENGLISH *flicorian* flutter.

flight OLD ENGLISH *flyht,* from *fleotgan.*

flimsy origin uncertain, perhaps from **film.**

flinch FRENCH *flenchir* bend.

flinders SCANDINAVIAN *flindra* splinter.

fling MIDDLE ENGLISH *flingen* rush, from OLD NORSE *flengja* whip.

flint Old English *flint* rock.

flip imitative.

flirt possibly from French *fleureter* move from flower to flower, from *fleur* flower, from Latin *flos*.

flit Old Norse *flytia* carry.

flivver origin uncertain.

float Old English *flotian.*

flock[1] (group) Old English *flocc.*

flock[2] (wool) French *floc* lock of wool.

floe probably from Norse *flo* layer, slab, from *flo.*

flog possibly from Latin *flagellare* whip.

flood Old English *flod.*

floor Old English *flor* bottom of a room.

flop See **flap**.

florid Latin *floridus* full of flowers, from *flos* flower.

florin Middle English, from French, from Latin *florem,* from *flos* flower.

floss French *floche*, from *floc*, from Latin *floccus* tuft of wool.

flotilla Spanish *flota* fleet.

flotsam French, from Dutch *vloten* float.

flounce[1] (body movement) Middle English, imitative origin, possibly related to Norse *flunsa* hurry.

flounce[2] (ruffle) Middle English *frounce* pleat, wrinkle, fold, from French *fronce* wrinkle.

flounder[1] (motion) perhaps from **founder,** influenced by Dutch *flodderen* flop about.

flounder[2] (fish) French *floundre*, from *flondre*, from Old Norse *flydhra.*

flour French *fleur de farine* flower (the best part of) the meal.

flourish French *florir* blossom, from Latin *flos* flower.

flout Middle English *flouten* play the flute, from French *flauter,* from *fleute.* See **flute.**

flow Old English *flowan.*

flower Middle English *flour*, from French *flor*, from Latin *florem.*

flub American, origin uncertain.

fluctuate Latin *fluctuare,* from *fluctus* wave.

flue possibly from French *fluie* a flowing.

fluent Latin *fluere* flow.

fluff French *velu* shaggy, from Latin *villus* shaggy hair.

fluid Latin *fluidus* flowing.

fluke[1] (fish, parasite) Old English *floc* flatfish.

fluke[2] (luck) origin unknown, originally a lucky shot at billiards.

fluke[3] (anchor) possibly from resemblance to the fish. See **fluke**[1].

flume French, from Latin *flumen* river, from *fluere* flow.

flummox British, origin uncertain.

flunk American slang, origin uncertain.

flunky See **flank.**

fluorescence Latin *fluere* flow + *escens* ending.

flurry See **flutter** + **hurry**.

flush blend of **flash** and Middle English *flusschen* fly up suddenly.

fluster probably from Scandinavian.

flute French *flaute,* possible imitative.

flutter Old English *flotorian* flap the wings.

flux LATIN *fluxus* flowing.

fly OLD ENGLISH *fleoge.*

foal OLD ENGLISH *fola.*

foam OLD ENGLISH *fam.*

foc'sle See **forecastle**.

focus LATIN floor of a fireplace, because this was the center of the home.

fodder OLD ENGLISH *foda* food.

foe OLD ENGLISH *fah.*

fog probably from SCANDINAVIAN.

foible weak point of a sword blade, from FRENCH *foible* weak, from *fieble* feeble.

foil MIDDLE ENGLISH *foilen* trample on, from FRENCH *fouler,* from LATIN *fullo* person who prepares woolen cloth.

foist probably from DUTCH *vuisten* take in the hand, as in concealing loaded dice in one's hand so as to cheat by switching them, from *vuist* fist.

fold OLD ENGLISH *fealdan.*

foliage FRENCH, from LATIN *follum,* from *foliatus* leafy.

folio LATIN *folium* leaf.

folk OLD ENGLISH *fole* people.

follicle LATIN *folliculus* little bag, from *follis* bellows, inflated ball.

follow OLD ENGLISH *folgian.*

folly FRENCH *folie* foolishness, from *fol* fool, from LATIN *follis* windbag.

foment LATIN *fomentare* help the body by putting wet heat on painful places, from *fomentum* keep warm.

fond MIDDLE ENGLISH *fonne* a fool.

fondle See **fond**.

fondue FRENCH, from *fondre* melt.

font[1] (bowl) OLD ENGLISH, from LATIN *fons* fountain.

font[2] (printing) FRENCH *fonte*, from *fondre.*

food OLD ENGLISH *foda.*

fool FRENCH *fol* foolish person, from LATIN *follis* windbag (person who talks a lot but doesn't say anything important).

foot OLD ENGLISH *fot.*

footling See **foot** + **-ling**.

fop MIDDLE ENGLISH *foppe* a fool, from DUTCH *foppen* fool, from GERMAN *foppen.*

for OLD ENGLISH.

for- OLD ENGLISH.

forage FRENCH *fourage,* from *forre* food for cattle, sheep, etc.

foray FRENCH *forrer* forage.

forbid OLD ENGLISH *forbeodan.*

force FRENCH strength, from LATIN *fortis* strong.

forceps LATIN, from *formus* hot + *capere* take, from a tool used by a blacksmith to grasp hot things.

ford OLD ENGLISH shallow place.

fore OLD ENGLISH before.

fore- OLD ENGLISH.

forebode OLD ENGLISH.

forecastle See **fore** + **castle**.

foreclose FRENCH *forclore* shut out, from LATIN *foris* outside + *claudere* shut.

foreign MIDDLE ENGLISH *foreyne* outside, from FRENCH *forain,* from LATIN *foris.*

forelock See **fore** + **lock**[2].

forensic LATIN *forensis* public, from *forum* marketplace.

foresee OLD ENGLISH *foreseon.*

forest FRENCH, from LATIN *forestis* wood not fenced in, from *foris* outside.

forestall MIDDLE ENGLISH *forestallen* prevent from going forward, from OLD ENGLISH *foresteall.*

forfeit FRENCH *forfaire* act beyond the law, from LATIN *foris* outside + *facere* do.

forfend See **for-** + **fend.**

forge MIDDLE ENGLISH, from FRENCH, from LATIN *fabrica* workshop, from *faber* worker.

forget OLD ENGLISH *forgitan.*

forgive OLD ENGLISH *forgifan* give.

forgo OLD ENGLISH *forgan* pass over.

fork OLD ENGLISH *forca,* from LATIN *furca.*

forlorn OLD ENGLISH *forleosan* lose.

form FRENCH *forme* shape, from LATIN *forma.*

-form See **form.**

formal LATIN *formalis* relating to form, from *forma* shape.

formaldehyde MODERN ENGLISH **formic** (acid) + *aldehyde,* from *al(cohol)* + *dehyd(rogenated),* alcohol without hydrogen.

Formalin See **formaldehyde** + **-ine** (trademark name for a solution of formaldehyde in water).

format FRENCH, from GERMAN, from LATIN *formare* shape.

former MIDDLE ENGLISH *formere* first, from OLD ENGLISH *forma.*

formic acid LATIN *formica* ant (the acid was obtained from red ants).

formidable FRENCH, from LATIN *formidare* be afraid of.

formula LATIN small pattern, from *forma* shape.

forsake OLD ENGLISH *for-* away + *sacan* work for.

forswear OLD ENGLISH *forswerian* swear falsely.

fort FRENCH, from LATIN *fortis.*

forth OLD ENGLISH.

fortify FRENCH *fortifier,* from LATIN *fortis* strong + *facere* do, make.

fortitude LATIN *fortis* strong.

fortnight OLD ENGLISH fourteen nights.

fortuitous LATIN *fortuitus,* from *fors* chance.

fortune FRENCH chance, from LATIN *fortuna* luck.

forum LATIN area out of doors.

forward OLD ENGLISH *foreweard.*

fossil LATIN *fodere* dig.

foster OLD ENGLISH *fostrian* feed.

foul OLD ENGLISH *ful* rotten.

found[1] (past tense of find) MIDDLE ENGLISH, from OLD ENGLISH *funden.*

found[2] (establish) MIDDLE ENGLISH *founden,* from FRENCH *fonder,* from LATIN *fundus* base.

found[3] (melt metal) FRENCH *fondre* pour out, melt, mix together, from *fondre,* from LATIN *fundere* melt, cast, pour out.

founder FRENCH *fondrer* sink, from LATIN *fundus* base.

foundling MIDDLE ENGLISH *fundeling,* from *fundan.* See **find** + **-ling.**

fount See **fountain,** influenced by FRENCH *font* fount.

fountain FRENCH *fontaine* water, from LATIN *fontana,* from *fons.*

fourchette FRENCH *fourchette,* from *fourche.* See **fork.**

fowl OLD ENGLISH *fugol* bird.

foyer FRENCH hearth (floor of a fireplace), from LATIN *focus.* Theatres in early times had hearths in their entrance halls.

fracas FRENCH *fracasser* break in small bits, from LATIN *frangere* break + *quassare* shake.

fraction LATIN *frangere* break.

fractious See **fraction**.

fracture LATIN *fractura.*

fragile FRENCH, from LATIN *fragilis,* from *frangere* break.

fragment LATIN *fragmentum* a piece.

fragrant LATIN *fragrare* give out a sweet smell.

frail FRENCH *fraile* weak, from LATIN *fragilis* easily broken.

fraise FRENCH, from *fraiser* ruffle.

frame OLD ENGLISH *framian* be helpful.

franchise FRENCH freedom, from *franc* free. See **frank**.

frank FRENCH *franc* free, from LATIN *francus* a Frank. The Frankish tribe had conquered the territory the Romans called Gaul and renamed it France. Only the ruling Franks were free men.

frantic FRENCH *frenetique,* from LATIN *phreneticus* mad, from GREEK *phrenetikos,* from *phren* mind.

fraternal FRENCH *fraternite,* from LATIN *frater* brother.

fraud FRENCH *fraude,* from LATIN *fraus* dishonesty.

fraught DUTCH *vracht* a load (for a ship).

fray FRENCH, from LATIN *fricare* rub.

frazzle possibly from GERMAN *faselen,* from OLD ENGLISH *fæs.*

freak possibly from OLD ENGLISH *grician* dance.

freckle OLD NORSE *freknur* small spots of the skin.

free OLD ENGLISH *fri.*

freebooter DUTCH *vrijbuiter*, from *vrijbuit* plunder, from *vrij* free + *buit* booty, from *buiten* exchange or plunder, from *buten.*

freeze OLD ENGLISH *freosan.*

freight DUTCH *vracht* a load (for a ship).

frenzy FRENCH *frenesie,* from LATIN *phrenesis.* See **frantic**.

frequent FRENCH, from LATIN *frequens* crowded.

fresco ITALIAN fresh, from GERMAN *frisc.*

fresh OLD ENGLISH *fersc* not salted.

fret OLD ENGLISH *fretan* eat up.

friar FRENCH *frere* brother, from LATIN *frater.*

fribble imitative.

fricassee FRENCH *fricasser* cut up and fry.

friction LATIN *fricare* rub.

Friday OLD NORSE *Friedaeg* Frigg's (the Norse goddess of love) + *tag* day.

friend OLD ENGLISH *freond.*

frieze FRENCH, from LATIN *frisium* embroidered cloth.

frigate FRENCH, from ITALIAN *fregata.*

fright OLD ENGLISH *fyrhto* terror.

frigid LATIN *fiigidus* cold.

frijole SPANISH.

frill MIDDLE ENGLISH, origin uncertain.

fringe FRENCH *frenge* border of cloth threads that hang, from LATIN *fimbriae* threads.

frippery FRENCH *frepe* a rag.

frisado SPANISH.

frisk French *frisque* lively, from German *frisc.*

frisson French, from Latin *frictionem,* from *frictio* shiver.

fritter possibly from French *fraiture* a breaking, from Latin *fractura.*

frivolous Latin *frivolus.*

frizz French *friser* curl, from Latin *frigere* fry, because fried meat can curl at the ends.

frizzle Middle English curl hair. See **frizz.**

frock French *froc* hood.

frog Old English *frogga.*

frolic Dutch *vrolijk* merry, from *vro* glad.

from Old English.

front Latin *frons* forehead.

frontier French *frontiere* border of a country, from Latin *frons* forehead.

frost Old English *froesan* freeze.

froth Old Norse *frotha* foam.

frown Middle English *frounen,* from French *fro(i)gnier,* from *frogne* angry look, grimace.

frowsty Middle English smelly, origin uncertain.

fructify French, from Latin *fructificare,* from *fructus* enjoy.

fructose Latin *fructus* fruit + chemical suffix *-ose.*

frugal Latin *frugalis* fit for food, from *frux* fruit.

fruit French *fruit,* from Latin *fructus.*

frustrate Latin *frustrari* disappoint, from *frustra* without success.

frustum Latin a piece.

fry Middle English *frien,* from French *frire* cook in a frying pan with fat, from Latin *frigere* fry.

fuddle Middle English get drunk, origin uncertain.

fudge Middle English *fadge* make suit, fit, origin uncertain.

fuel French *fouaille,* from Latin *focale,* from *focus* floor of a fireplace.

fugitive French *fugitif* fleeing, from Latin *fugere* flee.

-ful Old English complete.

fulcrum Latin.

fulfill Old English *fullfyllan* fill full.

full Old English.

fuller Old English.

fulminate Latin *fulminare* thunder.

fulsome See **full** + **some.**

fumble Dutch *fommelen.*

fume French *fum* smoke, from Latin *fumus.*

fumigate Latin *fumigare,* from *fumus* smoke + *agere* make.

fun Middle English *fonne* a fool.

function Latin *functio* performance.

fund Latin *fundus* bottom.

fundamental Middle English, from Latin *fundamentalis* of the foundation, from *fundamentum* foundation, from *fundus* bottom.

funeral Latin *funeralia,* from *funus* death.

fungus Latin mushroom, from Greek *spongos* sponge.

funicular Latin *funiculum,* from *funis* a rope.

funnel Latin *fundibulum,* from *infundibulum,* from *in-* in + *fundere* pour.

fur French *fuerre* a knife case.

furbelow French *falbala.*

furbish French *forbir* polish.

furious French *furieux* rage, from Latin *furiosus,* from *furia.*

furl French *ferlier* tie up, from *ferm* firm + *lier* tie.

furlong Old English *furh* a furrow + *lang* long.

furlough Dutch *verlof.*

furnace French *fornais* large oven, from Latin *fornax* oven.

furnish French *fornir* supply.

furniture French *fourniture,* from *fournir.* See **furnish**.

furor French *fureur,* from Latin *furor.*

furrow Old English *furh.*

further Old English *furthra* before.

furtive Latin *furtivus* stolen, from *fur* thief.

fury French, from Latin *furia furere* rage.

furze Old English *fyrs.*

fuse Italian *fuso* shaft, from Latin *fusus.*

fuselage French *fuselé* tapered, spindle-shaped.

fusiform Latin *fusus* spindle + French *forme* shape, from Latin *forma.*

fusillade French *fustiller* shoot.

fuss imitative.

fusty French *fuste* smell, from *fust* tree trunk, from Latin *fustis* stick.

futile Latin *futilis* worthless.

futtock nautical. See **foot** + **hook**.

future French *futur,* from Latin *futurus* about to be, from *esse* be.

fuzz Middle English *fusse.*

-fy (-ify, -efy) French *-fier,* from Latin *ficare,* from *facere* do, make.

G

gab French *gabba* make fun of.

gabble See **gab** + **-le**.

gable French, from Old Norse *gafl.*

gad possibly from Old English *gædeling* companion.

gadget from *gadjet* sailors' slang for any small mechanical thing or part of a ship, perhaps from French *gâchette* catchpiece of a mechanism, from *gâche* staple of a lock.

gadroon French *godron,* from *godet* cup without handle, from Dutch *kodde* log.

gaff French *gaffe,* from *gaf* boat hook.

gaffe French *gaffe* clumsy remark. See **gaff**.

gaffer See **grandfather** or **godfather**.

gag imitative.

gage French *pledge.*

gaggle Middle English *gagelen* cackle.

gain French *gaigner* win.

gainsay Old English *gegn* against + *secgan* say.

gait Old Norse *gata* path.

gaiter French *guêtre.*

gala Italian, from French *gale* enjoyment.

galaxy French *galaxie,* from Latin *galaxias,* from Greek *gala* milk.

gale Middle English *gaile* wind, origin uncertain.

galingale French *galingal,* from Arabic *khalanjan.*

galipot French possibly from *garipot* pine tree.

gall[1] (swelling) Middle English *galle,* from Old English *gealla,* from Latin *galla*, lump on a plant.

gall[2] (bile) Old English *galla.*

gall[3] (on a tree) French *galle*, from Latin *galla* the oak-apple.

gall bladder See **gall**[2] + **bladder**.

gallant French *galant* brave, from *gale* pleasure.

galleass (galliass) French *galeace,* from Italian *galeaza.*

galleon Spanish *galeón,* from Latin *galea.* See **galley**.

gallery French *galerie* long room, from Latin *galeria.*

galley Middle English, from French *galie* large ship, from Latin *galea,* from Greek.

galley-west British *colleywesson* awry, of unknown origin.

gallipot possibly from pottery that was brought in galleys (ships from the Mediterranean).

gallon French *galon,* from Latin *galo* jug.

gallop French *galoper.*

gallows Middle English *galwe*, from Old English *galga.*

gallus See **gallows.**

galore Irish *goleor* be enough.

galoshes French *galoche,* probably from *gallicula* small shoe.

galumph blend of *gallop* and *triumph*, coined by Lewis Carroll.

galvanism French, from Italian, from Luigi *Galvani* (1737–1798), Italian physicist.

gambit French, from Spanish *gambito* tripping, from Italian, from Latin *gamba,* from Greek *kampe* a joint.

gamble Middle English *gamenen,* from Old English *gamenian* play.

gambol French, from Italian *gambata* a kick.

gambrel possibly from French *gamberel.*

game Old English *gamen* sport.

gammer See **godmother**.

gammon French *gambe.*

gamut Latin *gamma ut,* from *gamma* the name of the last note of medieval music + *ut* another name for the first note.

gander Old English *gandra.*

gang Old Norse *gangr* a going.

gangling possibly from Scottish *gangrel* wandering beggar, from Middle English.

ganglion Greek *ganglion* tumor.

gangrene Latin *gangraena,* from Greek *gangriana* eat away at something.

gannet Old English *ganot.*

gantry French, from Latin *canterius* beast of burden, from Greek *kanthon.*

gap Old Norse *gap.*

gape Old Norse *gapa.*

gar See **garfish**.

garage French *garer* guard.

garantizados Spanish.

garb French *garbe* good fashion, from Italian *garbo* grace.

garbage Middle English *garbage* intestines of birds.

garble Italian *garbellare* sift, from Arabic *gharbala,* from Latin *cribrum* sieve.

garden French *gardin.*

garderobe French *garderobe*, from *garder* keep, guard + *robe* robe.

garfish Middle English *gare* spear + *fish* fish.

gargantuan a book about a huge king titled *Gargantua and Pantagruel* written in 1535 by the French writer François Rabelais, based on an early French legend about a kindly giant.

garget French *gargate, garguette* throat.

gargle French *gargouiller* make a bubbling sound, from *gargate* throat.

gargoyle French *gargouiller.* See **gargle**.

garibaldi Giuseppe *Garibaldi* (1807–1882), Italian patriot.

garland French *garlande.*

garment French *garnement* robe, from *garnir* protect.

garner French *gernier* place to store grain, from Latin *granarium.*

garnet French, from Latin *granatus* pomegranate.

garnish French *garnir* protect.

garret French *garite* tall tower for guards, from *garir* defend.

garrison French *garison,* from *garir* defend.

garrote Spanish a stick used to wind a cord or rope, from French.

garrulous Latin *garrire* talk quickly.

garter French *garet* the back of the knee.

garth Middle English, from Old Norse *garthr* farmyard.

gas Dutch, from Greek *chaos* empty space.

gash French *garser,* from Latin *charaxare* scratch, from Greek *charassein.*

gasket English *caskette* small rope used to secure a furled sail, origin uncertain.

gaskin probably short for *galligaskins* loose fitting pants, from French *garguesque*, from Italian *grechesca* Greek (as in Greek breeches).

gasp Old Norse *geispa* yawn.

gaster Greek stomach.

gastric See **gaster**.

gastronomy French *gastronomie*, from Greek *gaster* stomach + *nemein* regulate, from *nomos* rule.

gate Old English *geat.*

gather Old English *gaderian* bring together, from *geador* together.

gauche French left, from *gauchir* turn aside.

gaudy Middle English *gaude,* from Latin *gaudere* enjoy.

gauge French.

gaum possibly from Old English *guma.*

gaunt Middle English, from French *gant,* origin uncertain, perhaps from Scandinavian.

gauntlet Middle English, from French *gantelet* armored glove, from *gant* glove.

gauze French *gaze* thin cloth, which is supposed to first have come from Gaza, a city near the Mediterranean Sea.

gavel Scottish *gable* a tool.

gawk Old English *ga(gol)* foolish person.

gay French *gai* merry.

gaze Middle English, of Norse origin.

gazebo origin uncertain, perhaps with some humor based on the word *gaze.*

gazelle French *gazel.*

gazette French newspaper, from Italian *gazetta* coin worth little, also the price of a newspaper in Venice, Italy in the 16th century, from Latin *gaza* wealth, from Greek treasure.

gazogene French *gazogène*, from *gaz* gas + *-gène.* See **-gen**.

gear Old Norse *gervi* equipment.

gebel Arabic *jebel* mountain.

geezer French, from German *wisa* manner.

gefüllte fish Yiddish, from German *gefüllt* filled, stuffed, from *fullen* fill.

geisha Japanese.

gel See **gelatin**.

gelatin French *gélatine,* from Italian *gelatina* jelly, from Latin *gelare* freeze.

geld Old Norse *gelda* unable to reproduce.

gem French *gemme* jewel, from Latin *gemma.*

Gemini Latin *gemini* twins (plural of *geminus* twin).

-gen French *gène*, from Greek *genes* born.

gendarme French, from Latin *gens* a people + *de* of + *arma* arms.

gender French *gendre* sort, from Greek *genus.*

gene GERMAN *gen,* from GREEK *genos* race.

general FRENCH universal, from LATIN *generalis,* from *genus* kind, type.

generate LATIN *generare,* from *genus* race.

generic LATIN *genus* kind, type.

generous LATIN *generosus* noble birth, from *genus* kind, type.

genesis LATIN creation, from GREEK.

genial LATIN *genialis* pleasant, from *genius* guardian spirit.

genie FRENCH (in FRENCH version of Arabian Nights, for ARABIC *jinni, jinn* spirit), from LATIN genius.

genitive FRENCH, from LATIN *casus genitivus* case of origin.

genius LATIN guardian spirit.

genre FRENCH kind, from LATIN *genus* kind.

genteel FRENCH *gentil* noble birth, from LATIN *gentilis* same family (clan), from *gens* clan.

gentian FRENCH, from LATIN *gentiana.*

gentile LATIN *gentilis* of the same clan (group of families), from *gens* clan.

gentle FRENCH *gentil* noble birth, from LATIN *gentilis.* See **gentile**.

gentry FRENCH *genterise* rank, from *gentil* noble birth. See **gentle**.

genuflect LATIN *genu* the knee.

genuine LATIN *genuinus* natural.

genus LATIN kind, type.

geo- GREEK *gaia, ge* the earth.

geodesy GREEK *ge* the earth + *dalien* divide.

geography LATIN *geographia,* from GREEK *geographia* writing about the earth, from **geo-** + **-graphy**.

geology LATIN *geologia,* from GREEK **geo-** + **-logy**.

geometry FRENCH *geometrie,* from LATIN *geometria,* from GREEK *gaia, ge* the earth + *-metria* measurement.

geranium LATIN, from GREEK *geranion* bill of a crane, because the seed looks like it has a beak.

gerbil FRENCH *gerbille,* from *gerbo.*

germ LATIN *germinare* bud, from *germen* bud.

gesticulate LATIN *gesticulari* make gestures, from *gerere* carry on.

gesture LATIN *gestura* behavior, perform, from *gerere* carry on.

get OLD NORSE *geta.*

gewgaw MIDDLE ENGLISH *giuegoue, gugaw.*

geyser Icelandic *Geysir* name of a hot spring in Iceland, from OLD NORSE *geysa* gush.

ghastly OLD ENGLISH *gastlic* ghostly, from *gast* ghost.

ghetto perhaps from ITALIAN *getto* foundry, from *gettare* pour, from LATIN *jactare* throw. *Ghèto,* a part of Venice, Italy, was set aside in 1516 for Jews to live in. Before that time the area was a foundry (a place where metal is melted and poured into molds for making things).

ghost OLD ENGLISH *gast.*

ghoul ARABIC *ghul* demon.

giant FRENCH *geant,* from LATIN *gigas* a huge creature from mythology, from GREEK *gigas.*

gibber imitative.

gibbet FRENCH *gibet,* from *gibe* club.

gibbous LATIN *gibbosus,* from *gibba* a hump.

gibe FRENCH *giber* handle roughly.

giddy OLD ENGLISH *gidig* foolish.

gift Old Norse *gipt.*

gig Middle English *gigge, ghyg* spinning top (in *whyrlegyg*), also *giglet* giddy girl, from Old Norse *geiga* turn sideways.

gigantic Latin *gigas.* See **giant**.

giggle imitative.

gild Middle English *gilden,* from Old English *gyldan* cover with a layer of gold.

gill[1] (fish) Middle English *gile,* from Old Norse *giolnar* gills.

gill[2] (glen) Middle English, from Old Norse *gil* a deep glen.

gill[3] (measure) Middle English, from French *gille* a wine measure, from Latin *gillo* earthenware jar.

gilt[1] (gold) See **gild**.

gilt[2] (sow) Old Norse *gylt-r* young sow.

gimcrack Middle English *gibbecrak* an ornament.

gimlet French, from Dutch *wimmel* tool.

gimmick American, origin uncertain.

gimp[1] (limp) American slang, origin uncertain.

gimp[2] (cord) Dutch, origin uncertain.

gin[1] (machine) Middle English, from French *engin* machine, from Latin *ingenium* skill.

gin[2] (drink) French *genvre* juniper tree, from Latin *juniperus* from an alcoholic drink that was flavored with juniper berries.

ginger Old English *gingifer* the plant.

gingham Malay *ginggang* striped cloth.

gingivitis Latin *gingiva* gums + **-itis**.

giraffe French, from Italian *giraffa,* from Arabic *zarafa.*

gird Old English *gyrdan* surround.

girdle Old English *gyrdel* belt worn around the waist.

girl Middle English *girle* youngster (child).

girt Old English *gyrdan* surround.

girth Old Norse *gjörth* hoop.

gist French.

gittern French *guiterne,* from Spanish *guittarra* guitar.

give Old English *giefan.*

gizzard French *gisier,* from Latin *gigeria* cooked insides of poultry.

glacier French *glace* ice, from Latin *glacies.*

glad Old English *glæd* cheerful.

glade Middle English *glade, glode,* from Old Norse *gladr* bright.

gladiator Latin swordsman, from *gladius* sword.

gladius Latin.

glamour Scottish *gramarye* magic.

glance French *glacier* slip, from Latin *glaciare* turn into ice.

gland French *glande,* from Latin *glandual* gland of the throat.

glare German *glaren.*

glass Old English *glæs.*

glaze Middle English *glasen* make a glass surface, from Old English *glæs* glass.

gleam Old English *glæm* brightness.

glean French *glener,* from Latin *glennare.*

glede Old English *glida.*

glee Old English *gleo* joy.

glen Welsh *glyn.*

glib Dutch *globberig* slippery.

glide OLD ENGLISH *glidan* slide.

glimmer OLD ENGLISH *glæm.*

glimpse MIDDLE ENGLISH *glimsen* glow, from OLD ENGLISH *glæm* brightness.

glint possibly from SWEDISH *glinta* slip.

glisten OLD ENGLISH *glisnian.*

glitter OLD NORSE *glitra* sparkle.

glitzy probably from GERMAN *glitzern* glitter.

gloaming OLD ENGLISH *glow* twilight.

gloat OLD NORSE *glotta.*

glob possibly from a blend of **blob** and **gob**.

globe LATIN *globus* ball.

glockenspiel GERMAN *glocke* a bell + *spiel* play.

glom SCOTTISH.

gloom MIDDLE ENGLISH *gloumen,* possibly from OLD ENGLISH *glumian.*

glop possibly from **glue** + **slop**.

glory FRENCH *glorie,* from LATIN *gloria* honor, praise.

gloss[1] (shine) SCANDINAVIAN, from GERMAN *glos.*

gloss[2] (explanation) MIDDLE ENGLISH *glose,* from FRENCH *glosa,* from LATIN *glossa* word needing explanation, from GREEK *glossa* language.

glossary See **gloss**[2].

glottis GREEK *glotta,* from *glossa* tongue.

glove OLD ENGLISH *glof.*

glow OLD ENGLISH *glowan* shine.

glucose FRENCH *glucose*, from GREEK *gleukos* sweet wine, from *glyks* sweet.

glue FRENCH *glu,* from LATIN *glus,* from *gluten.*

glum MIDDLE ENGLISH *glomen.* See **gloom**.

glut FRENCH *gloutir* gulp down, from LATIN *gluttire.*

gluten LATIN glue.

glutton FRENCH *glouton* greedy eater, from LATIN *glutto.*

gnarled MIDDLE ENGLISH *knur* a knot.

gnash MIDDLE ENGLISH *gnasten,* from OLD NORSE *gnasten.*

gnat OLD ENGLISH *gnæt.*

gnaw OLD ENGLISH *gnagan.*

gnome FRENCH, from GREEK *gnome* thought.

gnomon LATIN, from GREEK *gignoskein* know.

go OLD ENGLISH *gan.*

goad OLD ENGLISH *gad.*

goal MIDDLE ENGLISH *gol* limit.

goat OLD ENGLISH *gat.*

gob FRENCH *gobe* lump.

gobble MIDDLE ENGLISH *gobben* drink with greed.

goblet MIDDLE ENGLISH, from FRENCH *gobelet* cup.

goblin FRENCH *gobelin,* from LATIN *gobelinus*, perhaps from *cabalus*, from GREEK *kobalos* sprite.

god OLD ENGLISH.

godfather See **god** + **father**.

godmother See **god** + **mother**.

goggle MIDDLE ENGLISH *gogelen.*

goiter FRENCH *goitron* throat, from LATIN *guttur.*

gold OLD ENGLISH.

golf possibly from SCOTTISH *gowf* strike.

golliwog name of a doll in an illustrated series of children's books written in the early part of the 20th century.

gombeen IRISH *gaimbín,* from LATIN *cambium* exchange.

-gon GREEK *gonia* an angle.

gondola ITALIAN *gondola*, from *gondula.*

gong MALAY probably imitative of the sound.

good OLD ENGLISH *god* excellent.

good-bye *God be with you* or *ye.*

goodness OLD ENGLISH *godnes* kindness.

goof FRENCH *goffe* stupid, from ITALIAN *goffo.*

goose OLD ENGLISH *gos.*

gore[1] (blood) OLD ENGLISH *gor* dirt.

gore[2] (pierce the skin) MIDDLE ENGLISH *goren,* from *gore* spear, from OLD ENGLISH *gar.*

gorge FRENCH throat, from LATIN *gurges* whirlpool.

gorilla GREEK *gorillai* tribe of hairy people, possibly from an African name.

gorse MIDDLE ENGLISH *gorst,* similar to LATIN *hordeum* barley.

gosling MIDDLE ENGLISH *goslynge.* See **goose** + **-ling**.

gospel OLD ENGLISH *godspel* teachings of Jesus, the Gospel, from *god* good + *spel* news.

gossamer MIDDLE ENGLISH *gosesomer* goose summer, the time in the fall when the geese are in season.

gossip OLD ENGLISH *godsibb* godparent (person who agrees to be responsible for the religious training of another's child), from *god* God + *sibb* relative.

Gothic LATIN, from GREEK *gothoi.*

gouge FRENCH, from LATIN *gubia.*

goulash HUNGARIAN *gulyashus*, from *gulyas* herdsman + *hus* meat. Originally beef or lamb soup made by herdsmen while pasturing.

gour HINDI *gaur* large ox.

gourd FRENCH, from LATIN *cucurbita.*

gourmet FRENCH winetaster.

gout FRENCH *goute,* from LATIN *gutta* drop, because in medieval times it was thought that drops of fluids in the body affected the places where two bones are joined (joints).

govern FRENCH *governor* rule, from LATIN *gubernare,* from GREEK *kybernan.*

gown FRENCH *goune* long coat, from LATIN *gumma* fur.

grab MIDDLE ENGLISH *grabben* hold firmly, probably from GERMAN.

grace FRENCH, from LATIN *gratia* favor, charm.

grade LATIN *gradus* step.

-grade LATIN *gradi* walk.

gradely MIDDLE ENGLISH *greithlic,* from OLD NORSE *griethligr.*

gradient LATIN *gradi* walk.

gradual LATIN *gradualis* by degrees, from *gradus* step.

graduate LATIN *graduari* take an academic degree, from *gradus* step.

graft MIDDLE ENGLISH *graffe,* from FRENCH *grafe,* from LATIN *graphium* pointed pencil, from GREEK *graphein* write.

grail FRENCH *graal,* from LATIN *gradalis* cup.

grain FRENCH, from LATIN *granum* seed.

gram FRENCH, from LATIN, from GREEK *gramma* small weight.

-gram GREEK *gramma* small weight.

grammar Middle English *gramarye,* from French *grammaire,* from Latin *grammatica,* from Greek *grammatike tekhne* art of letters, from *gramma* letter, from *graphein* draw or write.

grampus Middle English *grapays,* from French *graspeis,* from Latin *crassus piscis,* from *crassus* fat + *piscis* fish.

granary Latin *granum* grain.

grand French great, from Latin *grandis* large.

grandfather See **grand** + **father**.

grandiloquent Latin *grandiloquus,* from *grandis* great + *loqui* speak.

grandiose French, from Italian *grandioso,* from *grande* great, from Latin *grandis.*

grandmother See **grand** + **mother**.

grange French barn, from Latin *granum* seed.

granite Italian *granito* grained, from Latin *granum* grain.

granola See **grain** + **-ola**.

grant French *granter* promise, from Latin *credere* believe.

granule Latin *granulum,* from *granum* grain.

grape French bunch of grapes, from *graper* gather with a hook.

grapeshot See **grape** + *shot.* See **shoot**.

-graph Greek *graphos.*

graphic Latin *graphicus* relating to drawing, from Greek *graphikos,* from *graphein* write, draw.

-graphy Greek *-graphia* description, from *graphein* write.

grapnel Middle English, from French *grapin* hook.

grapple French *grape* hook.

grasp Middle English *graspen,* from Old English *gegræppian.*

grate[1] (grind) French *grater.*

grate[2] (frame) Latin *cratis* crate.

grateful Latin *gratus* pleasing + **-ful**.

gratify Latin *gratificari* please, from *gratus* pleasing + *facere* do, make.

gratis Latin *gratia* a favor.

gratitude French, from Latin *gratus* pleasing.

gratuitous Latin *gratuitus* free.

grave[1] (burial) Old English *græf.*

grave[2] (important) French, from Latin *gravis.*

gravel French *gravelem,* from *greve* stony or pebbly shore.

gravity Latin *gravitas* weight.

gravy Middle English *grave* spiced sauce, from Latin *granatus* having many grains, from *granum* seed, from gravies seasoned with the grains of spices.

gray Old English *græg.*

graze Middle English *grasen,* from Old English *grasian,* from *græs* grass.

grease French *graisse* animal fat, from Latin *crassus* fat.

great Old English *great* large.

grebe French.

greedy Old English *grædig.*

green Old English *grene, groeni,* related to *growan* grow.

greengage See **green** + Gage (the surname).

greensward See **green** + from Old English *sweard* a skin.

greet Old English *gretan.*

gregarious Latin *grex* flock.

gremlin Modern English, British Royal Air Force slang, origin unknown, possibly from Irish *gruaimin* bad-tempered little fellow.

grenade French small bomb, from Latin *granum* seed, because a grenade looks like a pomegranate, a fruit with many seeds.

grid See **gridiron**.

griddle French *gridil* grate. See **gridiron**.

gridiron Middle English *gredire* griddle, from French *gridil* grate.

grieve French *grever* burden, from Latin *gravare.*

griffin French *griffon,* from Latin *gryphus,* from Greek *grypos* curved, because of the curved beak.

grill French *gril,* from Latin *craticula.*

grille French, from Latin *graticula.*

grim Old English fierce.

grimace French *grimuche.*

grimalkin probably from Old English *græg* + *malkin* short form of the name *Matilda* or *Maud.*

grime possibly from Old English *grima* mask.

grin Old English *grennian.*

grind Old English *grindan* make into small parts.

grip Old English *gripe.*

gripe Old English *gripan* take.

grisly Old English *grislic.*

grist Old English.

grit Old English *greot.*

grizzle French *gris* gray.

groan Old English *granian.*

groat Dutch *grote.*

grocer French *grossier* person who sells goods in large amounts, from Latin *grossarius,* from *grossus* great.

grog "Old *Grog*", nickname for English Admiral Edward Vernon (1684–1757), because he wore a *grogram* (special kind of coat made of silk and wool).

groin probably from Old English *grynde.*

groom Middle English *grom* boy.

groove Dutch *groeve* channel.

grope Old English *grapian* touch.

gross French *gros* thick, from Latin *grossus.*

grotesque French fanciful, from Italian *pittura grottesca* cave painting, from *grotta* cave, from paintings found on the basement walls of Roman ruins. See **grotto**.

grotto Italian, from Latin *grupta,* from *crypta* burial place, from Greek *krypte* hidden.

grouch Middle English *grucchen.* See **grudge**.

ground Old English *grund* bottom.

groundsel Old English, possibly *gund* pus + *swelgan* swallow, from its use in healing.

group French *groupe,* from Italian *groppo* knot.

grouse Middle English *grows*, origin unknown.

grove Old English *graf.*

grovel Old Norse *agrufu* face downward.

grow Old English *growan.*

grub Middle English *grubben.*

grudge French *groucier* grumble.

gruel French *gru* oatmeal.

gruesome Scottish *grue* be terrified.

gruff Dutch *grof* heavy.

grumble probably from DUTCH *grommelen.*

grunge possibly from **grime** + **sludge**.

grunt OLD ENGLISH *grunnettan* make a sound like a pig.

guano SPANISH *huanu* droppings.

guarantee See **guaranty**.

guaranty FRENCH *guarantie,* from *garant* protection.

guard FRENCH *garder* protect.

guava SPANISH *guayaba.*

gudgeon FRENCH, from LATIN *gobio,* from GREEK *kobios.*

guerrilla SPANISH *guerilla,* from *guerra* war, from GERMAN *werra* quarrel.

guess probably from DUTCH *gessen.*

guest OLD NORSE *gestr* visitor.

guffaw imitative.

guide FRENCH *guider* lead.

guild OLD NORSE *gildi* payment.

guilder MIDDLE ENGLISH, from DUTCH *gulden florijn* golden florin (gold coin of medieval France).

guile FRENCH.

guillotine the French physician Joseph I. *Guillotin* (1738–1814), who recommended its use during the French Revolution.

guilt OLD ENGLISH *gylt* crime.

guimp See **gimp**[2].

guinea the country of *Guinea* in Africa.

guinea pig probably from *Guinea-men*, ships that traveled between England, Africa, and South America, in which the animals were first brought to England.

guise FRENCH way.

guitar FRENCH *guitare,* from SPANISH *guitarra,* from ARABIC *qitara* instrument with strings, from GREEK *kithara* type of lyre (small harp used by the ancient Greeks).

gulch imitative.

gules FRENCH *goules,* from LATIN *gulae.*

gulf FRENCH *golfe* bay, from ITALIAN *golgo,* from GREEK *lokpos.*

gull[1] (bird) MIDDLE ENGLISH, related to WELSH *gwylan* gull.

gull[2] (silly person) probably from MIDDLE ENGLISH *golle* silly person.

gullet FRENCH *goulet,* from LATIN *gula* throat.

gullible See **gull**[2].

gully[1] (channel) MIDDLE ENGLISH *golet* water channel, probably from FRENCH *goulet,* from LATIN *gula* throat.

gully[2] (knife) origin uncertain, perhaps related to **gullet**.

gulp DUTCH *gulpen.*

gum MIDDLE ENGLISH *gomme,* from FRENCH *gomme* sticky liquid from some trees, from LATIN *gummi,* from GREEK *kommi* from EGYPTIAN *kemai.*

gumption SCOTTISH common sense, shrewdness, possibly from MIDDLE ENGLISH *gome* attention, heed, from OLD NORSE *gaumr* heed.

gun OLD NORSE *Gunnhildr* female name, from *gunnr* war + *hildr* battle, from the Scandinavian habit of giving their weapons female names.

gunnel (gunwale) MIDDLE ENGLISH *gonne walle,* from **gun** + *wale* plank. Originally a platform on the deck of a ship to support the mounted guns.

gunny (sack) HINDI *goni* coarse fabric, from SANSKRIT *goni* sack.

gurgle imitative.

gurry MIDDLE ENGLISH diarrhoea (later applied to fish remains and to a wheelbarrow used to haul them).

guru HINDI *guru* teacher.

gush imitative.

gusset FRENCH *gouchet, gousset.*

gust OLD NORSE *gustr.*

gusto ITALIAN taste, from LATIN *gustus.*

gut OLD ENGLISH *guttas* intestines.

gutter FRENCH *goutiere* channel, from *goute* drop, from LATIN *gutta.*

guttural LATIN *guttur* throat.

guy[1] (person) *Guy* Fawkes (1570–1606), leader of the Gunpowder Plot attempt to blow up the British Parliament building in 1605.

guy[2] (line) FRENCH *guie* a guide, from *guier.*

gymkhana HINDI *gend-khana* ball-house, the name given to a racquet court.

gymnasium LATIN athletic school, from GREEK *gymnasion,* from *gymnos* naked, because ancient Greek athletes exercised naked.

gyp See **gypsy**.

gypsum LATIN *gypsum,* from GREEK *gypsos* chalk.

gypsy MIDDLE ENGLISH *gypcian* Egyptian, because it was mistakenly thought that Gypsies came from Egypt.

gyrate LATIN *gyrare,* from *gyrus* circle, from GREEK *gyros.*

gyrfalcon FRENCH *girfaucon,* from GERMAN *gir* hawk.

ha imitative.

haberdasher probably from French *hapertas* kind of cloth.

habergeon French *haubergeon,* from *hauberc* medieval coat of armor. See **hauberk.**

habit French, from Latin *habitus* condition, from *habere* have.

habitat Latin *habitare,* from *habere* have.

habituate Latin *habitus.* See **habit.**

hack[1] (chop) Old English *haccian* cut.

hack[2] (horse) See **hackney.**

hackamore probably from Spanish *jaquima* halter.

hackle Middle English *hechele,* from *hackle* bird feathers, from Old English *hacele.*

hackney Middle English *hakene* hackney horse, from *Hackney,* a town in England once famous for its horses. These horses were often worn out, from being overused.

had See **have.**

haddock Middle English, origin uncertain.

hafod Welsh summer house.

haft Old English *hæft.*

hag Old English *hægtesse* witch.

haggard French *hagard* not tamed.

haggle possibly from Scandinavian.

hail[1] (greet) Middle English *hailen* greet, from Old Norse *heill* well.

hail[2] (ice) Middle English *haile,* from Old English *hægel.*

hair Old English *hær.*

halberd German *helmbarie,* from *helm* handle + *barte* an ax.

halcyon Middle English *alcioun,* from Latin *alycon* kingfisher (bird), from Greek *(h)alkyon.* According to Greek mythology, *Alkyone,* the daughter of the god of the winds, threw herself into the sea when she learned her husband was dead. She was changed into a kingfisher. She built a floating nest on the sea, and whenever she laid eggs the sea was always calm at that place.

hale[1] (healthy) Old English *hal.* See **heal.**

hale[2] (summon) French *haler* pull, haul.

half Old English *h(e)alf.*

hall Old English *heall* large roofed place.

hallah Hebrew.

hallelujah Latin *alleluja,* from Greek *hallelouia,* from Hebrew *halelu* praise + *ya* God.

hallmark a *mark* first put on gold or silver items in the 1300s at the Goldsmith's *Hall* in London to show quality or purity.

hallo French *hola,* from *ho* ahoy + *la* there.

hallow Old English *halgian.*

hallucinate Latin *(h)allucinari* wander in the mind.

halo Latin *halos* circle of light around the sun or moon, from Greek *halos* circle or disk.

halogen Greek *hals, halo-* salt + *-gen* produce, because a salt is formed in reactions of these elements with metal.

halt German *halten* hold.

halter Old English *hælfter.*

halyard Middle English *halier,* from *halen* pull.

ham Old English *hamm.*

hamburger the German town of *Hamburg,* where hamburgers were first known to be made.

hame Dutch horse collar.

hamlet French *hamel* village, from German *hamm* enclosed area.

hammer Old English *hamor.*

hammock Spanish *hamaca,* origin uncertain.

hamper[1] (get in the way) Middle English *hamperen* surround.

hamper[2] (large basket) French *hanap* a cup.

hand Old English.

handicap Modern English *hand in cap,* a game where two players would put their hands (holding money) into a cap.

handiwork Old English *handgeweorc.*

handkerchief See **hand** + **kerchief**.

handle Old English *hand* hand.

handsome Middle English *handsom* easy to handle, ready at hand.

handy See **hand**.

hang Old English *hangian.*

hangar French *hangar* shed, from *hanghart,* from Latin *angarium* shed in which horses are shod.

hanger[1] (something hanging) See **hang**.

hanger[2] (woods) Old English *hangra.*

hank Old Norse *hankar.*

hanker probably from Dutch *hankeren* want.

hansom Joseph A. *Hansom* (1803–1882), Englishman who designed the cab.

hap Old Norse *happ* good luck.

haphazard See **hap** + **hazard**.

hapless See **hap** + **-less**.

happen Middle English *happenen,* from Old Norse *happ* good luck.

happy Old Norse *happ* good luck.

harangue Middle English speech, from Latin *harenga* speech made at a meeting.

harass French *harasser,* from *harer* set a dog to chase, from *hare* the hunting cry to urge the dog to chase.

harbinger French *herberge* temporary place to stay, from the idea of the person who went ahead of an army to find shelter.

harbor Old English *herebeorg* place to stay, from *here* army + *beorg* protection.

hard Old English *heard* solid.

hardy French *hardi* bold.

hare Old English *hara.*

harem Arabic *haram* women's rooms, from *harama* forbidden, because men were forbidden to enter.

haricot FRENCH possibly from *harigoter* tear into scraps.

hark MIDDLE ENGLISH *herkien,* possibly from OLD ENGLISH *heorcnian.*

harlequin ITALIAN, from FRENCH *Herlequin,* a devil in medieval legend.

harm OLD ENGLISH *hearm.*

harmonium GREEK *harmonion.*

harmony LATIN *harmonia* agreement of sounds, from GREEK *harmonia,* from *harmos* fitting.

harness FRENCH *harneis* armor, from OLD NORSE.

harp OLD ENGLISH *hearpe.*

harpoon DUTCH, from FRENCH *harper* claw, from OLD NORSE *harpa* squeeze.

harpsichord FRENCH *harpechorde* harp string, from LATIN *harpichordium*, from *harpa* harp + *chorda* string.

harpy FRENCH, from LATIN, from GREEK *harpazien* seize.

harridan FRENCH *haridelle* worn-out horse.

harrow probably from OLD NORSE *harfr.*

harry OLD ENGLISH *hergian* make raids, from *here* army.

harsh MIDDLE ENGLISH *harsk,* from DANISH bad smell or taste.

hart OLD ENGLISH *heorot.*

hartebeest AFRIKAANS, from DUTCH *harte* hart (deer) + *beest* beast.

harum-scarum probably from **harry** + **scare** + **them**.

harvest OLD ENGLISH *hærfest* season for gathering crops.

has See **have**.

hash FRENCH *hacher* chop with heavy blows, from *hache* ax.

hasp FRENCH *haepse.*

hassock OLD ENGLISH *hassue* grass that is not smooth. Hassocks were originally made from such grass.

haste MIDDLE ENGLISH, from OLD ENGLISH speed.

hastilude LATIN *hastiludus*, from *hasta* spear + *ludus* play.

hat OLD ENGLISH *hætt.*

hatch[1] (egg) MIDDLE ENGLISH *hacchen.*

hatch[2] (door) OLD ENGLISH *hæcc* a grate.

hatchet FRENCH *hatchette,* from *hache* ax.

hate OLD ENGLISH *hatian.*

hathi HINDI, from SANSKRIT *hastin* elephant, from *hasta* elephant's trunk.

hauberk FRENCH *hausberc* neck protector, from FRANKISH *hals* the neck + *bergan* protect.

haughty FRENCH *haut* high, from LATIN *altus.*

haul FRENCH *haler* pull, from DUTCH *halen* get.

haunch FRENCH *hanche* hip.

haunt FRENCH *hanter* be at a place often.

hauteur FRENCH *haut* high, proud, from LATIN *altus.*

have OLD ENGLISH *habban.*

haven OLD ENGLISH *hæfen* harbor, from OLD NORSE *höfn.*

haversack FRENCH, from GERMAN *habersack* sack of oats.

havoc FRENCH *havot* take by force.

haw OLD ENGLISH *haga* enclosure, hedge.

hawk OLD ENGLISH *hafoc.*

hawser French *hauceor,* from *halcier* pull up, from Latin *altus* high.

hawthorn Old English *haga* hedge + *thorn.*

hay Old English *hieg.*

hayron Middle English *heiroun,* from French *hairon,* from Latin *hagironem* heron.

hazard Middle English, from French *hasard* dice game, from Arabic *yasara* playing at dice.

haze[1] (mist) See **hazy**.

haze[2] (harass) Old English *haser* annoy.

hazy probably from Old English *hasu* like dusk.

he Old English *he.*

head Old English *heafod.*

headlong Middle English *hedlong.*

heal Old English *hælan* make whole.

health Old English *hælth* being well in body or mind.

heap Old English.

hearse Middle English frame for holding many candles over a coffin, from French *herse* large rake, from Latin *hirpex* harrow (a large rake used to prepare ground for planting), from *hirpus* wolf (from the long teeth on the harrow).

heart Middle English *herte,* from Old English *heorte.*

hearth Old English *heorth.*

heat Old English *hætu* great warmth.

heath Old English *hæth.*

heathen Old English *hæthen* person who lives on a heath (land that is empty), from *hæth* heath. Originally, people who lived in areas away from the city.

heather Middle English *haddyr.*

heave Old English *hebban* lift.

heaven Old English *heofon.*

heavy Old English *hefig.*

Hebrew Old English, from Hebrew *'ibhri* one from across (the river).

hecatomb Latin, from Greek *hecaton* a hundred + *bous* ox.

heckle Middle English *hechele.* See **hackle.**

hectic Latin *hectica* continuous, from Greek *hektikos,* from *hexis* condition of the body.

hecto- French, from Greek *hekaton* a hundred.

hector Greek *Hector*, a Trojan hero killed by Achilles.

heddle Old English, small cords on a loom, origin uncertain.

heder Hebrew *hedher* chamber.

hedge Old English *hecg.*

hedonism Greek *hedone* pleasure + *ismos.*

heed Old English *heden.*

heel[1] (of foot) Old English *hela.*

heel[2] (a boat) Middle English *hield*, from Old English *hyldan* incline.

heeled (provided) American slang. See **heel**[1]. Originally said of a gamecock furnished with a metal spur.

heft See **heave**.

hegemony Greek *hegemon* leader.

height Old English *heihthu.*

heinous French *haineus,* from *haine* hate.

heir French, from Latin *heres.*

heirloom See **heir** + **loom**[1].

heist See **hoist**.

helicopter French *héicoptèr,* from Greek *helix* spiral + *pteron* wing.

helio- Latin, from Greek *helios* sun.

heliostat Latin *heliostata,* from **helio-** + Greek *statos* standing.

heliotrope French, from Latin *heliotropium,* from Greek *heliotropion,* from *helios* sun + *tropos* turn.

helium Latin, from Greek *helios* sun, because it was first discovered in the sun.

helix Latin, from Greek spiral, from *helissein* turn around.

hell Old English hidden place.

hello German *hala* fetch, especially in calling for a ferryman.

helm Old English *helma* position of guidance, control.

helmet French.

help Old English *helpan.*

helter-skelter imitative of the sound of children's running feet.

helve Old English *helfe.*

hem Middle English, from Old English border of a piece of cloth.

hemisphere Latin *hemisphaerium* a half globe, from Greek *hemisphairion,* from *hemi* half + *sphaira* ball, sphere.

hemlock Old English *hymlic.*

hemorrhage French *hémorrhagie,* from Latin *haemorrhagia* dangerous bleeding, from Greek *haimorrhagia*, from *haima* blood + *rhegnynai* to burst.

hemp Old English *hænep.*

hen Old English *henn.*

henbane See **hen** + **bane**.

hence Middle English *hennes* away, from Old English *heonan.*

henchman Old English *hengst* horse + *-man* possibly meaning "groom".

hennin French.

hepatic Latin *hepaticus*, from Greek *hepatikos*, from *hepar* the liver.

hepta- Greek seven.

heptarchy See **hepta-** + **-arch**.

her Old English *hire.*

herald French *herau(l)t* royal officer.

herb French, from Latin *herba.*

herd Old English *heord.*

here Old English *her.*

heredity French, from Latin *hereditas,* from *heres* heir.

heresy French *heresie,* from Latin *haeresis,* from Greek *hairesis* choice.

heritage French inheritance, from *heriter* inherit, from Latin *hereditare,* from *heres* heir.

hermit French *(h)ermite,* from Latin *(h)ememita,* from Greek *eremites* person who lives in a desert, from *dremia* desert.

hernia Latin.

hero Latin *heros* man born from a god, from Greek.

heron French *hairon.*

herring Old English *hering.*

herringbone See **herring** + **bone**.

hesitate Latin *haesitare* stick fast, from *haerere* stick.

hew Old English *heawan* strike.

hex German *Hexe* witch.

hexamine GREEK *hex-* six + *amine.* See **amino-**.

hey MIDDLE ENGLISH *hei.*

hiatus LATIN *giatus* gap.

hibernate LATIN *hibernare,* from *hibernus* wintry.

hiccup imitative.

hick *Hick,* early nickname for Richard.

hide[1] (conceal) OLD ENGLISH *hydan.*

hide[2] (animal skin) OLD ENGLISH *hid.*

hideous FRENCH *hideus,* from *hide* terror.

hierarchy LATIN *hierarchia* rule of a priest, from GREEK *hierarchia,* from *hieros* sacred + *archein* rule.

hieroglyphic FRENCH, from LATIN, from GREEK *heros* sacred + *glyphein* carve.

high OLD ENGLISH *heah.*

hijack AMERICAN *high(way)* + *jacker* one who holds up.

hike See **hitch**.

hilarity FRENCH *hilarité,* from LATIN *hilaritas,* from GREEK *hilaros* merry.

hill OLD ENGLISH *hyll.*

hillock MIDDLE ENGLISH small hill, from OLD ENGLISH *hyll* + *-ock* small.

hilt OLD ENGLISH.

him OLD ENGLISH.

Himalayan SANSKRIT *himalayah,* from *hima* snow + *alaya* abode.

hind OLD ENGLISH *hindan.*

hinder OLD ENGLISH *hindrian.*

hinge MIDDLE ENGLISH *hengen* hang.

hint OLD ENGLISH *hentan* take.

hip OLD ENGLISH *hype.*

hippo- GREEK *hippos* a horse.

hippodrome See **hippo-** + GREEK *dromos* a course.

hippogriff See **hippo-** + **griffin**.

hippopotamus See **hippo-** + GREEK *ptoamos* river.

hire OLD ENGLISH *hyr* payment for the use of something.

his OLD ENGLISH.

hiss imitative.

history LATIN *historia* story of past events, from GREEK *historia,* from *histor* learned.

hit OLD ENGLISH *hittan.*

hitch MIDDLE ENGLISH *hicchen* move jerkily.

hithe See **hythe**.

hither OLD ENGLISH *hinder.*

hive OLD ENGLISH *huf.*

hoard OLD ENGLISH *hord* treasure.

hoarhound MIDDLE ENGLISH *horhowne*, from OLD ENGLISH *hare hune*, from *har* hoar, hoary + *hune* name of a plant.

hoarse OLD ENGLISH *has.*

hoax See **hocus-pocus**.

hob[1] (ledge) possible variation of **hub**.

hob[2] (goblin) old form of *Robin,* an elf in English folk tales.

hobbit stories by J.R.R. Tolkein, 20th century English writer.

hobble MIDDLE ENGLISH *hobelen,* from DUTCH *hobbelen* jolt.

hobby MIDDLE ENGLISH *hobyn* small horse, possibly from DUTCH *hobben* move back and forth.

hobnob OLD ENGLISH *habban* have + *nabban* not to have.

hoboy French *hautbois* high wood.

hock[1] (leg joint) Middle English *hockshin*, from Old English *hoh-sinu* heel sinew.

hock[2] (pawn) Dutch *hok* jail, pen, doghouse.

hockey French *hoquet* bent stick, from *hoc* hook.

hocus-pocus Latin rhyming words used by jugglers and magicians.

hodge-podge French *hochepot*, from *hocher* shake + *pot* pot.

hoe French *houe*, from German *houwan*.

hog Old English *hogg*.

hoist Dutch *hyssen* raise up.

hoity-toity rhyme based on obsolete *hoit* lively play.

hold Old English *h(e)aldan* keep.

hole Old English *hol*.

holiday Old English *haligdæg* holy day.

holler French *hola*, from *ho* ahoy + *la* there.

hollow Old English *holh* hole.

holo- French, from Latin, from Greek *holos* whole.

holocaust Middle English, from French *holocauste*, from Latin *holocaustum* whole burnt offering or sacrifice, from Greek *holokauston*, from *holos* whole + *kaiston* burnt.

holus-bolus humerous Latin-sounding term meaning whole bolus (lump of earth).

holy Old English *halig* sacred.

holystone See **holy** + **stone**, perhaps because sailors knelt as if in prayer while using it to scrub decks.

homage French duty owed to a lord, from *hom* man, from Latin *homo* man.

homburg *Homburg* the town in Germany where the hat originated.

home Old English *ham*.

homeopathy German *Homöopathie*, from Greek *homoios* same + *-patheia* effect.

homicide French, from Latin *homicidium*, from *homo* man + *-cidium*, from *caedere* kill.

homily Latin *homilia* sermon, from Greek *homilia* instruction.

hominy Native American *rockahominy* something ground.

homogeneous Latin *homogeneus* of the same kind, from Greek *homogenes*, from *homos* same + *genos* kind, race.

homonym Latin *homonymum*, from Greek *homonymos* having the same name.

honcho Japanese *hancho* leader, from *han* group + *cho* chief.

hone Old English *han* a stone.

honest French, from Latin *honestus* having honor.

honey Old English *hunig*.

honeymoon Middle English *hony moone*, referring to the sweetness of the first month of a marriage.

honky-tonk American *honk-a-tonk*, origin uncertain.

honor French, from Latin dignity.

hood Old English *hod* covering for the head and neck.

-hood Old English *had* order, condition, rank.

hoodlum probably from German *hudilump* miserable person.

hoof Old English *hof*.

hook Old English *hoc* bent piece of metal.

hookah ARABIC *huqqah* pipe for smoking.

hooky possibly from MIDDLE ENGLISH *hook it* escape.

hooligan possibly from the Irish family name *Hooligan.*

hoop OLD ENGLISH *hop.*

hoosegow SPANISH *juzgado* court of justice, from LATIN *judex* judge.

hoot imitative.

hop MIDDLE ENGLISH *hoppen,* from OLD ENGLISH *hoppian* leap.

hope OLD ENGLISH *hopa* trust.

hopscotch OLD ENGLISH *hoppian* leap + *scotch* line.

hora HEBREW *hōrāh,* from ROMANIAN *horă.*

horde FRENCH pack, from TURKISH *ordu* camp.

horehound OLD ENGLISH *harhune.*

horizon FRENCH, from LATIN, from GREEK *horos* limit.

hormone GREEK *hormon* that which sets in motion.

horn OLD ENGLISH highest part of the body.

hornet OLD ENGLISH *hyrnetu, hurnitu* large wasp, beetle.

hornswoggle AMERICAN, origin unknown.

horoscope FRENCH, from LATIN *horoscopus,* from GREEK *horoskopos,* from *hora* hour (of birth) + *skopos* watcher.

horrible FRENCH, from LATIN *horribilis,* from *horrere* tremble.

horror LATIN *horridus* frightful.

hors d'oeuvre FRENCH *hors d'oeuvre,* from *hors,* from *fors* outside + *de-* from + *oeuvre* work.

horse OLD ENGLISH *hors.*

horticulture LATIN *hortus* garden + *cultura* cultivate (grow).

hosanna LATIN *hosamma,* from GREEK *hosanna,* from HEBREW *hoshia na* save now, we pray.

hose OLD ENGLISH *hosa* clothes for the leg.

hospitable FRENCH, from LATIN *hospes* host.

hospital FRENCH place for persons in need, from LATIN *hospitale* guest room, from *hospes* guest.

host[1] (person) MIDDLE ENGLISH *hoste,* from FRENCH innkeeper, from LATIN *hospes* guest.

host[2] (large number) MIDDLE ENGLISH *host,* from FRENCH *host* army, from LATIN *hostis,* from enemy.

hostage FRENCH *(h)ostage,* from LATIN *obses.* See **host**[2].

hostel MIDDLE ENGLISH, from FRENCH, from LATIN *hospitale* guest room.

hostile LATIN *hostis* enemy.

hostler MIDDLE ENGLISH *hosteler* innkeeper, from FRENCH *hostelier.*

hot OLD ENGLISH *hat.*

hotel FRENCH inn, from *hostel,* from LATIN *hospitale* guest room, from *hospes* guest.

hound OLD ENGLISH *hund.*

houppelande FRENCH.

hour MIDDLE ENGLISH, from FRENCH *hore,* from LATIN *hora,* from GREEK *hora* time.

house OLD ENGLISH *hus.*

hovel MIDDLE ENGLISH roofed passage, vent for smoke, origin uncertain.

hover MIDDLE ENGLISH *hoveren* stay in the air.

how[1] (what way) OLD ENGLISH *hu.*

how[2] (hollow) SCOTTISH *howe,* from MIDDLE ENGLISH *holl* valley.

howdah Persian *haudah.*

howl Middle English *houlen.*

hoyden Dutch *heiden* uncivilized person.

huarache Spanish, from Native American *kwarachi.*

hub Middle English, perhaps from *hubbe* lump.

hubbub of uncertain origin, perhaps Irish, from *abu* a battle cry.

hubris Greek *hubris* outrage.

huddle possibly from Middle English *hoderen* cover up.

hue Middle English *hewe,* from Old English *heow* shape.

huff imitative.

hug probably from Old Norse *hugga* comfort.

huge French *ahuge.*

hulk Old English *hulc,* possibly from Latin *hulcus,* from Greek *holkas* trading ship.

hull Old English *hulu* shell of a seed.

hullabaloo imitative.

hum imitative.

human Latin *humanus*, from *homo* man.

humanity French *humanite* human nature, from Latin *humanitas.*

humble French, from Latin *humilis* low, from *humus* ground.

humbug British slang, origin uncertain.

humdinger possibly from **hum** + **ding**.

humdrum imitative rhyme.

humid Latin *(h)umidus.*

humiliate Latin *humiliare,* from *humilis.* See **humble**.

humility French *humilite,* from Latin *humilitas* lowness.

hummock Middle English, nautical term, origin uncertain.

humor Middle English juice of an animal or plant, from French, from Latin *umor* body fluid.

hump German *humpe* thick piece.

hunch Middle English push, thrust, origin unknown.

hundred Old English.

hunger Old English *hungor.*

hunk Dutch *hunke.*

hunker probably from Old Norse *hokra* creep.

hunt Old English *huntian.*

hurdle Old English *hyrdel* movable frame used as a fence.

hurl Middle English *hurlen,* from German *hurreln* toss.

hurly-burly earlier *hurling and burling,* rhyme based on **hurl**.

hurrah German *hurra* cheer.

hurricane Spanish *huracán* violent storm, from Native American *hurakan* name of an evil spirit.

hurry possibly from Middle English *horyed* rushed, from German *hurren* move quickly.

hurt French *hurter* strike.

hurtle Middle English *hurten.* See **hurt**.

husband Old English *husbonda* master of a house, from Old Norse *husbondi.*

hush Middle English *huscht* quiet.

husk Dutch *husken* little house, from *huus* house.

hussar HUNGARIAN *huszár* army horseman, from LATIN *cursarius* pirate, from *cursus* rob, from *corsus* course.

hustle DUTCH *hutslen* shake.

hutch FRENCH *huche* chest, from LATIN *hutica.*

huzza, huzzah originally a sailor's shout.

hyacinth GREEK *hyakinthos.*

hybrid LATIN *hybrida.*

hydrate FRENCH, coined by French chemist Joseph-Louis Proust, from GREEK *hydor* water.

hydraulic LATIN *hydraulicus* water engine, from GREEK *hydor* water + *aulos* pipe. The Greeks had a kind of pipe organ played by using water.

hydro- GREEK *hydor* water.

hydrogen FRENCH *hydrogène,* from GREEK *hydor* water + *gennan* produce, because water is produced when hydrogen is burned.

hydroponic GREEK *hydro-* water + *-ponic,* from *ponein,* from *ponos* labor.

hydrostatic See **hydro-** + **static.**

hygiene FRENCH, from GREEK *hygies* health.

hyla GREEK *hyle* wood.

hymn LATIN *hymnus* song of praise, from GREEK *hymnos.*

hype AMERICAN. See **hyperbole.**

hyper See **hyper-** + **active.**

hyper- GREEK above, over, beyond.

hyperactive See **hyper-** + **active.**

hyperbola See **hyperbole.**

hyperbole LATIN, from GREEK, from *hyperballein* throw over or beyond, from *hyper-* beyond + *bol-*, from *ballein* throw.

hypertrophy See **hyper-** + **-trophy.**

hyphen LATIN, from GREEK together, from *hypo-* under + *heis* one.

hypnotic LATIN *hypnoticus,* from GREEK *hypnotikos*, from *hypnos* sleep.

hypo- GREEK under, below.

hypochondria LATIN belly, from GREEK *hypo* under + *chondros* part of the breastbone, from an early belief that depression came from that part of the body.

hypocrisy FRENCH *hypocrisis* pretending, from GREEK *hypokrites,* from *hypo-* under + *krinesthai* argue.

hypodermic GREEK *hypo-* under + *derma* the skin.

hypothesis GREEK foundation, from *hypo-* under + *tithenai* place.

hyssop OLD ENGLISH *ysope*, from Latin *hyssopus*, from GREEK *hyssopos* a plant of Palestine, used in Jewish purification rites, from HEBREW *ezobh.*

hysteria LATIN, from GREEK.

hythe OLD ENGLISH *hyth* a river-landing.

I OLD ENGLISH *ic.*

-ia LATIN, from GREEK.

-ial LATIN *-ialis.*

-ian LATIN *-ianus.*

-ibility LATIN *-ibilitas.*

-ic FRENCH *-ique,* from LATIN *-icus,* from GREEK *-ikos.*

-ical LATIN *-icus.*

ice OLD ENGLISH *is.*

icicle OLD ENGLISH *is* ice + *gicel* piece of ice.

icon LATIN image, from GREEK *eikon.*

iconoclast LATIN *iconoclastes,* from GREEK *eikon* image + *klastes* breaker.

ichor GREEK, origin unknown.

-ide use in names of simple chemical compounds. See **oxide**.

idea LATIN model, from GREEK form, model.

ideal LATIN *idealis,* from *idea.* See **idea**.

identical LATIN *identicus.* See **identity**.

identity LATIN *identitas* sameness, from LATIN *idem* the same.

ideology GREEK *idea* form, model + *-logia,* from *logos* word.

ides FRENCH, from LATIN *idus.*

idiom LATIN *idioma,* from GREEK *idios* one's own.

idiosyncrasy GREEK *idio-* one's own + *synkrasis* mixture, from *syn-* together + *kerannynai* mix.

idiot MIDDLE ENGLISH *idiote,* from FRENCH, from LATIN *idiota* ignorant person, from GREEK private person, from *idios* one's own. A Greek private person (one without professional knowledge) could not work for the government because they were thought to be ill-informed.

idle OLD ENGLISH *idel* useless.

idol FRENCH, from LATIN *idollum* image, from GREEK *eidolon.*

idyll LATIN *idyllium,* from GREEK *eidyllion* little picture, from *eidos* picture.

if OLD ENGLISH *gif.*

igloo ESKIMO for house, dwelling.

igneous LATIN *igneus* of fire, fiery, from *ignis* fire.

ignite LATIN *ignire* set on fire, from *ignis* fire.

ignoble FRENCH, from LATIN *ignobilis* unknown, from *in-* not + *gnobilis* of noble birth.

ignominy FRENCH, from LATIN *ignomina,* from *in-* not + *nomen* name.

ignorant FRENCH, from LATIN *ignorare.* See **ignore.**

ignore FRENCH, from LATIN *ignorare,* from *in-* not + *gnarus* knowing.

iguana SPANISH *iuana.*

il- See **in-**[1], **in-**[2]. Used when the root word starts with the letter *l.*

-ile FRENCH *-il, -ile,* from LATIN *-ilis.*

ilk OLD ENGLISH *ilca* same.

ill OLD NORSE *illr* bad.

illimitable See **il-** + **limit** + **-able.**

illuminate LATIN *illuminare* cause to have light, from *in-* in + *lumen* light.

illusion FRENCH, from LATIN *illusio* deceive.

illustrate LATIN *illustrare* light up.

illustrious LATIN *illustris* bright.

im- See **in-**[1], **in-**[2]. Used when the root starts with *m.*

image FRENCH statue, from LATIN *imago.*

imagine FRENCH *imaginer* form in the mind, from LATIN *imaginari* imagination.

imbecile FRENCH weak, without support, from *in-* not + *bacillus* little staff.

imbibe LATIN *imbibere,* from *in-* in + *bibere* drink.

imbue LATIN *imbuere* stain.

imitate LATIN *imitari* copy.

immaculate LATIN *in-* not + *maculare* soil, from *macual* a spot.

immediate LATIN *immediatus,* from *in-* not + *medius* middle.

immense LATIN *immensus,* from *in-* in + *metiri* measure.

immerse LATIN *immergere,* from *in-* into + *mergere* dip.

immigrate LATIN *immigrare,* from *in-* in + *migrare* move from place to place.

imminent LATIN *imminere* threaten.

immolate LATIN *immolare* sprinkle grain on a sacrificial victim, from *in-* in, on + *mola* meal (grain).

immune LATIN *immunis* exempt, from *in-* without + *munia* duties.

imp OLD ENGLISH *impa* young plant, from LATIN *impotus* graft (putting a bud from one plant onto a cut made in another so there is one plant from two), from GREEK *emphytos.* In the 15th century the word meant to repair the wing of a falcon. Later it came to mean putting wings on a person, such as a small demon or wicked spirit.

impact LATIN *impingere,* from *in-* in + *pangere* drive in.

impair FRENCH *empeirer,* from LATIN *in-* in + *pejor* worse.

impala AFRICAN.

impale LATIN *in-* in, on + *palus* stake.

impart LATIN *impartire* share with, from *in-* in + *pars* share.

impasse FRENCH *in-* not + *passer* go across. See **pass.**

impeach FRENCH *empe(s)cher* get in the way of, from LATIN *impedicare* be in difficulty, from *in-* in, on + *pedicare* chain wound around the feet of criminals, from *pes* foot.

impeccable LATIN *impeccabilis,* from *in-* not + *peccare* sin.

impecunious LATIN *in-* not + *pecuniosus* rich, wealthy, from *pecunia* money.

impede LATIN *impedire* put chains on prisoners, from *in-* in + *pes* foot.

impediment LATIN *impedimentem.* See **impede.**

impel LATIN *impellere,* from *in-* on + *pellere* drive.

impend LATIN *impendere,* from *in-* in, on + *pendere* hang.

imperative LATIN *imperativus,* from *imperatum* command.

imperial LATIN *imperialis,* from *imperium* rule.

imperious LATIN *imperium* rule.

impersonate LATIN *in-* in + *persona* mask.

impetuous FRENCH, from LATIN *impetus.* See **impetus**.

impetus LATIN *impetere* attack, from *in-* in + *petere* rush at.

impinge LATIN *impingere,* from *in-* in + *pangere* strike.

implement LATIN *implementum* a filling up, from *implere,* from *in-* in + *plere* fill.

implicate LATIN *implicatus*, from *implicare* involve. See **imply**.

implicit LATIN *implicitus,* from *implicare* involve. See **imply**.

implore LATIN *implorare* beg, from *in-* very much + *plorare* cry out.

imply FRENCH *emplier* involve, from LATIN *implicare* involve, from *in-* in + *plicare* fold.

import LATIN *importare,* from *in-* in + *portare* carry.

important FRENCH, from LATIN *importare* be of weight, from carry in. See **import**.

importune FRENCH, from LATIN *importunus* causing trouble, from *in-* not + *(op)portunus* before the port, from *potrus* resting place.

impose FRENCH *imposer* put on, from LATIN *imponere,* from *in-* in + *ponere* place.

impostor LATIN *imponere* place on. See **impose**.

impotent LATIN *impotens* powerless, from *in-* not + *posse* be able.

impoverish FRENCH *empoverir* make poor, from LATIN *in-* in + *pauper* poor.

imprecate LATIN *imprecari* call down, from *in-* on + *precari* pray.

impregnable FRENCH *imprenable*, from LATIN *in-* not + *prenable,* from *prendere* take.

impress MIDDLE ENGLISH *impressen,* from LATIN *imprimere*, from *in-* in + *premere* press.

imprint FRENCH, from LATIN *imprimere,* from *in-* on + *premere* press.

impromptu FRENCH not prepared, from LATIN *in promptu* in readiness.

improve FRENCH *emprower* benefit, from *em-* in + *prou* a benefit, from LATIN *prodesse* be of advantage.

improvise ITALIAN *improvissare,* from LATIN *improvisus* not foreseen, from *in-* not + *providere* see ahead.

impudent LATIN *impudens,* from *in-* not + *pudere* feel shame.

impugn LATIN *impugnare,* from *in-* against + *pugnare* fight.

impulse LATIN *impulsus*. See **impel**.

impute LATIN *imputare* charge, from *in-* to + *putare* think, estimate.

in OLD ENGLISH.

in-[1] (not, without) LATIN *in-* not.

in-[2] (in) LATIN *in-* in, into, on, toward, against.

-ina LATIN.

inane LATIN *inanis* empty.

inaugurate LATIN *inaugurare* look for guidance, from omens (sign of something to come) before acting. See **augur**.

incandescent LATIN *incandescere* become hot, from *in-* in + *candescere,* from *candere* glow.

incantation LATIN *incantatio* enchantment, from *incantare,* from *in-* in + *cantare* chant.

incapable LATIN *incapabilis,* from *in-* not + *capabilis* able to hold.

incarcerate LATIN *incarcerare,* from *in-* in + *carcer* prison.

incarnate LATIN *incarnare,* from *in-* in + *caro* flesh.

incendiary LATIN *incendiarius* causing a fire, from *incendium* fire. See **incense**.

incense MIDDLE ENGLISH *encens,* from FRENCH, from LATIN *incensum,* from *incendere* set on fire, from *in-* in + *candere* glow.

incentive LATIN *incentivus* set the tune, from *incinere* sound, from *in-* in + *canere,* from *cantus* song.

incessant LATIN *in-* not + *cessare* cease.

inch OLD ENGLISH *ynce,* from LATIN *uncia* a twelfth part.

inchoate LATIN *inchohare* begin, harness, from *in-* in + *cohum* a strap that ties two parts of a plow together.

incident LATIN *incidere* happen, from *in-* on + *cadere* fall.

incinerate LATIN *incinerare* turn into ashes, from *in-* in + *cinis* ashes.

incipient LATIN *incipere,* from *in-* on + *capere* take.

incise FRENCH *inciser,* from LATIN *incidere,* from *in-* into + *caedere* cut.

incisor LATIN *incisor* that which cuts into, from *incisus.* See **incision**.

incision FRENCH, from LATIN *incisionem,* from *incidere,* from *in-* into + *-cidere* cut.

incite LATIN *incitare,* from *in-* in + *citare* excite.

inclement LATIN *inclemens* harsh, from *in-* not + *clementem* mild.

incline FRENCH *incliner,* from LATIN *inclinare,* from *in-* on + *clinere* lean.

include LATIN *includere,* from *in-* in + *claudere* close.

incognito ITALIAN unknown, from LATIN *incognitus,* from *in-* not + *cognoscere* know.

incommode FRENCH, from LATIN *incommodus* inconvenient, from *in-* not + *commodus* convenient.

incontinent FRENCH, from LATIN *incontinentem,* from *in-* not + *continentem,* from *continere* hold together.

incorporate LATIN *incorporatus,* from *incorporare,* from *in-* in + *corpus* body.

increase FRENCH *encrestre* grow, from LATIN *increscere,* from *in-* in + *crescere* grow.

increment LATIN *incrementum* increase.

incriminate LATIN *incriminare* accuse, from *in-* against + *crimen* charge.

incubate LATIN *incubare,* from *in-* on + *cubare* lie.

incubus LATIN nightmare, that which lies on one, from *incubare* lie on.

inculcate LATIN *inculcare* walk on with the heel, from *in-* in + *calx* heel.

inculpate LATIN *inculpare* blame, from *in-* on + *culpa* blame.

incumbent LATIN *incumbere* obtain, from *in-* on + *combere* lie down.

incur LATIN *incurrere,* from *in-* in + *currere* run.

indefatigable FRENCH, from LATIN *in-* not + *defatigare* tire out.

indelible LATIN *indelebilis,* from *in-* not + *delere* destroy.

indemnify LATIN *indemnis* not hurt, from *in-* not + *demnum* harm.

indent MIDDLE ENGLISH *indenten,* from FRENCH *endenter*, from LATIN *indentare* provide with teeth, make a V-cut in an edge, from *in-* in + *dens* tooth.

indenture MIDDLE ENGLISH *endenture,* from LATIN *indenture.* See **indent**. Copies of documents had jagged edges for identification.

index LATIN. See **indicate**.

Indian LATIN *Indianus,* from *India* India. When Columbus got to America he thought he had discovered India.

indicate LATIN *indicare* show, from *in-* in + *dicare* declare.

indict LATIN *indictare* accuse, from *in-* in + *dictare,* from *dicere* say.

indigenous LATIN *indigena,* from *indu* in + *gignere* be born.

indigent FRENCH, from LATIN *indigere* be in need, from *indu* in + *egere* need.

indignant LATIN *indignari* think not worthy, from *in-* not + *dignus* worthy.

indigo SPANISH, from LATIN *indicum,* from GREEK *Indikos* Indian, from *India.*

indite FRENCH *enditer* write down, from LATIN *in-* in + *dictare.*

individual MIDDLE ENGLISH, from LATIN *individualis,* from *individuus,* from *in-* not + *dividere* divide.

indolent LATIN *indolens* painless, from *in-* not + *dolere* feel pain.

indomitable LATIN *in-* not + *domare* tame.

induce LATIN *inducere,* from *in-* in + *ducere* lead.

indulge LATIN *indulgere* be kind to.

indurate LATIN *induratus*, from *indurare* make hard, from *in-* not + *durus* hard. See **endure**.

industry FRENCH *industrie* work, from LATIN *industria,* from *industrius* active.

-ine[1] (like) FRENCH, from LATIN *-inus.*

-ine[2] (feminine nouns) LATIN, from GREEK *-ine.*

inebriate LATIN *inebriare,* from *in-* thoroughly + *ebrius* drunk.

ineffable LATIN *ineffabilis*, from *in-* not + *ex-* out + *fari* speak.

inept LATIN *ineptus,* from *in-* not + *aptis* fit.

inert LATIN *in-* not + *ars* art.

inevitable LATIN *in-* not + *evitabilis* avoidable.

inexorable LATIN *inexorabilis*, from *in-* not + *exorare* change the mind by pleading, from *ex-* out + *orare* pray.

inexplicable LATIN *inexplicabilis,* from *in-* not + *explicabilis*, from *explicare*, from *ex-* out of + *plicare* fold.

infamy LATIN *infamia* bad reputation.

infant MIDDLE ENGLISH *infaunt,* from FRENCH *enfant,* from LATIN *infans* without speech, from *in-* not + *fari* speak.

infantry FRENCH *infanterie,* from ITALIAN *infanteria,* from *infante* child, foot soldier, from LATIN *infans* baby.

infatuate LATIN *infatuare* make a fool of, from *in-* in + *fatus* foolish.

infect LATIN *infecere* stain, from *in-* in + *facere* do, make.

infer LATIN *inferre,* from *in-* in + *ferre* bring.

inferior LATIN *inferior*, from *inferus* low.

infernal LATIN *infernalis* relating to the underworld, from *inferus* low.

inferno ITALIAN *inferno,* from LATIN *infernus* lying beneath, from *inferus* low.

infest LATIN *infestare* attack.

infidel LATIN *infidelis,* from FRENCH, from LATIN *in-* not + *fidelis* faithful.

infinite LATIN *infinite.* See **in-**[1] + **finite.**

infinitesimal LATIN *infinitus* infinite.

infinitive LATIN *infinitus* indefinite, from *in-* not + *finitius* definite.

inflate LATIN *inflare,* from *in-* in + *flare* blow.

inflect LATIN *inflectere,* from *in-* in + *flectere* bend.

inflict LATIN *infligere,* from *in-* against + *fligere* strike.

influence FRENCH power flowing, from the stars, from LATIN *influentia,* from *influere,* from *in-* in + *fluere* flow, from the belief that forces flowing from the stars affect human life.

influenza ITALIAN influence, from LATIN *influentia.* See **influence.**

inform FRENCH *enformer* give shape or form to, from LATIN *informare,* from *in-* in + *forma* shape, pattern.

infrared LATIN *infra-* below + OLD ENGLISH *read.*

infringe LATIN *infringere,* from *in-* in + *frangere* break.

infuriate LATIN *infuriare,* from *in-* in + *furia* rage.

infuse LATIN *infundere,* from *in-* in + *fundere* pour.

-ing[1] (action name) OLD ENGLISH *-ing, -ung.* Attached to verbs to mean their action, result, product, material, etc.

-ing[2] (going on) OLD ENGLISH *-ende.*

ingenious LATIN *ingenosus* smart, from *ingenium* talent, from *in-* in + *gignere* produce.

ingénue FRENCH, from LATIN *ingenuus.* See **ingenuous.**

ingenuous LATIN *ingenuus,* from *in-* in + *gignere* produce.

ingest LATIN *ingerere,* from *in-* into + *gerere* carry.

inglenook SCOTTISH *aingeal* fire + MIDDLE ENGLISH *nok,* from SCANDINAVIAN.

ingot OLD ENGLISH *in-* in + *goten* poured, from *geotan* pour.

ingrate FRENCH, from LATIN *in-* not + *gratis* grateful.

ingratiate LATIN *in-* in + *gratia* favor.

ingredient LATIN *ingredi* begin.

inhabit LATIN *inhabitare,* from *in-* in + *habitare* dwell, from *habitus.* See **habit.**

inhale LATIN *inhalare,* from *in-* in + *halare* breathe.

inherent LATIN *inhaerere,* from *in-* in + *haerere* stick.

inherit FRENCH *enheriter,* from LATIN *inhereditare,* from *in-* in + *heres* heir.

inhibit LATIN *inhibere* hinder, from *in-* in + *habere* hold.

inimical LATIN *inimicalis* like an enemy, from *inimicus* enemy.

iniquity FRENCH, from LATIN *iniquus* unequal, from *in-* in + *aequus* equal.

initial LATIN *initium,* from *in-* in + *ire* go.

initiate LATIN *initare.* See **initial.**

inject LATIN *injicere,* from *in-* in + *jacere* throw.

injunctive LATIN *injungere.* See **enjoin** + **-ive.**

injury LATIN *injuria,* from *in-* not + *jus* right.

ink FRENCH *enque,* from LATIN, from GREEK *enkauston* red ink, from *enkalein* burnt in.

inn OLD ENGLISH.

innate LATIN *innasci,* from *in-* in + *nasci* be born.

inning OLD ENGLISH *innung* a getting in.

innocent LATIN *innocens,* from *in-* not + *nocere* do wrong to.

innocuous LATIN *in-* not + *nocuus* harmful, from *nocere* harm.

innovate LATIN *innovare,* from *in-* in + *novare* change.

innuendo LATIN *innuere* nod to, from the use of a nod to suggest something without speaking.

inoculate MIDDLE ENGLISH *enoculaten,* from LATIN *incoulare* graft (putting part of a plant onto a cut made in another to make a better plant, from the parts of two), from *in-* in + *oculus* eye, bud. The idea of putting a germ into the body to make the body well is similar to grafting part of a plant to another to make a better plant.

inordinate LATIN *inordinatus,* from *in-* not + *ordo* order.

inositol GREEK *inos-* muscle + LATIN, from GREEK *ites* + the *-ol* ending of alcohol.

inquest FRENCH *enqueste,* from LATIN *inquirere* search for. See **inquire**.

inquire FRENCH, from LATIN *inquirere,* from *in-* into + *quaerere* search.

inquisitive See **inquire**.

inscribe LATIN *inscribere,* from *in-* in + *scribere* write.

inscrutable LATIN *inscrutabilis,* from *in-* not + *scrutari* examine.

insect LATIN *insectum* notched, from *in-* into + *secare* cut. Refers to the insect body having different parts.

inseminate LATIN *inseminare,* from *in-* in + *seminare* sow, from *semen* seed.

insert LATIN *inserere,* from *in-* in + *serere* join.

insidious LATIN *insidiosus,* from *insidiae* plot, from *in-* in + *sedere* sit.

insignia LATIN *insigne,* from *in-* in + *signum* a mark.

insinuate LATIN *insinare* bring in by winding or turning, from *in-* in + *sinus* curve, hollow.

insipid FRENCH, from LATIN *in-* not + *sapere* taste.

insist LATIN *insistere,* from *in-* in + *sistere* stand.

insolate LATIN *insolare* expose to the sun, from *in-* in + *sol* the sun.

insolent LATIN *insolens,* from *in-* not + *solere* used to.

insomnia LATIN *in-* without + *somnus* sleep.

inspect LATIN *inspicere,* from *in-* at + *specere* look.

inspire LATIN *inspirare,* from *in-* in + *spirare* breathe.

install LATIN *installare,* from *in-* in + *stallum* seat.

instance FRENCH, from LATIN *instantia* being present.

instant LATIN *instare,* from *in-* upon + *stare* stand.

instigate LATIN *instigare* cause action.

instill FRENCH, from LATIN *instillare,* from *in-* in + *stilla* a drop.

instinct LATIN *instinctus* impulse, from *instinguere* cause to move forward.

institute LATIN *instituere,* from *in-* in + *statuere* establish.

instruct LATIN *instruere,* from *in-* in + *struere* pile up.

instrument French, from Latin *instuere.* See **instruct**.

insula Latin island.

insular See **insulate**.

insulate Latin *insulatus,* from *insula* island.

insult Latin *insultare,* from *in-* on + *saltare,* from *salir* leap.

insurance See **ensure**.

insurgent Latin *insurgere,* from *in-* upon + *sugere* rise.

insurrection French, from Latin *insurgere,* from *in-* upon + *sugere* rise.

intact Latin *in-* not + *tangere* touch.

intaglio Italian *in-* in + *tagliare* cut, from Latin *taliare* split.

integer Latin whole.

integral See **integer**.

integrate Latin *integrare* make whole.

integrity Latin *integritas.* See **integer**.

intellect Latin *intellegere* understand, from *inter-* between + *legere* choose.

intelligence French, from Latin *intelligere.* See **intellect**.

intelligible Latin *intelligere.* See **intellect**.

intend Middle English, from Latin *intendere,* from *in-* at + *tendere* stretch.

intense Latin *intensus* stretch out. See **intend**.

inter French, from Latin *in-* in + *terra* earth.

inter- Latin *inter-* among, between.

intercede Latin *intercedere,* from *inter-* between + *cedere* go.

intercept Latin *intercipere,* from *inter-* between + *capere* take.

interchange French *entrechangier* change, from Latin *inter-* between + *cambiare.* See **change**.

interdict French, from Latin *interdictum* prohibit, from *inter-* between + *dicere* speak.

interest Latin of importance, from *inter-* between + *esse* be.

interfere French *entreferir* hit each other, from Latin *entre-* between + *ferire* hit.

interim Latin in the meantime, from *inter-* between.

interior French, from Latin *inter-* between.

interject Latin *interjicere,* from *inter-* between + *jacere* throw.

interlard French *entrelarder,* from *entre* between + *larder* lard, from French *lard* bacon fat.

interlocutor Latin *inter-* between + *loqui* talk.

interlude Latin *interludium* type of comic skit between mystery plays of the Middle Ages, from *inter-* between + *ludus* play.

intermediate Latin *inter-* between + *medius* middle.

intermit Latin *intermittere,* from *inter-* between + *mittere* send.

intern French *interne* internal, from Latin *internus.*

internal Latin *internus* internal.

interpolate Latin *inter-* between + *polire* polish.

interpose French, from Latin *inter-* between + *ponere* put.

interpret French, from Latin *interpretari* explain.

interrogate Latin *interrogare* question, from *inter-* between + *rogare* ask.

interrupt LATIN *interrumpere* break off, from *inter-* between + *rumpere* break.

intersect LATIN *intersecare* cut apart, from *inter-* between + *secare* cut.

intersperse LATIN *interspergere,* from *inter-* among + *spargere* scatter.

interval LATIN *intervallum* space between, from *inter-* between + *vallum* defense, wall.

intervene LATIN *intervenire* come between, from *inter-* between + *venire* come.

interview FRENCH *entrevue* meeting, from *entrevoir* see, from LATIN *inter-* between + *videre* see.

intestine LATIN *intestinus* internal, from *intus* within.

intimate[1] (close) FRENCH *intime* inward, from LATIN *intimus* farthest in.

intimate[2] (hint) LATIN *intimare* make known.

intimidate LATIN *intimidare,* from *in-* in + *timidus* afraid.

into See **in-**[1] + **to.**

intone FRENCH, from LATIN. See **in-**[2] + **tone.**

intoxicate LATIN *intoxicare* poison, from *in-* in + *toxicus* poison. See **toxic.**

intransigent FRENCH *intransigeant,* from SPANISH *intransigente,* from LATIN *in-* not + *transigere* come to agreement.

intrepid LATIN *intrepidus,* from *in-* not + *trepidus* alarmed.

intricate LATIN *intricare* tangle up, from *in-* in + *tricae* confusion.

intrigue FRENCH, from ITALIAN, from LATIN *intricare.* See **intricate.**

intrinsic FRENCH, from LATIN *intrinsecus* inward, from LATIN *intra-* within + *secus* close.

intro- LATIN into, within, inward.

introduce LATIN *introducere,* from *intro-* within + *ducere* lead.

introvert LATIN *intro-* to the inside + *vertere* turn.

intrude LATIN *intrudere,* from *in-* not + *trudere* force in.

intuition LATIN *intuitio* looking into, from *intueri,* from *in-* in + *tueri* look at.

inundate LATIN *inundare,* from *in-* upon + *unda* wave.

inure MIDDLE ENGLISH *in* in + *ure* practice, work, from FRENCH *ovre,* from LATIN *opera* a work.

invade LATIN *invadere,* from *in-* in + *vadere* go.

invalid FRENCH *invalide* make unable, from LATIN *invalidus* not well, from *in-* not + *validus* strong.

invect See **invective.**

invective FRENCH, from LATIN *invectus,* from *invehi.* See **inveigh.**

inveigh LATIN *invehi* attack with words, from *invehere* attack, from *in-* in + *vehere* carry.

inveigle FRENCH *aveugler* blind, from LATIN *ab-* from + *oculus* an eye.

invent LATIN *invenire,* from *in-* on + *venire* come.

inventory LATIN *inventorium* list, from *invenire* find. See **invent.**

invert LATIN *invertere,* from *in-* to + *vertere* turn.

invest LATIN *investire,* from *in-* in + *vestire* clothe, from *vestis* clothing.

investigate LATIN *investigare* trace out, from *vestigum* a track.

invidious LATIN *invidiosus,* from *invidia* envy.

invigorate See **vigor.**

invite LATIN *invitare* entertain.

invoke LATIN *invocare,* from *in-* on + *vocare* call.

involve LATIN *involvere* cover, from *in-* in + *volvere* roll.

iodine FRENCH *iode,* from GREEK *iodes* violet-colored.

iodoform LATIN *iodum* iodine + *formyl* formic acid.

ion GREEK *ienai* go.

-ion GREEK.

iota GREEK the name of the smallest Greek letter.

ipecacuanha PORTUGUESE.

ir- See **in-**[1], **in-**[2].

irascible FRENCH, from LATIN *irascibilis,* from *irascit* become angry.

irate LATIN *ira* anger.

ire FRENCH, from LATIN *ira* anger.

iridescent LATIN *iris* rainbow. See **iris.**

iris MIDDLE ENGLISH, from LATIN rainbow, from GREEK.

irk MIDDLE ENGLISH *irken* be tired of.

iron MIDDLE ENGLISH *iren,* from OLD ENGLISH.

ironmonger See **iron** + **monger.**

irony LATIN *ironia* hide one's feelings while speaking, from GREEK *eironeia,* from *einein* speak.

irradiate LATIN *irradiare* send out rays.

irrational See **ir-** + **rational.**

irrigate LATIN *irrigare,* from *ir-* in + *rigare* make wet.

irritate LATIN *irritare* excite.

irrupt LATIN *irrumpere,* from *ir-* into + *rumpere* break.

is OLD ENGLISH.

-ish OLD ENGLISH *-isc.*

isinglass probably from DUTCH *huizen* sturgeon (type of fish) + *blas* bladder.

Islam ARABIC *islam* submission (to the will of God).

island MIDDLE ENGLISH, from OLD ENGLISH *igland* piece of land surrounded by water.

-ism GREEK *-ismos.*

iso- GREEK *isos* equal.

isobar GREEK *isos* equal + *baros* weight, from *barys* heavy.

isolate ITALIAN *isolato* separated, from *isola* island, from LATIN *insula.*

isometric GREEK *isos* equal + *metron* a measure.

isosceles LATIN having two legs, from GREEK *isoskeles,* from *isos* equal + *skelos* leg.

isotherm GREEK *isos* equal + *therme* heat, from *thermos* hot.

Israel HEBREW *y isra'el* "God strives" also "he who wrestles with God".

issue FRENCH way out, from *issir* go out, from LATIN *exire,* from *ex-* out + *ire* go.

-ist FRENCH, from LATIN, from GREEK *-istes.*

it OLD ENGLISH *hit.*

italic LATIN *italicus* Italian. The first use of the type style was in an Italian edition of the work of Virgil (an early Roman poet).

itch OLD ENGLISH *giccan.*

-ite LATIN, from GREEK *ites.*

item LATIN *ita* so, thus.

itinerant LATIN *itinerari* travel, from *iter* walk.

itinerary LATIN *itinerarium* report of a journey, from *iter* walk.

-ition FRENCH *-ition* or LATIN *-itio.*

-itis LATIN, from GREEK inflammation.

its See **it**.

-ity FRENCH *-ite,* from LATIN *-itas.*

-ive FRENCH *-if,* from LATIN *-ivus.*

ivory MIDDLE ENGLISH *ivorie,* from LATIN *eboreus* made of ivory, from *ebur* ivory, from EGYPTIAN *ebou* elephant.

-ize FRENCH, from LATIN, from GREEK *-izein.*

J

jab Middle English *jobben* peck.

jabber imitative.

jabot French, gizzard, unknown origin.

jack French, from Latin *Jacobus* Jacob.

jackal Turkish *çakal*, from Persian *shaghal*, from Sanskrit *srgala* the howler.

jackanapes apparently from "*Jack an ape*" a monkey.

jackdaw common name of the daw (bird).

jacket French *jaquette* sleeveless coat, from Spanish *jaco* coat, from Arabic *shakk.*

jade[1] (gem) Spanish *piedra de ijada* stone of the side, because it was thought that jade could cure pains in the side.

jade[2] (horse) Old Norse *jalda* a mare.

jaeger German *jäger* one who hunts.

jag[1] (sharp point) Middle English *jagge.*

jag[2] (active time) American a quantity, a lot, from Modern English load of hay or wood.

jail French *gaole* prison, from Latin *gabiola* cage, from *cavea.*

jake probably from the name Jake.

jalap French, from Spanish *jalapa* the plant, from *Jalapa,* Mexican town where the plant was first used.

jalopy origin uncertain, perhaps from *Jalapa,* Mexico, where many U.S. used cars went.

jam Modern English, origin uncertain.

jamb French *jambe* leg, from Latin *gamba* leg, from Greek *kampe* bend.

jangle French *jangler* chatter.

janitor Latin doorkeeper, from *janua* door, from *Janus* Roman god of gates.

January Middle English *Janyuere* first month of the ancient Roman year, from Latin the god *Janus*, god of gates and beginnings.

japonica Latin *japonicus* having to do with Japan.

jar[1] (container) Middle English *jarre,* from French, from Spanish *jarra,* from Arabic large earthen container for keeping water.

jar[2] (shake) Middle English, imitative, representing a harsh vibratory sound.

jargon French chatter.

jaundice French *jaune* yellow, from Latin *galbinus* greenish yellow, from *galbus* yellow.

jaunty French *gentil* pleasing, from nobly born, from Latin *gens* race.

javelin French *javeline* long, thin dart.

jaw French *jawe,* from *joe* cheek.

jay French *gal,* from Latin *gaius* a jay.

jazz AMERICAN, origin uncertain, possibly a style of ragtime dancing.

jealous FRENCH *jalous,* from LATIN *zelosus,* from GREEK *zelos.*

jeameses *James* the name of a footman, and therefore his costume.

jeep U.S. Army *G.P.* (general purpose).

jeer possibly from OLD ENGLISH *cegan* call out.

jehoshaphat biblical name.

jelly FRENCH *gelee* frost, from LATIN *gelare* freeze.

jennet FRENCH, from SPANISH *jinete* horseman, from ARABIC *Zenata* a tribe.

jenny the name *Jane.*

jeopardy MIDDLE ENGLISH *jeuparti,* from FRENCH *je parti* even chance, from LATIN *jocus* game + *partire* divide.

jerfalcon See **gyrfalcon.**

jerk imitative.

jerkin MIDDLE ENGLISH, origin uncertain.

jersey the British island *Jersey,* where the cloth and the cow originally came from.

jess FRENCH *ges* throw, from LATIN *jactus* metal mold.

jest FRENCH *geste* tale, from LATIN *gerere* perform.

Jesuit LATIN *Jesusta,* from **Jesus** + **-ite.**

Jesus LATIN *Iesus,* from GREEK *Iesous,* from HEBREW *hesha'a* help of Jehovah.

jet FRENCH *jeter* throw, from LATIN *facere.*

jetsam MIDDLE ENGLISH *jetteson.* See **jettison.**

jettison FRENCH *getaison* throw, from LATIN *jactionem,* from *jectare* toss about.

jetty FRENCH *jetée.* See **jet.**

jewel FRENCH *jouel* gem, from LATIN *jocus* game.

jib DANISH *gibbe* jibe.

jibe DUTCH *gijpen.*

jig MIDDLE ENGLISH, possibly from FRENCH *giguer* dance, from *gigue* a fiddle.

jigger (to damn) probably from some sense of **jig.**

jiggle See **jig.**

jilt a made-up begger term in England about 1640.

jimson weed originally *Jamestown weed* after *Jamestown* Colony, an early English settlement in North America, where it was first found.

jingle imitative.

jinrikisha JAPANESE *jin* a man + *riki* power + *sha* carriage.

jinx LATIN *iynx,* from GREEK *iynx* the wryneck, a bird used in black magic.

job MIDDLE ENGLISH, origin uncertain.

jobberknoll MIDDLE ENGLISH *jobard* fool + *noll,* from OLD ENGLISH *knol* head.

jockey SCOTTISH *Jock,* nickname for John.

jocular LATIN *joculus* little joke, from *jocus* game.

jodhpur *Jodhpur* former state in India.

jog MIDDLE ENGLISH *joggen* urge on.

johnnycake possibly from *journey cake.*

join FRENCH *joindre* connect, from LATIN *jungere* join.

joint FRENCH, from LATIN *jungere* join.

joist FRENCH *giste* a bed, from LATIN *jacere* rest.

joke LATIN *jocus* game.

jolly French *jolif* festive, perhaps from Old Norse *jol* feast.

jolt Middle English combination of *jot* to jolt and *joll* to bump.

jonquil French, from Spanish *junquillo,* from Latin *juncus* grasslike plant.

joree imitative.

jorum possibly from Biblical *Joram* who "brought with him vessels of silver, and vessels of gold, and vessels of brass."

josh American, probably from the name *Josh,* from *Joshua.*

joss Portuguese *deos,* from Latin *deus* a god.

jostle See **joust**.

jot Latin *iota* the smallest letter, from Greek letter.

jour French, from Latin *diurnus,* from *dies* day.

journal French daily, from *journal,* from Latin *diurnalis,* from *dies* day.

journey French *journee* day, from Latin *dies.*

journeyman Middle English *journee* day's work + *man.*

joust French *jouste,* from *jouster* meet, from Latin *iuxtare,* from *iuxta* near.

jovial French, from Italian *joviale,* from Latin *Jovialis* of Jupiter, from *Jovius* Jupiter, Roman god of the sky. From the idea that people were affected by the planets. The planet Jupiter was thought to be the source of joy and happiness.

jowl Old English *ceafl* jaw.

joy French *joie,* from Latin *gaudium.*

jubilant Latin *jubilare* shout with joy.

jubilee French *jubile,* from Latin *jubilaeus* year of jubilee, from Greek *iobelos,* from Hebrew *yovel* ram's horn, which was blown on the year of the jubilee.

judge French *juge,* from Latin *judex* juror, from *jus* law + *dicere* say.

judicious French *judicieus,* from Latin *judicium* judgment.

jug nickname for the girl's name *Joan,* which a jug was jokingly called.

juggernaut Hindi *jagat* world + *natha* lord.

juggle French *jogler,* from Latin *joculari* joke.

jugular Latin *jugularis,* from *jugulum* collarbone, from *jugum* yoke (a wooden frame that fits around the necks of oxen to join them together for use in pulling wagons, etc.).

juice French *jus* sauce, from Latin *jus.*

jujube French, from Latin *zizyphum,* from Greek *zizyphon.*

julep French, from Arabic *gul* rose + *ab* water.

July Middle English *Julie,* from French *Julie,* from Latin *Julius,* from the Roman leader Julius Caesar, who was born in this month.

jumble possibly from a combination of **jump** and **tumble**.

jumby African *zumbi* evil spirit.

jump German *gumpen.*

jumper Modern English *jump* short coat, from French *jupe* skirt, from Arabic *jubbah* loose outer garment.

junco Spanish *junco* reed, bush.

junction Latin *junctio* a joining.

June French, from Latin *Junius* the name of the goddess *Juno,* protector of women and marriage.

jungle Hindi *jangal* forest.

junior Latin *juvenis* young.

juniper Latin *juniperus.*

junk[1] (boat) Spanish and Portuguese *junco.*

junk[2] (trash) Portuguese *junco* a reed, from Latin *juncus.*

junket Latin *juncus* a grasslike plant.

junta Spanish *junta* council, meeting, from Latin *juncta* joint, from *juncta*, from *jungere* join.

jupe French *jube,* from Arabic *aljuba.*

Jupiter Latin *Iupeter.*

Jurassic French *Jurassique*, from the *Jura* Mountains between France and Switzerland where fossils of the period were found.

jurisdiction French, from Latin *jurisdictio*, from *jus* law + *dicere* say.

jurisprudence Latin *jurisprudentia*, from *juris* of right, of law + *prudentia* knowledge, a foreseeing.

jury French *juree* oath, from *jurer* swear, from Latin *jurare.*

just Middle English, from French right, from Latin *justus,* from *jus* law.

justaucorps French *juste* fitting closely + *au corps* to the body

justice See **just**.

justify French *justifier* prove the innocence of, from Latin *justus* fair + *facere* do, make.

jut origin uncertain.

jute Hindi *jhuto* matted hair.

juvenile Latin *juvenilis,* from *juvenis* young.

juxtapose French *juxta,* from Latin near.

ka Egyptian.

kaiser Latin *Caeser.*

kajawah Persian.

kale Scottish, from *cole* cabbage, from Middle English *cawul.*

kaleidoscope Greek *kalos* beautiful + *eidos* form + *skopen* examine.

kangaroo Australian Aboriginal.

kaolin French, from Chinese *kao-ling* name of the place where it is found.

karate Japanese *kara* empty + *te* hand.

karma Sanskrit *karman* fate.

katydid imitative.

kayak Eskimo.

kedge Middle English *caggen* fasten.

keel[1] (central bottom boat frame piece) Middle English *kele,* from Old Norse *kjölr.*

keel[2] (flat bottomed ship) Middle English *kele,* from Dutch *kiel* boat.

keel[3] (stir) Middle English *kelen,* from Old English *celan,* from *col* cool.

keel[4] (red stain) Irish *cil.*

keen[1] (sharp) Middle English *kene,* from Old English *cene* wise.

keen[2] (wailing) Irish *caoinim* I wail.

keep Old English *cepan.*

keg Old Norse *kaggi.*

kelp Middle English *culp.*

ken Old English *cennan* make known.

kennel French *chenil,* from Latin *canis* dog.

kerchief French *couvrechief* cover the head, from *couvrir* cover + *chef* head, from Latin *caput.*

kernel Old English *cyrnel.*

kerosene Greek *keros* wax, because a wax is used in making it.

kersey possibly from the village of Kersey in Suffolk, England.

kestrel French *cresserelle.*

ketch Middle English *cacchen* catch.

ketchup Chinese *ke-tsiap* sauce used with fish.

kettle Old Norse *ketill,* from Latin *catillus* small bowl.

key[1] (for lock) Middle English *keye,* from Old English *cæg.*

key[2] (island) Spanish *cayo.*

khaki Hindi *khak* dust.

kibbutz Hebrew.

kick Middle English *kiken,* origin uncertain.

kid Old Norse *kith* young goat.

kidney Middle English *kidenere,* possibly from Old English *cwith* womb + *ey* egg, because of the likeness in shape.

kike possibly from *-ki* or *-ky,* endings on the names of Eastern European Jews who came to the U.S. in the early 1900s.

Kilkenny the name of an Irish town.

kill Middle English *killen,* possibly from Old English *cwellan.*

kiln Old English *cylene* oven, from Latin *culina* kitchen.

kilo- French, from Greek *chillioi* thousand.

kilt Middle English *kilten,* probably of Scandinavian origin.

kimono Japanese.

kimquat See **kumquat**.

kin Old English *cynn* family.

-kin Middle English, from Dutch suffix meaning "little."

kind Middle English *kynde,* from Old English *gecynde* natural.

kindergarten German *kind* child + *garten* garden.

kindle Middle English *kindlen,* from Old Norse *kynda* light a fire.

kindred Old English *cynn* family + *ræden* condition.

kine Old English *cyna.*

kinesthesia Greek *kinein* move + *aisthesis* sensation.

kinetic Greek *kinetikos* moving, from *kinetos* moved, from *kinein* move.

king Old English *cyning* male ruler.

kingdom Old English *cyningdom.*

kink Dutch twist in a rope.

kiosk French *kiosque,* from Persian *kushk* palace, villa.

kip[1] (hides) Middle English *kyppe,* from Dutch *kijp* hides.

kip[2] (bed) Danish *kippe* alehouse.

kip[3] (money) Thai.

kip[4] (weight) *kilopound.* See **kilo-** + **pound**.

kipper Old English *cypera* male salmon, perhaps from *coper,* copper metal, by similarity of color.

kiss Old English *cyssan.*

kissel Russian *kisel.*

kit Dutch *kitte* large wooden bowl.

kitchen Old English *cycene,* from Latin *coquina,* from *coquere* cook.

kite Old English *cyta.*

kith Old English *cyththu* relationship.

kithe (kythe) Middle English *kithen,* from Old English *cythan* make known.

kittel Yiddish *kitl.*

kiver See **cover**.

kiwi Maori.

klaxon trademark for a kind of loud horn.

knack Middle English *knak* sharp hit.

knave Old English *cnafa* boy, servant.

knead Old English *cnedan.*

knee Old English *cneow.*

kneel Old English *cneowlian,* from *cneow* knee.

knell Old English *cnyllan* ring a bell.

knickerbocker the pen name used by Washington Irving to publish his *History of New York*.

knickers See **knickerbocker**, by resemblance to short trousers worn by Dutchmen pictured in Washington Irving's *History of New York*.

knife OLD ENGLISH *cnif.*

knight OLD ENGLISH *cniht* boy.

knit OLD ENGLISH *cnyttan* tie by knotting.

knob MIDDLE ENGLISH *knobe.*

knock OLD ENGLISH *cnocian* hit hard.

knoll[1] (hilltop) OLD ENGLISH *cnoll.*

knoll[2] (bell sound) See **knell**.

knot OLD ENGLISH *cnotta.*

know OLD ENGLISH *cnawan* understand.

knuckle GERMAN *knokel* little bone.

knurl probably from MIDDLE ENGLISH *knur* a knot.

kobold GERMAN *kobold, kobolt.*

kow-tow CHINESE *k'o-t'ou* knock head.

kremlin FRENCH, from RUSSIAN *kreml.*

krone GERMAN *krone* crown.

krypton LATIN, from GREEK, from *kryptos* hidden.

kudos GREEK *kydos* glory.

kudu AFRICAN *koedoe.*

kugel YIDDISH, from GERMAN *kugel, kugele* ball, globe.

kumquat CHINESE *kamkwat*, from *kam* golden + *kwat* orange.

L

labboard See **larboard**.

label French ribbon.

labor French *labour* trouble, from Latin *labor* work, pain.

laboratory Latin *laboraterium* workshop, from *laborare* work.

laburnum Latin.

labyrinth Latin *labyrinthos* maze, from Greek *labyrinthos.*

lac Hindi *lakh*, from Sanskrit *laksa.*

lace French *las* knotted rope, from Latin *laqueus.*

lacerate Latin *lacerare,* from *lacer* hurt badly.

lachrymose Latin *lacrima* teary-eyed.

lack possibly from Dutch *lac.*

lackadaisical Modern English *lackadaisy*, from *lack-a-day*, from *alack the day.*

lackey French *laquais* footman (man who helps in the house), from Turkish *ulak* man who carried messages.

laconic Latin *Laconicus*, the ancient country Laconia (*Lakonikos* in Greek), near Greece, where a race of people called the Spartans lived. The Spartans used few words to express themselves.

lacquer French, from Portuguese *laca* gummy substance.

lactic Latin *lactis,* from *lac* milk.

ladder Old English *hlæder* frame with steps.

lade Old English *hladan* load up, heap.

laden Old English *hladan* load up, heap.

ladle Old English *hlædel,* from *hladan,* load up, heap.

lady Old English *hlæfdige* loaf-kneader (mistress of the house who kneads bread).

lag possibly from Dutch *lakke* go slowly.

lagoon Italian *laguna* pool, from Latin *lacuna* pond.

lair Old English *leger* bed.

lake French *lac* pond, from Latin *lacus* large body of water.

lam Old Norse *lemja* lame.

lamb Old English.

lambent Latin *lambentem*, from *lambere* lick.

lame Old English *lama* not able in body.

lament French, from Latin *lamentari* make a long sound of grief or pain.

laminate Latin *laminare* thin piece.

laminitis LATIN *lamina* thin piece of metal or wood + **-itis.**

lamp FRENCH *lampe* something that lights, from LATIN *lampas* torch, from GREEK *lampas.*

lampoon FRENCH *lampons* let us drink (part of a drinking song).

lamprey FRENCH *lampreie,* from LATIN *lampreda.*

lance MIDDLE ENGLISH, from FRENCH spear, from LATIN *lancea* light spear.

lancet FRENCH *lancette* small lance.

land OLD ENGLISH *land* solid piece of Earth.

landau the German town *Landau* where the carriage was originally made.

landscape DUTCH *landschap* painting of land scene, from *land* land + *-schap* shape.

lane OLD ENGLISH.

langouste FRENCH.

language FRENCH *langage,* from *langue* tongue, from LATIN *lingua* tongue, speech.

languid FRENCH *languide,* from LATIN *languidus,* from *languere* be faint or listless from lack of energy.

languish FRENCH *languir* grieve, become ill, from LATIN *languere* be faint or listless from lack of energy.

lank OLD ENGLISH *hlanc.*

lantern FRENCH *lanterne* box with clear sides that contains a light, from LATIN *lanterna* lamp, from GREEK *lampein* shine.

lanthorn See **lantern.**

lanyard FRENCH *laniere,* from *lasne* noose.

lap OLD ENGLISH *lapian* take up liquid with the tongue.

lapel OLD ENGLISH *læppa* part of clothing.

lapstrake MODERN ENGLISH (shipbuilding) *lap* overlap + *strake* line of planking.

lapis lazuli LATIN *lapis* a stone + *lazulus* azure (sky blue color).

laporotomy GREEK remove part of the intestine.

lapse LATIN *lapsus* fall.

larboard OLD ENGLISH *hladan* bring up water + *bord* table.

larceny FRENCH, from LATIN *latrocinari* rob, from *latro* robber.

lard FRENCH bacon fat, from LATIN *lardum.*

larder FRENCH tub in which bacon is kept, from *lard* bacon. See **lard.**

large FRENCH, from LATIN *largus* having more than enough.

largess FRENCH *largesse,* from LATIN *largus* more than enough.

lariat SPANISH *la reata* the rope.

lark[1] (bird) OLD ENGLISH *lawerce.*

lark[2] (play) OLD NORSE *leika* play.

larva LATIN *ghost.*

larynx GREEK.

lasagna ITALIAN, from LATIN *lasanum,* from GREEK *lasanon* a pot.

lascar HINDI *lashkar,* from ARABIC *al-askar* army.

lascivious LATIN *lasciviosus,* from *lascivia.*

lash[1] (whip) MIDDLE ENGLISH *lassche.*

lash[2] (bind) MIDDLE ENGLISH *lashen,* from FRENCH *lachier,* from *lacier* lace.

lashings IRISH plenty.

lass MIDDLE ENGLISH *lasse,* probably from OLD NORSE.

lassitude LATIN *lassitudo.*

lasso SPANISH *lazo,* from LATIN *laqueus.*

last[1] (slowest) MIDDLE ENGLISH *laste,* from OLD ENGLISH *latost,* from *læt.*

last[2] (continue) OLD ENGLISH *læstan.*

latch OLD ENGLISH *læccan* take.

late OLD ENGLISH *læt* slow.

lateen FRENCH *voile latine,* Latin sail.

latent LATIN *latere* hidden.

lateral LATIN *lateralis,* from *latus* side.

lath OLD ENGLISH *lætt* narrow piece of wood used in building.

lathe probably from DUTCH *lade,* from *drejelad* supporting framework.

lather OLD ENGLISH *leathor.*

latitude FRENCH, from LATIN *latitudo,* from *latus* wide.

latke RUSSIAN *latka* pastry.

latrine LATIN *latrina,* from *lavatrina* washbasin, washroom, from *lavatus,* from *lavare* wash + *-trina* workplace.

latter OLD ENGLISH *lætra* slower, from *læt* slow.

lattice FRENCH *lattis,* from GERMAN *latte* a lath (narrow strip of wood used in building lattices, etc.).

laud FRENCH, from LATIN *laudes,* from *laus* praise.

laudanum LATIN variation of *ladanum* used by a 16th century Swiss physician to name a remedy based on opium.

laugh OLD ENGLISH *hlæhhan.*

launch FRENCH *lancher,* from *lancier* throw, from *lance* spear. See **lance**.

laund FRENCH *launde* wooded ground, from early IRISH *lann.* See **land**.

launder MIDDLE ENGLISH one who washes clothes, from FRENCH *lavandier,* from LATIN *lavanda* things to be washed, from *lavare* wash.

laureate MIDDLE ENGLISH, from LATIN *laureatus* crown with flowers, from *laurea corona* laurel (type of flower) crown, because of the ancient Roman custom of honoring poets, athletes and other heroes by crowning them with a laurel wreath.

laurel FRENCH, from LATIN *laurus.*

lava ITALIAN *lave,* from LATIN *labes* a fall, from *labi* slide.

lavabo LATIN *lavare* wash.

lavage FRENCH, from *laver* wash.

lavatory LATIN *lavatorium* place for washing, from *lavare* wash.

lavender FRENCH, from LATIN *lavandria,* from *lavare* wash. The plant was used to scent washed fabrics and as a bath perfume.

lavish FRENCH *lavasse* rain, from *laver* wash, from LATIN *lavare* wash.

law MIDDLE ENGLISH *lawe,* from OLD ENGLISH *lagu* body of rules, from OLD NORSE *lag* a law, something laid down and fixed or set.

lax LATIN *laxus* loose.

lay[1] (hire) OLD NORSE *leiga* hire.

lay[2] (law term) FRENCH *lie,* from ITALIAN *legge,* from LATIN *lex* law.

lay[3] (put down) OLD ENGLISH *lecgan.*

lay[4] (poem) FRENCH *lai.*

lazy MIDDLE ENGLISH *laysy,* origin uncertain.

-le MIDDLE ENGLISH *-el,* from OLD ENGLISH *-ol.*

leach OLD ENGLISH *leccan* moisten. See **leak**.

lead[1] (to guide) OLD ENGLISH *lædan.*

lead[2] (metal) OLD ENGLISH.

leaf OLD ENGLISH.

league French *ligue,* from Italian *liga,* from Latin *ligare* bind.

leak Old Norse *leka* drip.

lean[1] (bend) Old English *hleonian* bend.

lean[2] (thin) Old English *hlæne* thin.

leap Old English *hleapan* jump.

learn Old English *leornian* get knowledge.

lease French, from Latin *laxare* loosen.

leash French, from Latin *laxus* lax.

least Old English *læst* smallest.

leather Old English *lether.*

leave Old English *læfan* allow to remain.

leaven French *levain,* from Latin *levamen* rising.

lecithin French *lécithine,* from Greek *lethikos* yolk of an egg.

lectern French *letrun* reading desk, from Latin *lectrum,* from *legere* read.

lecture Latin *lectura* a reading, from *legere* read.

lede Old English *leod* people.

ledge probably from Middle English *leggen.*

ledger Middle English *legger* record book, from Old English *lecgan* place.

leduc French the duke.

lee Old English *hleo* protection.

leech Old English *læce.*

leek Old English *leac.*

leer Old English *hleor* face.

left Middle English *lift* left side, from Old English *lyft* weak.

legacy French *legacie* office of an official, from Latin *legare* choose someone for an official job.

legal French, from Latin *legalis* having to do with the law, from *lex* law.

legate French, from Latin *legare,* from *lex* law.

legend French *legende* a writing, from Latin *legenda* thing to be read, from *legere* read.

legerdemain French *leger de main* light of hand.

legible Latin *legibilis,* from *legere* read.

legion French Roman body of soldiers, from Latin *legio,* from *legere* choose.

legislation Latin *legislationem* bringing of a law, from *legis,* from *lex* law + *lationem* bringing.

legitimate Latin *legitimare* make lawful, from *legitimus* lawful.

legume French, from Latin *legumen,* from *legere* gather.

leisure French *leisir* free time, from Latin *licere* be allowed.

lemon French, from Arabic *laimun.*

lend Old English *lænan.*

length Old English *lengthu.*

lenient Latin *lenire* soften, from *lenis* soft.

lens Latin lentil, because the shape of a glass lens looks like a lentil seed.

-lent Latin *-lentus.*

lenticular Latin *lenticularis,* from *lenticula,* from *lens* lentil. See **lens**.

leopard French, from Latin, from Greek *leopardos,* from *leon* lion + *pardos* panther.

leotard J. *Léotard,* 19th century tightrope walker.

leper French *lepre,* from Latin *lepra,* from Greek *lepros* rough, having scales, from *lepein* peel.

leprechaun IRISH *lupracan* very small body, from *lu* little + *corpan* small body, from LATIN *corpus* body.

leprosy See **leper**.

lesion FRENCH, from LATIN *laesio,* from *laedere* harm.

less OLD ENGLISH *læsa* smaller.

-less OLD ENGLISH *-leas.*

lesson FRENCH *leçon* lecture, from LATIN *lectio* a reading.

lest OLD ENGLISH *thy læs the* by the less that.

let OLD ENGLISH *lætan* allow.

-let FRENCH *-el,* from LATIN *-ellus.*

lethal LATIN *lethalis,* from *letum* death.

lethargy LATIN *lethargia* sleepiness, from GREEK *lethargia,* from *lethargos,* from *lethe* forgetful + *argos* not busy, from *a-* not + *ergon* work.

letter FRENCH *lettre* letter of the alphabet, from LATIN *littera.*

lettuce FRENCH, from LATIN *lactuca,* from *lac* milk, from its milky juice.

leukemia GREEK *leukos* white + *haima* blood.

levee FRENCH *lever* raise.

level FRENCH *livel* carpenter's level (tool that tells if a surface is level), from LATIN *libella* balance.

lever FRENCH *levier* crowbar (tool that helps to get a box lid open), from *lever* raise, from LATIN *levare.*

leverat FRENCH *levre,* from LATIN *lepus* hare.

leviathan LATIN *leviathon* sea monster.

levity LATIN *levitas* lightness. See **light**[2].

levy See **lever**.

lexicon GREEK *lexikon,* from *lexis* a word, from *legein* speak.

liable FRENCH *lier* bind, from LATIN *ligare.*

liaison FRENCH *liason*, from LATIN *ligare* bind.

liana MODERN ENGLISH, from FRENCH *liane.*

libation LATIN *libatio* liquid poured out as an offering to a god.

libel LATIN *libellus* little book. In ancient Rome little books were written and sent around for the purpose of damaging reputations.

liberal FRENCH, from LATIN *liberalis* free man, from *liber* free.

liberate LATIN *libarare* set free.

liberty FRENCH *liberte* freedom, from LATIN *liberatas.*

libido LATIN, from *libere* to please.

library FRENCH *librairie* collection of books, from LATIN *librarius*, from *liber* book.

lice plural of **louse**.

license FRENCH granting permission to do something, from LATIN *licentia.*

lichee CHINESE *li-chih.*

lichen LATIN, from GREEK, probably from *leichein* lick.

licit LATIN *licere* be permitted.

lick OLD ENGLISH *liccian.*

licorice FRENCH, from LATIN *liquiritia,* from GREEK *glykys* sweet + *rhiza* root.

lie OLD ENGLISH *leogan* make a false statement.

lief OLD ENGLISH *leof* dear.

liege probably from FRENCH *liege* person owned by a lord, from LATIN *laetus* serf.

lieutenant FRENCH *lieu* place + *tenant* holding, from LATIN *tenere* hold.

life Old English *lif* time from birth to death.

lift Old Norse *lypia* raise.

ligament Latin *ligamentum* band, tie, from *ligare* bind.

ligature French, from Latin *ligatura* a band, from *ligatus*, from *ligare* bind.

light[1] (brightness) Old English *leht*, from *leoht.*

light[2] (weight) Old English *leoht.*

light[3] (dismount) Old English *lihtan.*

lightning Old English *lightnen* lighten (make bright).

lignite Latin *lignum* wood + Greek *ites.*

like Old English *(ge)lic* similar.

lilac French, from Arabic *nilac* bluish.

lilt Middle English *lulte.*

limb Old English *lim.*

limber Middle English, origin uncertain.

limbo Latin border.

limerick *Limerick*, Ireland, place where at parties the same song would be sung after each person who came up with a nonsense verse.

limit French *limiter*, from Latin *limes* boundary.

limousine French coat worn by people in *Limousin*, France, where a horse-drawn car was built.

limp Old English *limpan* have happen to one.

limpet Old English, from Latin *lempreda.*

limpid French *limpide,* from Latin *limpidus,* from *limpa* water.

limpsy See **limp**.

linchpin possibly from Middle English *lynspin,* from Old English *lynis* axle pin.

line Old English *line* rope, from Latin *linea* linen thread.

lineament Latin *lineamentum,* from *lineare* make a straight line.

linen Old English.

-ling Old English.

linger Middle English *lengeren* wait, from Old English *lengan* cause to wait longer than needed.

lingo probably from Latin *lingua* tongue.

linguist Latin *lingua* tongue.

liniment Latin *linimentum,* from *linire* spread.

linimentum Latin. See **liniment**.

link Old Norse *hlekkr* chain.

linnet French *linette,* from *lin* flax, because the bird eats the seeds of the flax plant.

linoleum Latin *linum* flax + *oleum* oil.

linseed Old English.

linsey-woolsey Middle English *lin* flax + *wolle* wool.

linstock Dutch *lontstok,* from *lont* wooden match + *stok* stick.

lintel French *lintel,* from Latin *limes* boundary.

lion French, from Latin *leonis,* from Greek *leon.*

lip Old English *lippa.*

lipoma Latin, from Greek *lipos* fat + *-oma* tumor.

lipoprotein Greek *lipos* fat + German, from French, from Greek *proteios* primary, from *protos* first.

lipper nautical usage, related to **lip** or **lap**.

liquid French, from Latin *liquidere.*

liquidate Latin *liquidare.*

liquor FRENCH *licor,* from LATIN *liquor.*

lisp MIDDLE ENGLISH *lispen,* from OLD ENGLISH *wlisp.*

list[1] (items) MIDDLE ENGLISH *liste*, from OLD ENGLISH *liste* border.

list[2] (lean) MIDDLE ENGLISH *listen*, from OLD ENGLISH *lystan* desire.

list[3] (listen) MIDDLE ENGLISH *listen*, from OLD ENGLISH *hlystan*, from *hlyst* hearing.

listen OLD ENGLISH *hlysnan.*

litany FRENCH *litanie*, from LATIN *litania* form of prayer, from GREEK *litaneia* prayer.

liter FRENCH *litre,* from LATIN, from GREEK *litra* a pound.

literal LATIN *litteralis* relating to a letter, from *littera*. See **literate**.

literate LATIN *littera* a letter of the alphabet.

literature FRENCH, from LATIN *litteratura* learning, from *littera*. See **literate**.

lithe OLD ENGLISH soft, mild.

lithium GREEK *lithos* stone.

litho- GREEK *lithos* stone.

litigate LATIN *litigare* argue, from *lit* quarrel + *agere* go.

litter FRENCH *litiere* bed, from LATIN *lectus* bed.

little OLD ENGLISH *lytel.*

liturgy LATIN *liturgia,* from GREEK *leitourgia* public service, from *leos* people + *ergon* work.

live OLD ENGLISH *lifian* have life.

lively OLD ENGLISH *liflic.*

liver OLD ENGLISH *lifer.*

livery FRENCH *livree* gift of clothes to a servant, from *livrer* deliver, from LATIN *liberare* set free.

livid FRENCH, from LATIN *lividus* blueish. Early use of the word described someone pale with anger, then came to mean someone red-faced with anger.

livre FRENCH money, from LATIN *libra* scales for weighing.

lizard FRENCH *lesard,* from LATIN *laceria.*

load OLD ENGLISH *lad* journey.

loaf OLD ENGLISH *hlaf.*

loam OLD ENGLISH *lam.*

loan OLD NORSE *lan.*

loath OLD ENGLISH *lath* hostile.

loathe OLD ENGLISH *lath* hateful.

lob[1] (toss) MIDDLE ENGLISH *lobbe* heavy

lob[2] (spider) OLD ENGLISH *lobbe.*

lobby FRENCH *loge* small house, from LATIN *lobia* covered area.

lobe LATIN *lobos,* from GREEK.

lobscouse DANISH *lobskous.*

lobster OLD ENGLISH *loppestre,* corruption of LATIN *locusta* lobster, locust (influenced by OLD ENGLISH *loppe*, a variant of *lobbe,* spider).

local FRENCH, from LATIN *localis* relating to a place, from *locus* place.

locate LATIN *locare* place.

lock[1] (fasten) OLD ENGLISH *loc* bolt, fastening, enclosure.

lock[2] (hair) OLD ENGLISH *locc.*

loco SPANISH insane, origin uncertain.

loco- LATIN *locus* a place.

locomotive See **loco-** + **motion**.

locus LATIN *locus* place.

locust LATIN *locusta.*

lode OLD ENGLISH *lad* way.

lodestone Middle English, from Old Norse *leith* way + Old English *stan.*

lodge French *loge* small house, from Latin *lobia* covered area.

loft Old Norse *lopt* upper room.

log Middle English *logge,* probably from Old Norse *lag* tree cut down.

logarithm Latin *logarithmus* ratio-number, from Greek *logos* proportion, ratio, word + *arithmos* number.

logic Latin *logica* art of reasoning, from Greek *logike,* from *logos* word, reason.

logistics French *logistique,* from *logis* lodging, from *loger* lodge, from *loge* small house.

logo Greek *logogram* sign for a word, from *logos* word + *gram* written.

-logy Greek *-logia,* from *logos* word.

loin French *loigne,* from Latin *lumbus.*

loiter possibly from Dutch *loteren* delay.

loll Dutch *lollen.*

lollop See **loll**.

lone See **alone**.

lonely See **alone**.

long[1] (distance) Old English *lang* not short.

long[2] (want) Old English *langian.*

longevity Latin *longus* long + *aevum* age.

longitude Latin *longitudo* length.

longshore See **along** + **shore**.

look Old English *locian.*

loom[1] (machine) Middle English *lome,* from Old English *loma* tool.

loom[2] (appear large) Scandinavian.

loon Middle English *loom* diving bird.

loony See **lunatic**. (Also, from the wild cry of the **loon**.)

loop Old Norse *hlaup* leap.

loose Old Norse *lauss* free.

loot Hindi *lut,* from Sanskrit *lota* stolen property.

lop Middle English *loppen,* from Old English *loppian.*

lope Old Norse *hiaupa* lead.

loquacious Latin *loquax,* from *loqui* speak.

lord Old English *hlaford,* from *hlaf* loaf + *weard* keeper, from master of a household with dependents who eat his bread.

lore Old English *lar* teaching.

lorgnette French *lorgner* squint + **-ette**.

lorry British railroad usage, probably from *lurry* pull.

lose Old English *losian* escape.

loss possibly from Old English *los* ruin.

lot Old English *hlot* share, what is used as a playing piece in a game of chance.

lotion Latin *lotio* washing.

lottery French, from Dutch *lot* lot.

lotus Latin plant, from Greek *lotos.*

loud Old English *hlud.*

lounge Scottish, origin uncertain.

louse Old English *lus.*

lout Middle English *lutien* stay hidden.

louver Middle English *luver,* from French *lover.*

love Old English *lufu.*

low Old Norse *lagr.*

lox Yiddish *laks,* from German *lachs* salmon.

loyal FRENCH, from LATIN *legalis* relating to the law, from *lex* law.

lozenge MIDDLE ENGLISH rhombus, from FRENCH *losenge,* diamond-shaped.

lubber MIDDLE ENGLISH *lobbe* heavy, from GERMAN *lobbe* hanging lump of flesh.

lubricate LATIN *lubricare* make slippery.

lucid LATIN *lucidus* bright.

luck DUTCH *luc* good fortune.

lucrative LATIN *lucrum* gain.

ludicrous LATIN *ludicrus* playful, from *ludus* play.

lug MIDDLE ENGLISH *luggen,* probably of SCANDINAVIAN origin.

luggage See **lug** + **-age.**

lugubrious LATIN *lugubris* very sad.

lukewarm MIDDLE ENGLISH *lukewarme* (slightly warm, tepid), origin uncertain.

lulav HEBREW *lulabh* branch.

lull MIDDLE ENGLISH *lullen* origin imitative.

lullaby MIDDLE ENGLISH *lullai* cradlesong words + *-by* as in *bye-bye.*

lullian 13th century philosopher Raymund *Lull.*

lumber MIDDLE ENGLISH *lomeren.*

luminary FRENCH, from LATIN *luminarium,* from *lumen* light.

lump MIDDLE ENGLISH *lumpe.*

lunar LATIN *luna* moon.

lunatic MIDDLE ENGLISH *lunatik,* from FRENCH *lunatique,* from LATIN *lunaticus* moonstruck, from *luna* moon, from a belief that insanity is related to or caused by the phases of the moon.

lunch See **luncheon.**

luncheon MIDDLE ENGLISH *nonechenche* light mid-day meal, from *none* noon + *schench* drink, from OLD ENGLISH *scenc,* from *scencan* pour out.

lung OLD ENGLISH *lungen.*

lunge FRENCH *allonger* lengthen, from LATIN *ad-* to + *longus* extended.

lupine LATIN *lupis* wolf, origin uncertain for name of plant.

lurch nautical *lee-larch* sudden roll to leeward, perhaps from FRENCH *lacher* let go, from LATIN *laxus* loose.

lure FRENCH *loirre.*

lurid LATIN *luridus* pale yellow.

lurk MIDDLE ENGLISH *lurken,* from *lurne* frown.

luscious MIDDLE ENGLISH *lucius.* See **delicious.**

luster FRENCH *lustre* bright, from ITALIAN *lustro,* from LATIN *lustrare.*

lute FRENCH *lut,* from ARABIC *al`ud* the wood.

luxury FRENCH, from LATIN *luxeria* too much.

-ly OLD ENGLISH *-lic.*

lye OLD ENGLISH *leag.*

lymph FRENCH *lymphe,* from LATIN *lympha* clear water.

lymphosarcoma See **lymph** + GREEK *sarkoma* fleshy.

lynch *Lynch's law,* possibly from Charles *Lynch,* 1736–86, a Virginia planter who organized bands of patriots to punish people who supported the British during the American Revolution.

lynx GREEK.

lyre LATIN, from GREEK *lyra.*

lyric LATIN *lyricus* relating to the lyre, an early stringed instrument.

macabre French *danse macabre* dance of death.

macadam J. L. *McAdam* (1756–1836) Scottish engineer.

macaroni Italian *maccaroni.*

macaroon French *macaron,* from Italian *maccarone.*

mace[1] (club) Middle English, from French large hammer, from Latin *matteola.*

mace[2] (spice) Middle English, from French *macis,* from Latin *macir* red spice from India, from Greek *makir.*

machete Spanish *macho* hammer, from Latin *marculus* small hammer.

machine French engine, from Latin *machina,* from Greek *machos* something built in a skillful way.

macho Spanish male, from Latin *masculus.* See **masculine.**

mackeral French *makerel.*

mackinaw *Mackinac* Island, a small island in the area between Lake Michigan and Lake Huron.

mackintosh C. *Macintosh* (1766–1843), Scottish inventor.

macramé French, from Italian, from Turkish *makrama* towel, from Arabic *miqrama* embroidered cloth (cloth decorated using needle and thread).

macro- Greek *makros* long.

mad Old English *(ge)mæded* drive mad.

madam French *ma dame* my lady, from Latin *mea* my + *domina* lady.

madras *Madras,* India, where it was first made.

madrigal Italian *madrigale,* from Latin *mandra* pastoral song.

maelstrom Dutch name of a well-known whirlpool off the coast of Norway that was reputed to destroy everything that came near it, from *maalen* whirl, grind + *stroom* stream.

maestro Italian *maesta* master, from Latin *magister.*

magazine French *magasin* store, from Italian *magazzino,* from Arabic *makhzan* storehouse. In the 16th century *"Magazine"* was used in the titles of books, to give the idea that the book was a "storehouse of knowledge".

maggot Middle English *magot,* from Old English *matha,* from Old Norse *mathkr.*

magic French *magique,* from Latin *magice,* from Greek *magikos* of the Magi.

magistrate Latin *magistratus* public person, from *magister* master.

magma Middle English dregs, from Latin dregs of an ointment, from Greek ointment.

magnanimous Latin *magnanimus* high-minded (having high ideals), from *magnus* great + *animus* mind.

magnate Latin *magnas* great man, from *magnus* great.

magnesium Latin *magnesia*, from Greek *Magnesia,* region in Thessaly.

magnet Middle English *magnete,* from Latin *magnetum* lodestone, from Greek *ho Magnes lithos* the Magnesian stone, from *Magnesia,* source of magnetized ore.

magnificent French *magnificient* grand, from Latin *magnificus* noble, from *magnus* great + *facere* do, make.

magnify French *magnifier,* from Latin *magnificare,* from *magnus* great + *facere* do, make.

magnitude Latin *magnitudo* greatness.

magnolia P. *Magnoll* (1638–1715) French botanist.

magpie *Mag* short for Margaret + *pie* earlier name of the bird.

maharajah Hindi *maharaja* great king, from *maha* great + *raja* king.

mahogany Spanish *mahogani.*

mahout Hindi *mahaut, mahawat.*

maiden Old English *mægden.*

mail[1] (postal) Middle English *male* bag, from French, from German *malhe,* from *malaha* wallet, bag.

mail[2] (armor) French *maille,* from Latin *macula* net.

maim French *mahaignier* wound.

main Old English *mægen* strength.

maintain Middle English, from French *maintenir,* from Latin *manu tenere* hold in one's hand, from *manus* hand + *tenere* hold.

maize Spanish *maíz* Indian corn.

majesty French *majeste,* from Latin *majestas* authority, from *major* greater. See **major**.

major Latin greater, from *magnus* great.

majordomo Spanish or Italian, from Latin *major* greater + *domus* house.

majority French *majorité,* from Latin *major* greater. See **major**.

make Old English *macian* produce.

mal- French badly, from Latin *male.*

malachite Latin *molochitis*, from Greek *molochitis lithos* mallow stone, from *molokhe* mallow.

malady French *maladie* sickness, from *malade,* from Latin *male habitus* badly kept.

malaise French *mal* bad + *aise* ease.

malapert French *mal apert* ill-skilled, from *mal-* badly + *apert* skillful, from *espert*, from Latin *expertus.* See **expert**.

malaria Italian *mala aria* bad air, because it was once thought that bad air from swamps caused the disease, from Latin *malus* bad + *aer* air.

male French *ma(s)le* manly, from Latin *mas* male.

malefactor Latin person who does evil, from *maleficus* wicked, from *male* evil + *facere* do, make.

malevolent Latin *malevolens* jealous, from *male* evil + *velle* wish.

malfeasance Latin *malus* evil + *facere* do, make.

malice FRENCH wickedness, from LATIN *molus* bad.

malign LATIN *malignare,* from *malignus* wicked.

malinger FRENCH *malingre* sickly, from *mal* bad + *heingre* tired look, from being ill.

mall MODERN ENGLISH, from *The Mall* in London, a broad, tree-lined promenade, formerly used for a game called *pall-mall* played with a ball and a mallet, from FRENCH *pallemaille,* from ITALIAN *pallamaglio,* from *palla* ball + *malleus* mallet.

mallender FRENCH *malandre*, from LATIN *malandria.*

mallet FRENCH *maillet,* from *mail* hammer, from LATIN *malleus.*

malodorous See **mal-** + **odor** + **-ous**.

malt OLD ENGLISH *mealt* barley or other grain used for making beer or a similar drink.

mammal LATIN *mammalia,* from *mamma* breast.

mammee SPANISH *mamey.*

mammoth RUSSIAN *mamont,* from *mamma* earth, because mammoths were thought to dig in the earth.

man OLD ENGLISH *mann.*

manacle FRENCH, from LATIN *manicula* little hand, from *manus* hand.

manage ITALIAN *maneggiare* handle, from *mano* hand, from LATIN *manus.*

manchet MIDDLE ENGLISH, origin uncertain.

mandarin[1] (Chinese official) PORTUGUESE *mandarim,* from MALAY *mantri*, from HINDI, from SANSKRIT, from *mantrin* counsellor, from *mantra* counsel.

mandarin[2] (fruit) **mandarin**[1], from the similarity of color to the yellow silk robes worn by Chinese officials.

mandate LATIN *mandatum* order, from *manus* hand + *dare* give.

mandible FRENCH, from LATIN *mandibula* jaw, from *mandere* chew.

mandolin FRENCH *mandoline,* from ITALIAN *mandolino,* from LATIN, from GREEK *pandoura* a kind of stringed instrument.

mane MIDDLE ENGLISH, from OLD ENGLISH *manu.*

maneuver FRENCH *manoeuvre* manual labor, from *manuevre,* from LATIN *manu operare* work by hand, from *manu* hand + *operare* work.

mange FRENCH *mangeue* an itch, from LATIN *manducare* eat.

mangel-wurzel GERMAN *mangold* beet + *wurzel* root.

manger MIDDLE ENGLISH, from FRENCH *mangeure,* from *mangier* eat, from LATIN *manducare,* from *mandere* chew.

mangle FRENCH *mehaigner* injure greatly.

mania LATIN, from GREEK *mania* madness.

manicure FRENCH, from LATIN *manus* hand + *cura* care.

manifest FRENCH, from LATIN *manifestus* struck by the hand.

manifold OLD ENGLISH *manigfeald* various.

manikin DUTCH *manneken* little man, from *man* man.

manipulate See **manipulation**.

manipulation FRENCH clever trick, from LATIN *manipulus* handful.

manna LATIN, from GREEK, from ARABIC, from HEBREW *man.*

manner FRENCH *manere* way of behaving, from LATIN *manuarius* of the hand, from *manus* hand.

manometer GREEK *manos* thin + FRENCH *mètre,* from GREEK *metron* measure.

manor FRENCH *manoir* live in, from LATIN *manere* remain.

mansard FRENCH *mansarde,* from *toit à la mansarde,* from architect Nicholas François *Mansart.*

mansion FRENCH *manse,* from LATIN *mansio* a dwelling.

manta SPANISH *manta* blanket (wrap or cloak), from LATIN *mantellum* cloak.

manteau See **mantle.**

manticore MIDDLE ENGLISH, from LATIN *manticora,* from GREEK *mantikhoros,* possibly from a PERSIAN word meaning "maneater."

mantis GREEK prophet.

mantle FRENCH *mantel* cloak, from LATIN *mantellum.*

manual MIDDLE ENGLISH *manuel,* from FRENCH, from LATIN *manus* a hand.

manufacture FRENCH, from LATIN *manufactura* work done by hand, from *manufactura,* from *manus* a hand + *facere* do, make.

manumit LATIN *manumittere,* from *manus* a hand + *mittere* send.

manure FRENCH *manouvrer* work with the hands.

manuscript LATIN *manuscriptum* something written by hand, from *manu scriptus* written by hand, from *manu* hand + *scriptus* written, from *scribere* write.

many OLD ENGLISH *manig.*

manzanita SPANISH *manzana* apple.

map LATIN *mappa mundi* map of the world, from *mappa.*

mar OLD ENGLISH *merran* hinder.

maraca PORTUGUESE.

marae MAORI, cleared space, free of trees.

marathon the legend of an ancient Greek soldier's run (approximately 26 miles), from the city of *Marathon* to Athens, to announce a military victory at Marathon.

marauder FRENCH steal, from *maurad* person who wanders, from *maraud* tomcat.

marble FRENCH *marbre* the stone, from LATIN *marmor,* from GREEK *marmaros* white shiny stone.

marcel *Marcel* Grateau, early 20th century French hairdresser.

march[1] (measured walk) FRENCH *marcher,* from *marchier* trample.

March[2] (month) MIDDLE ENGLISH *marche,* from FRENCH *marz,* from LATIN *Martius* month of Mars (the god of war).

march[3] (boundary) FRENCH *marche.*

mard See **mar.**

mare OLD ENGLISH *mere* horse.

margarine FRENCH, from GREEK *margaron* pearl.

margin LATIN *margo* border.

marina ITALIAN or SPANISH seashore, from LATIN *marinus,* from *mare* sea.

marinade FRENCH *marin* relating to the sea, from LATIN *marinus.* See **marine.**

marinate ITALIAN *marinare* pickle.

marine MIDDLE ENGLISH *maryne,* from FRENCH *marin,* from LATIN *marinus,* from *mare* sea.

marionette FRENCH *Marion,* from *Mary* the mother of Jesus, probably from the "little Mary" in an early religious puppet play.

maritime French, from Latin *maritimus,* from *mare* sea + *-timus,* from *intimus* inmost or *ultimus* last, here indicating association with.

marjoram French, probably from Latin *amaracus,* from Greek *amarakos.*

mark Old English *mearc* boundary.

market French trade, from Latin *mercatus,* from *merx* merchandise (things that are bought and sold).

marlin See **marlinspike**, by similarity of shape of its snout to the ropeworking tool.

marline Dutch *marlijne,* from *marren* tie + *lijn* line. See **line**.

marlinspike Dutch *marlijn* small cord, from *marlen* fasten or secure (a sail), probably from *maren* tie, moor + **spike**.

marmalade French *marmelade,* from Latin, from Greek *melimelon,* from *meli* honey + *melon* apple.

marmite French pot or kettle.

marmot French *marmottiane* probably from Latin *mus montanus* mountain mouse.

maroon[1] (abandon) Modern English *maron* fugitive black slave in West Indies jungle, from French *marron,* possibly from Spanish *cimmaron* wild, untamed, from *cimarra* thicket.

maroon[2] (dark red) French *marron* chestnut.

marplot See **mar** + **plot**.

marque Italian *marca* a mark.

marquee French *marquise* banner over an officer's tent.

marriage French *mariage,* from *marier* marry. See **marry**.

marrow Old English *mearh.*

marry Middle English *marien,* from French *marier,* from Latin *maritare* marry, from *maritus* husband.

Mars Latin.

marsh Old English *merisc.*

marshal French *mareschal* person in charge, from German *marah* horse + *scalc* servant. The medieval marshal's job was to provide good war horses for soldiers to ride.

marsupium Latin, from Greek *marsypion,* from *marsypos* pouch, purse.

martello tower Cape *Martella* in the Mediterranean, which was taken by the British in 1794.

marten French *martrine.*

martial Middle English *martialle,* from Latin *martialis* relating to Mars, the Roman god of war.

martinet Gen. J. *Martinet,* 17th century French drillmaster.

martingale French, probably from Spanish *amlariaga* rein, from Arabic.

martlet French *martelet,* from *martinet* marten (like a weasel).

martyr Old English, from Latin, from Greek a witness.

marvel French *merveille* wonder, from Latin *mirabilia* wonderful things, from *marari* wonder.

mascara Spanish mask, possibly from Arabic *maskharah* person in costume.

mascot French *mascotte,* from *masco* magician.

masculine Latin *mansulinus* male, from *masculus,* from *mas* male.

mash Old English *mascewyrt* crushed grain used in making beer or other such liquids.

mask French *masque,* from Italian *maschera,* possibly from Arabic *maskharah* person in costume.

masochism Leopold von Sacher-*Masoch,* 1836–95, Austrian writer who first described it.

mason French *masson,* from Latin *matio.*

masque See **mask**.

masquerade French *mascarade* group of masked persons, from Italian *mascherata,* from *maschera* masked person. See **mask**.

Mass Old English *mæsse,* from Latin *missa,* from *mittere* send, dismiss.

mass Latin *masse,* from Greek *maza* barley cake.

massacre French *macacre* mess.

massage French *masser,* from Arabic *mass* touch.

mast Old English *mæst.*

mastaba Arabic.

master Middle English *maistre,* from Old English *magister* teacher, from Latin *magister,* from *magnus* great.

masticate Latin *masticare* chew, from Greek *mastichan,* from *mastax* a mouth.

mastiff French *mestif,* from *mastin,* from Latin *mansuetus* tame.

mastitis Greek *mastos* the breast + **-itis**.

mastoid Greek *mastoeides,* from *mastos* breast + *eidos* form.

mat[1] (floor covering) Middle English *matte,* from Old English, from Latin *matta.*

mat[2] (frame) French faded.

match[1] (wood) Middle English *macche* wick of a candle, from French *mesche,* from Latin *myxa.*

match[2] (pair) Old English *mæcca,* from *gemæcca* companion, from *macian* make.

mate Dutch *gemate.*

materia Latin.

material Latin *materialis,* from *materia* wood.

maternal Latin *maternus,* from *mater* mother.

mathematics Latin *mathematica,* from Greek *mathematike,* from *mathema* something learned.

mathetic Greek *mathetikos.*

matinee French *matin* morning, from Latin *Matuta* ancient Roman goddess of dawn.

matins French morning prayer, from *matin* morning, from Latin *Matuta* ancient Roman goddess of dawn.

matriarch Latin *mater* mother + Greek *archos* ruler.

matriculate Latin *matriculare* enroll, from *matricula* list.

matrix Latin womb, from *mater* mother.

matron French *matrone* married woman, from Latin *matrona,* from *mater* mother.

matte French faded.

matter Middle English *matiere,* from French, from Latin *materia.*

mattock Old English *mattuc.*

mattress French *materas* blanket to lie on, from Arabic *matrah* cushion.

mature Latin ripe.

matzoh Hebrew *matsa.*

maudlin *Maudlin* an early English name, from MIDDLE ENGLISH *Maudelen,* from LATIN *Magdalene,* from GREEK *Madalene* Mary Magdalene, woman in the Bible who cried because of her sins.

maul FRENCH *mail* hammer, from LATIN *malleus.*

mauna (must not) SCOTTISH.

mauve FRENCH mallow (plant), from LATIN *malva.*

maven HEBREW *mevin.*

maverick Samuel A. *Maverick,* 1803–70, Texan who decided not to brand his calves because his ranch was on an island.

maxilla LATIN upper jaw, from *mala* jaw, cheekbone.

maxillary See **maxilla** + **-ary**.

maxim FRENCH *maxime,* from LATIN *maxima,* from *maximus* greatest. See **maximum.**

maximum LATIN *maximus* greatest, from *magnus* great.

May FRENCH *Mai,* from LATIN *Maias* month of Maia, Roman earth goddess.

mayhap See **may** + **happen.**

mayhaw See **may** + **hawthorn.**

mayhem FRENCH *mahaym* injury, from *mahaignier* injure.

mayonnaise FRENCH *mayonaisse,* from *Mahón,* chief town of Minorca (Spanish island), which was captured by the French in 1756. The sauce is said to have been named in honor of this event.

mayor FRENCH *maire,* from LATIN *major* greater.

maze OLD ENGLISH *amasian* great surprise.

mead MIDDLE ENGLISH *mede,* from OLD ENGLISH *me(o)du.*

meadow OLD ENGLISH *mæd* land used for growing hay.

meager FRENCH *maigre* thin, from LATIN *macer.*

meal MIDDLE ENGLISH *meel* mealtime, from OLD ENGLISH *mæl,* from LATIN *metiri* measure.

mean[1] (intend) MIDDLE ENGLISH *menen,* from OLD ENGLISH *mænan.*

mean[2] (middle) MIDDLE ENGLISH *mene,* from FRENCH *meien,* from LATIN *medianus.*

mean[3] (not kind) MIDDLE ENGLISH *mene* common, from OLD ENGLISH *mæne.*

meander LATIN *maeander* winding pattern, from GREEK *maiandros,* from *Maiandros* the name of a winding river in Asia.

measles DUTCH *masel.*

measure FRENCH *mesure* measure, from LATIN *mensura.*

mecca ARABIC.

mechanic LATIN *mechanicus,* from GREEK *mechanikos,* from *mechane* a machine.

meconium LATIN, from GREEK *mekonion,* from *mekon* poppy (flower).

medal FRENCH *médaille,* from ITALIAN *medaglia,* from LATIN *metallum* metal.

medallion FRENCH *médaillon* large medal, from ITALIAN *medaglione,* from *medaglia* medal. See **medal.**

meddle FRENCH *medler* mix, from LATIN *miscere.*

medial LATIN *medialis* middle, from *medius.*

median LATIN *medianus* middle, from *medius.*

mediate LATIN *mediare* divide in the middle, from *medius* middle.

medic LATIN *medicus* physician.

medica Middle English *medice*, from Latin *medica*, from Greek, from *medike poa* Median grass, a kind of clover from Media.

medical French, from Latin *medicus* physician.

medicate Latin *medicari* heal.

medicine French *medecine*, from Latin *medicina* healing art.

medieval Latin *medius* middle + *aevum* age.

mediocre French, from Latin *mediocris* halfway up a mountain, from *medius* middle + *ocris* a peak.

meditate Latin *meditari* think about.

Mediterranean Latin *mare Mediterranean* Mediterranean Sea.

medium Latin the middle.

medley French *medlee* mixture, from Latin *miscere.*

meech French *muchier* hide.

meek Middle English *meke,* from Old Norse *mjukr* gentle.

meet Old English *metan* find.

mega- Greek *megas* great.

megalomania French *mégalomanie*, from Greek, from *megalou* + *mania.* See **mega** + **mania.**

megaron Greek hall.

meiosis Latin, from Greek *meioun* make smaller.

melagris Greek a type of bird.

melancholy French *melancolie* gloomy, from Latin *melancholia,* from Greek *melas* black + *chole* bad taste.

Meleager Greek *Meleagros* one of the Argonauts.

melee French *méler* mix, from *mesler,* from Latin *miscere.*

mellay French *mellée.* See **melee.**

mellifluous Latin *mellifluus* flowing with honey, from *mel* honey + *fluere* flow.

mellow Old English *melu* flour.

melodeon melody, made up by the inventor of the musical instrument.

melodrama French *mélodrame,* from Greek *melos* song + *drama* play, from the early dramas that included songs.

melody Latin *melodia* song, from Greek *melos* song + *aiden* sing.

melon French, from Latin, from Greek *melopepon.*

melt Old English *meltan.*

member French *membre* arm or leg, from Latin *membrum.*

membrane Middle English, from Latin *membrana.* See **member.**

membrillo Spanish.

memento Latin remember.

memoir French *mémoire* record, account, from Latin *memoria* account of history.

memorandum Middle English, from Latin *memorandus,* from *memorare* have in mind.

memory French *memorie,* from Latin *memoria,* from *memor* mindful.

menace French threat, from Latin *minacia.*

menagerie French place for keeping animals of the house, from *ménage* having to do with the home, from Latin *mansio* place to live in.

mend Middle English *menden* shortened from *amenden.* See **amend.**

mendacious Latin *mendax* lying.

menial Middle English *meineal* servant, from *meine(e)* having to do with the house, from Latin *mansio* home.

menopause Greek *men* month + *pausis* a stopping.

menses Latin *mensis* month.

menstruate Latin *menstruare,* from *mensis* month.

mensuration Latin *mensuratio* measuring, from *mensura.* See **measure.**

-ment French, from Latin *-mentum.*

mental French, from Latin *mentalis,* from *mens* mind.

mention French, from Latin *mentio.*

menu French small, from Latin *minutus.*

mezzanine French, from Italian *mezzanino,* from *mezzano* middle, from Latin *medianus* of the middle, from *medius.*

mercantile French, from Italian, from Latin *mercari* merchant.

mercenary Latin *mercenarius* hired for pay, from *merces* reward.

mercer French *mercier* trader, from Latin *merx.*

merchandise French *marchaundise,* from *marchaunt.* See **merchant.**

merchant French *marcheant* trader, from Latin *mercari* trade.

mercury Latin *Mercurius.*

mercy French *merci* thanks, from Latin *merces* reward.

mere[1] (only) Latin *merus* not mixed.

mere[2] (lake) Old English.

merge Latin *mergere* dip.

meridian French *meridien,* from Latin *meridianus* midday, from *meridies.*

meridienne French. See **meridian.**

meringue French.

merit French, from Latin *meritum* value, from *merere* earn.

merlon French, from Italian *merlone,* from *merlo* battlement.

merry Old English *myrge* pleasant.

mesa Spanish table, from Latin *mensa.*

mesalliance French *mésalliance,* from *mes-* bad + *alliance.* See **alliance.**

mesh Dutch *maesche* net.

mesmerism F. A. *Mesmer* (1734–1815), Austrian physician who developed a system of treatment through hypnotism.

mesquite Spanish *mesquite,* from Native American *mizquitl.*

mess French *mes* course (part of a meal served at one time), from Latin *missus,* from *mittere* send.

message French, from Latin *mittere* send.

Messiah Latin, from Greek *Messias,* from Hebrew *mashiah* anointed.

meta- Greek *meta* in the midst of, among, with, after.

metabolism Greek *metabole* change, from *meta* beyond + *ballein* throw.

metacarpus Latin, from *metacarpium,* from Greek *metakarpion,* from *meta* between + *karpos* wrist.

metal Latin *metallum,* from Greek *metallon.*

metallurgy Latin, from Greek *metallon* metal, mine + *ergon* work.

metamorphosis Latin, from Greek change, from *meta* over + *morphe* form.

metaphor Latin *metaphora,* from Greek *metaphora,* from *meta* over + *pherein* carry.

metatarsus GREEK *meta-* after + *tarsus* sole of the foot.

metathesis LATIN, from GREEK *metathesis,* from *metatithenai* transpose, from *meta-* change + *tithenai* place.

mete OLD ENGLISH *metan* measure.

meteor LATIN *meteorum,* from GREEK *meteoron* thing in the air, from *meta* beyond + *eora* in the air.

meter FRENCH *mètre,* from GREEK *metron* measure.

methane See **methyl** + **-ane**.

method FRENCH *methode,* from LATIN *methodus,* from GREEK *methodos* system.

methyl FRENCH, from GREEK *methy* wine + *hyle* wood.

methylcellulose See **methyl** + **cellulose**.

methylene FRENCH *méthylène.* See **methyl**.

meticulous LATIN *meticulosus* full of fear, from *metus* fear.

métier FRENCH, from LATIN *ministerium.*

metric See **meter**.

metronome GREEK *metron* measure + *nomos* rule.

metropolis LATIN mother city, from GREEK *meter* mother + *polis* city.

mettle variation of **metal**.

mew[1] (cage) FRENCH *muer,* from LATIN *mutare* change.

mew[2] (cat sound) imitative.

mews See **mew**[1].

mezuzah HEBREW door post.

mezzo ITALIAN middle, from LATIN *medius.*

miasma LATIN, from GREEK *miainein* make dirty or not pure.

mica LATIN *micare* shine.

Mick shortened form of the name Michael.

mickle MIDDLE ENGLISH *mikel,* from OLD ENGLISH *micel.*

micro- GREEK *mikros* small.

microbe FRENCH, from GREEK *mikros* small + *bios* life.

microscope See **micro-** + **-scope**.

mid- OLD ENGLISH *midde* middle.

midday OLD ENGLISH *middæg* noon.

middle OLD ENGLISH *middel.*

middy See **midshipman**.

midge OLD ENGLISH *mycg* gnat.

midget MODERN ENGLISH **midge** + *-et* little sand fly.

midriff OLD ENGLISH *midhrif,* from *midd* middle + *hrif* belly.

midshipman See **mid-** + **ship** + **man**.

midst MIDDLE ENGLISH *middes* middle, from OLD ENGLISH *on midden* in the middle.

midwife MIDDLE ENGLISH *midwif,* from OLD ENGLISH *mid* with + *wif* woman.

mien FRENCH *mine* look.

might MIDDLE ENGLISH *myghte* power, from OLD ENGLISH *might.*

migraine FRENCH, from LATIN *hemicrania* pain on one side of the head, from GREEK *hemikrania,* from *hemi* half + *kranion* skull.

migrate LATIN *migrare.*

milch OLD ENGLISH *milce.*

mild OLD ENGLISH *milde* kind.

mildew MIDDLE ENGLISH *mildeau* honeydew (from aphids), from OLD ENGLISH *meledeaw.* First used to describe the fungus in 14th century, from similarity of appearance.

mile Old English *mil,* from Latin *milia* Roman unit of measure, 1,000 paces.

milieu French middle place, from Latin *medius* middle + *locus* place.

militant Latin *militare* serve as a soldier.

military Latin *militaris,* from *miles* soldier.

milk Old English *meolc.*

mill Middle English *melle,* from Old English *mylen,* from Latin *mola* millstone (flat stones that grind grain).

millennium Latin *mille* thousand + *annus* year.

millet French *mil,* from Latin *millum* millet.

milli- Latin *mille* thousand.

milliliter See **milli-** + **liter**.

milliner *Milan,* Italy, a city famous for its cloth, hats, gloves, etc.

million French, from Italian *millione,* from *mille* thousand, from Latin.

mime Latin *mimus* actor, from Greek *mimos.*

mimic Latin *mimicus,* from Greek *mimikos,* from *mimos* actor.

miminy-piminy imitative.

minaret French minarete, from Italian *minaretto,* from Arabic *manara* lighthouse, from *nar* fire, light.

mince French *mincier* cut into small pieces, from Latin *minutia.*

mind Old English *gemynd* memory.

mine Middle English, from French, mine, tunnel, ore.

mineral French *miniere,* from *miner.* See **mine**.

mingle Middle English *menglen* join, from Old English *mengan* mix.

miniature Italian small picture, from Latin *miniare* paint red, from *minium* red lead (soft metal). In the Middle Ages texts of books were hand printed in black ink. Red ink was used for titles, headings and decorations, which were small pictures.

minimum Latin *minimus* smallest.

minion French *mignon* pretty.

minister French *ministre* servant, from Latin *minister,* from *minor* minor.

ministry Latin *minium* service.

mink Scandinavian.

minnow Old English *myne.*

minor Latin *minor* less.

minotaur Greek *minotauros*, from *Minos,* king of Crete + *tauros* bull.

minstrel French *menestrel* servant, from Latin *ministerialis,* from *ministerium* service.

mint[1] (plant) Middle English *mynte,* from Old English *minte,* from Latin *menta, mentha*, from Greek *minthe* herb.

mint[2] (money) Old English *mynet* coin, from Latin *moneta,* from *Moneta,* name of a goddess in whose temple in Rome money was coined.

minuet French *menu* small, from Latin *minutus*, from the small steps of this dance.

minus Latin *minor* less.

minute Latin *minutus* small.

minx Middle English *mynx* pet dog.

miracle French, from Latin *miraculum* wonderful thing, from *mirus* wonderful.

mirage French *mirer* look at, from Latin *mirare* see, from *mirari* wonder at.

mire Old Norse *myrr* swamp.

mirror FRENCH *mirour,* from LATIN *mirare* see, from *mirari* wonder at.

mirth OLD ENGLISH *myrgth.*

mis- OLD ENGLISH *mis-* and FRENCH *mes-* badly, wrongly.

misanthrope GREEK *misanthropos* hating mankind, from *misein* hate + *anthropos* man.

miscellaneous LATIN *miscellaneus* mixed, from *miscellus.*

mischief FRENCH *meschief* damage, from *meschever,* from *mes-* wrong + *chief* head.

miscreant FRENCH *mescroire* not believe, from *mes-* wrong + LATIN *credere* believe.

miser LATIN.

miserable FRENCH, from LATIN *miserabilis,* from *miser.*

misfeasance FRENCH *mesfaisance,* from *mesfaire* do wrong, from *mes-* wrong + LATIN *facere* do, make.

misnomer FRENCH *mesnommer* name incorrectly, from *mes-* wrong + LATIN *nominare* name.

miss OLD ENGLISH *missan.*

missal LATIN *missa* Mass.

missile LATIN *mittere* send, throw.

mission LATIN *missio* a sending.

Mississippi FRENCH *Messipi,* from NATIVE AMERICAN *Missi-ziibi* Big River.

missive FRENCH, from LATIN *mittere* send.

mistake OLD NORSE *mistaka* take by mistake.

mistress MIDDLE ENGLISH *maistresse,* from FRENCH *maistresse,* from *maistre* chief. See **master** + **-ess.**

mite OLD ENGLISH.

miter MIDDLE ENGLISH *mitre,* from FRENCH, from LATIN *mitra,* from GREEK *mitra* headband.

mitigate LATIN *mitigare* make soft.

mitochondrion GREEK *mitos* a thread + *chondrion* a small cartilage (the tough tissue that forms a part of the skeleton).

mitten FRENCH *mitaine.*

mix LATIN *mixcere.*

mizzen FRENCH *misaine,* from ITALIAN, from LATIN *medianus.* See **median.**

mnemonic GREEK *mnemonikos,* from *mneme* memory.

moan possibly from OLD ENGLISH *mænan* complain.

moat FRENCH *mote* mound.

mob LATIN *mobile vulgus* movable crowd.

mobcap DUTCH *mop* woman's cap + OLD ENGLISH *cæppe* hood, from LATIN *cappa.*

mobile LATIN *mobilis,* from *movere* move.

moccasin NATIVE AMERICAN.

mock FRENCH *mocquier.*

mode LATIN *modus* manner, measure.

model FRENCH *modelle* pattern, from ITALIAN *modello,* from LATIN *modulus,* from *modus* manner, measure.

moderate LATIN *moderari* control.

modern LATIN *modernus* of the present, from *modo* just now, from *modus* manner, measure.

modest LATIN *modestus,* from *modus* manner, measure.

modify FRENCH *modifier* change, from LATIN *modificare* control, from *modus* measure + *facere*to do, make.

modulate LATIN *modulari,* from *modus* manner, measure.

module French, from Latin *modus* manner, measure.

moider possibly from **muddle**.

moiety French *moitie,* from Latin *medietas* half.

moil French *moillier* moisten, from Latin *mollis* soft.

moist French *moiste* wet, from Latin *mucidus* moldy, from *mucus* slime. Probably influenced by Latin *musteus* fresh, new, from *musteum* new wine.

moke[1] (net) Old English *max* net.

moke[2] (donkey) British slang, origin unknown.

moke[3] (fog) British, origin unknown.

molar Middle English, from Latin *molaris dens* grinding tooth, from *mola.* See **mill**.

molasses Latin *mel* honey.

mold[1] (form) Middle English *molde,* from French *modle,* from Latin *modus* measure.

mold[2] (growth) Middle English *mold.*

mole[1] (animal) Middle English *mouldwarp* earth-thrower, from Old English *molde* earth + *weorpan* throw away.

mole[2] (skin spot) Old English *mal* spot, mark.

mole[3] (harbor wall) French *môle* breakwater, from Latin *moles* barrier.

molecule French, from Latin *molecula,* from *mole* mass.

molest French *molester,* from Latin *molestus* troublesome, from *moles* a burden.

moletta See **mulatto**.

mollify French *mollifier,* from Latin *mollificare* soften, from *mollis* soft + *facere* do, make.

mollusk French *mollusque,* from Latin *mollis* soft + *facere* do, make.

molt Middle English *mouten,* from Old English, from Latin *mutare* change.

molten See **melt**.

moment Latin *momentum,* from *movere* move.

mon Japanese family crest.

monarch Latin *monarcha* only ruler, from Greek *monarches,* from *monos* alone + *archein* rule.

monastery Latin *monasterium,* from Greek *monasterion,* from *monazein* live alone, from *monos* alone.

Monday Middle English, from Old English *Monandæg* moon's day, from Latin *lunae dies.*

money French *moneie* coin, from Latin *moneta* place for making money. See **mint**[2].

monger Old English *mangere* dealer, from Latin *mango.*

mongoose Hindi *mungus.*

mongrel Old English *mengan* mixture.

monitor Latin *monitor* advisor, from *monere* warn.

monk Old English *munuc,* from Latin, from Greek *monos* alone.

monkey German *Moneke,* from a medieval story about animals.

mono- Greek *monos* one, single, alone.

monocle French, from Latin *monoculus* one-eyed, from Greek *monos* single + Latin *oculus* eye.

monody Latin, from Greek *monodidia,* from *monos* single + *aeiden* song.

monogamy French, from Latin *monogamia,* from Greek *monos* single, alone + *gamos* marriage.

monogram LATIN, from GREEK *monos* single + *gramma* letter.

monolith FRENCH, from LATIN *monolithus* made of one stone, from GREEK *monolithos,* from *monos* single, alone + *lithos* stone.

monologue FRENCH, from GREEK *monologos* speaking alone, from *monos* single + *logos* word.

monomachy FRENCH *monomachie,* from LATIN *monomachia,* from GREEK *monomaxia,* from *mono* single + *maxia* fight.

monopoly LATIN *monopolium,* from GREEK *monopolion,* from *monos* single, alone + *polein* sell.

monotonous LATIN, from GREEK *monotonia,* from *monos* single + *tonos* sound.

monsieur FRENCH *mon* my + *sieur* lord.

monsoon DUTCH *monssoen,* from PORTUGUESE *monçao,* from ARABIC *mausim* season.

monster FRENCH *monstre,* from LATIN *monstrum,* from *monere* warn.

montage FRENCH *monter* put together. See **mount**.

Montgolfier FRENCH name of the brothers J. M. and J. E. *Montgolfier* who invented the hot air balloon.

month OLD ENGLISH *monath.*

monument LATIN *monumentum,* from *monere* warn.

mood OLD ENGLISH *mod* mind.

moon MIDDLE ENGLISH *mone,* from OLD ENGLISH *mona.*

Moor FRENCH *More*, from LATIN *Morus*, from *Maurus*, from GREEK *Mauros* inhabitant of Mauritania.

moor[1] (dock a ship) MIDDLE ENGLISH, possibly from GERMAN *moren* tie.

moor[2] (land) MIDDLE ENGLISH *more,* from OLD ENGLISH *mor.*

moot OLD ENGLISH *mot* meeting.

mop MIDDLE ENGLISH *mappe,* from FRENCH *mappe* napkin, from LATIN *mappa.*

mope possibly from DUTCH *mopen.*

mopoke imitative.

moppet MIDDLE ENGLISH *moppe* rag doll.

moraine FRENCH.

moral LATIN *moralis* relating to manners, from *mos* custom.

morale FRENCH *moral,* from LATIN *moralis.* See **moral**.

morass DUTCH *moeras* marsh, from FRENCH *mareis.*

moray LATIN *muraena* kind of fish, from GREEK *myraina.*

morbid LATIN *morbidus* sick, from *morbus* disease.

more OLD ENGLISH *mara.*

morganatic FRENCH *morgenatique* morning gift, from LATIN *matrimonium ad morganaticam* marriage of the morning, probably from GERMAN *morgan geba* morning gift. From the custom of the husband giving a wife of lower rank a gift the morning after their marriage.

morgue FRENCH, originally a building in Paris where bodies were kept awaiting identification.

morning MIDDLE ENGLISH *morwening,* from *morwen,* from OLD ENGLISH *morgen.*

moron GREEK *moros* foolish.

morose LATIN *morosus* bad tempered, from *mos* manner.

morphine LATIN *Morpheus* the god of dreams.

morrow Old English *morwe,* from *morgen* morning.

morsel French *mors,* from Latin *morsum* a bite.

mort[1] (death) French *mort,* from Latin *mortuum* dead.

mort[2] (quantity) British, origin uncertain.

mortal French, from Latin *mortalis,* from *mors* death.

mortar French *mortier* cement, from Latin *mortarium* bowl for mixing or pounding.

mortgage French *mort* dead + *gage* pledge.

mortify French *mortifier* put to death, from Latin *mortificare* kill, from *mors* death + *facere* do, make.

mortuary Latin *mortuarius,* from *mortuus* dead.

mosaic French *mosaïque,* from Italian *mosaico,* from Latin *mosaicus,* from *musivum,* from *Musa.* See **muse**[2].

mosque French *mosquée,* from Italian, from Spanish, from Arabic *masjid* place of worship, from *sajada* pray.

mosquito Spanish *mosca* fly, from Latin *musca.*

most Old English *mast.*

-most Old English *-mest.*

mote Old English *mot.*

motel combination of **motor** + **hotel**.

moth Old English *moththe.*

mother Old English *modor.*

motif French theme, from Latin *motivum* something that causes an action. See **motive**.

motile Latin *motus,* from *movere* move.

motion Latin *motio* movement.

motive French *motif,* from Latin *motivum* something that causes an action, from *motivus* moving, from *movere* set in motion.

motley Middle English, from French *motteley,* probably from Old English *mot* speck.

motor Latin mover, from *movere* move.

mottle See **motley**.

motto Italian a saying, from Latin *muttum* word, from *muttire* mutter.

mouflon French, from Latin *mufron.*

moulage French *moul(er)* mold.

mould British spelling for mold. See **mold**[1] and **mold**[2].

moulinet French *moulin* mill.

moult See **molt**.

mound possibly from Dutch *mond* protection.

mount French *monter* go up, from Latin *mons* mountain, high hill.

mountain French *montaigne* high hill, from Latin *monanus,* from *mons.*

mountebank Italian *montabanco* climb on the bench (to speak in front of an audience), from *montare* climb + *in* on + *banco* bench.

mourn Old English *murnan* feel sadness.

mouse Old English *mus.*

mousse French froth, from Latin *mulsa,* from *mulsum* honey wine.

mouth Old English *muth.*

move French *mover,* from Latin *movere* put in motion.

mow Old English *muga* cut down crops.

much Old English *mycel.*

mucilage FRENCH *mucilago* stale juice, from LATIN *mucere* be moldy.

muck OLD NORSE *myki* manure.

mucous LATIN *mucus.*

mud MIDDLE ENGLISH *mudde,* from GERMAN *mudde.*

muddle See **mud**.

muezzin ARABIC *mu'adhdhin,* from *adhana* announce.

muff DUTCH *mof* covering for the hands, from *moffel* thick glove, from LATIN *muffula.*

muffin MODERN ENGLISH *moofin,* possibly from GERMAN *muffen.*

muffle FRENCH *enmoufler* wrap up, from *moufle,* from LATIN *muffula* thick glove.

mug probably from SCANDINAVIAN.

mulatto SPANISH *mulato,* from *mulo* mule (whose mother is a horse and whose father is a donkey), from LATIN *mulus.*

mulberry OLD ENGLISH *morberie,* from LATIN *morum* mulberry.

mulch MIDDLE ENGLISH *molsh* soft, moist, from OLD ENGLISH *melsc, milisc* mellow, sweet.

mule OLD ENGLISH *mul,* from LATIN *mulus.*

mullein FRENCH *moleine,* from LATIN *mollis* soft.

mullet FRENCH *mulet,* from LATIN *mullus.*

mulligatawny TAMIL *miakutannil* a spicy soup, from *milaku* pepper + *tanni* water.

multifarious LATIN *multifarius,* from *multifariam,* from *multi-* many + *-fariam* parts.

multiple FRENCH, from LATIN *multiplus,* from *multus* many + *plex* fold.

multiply FRENCH *multiplier,* from LATIN *multiplicare.* See **multiple**.

multitude FRENCH, from LATIN *multitudo* a great number.

mum FRENCH *momer,* from *momo* imitative.

mumble MIDDLE ENGLISH *momelen,* from *mom* unclear sound.

mumblety-peg *mumble the peg.* Formerly the loser of the game had to pull a peg out of the ground with his teeth.

mummy FRENCH *momie,* from Latin *mumia,* from ARABIC *mumiyah* embalmed body.

mumps GERMAN *mimpfeln* mumble while eating.

mundane FRENCH, from LATIN *mundus* world.

municipal LATIN *municipalis,* from *munia* official duties + *capere* take.

munificent LATIN *munificens,* from *munus* gift + *facere* do, make.

munitions FRENCH *munition,* from LATIN *munitio* defense.

muntin FRENCH *montant* an upright blow or thrust.

mural FRENCH relating to a wall, from LATIN *muralis,* from *murus* wall.

murder OLD ENGLISH *morthor.*

murky OLD NORSE *myrkr* dark.

murmur FRENCH imitative.

murrey FRENCH *moré,* from LATIN *moratus,* from *morum* mulberry.

muscle LATIN *musculus* little mouse, from *mus* mouse, because some muscles look like a mouse when they are in use.

muse[1] (think about) FRENCH *muser,* from *muse* nose of an animal.

Muse[2] (inspiration) LATIN *Musa,* from GREEK *Mousa* any of the nine Greek goddesses of art, literature and science.

museum Latin, from Greek *mouseion* shrine (place of worship), from *Mousa.* See **muse**[2].

mush See **mash.**

mushroom French *moisseron,* from Latin *mussirio.*

music Latin *musica,* from Greek *mousike,* from *Mousa.* See **muse**[2].

musicale French *soirée musicale* musical evening, from *musique* art of music, from Latin *musica.* See **muse**[2].

musk Middle English, from French *musc,* from Latin *muscus,* from Greek *moskhos,* from Persian *mushk,* from Sanskrit *muska* testicle, from *mus* mouse.

musket French *mousquet,* from Italian *moschetto* originally meant arrow of a bow, from Latin *musca* fly.

muslin French *mousseline,* from Italian *mussolino,* from *Mosul* city in Iraq where it was first produced.

mussel Old English *muscle,* from Latin *musculus.*

must Old English *moste.*

mustache French *moustache,* from Italian *mostaccio,* from Greek *mystax* upper lip.

mustachio Spanish *mostacho* or Italian *mostaccio.*

mustang Spanish *mestengo* animal that strays, from *mesta* roundup of stray animals, from Latin *mixta* mixed. Originally applied to stray animals that got mixed with a herd.

mustard French *moustarde,* from Latin *mustum* new wine.

muster French *monstrer* show, from Latin *monstrare.*

musty possibly from **moist.**

mutation French *mutacion,* from Latin *mutatio* change.

mute[1] (silent) French *muet,* from *mut, mo,* from Latin *mutus* silent, dumb.

mute[2] (bird dropping) French *émeut.*

mutilate Latin *mutilare* maim (hurt a body part so badly that it can no longer be used).

mutiny French *mutin,* from *muete* revolt, from Latin *movere* move.

mutter Middle English *moteren.*

mutton French *moton* a ram, from Latin *multo* sheep.

mutual French *mutuel,* from Latin *mutuus.*

mux See **muck.**

muzzle French *musel,* from *muse* snout (the nose and jaws of some animals).

my Old English *min.*

myopia Latin, from Greek *myein* shut + *ops* eye.

myriad Greek *myrias* ten thousand, from *myrios* countless.

myrrh French *mirre,* from Latin *murra,* from Greek *myrrha,* from Arabic *murr.*

myrtle French *myrtille,* from Latin *myrtus,* from Greek *myrtos.*

mystery Latin *mysterium* secret worship, from Greek *mysterion,* from *myein* close lips and eyes.

mystic Latin, from Greek *mystikos,* from *mystes* initiate.

myth Latin *mythos* fable, from Greek.

mythology Latin *mythologia,* from Greek legend, from *mythos* fable + *logos* word.

nab probably from DANISH *nappe* grab.

nabob ARABIC *nâ'ib* governor.

nacelle FRENCH *nacelle,* from LATIN *naucella,* from *navis* a ship.

nadir FRENCH, from LATIN, from ARABIC *nazir* opposite to the zenith (point in the sky directly overhead).

naffy BRITISH *NAAFI* for N(avy), A(rmy), and A(ir) F(orce) I(nstitutes) (military canteen service).

nag[1] (horse) MIDDLE ENGLISH *nagge* small riding horse, origin uncertain.

nag[2] (annoy) OLD NORSE *gnaga* eat at bit by bit.

naiad FRENCH, from LATIN, from GREEK *naein* flow.

nail OLD ENGLISH *nægel.*

nainsook HINDI *nain* the eye + *sukh* pleasure.

naive FRENCH *naïf* natural, from LATIN *nativus.*

naked OLD ENGLISH *nacod* bare.

namby-pamby nickname given the poet *Ambrose* Phillips (1674–1749) by more skilled poets of the time who thought his poems childish and silly.

name OLD ENGLISH *nama.*

nankeen *Nanking* in China, from where the cloth was first exported.

nanny baby talk for *Anna,* a woman's name.

nap OLD ENGLISH *hnappian.*

nape MIDDLE ENGLISH.

napery FRENCH *naperie,* from *nape.*

napkin FRENCH *nappe* linen.

narcissus LATIN, from GREEK *narkissos,* from *narke* numbness. From a Greek myth about *Narcissus,* who fell in love with his reflection in a pool of water, and could do nothing else but look at it. He wasted away and died and his body turned into the flower called narcissus.

narcotic FRENCH *narcotique,* from GREEK *narkotikos,* from *narke* numbness.

narrate LATIN *narrare* tell.

narrow OLD ENGLISH *nearu.*

nasal FRENCH, from LATIN *nasus* nose.

nasty possibly from DUTCH *nestig* dirty.

nation FRENCH, from LATIN *natio* people.

native FRENCH, from LATIN *nativus* born.

natron FRENCH, from SPANISH, from ARABIC *natrun,* from GREEK *nitron.*

natty See **neat.**

natural FRENCH, from LATIN *naturalis* by birth.

nature FRENCH, from LATIN *natura* course of things, from *nasci* be born.

naturopathy **nature** + **-pathy** a particular system of treatment.

naught OLD ENGLISH *nawiht* nothing, from *na* no + *wiht* person.

naughty MIDDLE ENGLISH *naught* wicked act.

nausea LATIN seasickness, from GREEK *nausie,* from *naus* ship.

nautical LATIN, from GREEK *nautes* sailor, from *naus* ship.

nave MIDDLE ENGLISH *navis,* from LATIN ship.

navette FRENCH little boat, from LATIN *naveta,* from *navis* ship.

navigate LATIN *navigare* sail, from *navis* ship + *agere* drive.

navy FRENCH *navie* ships, from LATIN *navis* ship.

nay OLD NORSE *nei* no, from *ne* not + *ei* ever.

near OLD ENGLISH.

neat FRENCH *net* clean, from LATIN *nitidus* shining.

neatherd See **neat** + **herd**.

nebula LATIN cloud.

necessary LATIN *necessarious,* from *necesse,* from *ne-* not + *cedere* go.

neck OLD ENGLISH *hnecca.*

necromancy FRENCH *nygromancie,* from LATIN *nigromantia,* from LATIN *necromantia,* from GREEK *nekros* dead body + *manteia,* from *mantis* prophet.

nectar LATIN drink of the gods, from GREEK *nektar.*

nectarine See **nectar** + **-ine**[1].

need OLD ENGLISH *nied.*

needle OLD ENGLISH *ned.*

nefarious LATIN *nefus* crime, from *ne-* not + *fas* lawful.

negation FRENCH, from LATIN *negare* deny.

neglect LATIN *negligere,* from *neg-* not + *legere* gather.

negligee FRENCH *négliger* neglect.

negligent FRENCH, from LATIN *negligere.* See **neglect**.

negotiate LATIN *negotiari,* from *negotium* business, from *nec-* not + *otium* ease.

Negro FRENCH *negre,* from SPANISH *negro* black, from LATIN *nigrum* dark, black (applied to the sky, to skin color, etc.)

Negus AMHARIC *n'gus* king, from *nagasha* he ruled.

neighbor OLD ENGLISH *neahgebur* farmer.

neither OLD ENGLISH *na-hwæther* nor whether.

neo- GREEK *neos* new.

neon GREEK *neon,* from *neos* new.

neoprene GREEK *neos* new + *(chloro)prene* a colorless liquid.

nephew FRENCH *nevue,* from LATIN *nepos.*

nephritis LATIN, from GREEK, from *nephros* kidney + *-itis* inflammation.

ne plus ultra LATIN no more beyond.

nepotism FRENCH *népotisme,* from ITALIAN *nepotismo,* from *nepote* nephew, from LATIN *nepos.* Originally, privileges granted to "nephews" (actually sons) of Catholic popes.

Neptune LATIN *Neptunus* the Roman god of the sea.

nerve LATIN *nervus* strength.

nesh OLD ENGLISH *hnesce.*

-ness OLD ENGLISH *-nes(s).*

nestle Old English *nestlian* bird's nest.

net Old English *net* mesh.

nettle Old English *netele.*

network See **net** + **work.**

neuro- Greek *neuro-*, from *neuron* nerve (originally sinew, tendon, cord, bowstring).

neurocranium See **neuro-** + **cranium.**

neuron Greek nerve.

neurosis Greek nerve + Latin *-osis* abnormal condition.

neuter French, from Latin *neiture* neither, from *ne-* not + *uter* either.

neutral French, from Latin *neutralis,* from *neuter,* from *ne-* not + *uter* either.

never Old English *næfre* at no time, from *ne-* not + *æfre* always.

new Old English *niwe.*

newel French, from Latin *nucalis* like a nut, from *nux* nut.

newfangled Middle English *newefangel,* from Old English *niwe* new + *fon* take.

newt Middle English *an eute,* from Old English *efeta.*

nexamine Latin *nex* binding + *amine* protein.

next Old English *nehst.*

nexus Latin binding together.

niagara Native American town name.

nibble probably from German *nibbelen.*

nibblish See **nibble.**

nice Middle English stupid, from French, from Latin *nescius* ignorant, from *nescire,* from *ne-* not + *scire* know.

niche French corner, from Latin *nidus* nest.

nick possibly from Old Norse *hnykla* wrinkle.

nickel Swedish, from German *kupfernickel* false copper (copper-colored but containing no copper), from *kupfer* copper + *nickel* devil.

nicker imitative.

nickname Old English *eaca* addition + *nama* name.

nicotiana See **nicotine.**

nicotine Jean *Nicot* (1530–1600), who introduced tobacco into France.

nictate (nictitate) Latin *nictitare,* from *nictare* wink.

niece French *n(i)ece,* from Latin *neptis.*

niggard Middle English *nygart*, origin uncertain.

nigger (offensive term of contempt). See **Negro.**

niggle probably from Norwegian *nigla.*

nigh Old English *neah.*

night Old English *niht.*

nightingale Old English *nihtegale,* from *niht* night + *galan* sing.

nightmare Middle English *niht* night + *mare* demon.

nihilism Latin *nihil* nothing + Greek *-ismos.*

nimble Middle English *nymel* quick, from Old English *niman* take.

nimbus Latin.

nincompoop earlier *nicompoop*, origin unknown.

nip Middle English *nippen* pinch, from German or Old Norse *hnippa.*

nipple Middle English *nyppell*, *neble*, from Old English *neb* bill, beak, snout.

nirvana Sanskrit *nirvana* extinction, disappearance.

niter FRENCH *nitre,* from LATIN *nitrum,* from GREEK *nitron.*

nitric FRENCH *nitrique.* See **niter**.

nitrogen FRENCH *nitrogène,* from GREEK *nitron.*

nit-wit GERMAN *nit,* from *nicht* not + OLD ENGLISH *wit* understanding.

nix GERMAN *nichts* nothing.

no OLD ENGLISH *ne a* not ever.

nob SCOTTISH *knabb.*

noble FRENCH upper classes, from LATIN *nobilis* famous.

nock DUTCH *nocke* notch.

nocturne FRENCH, from LATIN *nocturnus* relating to night.

nod MIDDLE ENGLISH *nodden.*

noddle MIDDLE ENGLISH *nodle.*

node LATIN *nodus* knot.

nodule LATIN *nodus* knot.

noggin MIDDLE ENGLISH small cup, mug, possibly from *nog* strong ale.

noise MIDDLE ENGLISH clamor, shouting, from FRENCH *noise* uproar, brawl; apparently from LATIN *nausea* annoyance.

nomad LATIN *nomas* wanderer, from GREEK *nomos* pasture.

nombril FRENCH the navel.

nomenclature LATIN *nomenclatura* call by name, from *nomen* name + *calare* call.

nominal LATIN *nominalis,* from *nomen* name.

nominate LATIN *nominare* name, from *nomen* name.

nominative FRENCH *nominatif,* from LATIN *nominativus* pertaining to naming, from *nominare.* See **nominate**.

non- LATIN not.

non sequitur LATIN *non-* not + *sequor* follow.

nonchalant FRENCH, from LATIN *non-* not + *calene* be warm.

nondescript LATIN *non-* not + *describere,* from *de-* down + *scribere* write.

none OLD ENGLISH *nan.*

nonpareil FRENCH, from LATIN *non-* not + *pareil* equal, from *par.*

nonplus LATIN *non-* not + *plus* more.

noodle[1] (dough) GERMAN *Nudel.*

noodle[2] (head) MIDDLE ENGLISH *nodle.*

nook MIDDLE ENGLISH *nok*, from SCANDINAVIAN.

noon OLD ENGLISH *non* ninth hour after sunrise, from LATIN *nona hora* ninth hour (about 3 PM). The change to noon meaning midday occurred during the 14th century.

noose LATIN *nodus.*

nor MIDDLE ENGLISH *nother* neither.

norm LATIN *norma* carpenter's tool.

normal LATIN *normalis,* from *norma* rule, pattern.

north OLD ENGLISH.

nose OLD ENGLISH *nosu.*

nostalgia LATIN, from GREEK *nostos* return home + *algos* pain.

nostril OLD ENGLISH *nosthyrl,* from *nosu* nose + *thyrel* hole.

nostrum MODERN ENGLISH, from LATIN *nostrum remedium* our remedy, from *noster* ours. Originally, medicines offered by people who made their own mixtures.

not OLD ENGLISH *ne.*

notable LATIN *notabilis,* from *notare* note.

notary Latin *notare* note.

notation Latin *notatio*, from *notare* note.

notch French *oche* nick.

note Latin *nota* sign.

nothing Old English *na thing.*

notice French, from Latin *notitia.* See **note**.

notify French *notifier* make known, from Latin *notus* known + *facere* do, make.

notion Latin *notio* idea, from *noscere* come to know.

notorious Latin well-known, from *notus* known.

nought Old English *nowiht.*

noun French name, from Latin *nomen.*

nourish French *norir* bring up, from Latin *nutrire.*

nova Latin *nova stella* new star, from *novus* new.

noveau French *novel* new, from Latin *novellus*. See **novel**.

novel French new, from Latin *novellus,* from *novus* new.

November Latin *November* ninth month of the early Roman calendar, which started with March as the first month, from *novem* nine.

novena Latin *novem* nine.

novice French, from Latin *novicius,* from *novus* new.

novocaine Latin *novus* new + *-caine*, from *cocaine* (used as a local anesthetic).

now Old English *nu.*

noxious Latin *noxa* harm.

nozzle See **nose**.

nuance French *nuer* shade, from *nue* cloud, from Latin *nubes.*

nub German *knubbe* knob.

nubbin German *knubbe* knob.

nubia Latin *nubes* cloud.

nubile Latin *nubilis,* from *nubere* marry.

nucleus Latin a kernel.

nudge possibly from Norwegian *nyggia* push.

nugatory Latin *nugatorius* worthless, futile, from *nugator* trifler, from *nugae* jests, trifles.

nugget origin unknown, possibly from British *nug* lump.

nuisance French *nuire,* from Latin *nocere* annoy.

null French, from Latin *nullus* not any, from *ne-* not + *ullus* any.

nullify Latin *nullificare,* from *nullus* not any + *facere* do, make.

numb Middle English *nimen* take, from Old English *niman.*

number French *nombre* unit, from *numerus.*

numeral Latin *numeralis,* from *numerus* unit.

numerator Latin *numerare* count.

numerous Latin *numerus* a number.

numinous Latin *numen* divine approval (expressed by nodding the head), from *nuere* nod.

nun Old English *nunne,* from Latin *nonna.*

nuptial Latin *nuptiae* marriage, from *nubere* marry.

nurse French *nurrice* one who nurses a baby, from Latin *nutrire* nourish.

nurture French, from Latin *nutrire* nourish.

nut Old English *hnutu.*

nutgall See **nut** + **gall**.

nutmeg MIDDLE ENGLISH *notemygge,* from FRENCH *noiz muscade* musky (strong odor) nut.

nutrition LATIN *nutritio,* from *nutrire* feed.

nux vomica LATIN *nux* nut + *vomere* vomit.

nuzzle OLD ENGLISH *nosu.*

nylon made-up word.

nymph FRENCH, from LATIN *nympha,* from GREEK *nymphe.*

nystagmus LATIN *nystagmos* drowsiness, from GREEK *nystazein* be sleepy.

O

-o[1] (combining) Greek usage, in combinations such as Anglo-Saxon (where *Angle* + *-o* makes the combining form *Anglo*).

-o[2] (ending) Modern English slang usage, as in wino, weirdo, combo.

o'clock Middle English *of the clock.*

oaf Old Norse *alfr* elf, from an early idea that babies not beautiful or normal had been put there by an elf.

oak Old English *ac.*

oasis Latin, from Greek, from Egyptian word for "fertile place in the desert".

oath Old English *ath* promise to God to do something, or that what one says is true.

ob- Latin toward, against, over, opposite, entirely.

obbligato Italian obliged, from Latin.

obdurate Latin *odburare,* from *ob-* very much + *burare* make hard.

obedient French, from Latin *obedire* serve. See **obey**.

obeisance French *obeissance,* from *obeir* obey, from Latin *obedire* serve. See **obey**.

obese Latin *obesus* fat, from *obedere* eat.

obey French *obeïr,* from Latin *obedire* serve, from *ob-* to + *audire* hear.

obfuscate Latin *obfuscare* darken, from *ob-* toward, against + *fuscus* dark.

obituary Latin *obituarius,* from *obitus* death, from *ob-* toward + *ire* go.

object Latin *objectus* something thrown in the way, from *objicere,* from *ob-* against + *jacere* throw.

objective Latin *objectivus,* from *objectus.* See **object**.

oblation Latin *oblatio* offering, from *offere,* from *ob-* toward + *ferre* bring.

obligate Latin *obligare* bind. See **oblige**.

oblige French *obliger* bind, from Latin *obligare,* from *ob-* toward + *ligare* bind.

oblique Latin *obliiquus* slanting, from *ob-* toward + *liquis* slanted.

obliterate Latin *oblitarare* erase, from *ob-* over + *littera* letter.

oblivion Latin *obliviosus,* from *oblivisci* forget.

oblong Latin *oblongus* long, from *ob-* toward + *longus* long.

obnoxious Latin *obnoxius,* from *ob-* against + *noxa* injury.

oboe Italian, from French *hautbois,* from *haut* high + *bois* wood.

obscene Latin *obscenus* very bad.

obscure FRENCH *obscur* dark, from LATIN *obscurus,* from *ob-* over + *scurus* covered.

obsequious LATIN *obsequium,* from *ob-* to + *sequi* follow.

observe FRENCH *observer* examine, from LATIN *observare* watch, from *ob-* over + *servare* keep.

obsess LATIN *obsidere* sit at, from *ob-* toward + *sedere* sit.

obsolete LATIN *obsolescere,* from *ob-* opposite + *solere* be used to.

obstacle FRENCH *o(b)stacle,* from LATIN *obstaculum,* from *obstare* stand in the way, from *ob-* against + *stare* stand.

obstetrics LATIN *obstetricus* relating to a midwife (woman whose work is helping to deliver babies), from *obstetrix* midwife, she who stands by, from *ob-* against + *stare* stand.

obstinate LATIN *obstinare* continue trying, from *ob-* toward + *stare* stand.

obstreperous LATIN *obstreperous* clamorous, from *obstrepere* oppose noisily, from *ob-* against + *strepere* make a noise.

obstruct LATIN *obstruere* block, from *ob-* against + *struere* pile up.

obtain FRENCH *obtenir* get, from LATIN *obtinere* take hold of, from *ob-* entirely + *tenere* hold.

obtrude LATIN *obtrudere* push with force against, from *ob-* against + *trudere* push.

obtuse LATIN *obtundere* beat against, from *ob-* against + *tundere* strike.

obverse LATIN *obvertere* turn against, from *ob-* against + *vertere* turn.

obviate LATIN *obviare* prevent, from *ob-* against + *via* way.

obvious LATIN *obvius* at hand, from *ob-* toward + *via* way.

occasion LATIN *occasio* opportunity, from *ob-* toward + *cadere* fall.

occipital FRENCH, from LATIN *ob-* toward + *caput* head.

Occitan FRENCH.

occlude LATIN *occludere,* from *ob-* to + *claudere* close.

occult LATIN *occulere,* from *ob-* to + *celere* cover up.

occupy FRENCH *occuper* to take, from LATIN *occupare,* from *ob-* to + *capere* take.

occur LATIN *occurrere,* from *ob-* towards + *currere* run.

ocean FRENCH, from LATIN *oceanus,* from GREEK *okeanos.*

ocellus LATIN *oculus* eye.

ocher LATIN, from GREEK *ochros* pale yellow.

octa- GREEK *okto* eight.

octagon See **octa-** + GREEK *gonia* angle.

octave LATIN *octava,* from *octo* eight.

October LATIN *October* eighth month of the early Roman calendar, which started with March as the first month, from *octo* eight.

octopus GREEK *okto* eight + *pous* a foot.

odd OLD NORSE *oddi* triangle, third.

oddments See **odd** + **-ment**.

ode FRENCH, from LATIN song, from GREEK *oide.*

odious FRENCH *odieus,* from LATIN *odiosus,* from *odium* hatred.

odor FRENCH *odeur* smell, from LATIN *odor.*

odyssey the ancient GREEK poem which told about the adventures of *Odysseus* on his way home from war.

oedematous See **edema** + **-ous**.

of OLD ENGLISH.

off OLD ENGLISH.

offal MIDDLE ENGLISH *ofall* off-fall.

offence See **offend.**

offend FRENCH *offendre* hurt, from LATIN *offendere,* from *ob-* against + *fendere* hit.

offense See **offend.**

offer OLD ENGLISH *offrian* sacrifice, from LATIN *offerre* bring before, from *ob-* toward + *ferre* bring.

office FRENCH duty, from LATIN *officium,* from *opificium,* from *opus* work + *facere* do, make.

official See **office.**

officiate See **office.**

offshoot See **off** + **shoot.**

ogle probably from GERMAN *oegeln,* from *oog* the eye.

ogre FRENCH giant, from LATIN *Orcus* Roman god of the lower world.

ohm G.S. *Ohm* (1789–1854) German scientist.

-oid GREEK *eidos* form, shape.

oil FRENCH *huile,* from LATIN *oleum* olive oil, from GREEK *elaion.*

Ojibwa NATIVE AMERICAN *O'chepe'wag* plaited shoes, describing their moccasins. Also spelled *Ojibway.*

OK abbreviation of "oll korrect", AMERICAN folk spelling of "all correct".

okra AFRICAN *nkrumah.*

-ol the *-ol* ending of **alcohol.**

-ola AMERICAN, probably originally in *pianola.*

old OLD ENGLISH *ald* of the past.

oleander LATIN.

olfactory LATIN *olfacere* smell, from *olere* have a smell + *facere* do, make.

oligarchy GREEK *oligarchia* government by a few, from *oligos* few + *archein* rule.

oliphant See **elephant.**

olive FRENCH, from LATIN *oliva,* from GREEK *elaia.*

-ology GREEK *-ologia* has to do with.

ombudsman SWEDISH *ombud* deputy + *man* man.

omelet FRENCH *omelette,* from LATIN *lamella* thin plate.

omen LATIN.

ominous LATIN *ominosus,* from *omen* omen.

omit LATIN *omittere,* from *ob-* very much + *mittere* let go, send.

omnibus FRENCH, from LATIN for all, from *omni* all, because the transportation was for the use of all classes of people.

omnipotent LATIN *ominipotens,* from *omnis* all + *potens* powerful.

omnivorous LATIN *omnivorus,* from *omnis* all + *vorare* eat in a greedy way.

on OLD ENGLISH.

once MIDDLE ENGLISH *ones.*

one OLD ENGLISH *an.*

onerous LATIN *onerosus,* from *onus* burden.

onion FRENCH, from LATIN *unio* unity, a single onion, even though it has many layers.

only OLD ENGLISH *anlic.*

onomatopeia LATIN, from GREEK *onomatopoiia,* from *onomatos* name + *poiein* make.

onslaught DUTCH *annslag,* from *slagen* strike.

ontology LATIN *ontologia*, from GREEK *ontos* being + *-logia* study of.

onus LATIN.

onyx FRENCH, from LATIN, from GREEK nail.

ooze OLD ENGLISH *wos* sap.

opal LATIN, from GREEK *spallios*, from *upala* precious stone.

opaque LATIN *opacus* shady.

open OLD ENGLISH.

opera ITALIAN *opera in musica* work set to music, from LATIN *opera* a work.

operate LATIN *operari* work, from *opus* work.

opiate LATIN *opiatus* bringing sleep, from *opium.* See **opium**.

opinion FRENCH belief, from LATIN *opinio.*

opium LATIN, from GREEK *opion,* from *opos* vegetable juice.

opponent LATIN *opponere,* from *ob-* against + *ponere* set.

opportune LATIN *opportunus* toward the harbor, from *ob-* toward + *portus* harbor, referring to the helpful winds in the harbor.

oppose FRENCH *opposer*, from LATIN *opponere.* See **opponent**.

oppress FRENCH *oppresser,* from LATIN *oppressare*, from *opprimere,* from *ob-* against + *premere* press.

opprobrium LATIN *opprobare* blame, from *ob-* against + *probrum* a disgrace.

opt FRENCH *opter* choose + LATIN *optare.*

opthalmic GREEK *ophthalmos* eye

opthalmoscope See **opthalmic** + **-scope**.

optic FRENCH *optique,* from LATIN, from GREEK *optikos.*

optimism FRENCH *optimisme,* from LATIN *optimum* the best.

optimum LATIN *optimus* best, from *ops* riches.

option FRENCH, from LATIN *optio* choice, from *optare* wish.

opulent LATIN *opulentus* rich, from *ops.*

opus LATIN work.

or OLD ENGLISH *oththe* other.

-or FRENCH, from LATIN.

oracle FRENCH, from LATIN *orare* speak, pray.

oral LATIN *oris,* from *os* mouth.

orange FRENCH *orenge*, from ARABIC *nāranj*, from PERSIAN *nāranga.*

orangutan MALAY *orang* man + *hutan* forest.

oration LATIN *oratio* speech.

oratory LATIN *oratoria.*

orb LATIN *orbis* circle.

orbit FRENCH, from LATIN *orbita* path, from *orbis* circle.

orc OLD ENGLISH *orcthyrs, orcneas* ogre, from LATIN *Orcus* hell.

orca MIDDLE ENGLISH *orc, ork* large whale, from FRENCH *orque* sea monster, from LATIN *orca*, a kind of whale.

orchard OLD ENGLISH *ortgeard,* from LATIN *hortus* a garden + OLD ENGLISH *geard* yard.

orchestra LATIN, from GREEK place in the Greek theatre where the chorus danced, from *orcheisthai* dance.

ordain FRENCH *ordeiner*, from LATIN *ordinare* set in order.

ordeal OLD ENGLISH *ordel* judgment. From an ancient method of deciding guilt or innocence in which the accused person had to do a dangerous action. If he didn't get hurt, the gods had found him innocent.

order French *ordre,* from Latin *ordo.*

ordinal Latin *ordinalis,* from *ordo* straight row.

ordinance French *ordenance* rule, from Latin *ordinare* set in order, from *ordo* straight row.

ordinary French, from Latin *ordinarius* regular, from *ordo* order.

ore Old English *ar.*

oregano Spanish, from Latin *origanus,* from Greek *oreiganon,* from *oros* mountain + *ganos* brightness, ornament.

organ Latin *organum* musical instrument, from Greek *organon* tool.

organdy French *organdi,* origin uncertain.

organize Latin *organizare* arrange, from *organum.* See **organ.**

orgy French, from Latin, from Greek *orgia* secret ceremony.

orient French east, from Latin *oriens* rising sun, east, from *oriri* rise.

orienteering Swedish *orientering.* See **orient.**

orifice French, from Latin *orificium* opening, from *or,* from *os* mouth + *facere* do, make.

origin Latin *origo* beginning.

Orkney Old Norse *Orkney-jar* Seal Islands, from *orkn* seal.

ornament French *ornement,* from Latin *ornamentum* decoration.

ornate Latin *ornare* decorate.

ornery contraction of **ordinary**.

orphan Latin *orphanus,* from Greek *orphanos.*

orrery Charles Boyle, Earl of *Orrery* (1676–1731), for whom one was made.

ortho- Greek *orthos* straight.

orthodontics Greek *orthos* straight + *odontos* tooth + French *-ique,* from Latin *-icus,* from Greek *-ikos.*

orthodox Latin *orthodoxus* having the right faith, from Greek *orthodoxos,* from *orthos* right + *doxa* opinion, from *dokein* think.

orthography See **ortho-** + **-graphy**.

oscillate Latin *oscillare* swing.

-ose[1] (full of) Latin *-osus.*

-ose[2] (chemical) French, originally in *glucose.*

osier French, from Latin *auseria.*

osmosis Latin, from Greek *osmos* force into.

ossicone Latin.

ostensible French open, from Latin *ostendere* to show, from *obs-* against + *tendere* stretch.

ostentation Latin *ostendere.* See **ostensible.**

osteopathy Greek *osteon* bone + *-pathy,* from *pathos* suffering, disease, feeling.

ostler See **hostler**.

ostracize Greek *ostrakízein* order away from a group by voting on it. Pieces of broken pots were used as voting pieces, from *oístrakon* shards (pieces of broken pots).

ostrich French, from Latin *ans* bird + *struthio* ostrich, from Greek *strouthos.*

otoscope Greek *oto-* ear + Italian *scopo* target, from Greek *skopos.*

otter Old English *oter.*

ottoman French, from Italian *Ottomano,* from Arabic *Uthmani,* from *Uthman* founder of the empire.

ounce French *once* unit of weight, from Latin *uncia* one of twelve.

-ous Latin *-osus* full of.

ousel Old English *osle.*

oust French *oster,* from Latin *obstare* get in the way, from *obs-* against + *stare* stand.

out Old English *ut.*

outlaw Old English *utlaga* one put outside of the law, from Old Norse *utlagr* sent away from the group.

outrage French, from Latin *ultra* beyond.

oval Latin *ovalis,* from *ovum* egg.

ovary Latin *ovum* egg.

ovation Latin *ovatio* celebration honoring a general who won.

over- Old English *ofer-* too much, above.

overt French *ovrir* open, from Latin *aperire.*

overture French opening, from Latin *apertura.*

overwhelm See **over-** + **whelm.**

ovipositor Latin *ovum* egg + *positor* one who places, from *ponere* place.

ovule French *ovule,* from Latin *ovulum* small egg, from *ovum* egg.

ovum Latin egg.

owe Old English *agan* have to pay.

owl Old English *ule.*

own Old English *agan.*

ox Old English *oxa.*

oxide French *ox(ygène)* + *-ide,* from *acide* acid. See **oxygen.**

oxygen French *oxygène,* from Greek *oxys* acid + *-genes* produced, from the idea that oxygen was essential in the formation of acids.

oyster French *oistre,* from Latin *ostrea, ostreum* oyster, from Greek *ostreon.* Related to Greek *ostrakon* hard shell and *osteon* bone.

ozone German *Ozon* the gas, from Greek *ozon* smelling, from *ozein* smell.

P

pace FRENCH *pas* step, from LATIN *passus.*

pacific FRENCH *pacifique*, from LATIN *pacificus* peaceful. See **pacify**.

pacify FRENCH *pacefier*, from LATIN *pacificare* make peace, from *pax* peace + *facere* do, make.

pack DUTCH and GERMAN *pak* bundle.

pact FRENCH, from LATIN *pactum*, from *pax* peace.

pad MIDDLE ENGLISH bundle of straw to lie on.

paddle MIDDLE ENGLISH *padell* small spade, from LATIN *padela* perhaps from *patella* pan, plate.

paddock OLD ENGLISH *pearruc.*

paddy MALAY *padi.*

padlock MIDDLE ENGLISH *pad* (meaning uncertain) + *lokke* lock.

padre LATIN *pater* father.

paduasoy FRENCH *pou de soie* pelt of silk.

paean LATIN, from GREEK *paian* song to Apollo (who is also called *Paian*).

pagan LATIN *paganus* villager, from *pagus* village.

page[1] (book) FRENCH, from LATIN *pagina* page for writing.

page[2] (boy) FRENCH young boy, from GREEK *paidion*, from *pais* child.

pageant LATIN *pagina* scene of a play, from *pagina* page for writing.

pagoda PORTUGUESE *pagode*, from PERSIAN *butkadah*, from *but* idol + *kadah* house.

pail OLD ENGLISH *pægel* small measure, from LATIN *pagella*, from *pagina* page for writing.

pain FRENCH *peine* punishment, from LATIN *poena*, from GREEK *poine.*

paint FRENCH *peindre* color, from LATIN *pingere.*

painter[1] (artist) See **paint**.

painter[2] (rope) FRENCH, from LATIN *pendere* hang.

paiocke Shakespeare's *Hamlet*, a variation of peacock.

pair FRENCH *paire* a set of two, from LATIN *par* equal.

paisley the city in Scotland where it was first made.

pajama HINDI, probably from PERSIAN *paejamah*, from *pae* leg + *jamah* clothing.

pajock possibly from **peacock**.

pal GYPSY *phal* brother, friend, comrade.

palace FRENCH *palais* royal house, from LATIN *palatium,* from *Palatium* Palatine Hill in Rome, hill where the first very beautiful royal palace was built.

palanquin PORTUGUESE *palanquim*, from MALAY *palangki,* from SANSKRIT *palyanka* couch, bed, from *pari* around + *ancati* it bends, curves.

palate LATIN *palatum* roof of the mouth.

palatinate See **palatine**.

palatine FRENCH, from LATIN *palatium* palace.

palaver PORTUGUESE *palavra* work, from LATIN *parabola* comparison, parable (short story that teaches a moral lesson), from GREEK *parabole.* See **parable**.

pale[1] (little color) FRENCH not having color, from LATIN *pallidus.*

pale[2] (stake) FRENCH, from LATIN *palus* stake.

paleo- GREEK *palaio-* old, ancient, from *palai* long ago, far back.

paleoscincus See **paleo-** + LATIN *scincus*, from GREEK *skinkos* lizard.

palestra FRENCH *palestre*, from LATIN *palaestra*, from GREEK *palaistra* wrestling school, from *palaiein* wrestle + *-tra* place.

palette FRENCH, from LATIN *pala* tool for digging.

palfrey FRENCH *palefrei*, from LATIN *palafredus*, from *paraveredus* extra horse, from GREEK *para* beside + LATIN *verdus* post horse (provided for travelers).

palimsest LATIN *palimpsestus*, from GREEK *palimpsestos* scraped again, from *palin* again + *psen* rub smooth.

palindrome GREEK *palin* again + *dramein* run.

palisade FRENCH *palissade,* from LATIN *palus* stake.

pall[1] (covering) OLD ENGLISH *pæll* robe, from LATIN *pallium* covering.

pall[2] (boring) from **appall**.

pallet FRENCH *paillete* straw, from LATIN *palea.*

palliate LATIN *palliatus* covered with a cloak, from *pallium* cloak.

pallid LATIN *pallidus.*

pallor LATIN.

palm FRENCH *paume* inner part of the hand, from LATIN *palma.*

palmar LATIN *palmaris.*

palmette See **palm** + **-ette**.

palmetto SPANISH *palmito,* from *palma,* from LATIN palm.

palomino SPANISH coloring of a dove, from LATIN *palumbes* dove.

palpable LATIN *palpabilis* can be touched, from *palpare* touch.

palpitate LATIN *palpitare* beat rapidly.

palsy FRENCH *paralysie,* from LATIN *paralysis,* from GREEK nerves not working properly.

paltry probably from GERMAN *palte* rag.

pamper MIDDLE ENGLISH *pamperen,* from DUTCH *pameren.*

pamphlet LATIN *panfletus* little book, from FRENCH *Pamphilet* a medieval Latin poem that was first published in a small booklet of a few pages.

pan OLD ENGLISH *panne.*

pan- GREEK *pas* all, every.

panache FRENCH, from LATIN *penna* feather.

pancreas LATIN, from GREEK *pankreas,* from *pan-* all + *kreas* flesh, because it has no bone.

pandemic GREEK *pandemos,* from *pan-* all + *demos* the people.

pandemonium Latin, from Greek *pan-* all + *daimon* demon, invented by the English poet John Milton (1608–1674) as the name for the capital of hell.

pander Greek *Pandarus* a character in a medieval legend who was the communicating person between a girl and a man who were separated.

pandowdy American, origin uncertain.

pane French *pan* piece, from Latin *pannus* piece of cloth.

panegyric French *panegryique,* from Latin *panegyricus,* from Greek *panegyris* public meeting, from *pan-* all + *ageirein* bring together.

panel French piece, from Latin *pannus* piece of cloth.

pang Middle English, origin uncertain.

pangolin Malay *peng-goling* roller, from *goling* roll. The animal curls into a ball.

panic French *panique* sudden fear, from Greek *Panikos* relating to Pan, god of forests and shepherds, who was said to scare people when he showed up unexpectedly.

pannier French *panier* basket, from Latin *panarium* breadbasket, from *panis* bread.

pannikin See **pan** + Dutch *kin* little.

panoply Greek *panoplia* armor, from *pan-* all + *hopla* arms.

panorama Greek *pan-* all + *horama* view.

pant[1] (quick breath) probably from French *pantaisier* gasp, from Greek *phantasia* imagination, nightmare.

pant[2] (clothes) See **pantaloon.**

pantaloon French, from *Pantalone* character in a 16th century Italian comic play who wore tight pants, from Italian *Pantaleone* name of a 4th century saint.

pantelette See **pantaloon.**

pantheon Latin *Pantheon* Roman temple, from Greek *pantheios* common to all the gods, from *pan-* all + *theos* a god.

panther French, from Latin, from Greek.

pantler (panter) Middle English *paneter,* from Latin *panetarius* baker. See **pantry.**

pantograph French *pantographe,* from Greek *pant* all + *graphe* write.

pantomime Latin *pantomimus,* from Greek *pantomimos* actor (imitator of all), from *panto-* all + *mimos* imitator.

pantry French *paneterie* place where bread is kept, from Latin *panetaria,* from *panis* bread.

papa French, from Latin, originally a child's word.

papaw See **pawpaw.**

papaya Spanish.

paper French *papier,* from Latin *papyrus* paper made from papyrus, from Greek *papyros* the plant.

papillae Latin nipples.

papilloma Latin *papula* pimple.

papist Latin *papista,* from *papa.* See **pope.**

papoose Native American *papoos.*

papyrus Latin, from Greek.

par Latin equal.

para- Greek beside, beyond, aside from.

parable French, from Latin, from Greek *parabole* comparison, from *para-* beside + *ballein* throw.

parabola Greek *parabole.* See **parable.**

parachute French *para-* guarding against + *chute* fall.

parade French display, from Spanish *parada,* from Latin *parare* make ready.

paradigm Latin *paradigma* example, from Greek *paradeigma,* from *para-* beside + *deigma* example.

paradise French, from Latin *paradisus* heaven, from Greek *paradeisos* a garden.

paradisiacal See **paradise** + Greek *-iacal* like.

paradox Latin *paradoxum* something unexpected, from Greek *paradoxos,* from *para-* beyond + *doxa* opinion, from *dokein* think.

paraffin German wax, from Latin *parum* too little + *affinis* having to do with, because things don't stick to it well.

paragon Italian *paragone* standard of value, from Greek *para-* beside + *akone* whetstone (stone used for sharpening).

paragraph Latin *paragraphus,* from Greek *paragraphos,* from *para-* beside + *graphein* write.

parakeet Spanish *perquito.*

parallax Greek *parallaxis,* from *para-* beyond + *allassein* change.

parallel French, from Latin *parallelus,* from Greek *parallelos,* from *para-* side by side + *alleos* one another.

parallelogram French *parallélogramme,* from Latin *parallelogrammum,* from Greek *parallelogrammon,* from *parallelos* parallel + *graphein* write.

paralysis Latin, from Greek *paralyein* loosen at the side, from *para-* beside + *lyein* loose.

parameter Greek *para-* beside + *metron* measure.

paramount French *par amont* at the top, from Latin *per-* beyond + *admontem* uphill.

paramour French *par amour* with love.

paranoia Latin, from Greek *para-* beside + *nous* the mind.

parapet Italian *parapetto* chest-high wall, from *para-* against + *petto* chest, from Latin *pectus.*

paraphernalia Latin things a bride brings to her marriage in addition to her dowry, from Greek *parapherna,* from *para-* beside + *pherne* dowry. See **dowry**.

paraphrase French, from Latin *paraphrasis,* from Greek *paraphrasis,* from *para-* beyond + *phrazein* tell.

paraplegia Latin, from Greek *paraplegia* paralysis of one side of the body, from *para-* beside + *plege* paralysis.

parasite Latin *parasitus* one who lives off another, from Greek *parasitos* one who eats at the table of another, from *para-* beside + *sitos* food, from ancient Greek and Roman men who offered praise and kind words in return for food or support.

parasol French, from Italian *parasole,* from *parare* guard against + *sole* sun, from Latin *sol.*

paratyphoid See **para-** + **typhoid**.

parboil French *par* through + *boullir* boil.

parcel French *parcelle* small part, from Latin *pars.*

parch Middle English, possibly from *perchen, perishen* perish.

parcheesi Hindi *pachisi,* from *pachis* twenty-five (highest throw of the dice), from Sanskrit *panca* five + *vinsati* twenty.

parchment French *parchemin* skin, from Latin *pergamina,* from Greek *Pergamon* city where parchment was first made.

pardon French *pardonner* forgive, from Latin *perdonare,* from *per-* through + *donare* give.

pare French *parer* trim, from Latin *parare* make ready.

parent FRENCH, from LATIN *parens* father or mother.

parenthesis LATIN something put in, from GREEK *para-* beside + *entithenai* put in.

parfait FRENCH perfect.

parfleche FRENCH *parer* deflect + *fleche* arrow.

pariah TAMIL *paraiyan* drummer, member of a low caste (rank) whose duty it is to beat drums at festivals, from *parai* drum.

parietal LATIN *parietalis*, from *paries* wall.

parimutuel FRENCH a mutual bet.

parish FRENCH *paroisse* religious area, from LATIN *parchia,* from GREEK *paroilia,* from *para-* beside + *oikos* house.

parity LATIN *paritas,* from *par* equal.

park FRENCH *par,* from LATIN *parricus.*

parka RUSSIAN.

parkin perhaps from proper name *Perkin* or *Parkin.*

parlance FRENCH *parler* speak.

parlay FRENCH *paroli,* from ITALIAN *paro* equal, from LATIN *par* equal.

parley FRENCH *parlee* conversation, from *parler* speak, from LATIN *parabolare,* from *parabola.* See **parable.**

parliament FRENCH *parlement* conference, from *parler* speak. See **parable.**

parlor FRENCH *parleor* place for conversation, from *parler* speak. See **parable.**

parochial FRENCH, from LATIN *parochia* parish. See **parish.**

parody FRENCH, from LATIN, from GREEK *paroidia,* from *para-* beside + *oide* song.

parole FRENCH promise, from LATIN *parabola* story with a moral, from GREEK *parabole.* See **parable.**

paroxysm FRENCH, from LATIN, from GREEK *para-* beyond + *oxynein* sharpen, from *oxys* sharp.

parquet FRENCH *parc* a park.

parrot FRENCH *perrot.*

parry FRENCH *parer* defend, from LATIN *parare* make ready.

parse LATIN *pars orationis* part of speech.

parsley possibly from GERMAN *petarsile,* from LATIN *petrosilium.*

parsnip MIDDLE ENGLISH *nepe* turnip.

parson FRENCH *persone,* from LATIN *persona* priest. See **person.**

part LATIN *pars* share.

partake MIDDLE ENGLISH part taking, from LATIN *participatio* participation.

partial FRENCH, from LATIN *partialis,* from *pars* share.

participate LATIN *participare* share in, from *pars* share + *capere* take.

participle FRENCH *participe,* from LATIN *participium* sharing, from *pars* share + *capere* take.

particle LATIN *particula* small part, from *pars* share.

particular FRENCH *particuler* special, from LATIN *particularis* small part, from *particula.* See **particle.**

partisan FRENCH, from ITALIAN *partigiano* partner, from *parte* part, from LATIN *pars* share.

partition FRENCH *particion,* from LATIN *partitionem,* from *partire* part (divide).

partner FRENCH *parçoner* one who shares, from LATIN *partionarius,* from *partitio* sharing.

partridge FRENCH *perdriz,* from LATIN *perdix,* from GREEK.

parturition LATIN, from *parturire* be in labor, from *parere* bear.

party FRENCH *partie* side, from *partir* divide, from LATIN *pars* share.

parvenu FRENCH *parvenir* arrive, from LATIN *pervenire.*

pasque-flower FRENCH *passefleur*, from *passer* a step + *fleur* flower, from *pasque* Easter.

pass FRENCH *passer* go across, from LATIN *passus* step.

passage FRENCH *passage* going across, from *passer* move on. See **pass**.

passel variant of **parcel**.

passenger FRENCH. See **passage**.

passion FRENCH suffering, from LATIN *passio,* from *pati* suffer.

passive LATIN *passivus* able to suffer.

passport FRENCH *passeport,* from *passer* move + *port* harbor.

paste GREEK *pasta* barley cereal.

pastel FRENCH crayon, from ITALIAN *pastello,* from LATIN *pastellus,* from GREEK *pasta* barley cereal.

pastern MIDDLE ENGLISH shackle for an animal, from FRENCH *pasturon*, from LATIN *pastor*. See **pastor**.

pasteurize Louis *Pasteur* (1822–1895), French scientist who discovered the process.

pastiche FRENCH, from ITALIAN *pasticcio* mixture, from LATIN *pasta* dough. See **paste**.

pastor LATIN shepherd, from *pascere* feed.

pastoral LATIN *pastoralis* relating to shepherds, from *pastor*. See **pastor**.

pastry FRENCH *paste* dough, from LATIN *pasta,* from GREEK *pasta* barley cereal + FRENCH *erie* place of business, from LATIN *arius.*

pasture FRENCH food, from LATIN *pastura,* from *pascere* feed.

pasty See **paste**.

pat imitative.

pat-a-cake the first words of a nursery rhyme, said or chanted to accompany the action of patting or gently clapping together a child's hands.

patch FRENCH *pieche,* from *piece* part of a whole. See **piece**.

pate (top of head) perhaps from FRENCH *patene* or LATIN *patena,* both from *patina* pan, dish.

patella LATIN *patella* pan, kneecap, from *patina* pan.

patent FRENCH, from LATIN *patere* lie open, because the paper of the patent was open for the public to see.

patera LATIN *patera*, from *patere* be open.

paternal LATIN *paternalis,* from *pater* father.

path OLD ENGLISH *pæth.*

pathetic LATIN *patheticus,* from GREEK *pathetkios* able to experience emotion, from *pathein* suffer, from *pathos* suffering.

pathogenic FRENCH *pathogénique*, from GREEK *pathos* disease + FRENCH *génique* producing.

pathos GREEK suffering, emotion.

-pathy See **pathos**.

patient FRENCH one who is waiting to get medical care, from LATIN *pati* suffer.

patio SPANISH.

patriarch FRENCH *patriarche,* from LATIN *patriarcha* father of a tribe, from GREEK *patriarches,* from *pater* father + *archein* rule.

patrician LATIN *patricius* noble, from *pater* father.

patrimony FRENCH *patrimoine* inheritance, from LATIN *pater* father.

patriot FRENCH *patriote,* from LATIN *patriota* persons of the same country, from GREEK *patriotes.*

patrol FRENCH *patrouiller* paddle in mud, because guards often had to walk back and forth in mud, from *patte* paw.

patron FRENCH protector, from LATIN *patronus,* from *pater* father.

patsy ITALIAN *pazzo* crazy person.

patten FRENCH *patin* clog.

patter[1] (tapping) imitative.

patter[2] (fast or easy talk) MIDDLE ENGLISH *pater* mumble prayers rapidly, from LATIN *pater noster* the prayer "Our Father," which priests recited rapidly.

pattern See **patron**, from the idea of the father setting a good example for the child to copy.

patty FRENCH *pâté* pastry, from *pastee* pie, from *paste* dough. See **paste**.

paucity FRENCH, from LATIN *paucus* few.

paunch FRENCH *panche* belly, from LATIN *pantex.*

pauper LATIN poor person.

pause FRENCH, from LATIN *pausa* stop, from GREEK *pausis.*

pave FRENCH *paver* cover ground with stones, from LATIN *pavire* hit with force.

pavilion MIDDLE ENGLISH, from FRENCH *paveillun* tent, from LATIN *papilio* butterfly, because the tents looked somewhat like a butterfly.

paw FRENCH *poue.*

pawky SCOTTISH dialect, origin unknown.

pawn FRENCH *pan* promise.

pawpaw probably from **papaya**.

pax MIDDLE ENGLISH, from LATIN peace.

pay FRENCH *paier,* from LATIN *paccare* make peace, from *pax* peace.

pea MIDDLE ENGLISH *pese,* from OLD ENGLISH.

peace FRENCH *pais,* from LATIN *pax.*

peach FRENCH *pesche,* from LATIN *pessica,* from *persicum malum,* Persian apple.

peacock MIDDLE ENGLISH *poucock,* from *po,* from OLD ENGLISH *pawa* peafowl + MIDDLE ENGLISH *coc.* See **cock**[1].

peak GERMAN *pek* pike.

peal MIDDLE ENGLISH *pele,* from *apele* appeal.

pearl FRENCH *perle,* from LATIN *perna* a sea animal that sometimes contains pearls.

peart See **pert**.

peasant FRENCH *pais* country, from LATIN *pagus* village.

pease MIDDLE ENGLISH *paisen,* from FRENCH *paiser,* from *pais.* See **peace**.

peat MIDDLE ENGLISH *pete,* from LATIN *peta.*

pebble FRENCH *papolstan* pebble stone.

peccary NATIVE AMERICAN *pakira.*

peck MIDDLE ENGLISH *picken* pierce.

pectoral LATIN *pectoris,* from *pectus* breast.

peculiar LATIN *peculiaris* one's own.

pecuniary LATIN *pecunia* money.

pedagogue FRENCH, from LATIN *paedagogus* name for slaves who helped boys get to school, from GREEK *paidagogos,* from *pais* boy + *agogos* leader.

pedal LATIN *pedalis,* from *pes* foot.

pedant ITALIAN *pedante* teacher.

peddle See **peddler**.

peddler Middle English *peoddere, peddere,* origin uncertain.

pedestal French *piédestal* support, from Italian *piedistallo* support, from *pie* foot, from Latin *pes* + *di* of + *stallo* a rest.

pedestrian Latin *pedester,* from *pes* foot + Latin *-ianus.*

pedi- Latin *pes, pedem* foot.

pediatrics Greek *pais* child + *iatreia* medical help.

pedicab See **pedi-** + **cab**.

pedicel Latin *pedicellus* little foot.

pedigree French *pie de grue* foot of a crane (type of bird with long feet). Some charts that show the family tree have connecting lines that look like the foot of a crane.

pediment Modern English alteration of *periment, peremint,* origin uncertain.

pedlar British spelling of **peddler**.

peedoodle probably a made-up word.

peel[1] (fruit skin) Old English *pilian* and French *pillier* take off, from Latin *pilare* make bald, from *pilus* hair.

peel[2] (baker's shovel) Middle English, from French *pele,* from Latin *pala* spade, shovel.

peel[3] (stake) Middle English *pel, pele,* from French *pel, piel* stake, from Latin *palus.*

peep[1] (sound) imitative.

peep[2] (look) Middle English *pepe.*

peer[1] (equal) French *per* of equal rank, from Latin *par* equal.

peer[2] (look) short for **appear**.

peevish Middle English *peyvsh.*

peg probably from Dutch *pegge* little wooden pin for attaching.

pejorative Latin *pejorare* make worse, from *pejor* worse.

pelerine French *pèlerin* a pilgrim, from Latin *peregrinus* foreign.

pelican Latin *pelicanus,* from Greek *pelekan,* from *pelekys* ax, from the way the pelican's bill looks.

pellet French *pelote* small ball, from Latin *pila* ball.

pell-mell French *pêle-mêle* mix, from *pesle-mesle,* from *mesler* mix.

pellucid Latin *pellucidus,* from *per-* through + *lucere* shine.

pelt[1] (strike) Latin *pillare* drive.

pelt[2] (animal skin) French *pelterie,* from *pel* skin, from Latin *pellis.*

peltry[1] (skins) See **pelt**[2].

peltry[2] (trash) See **paltry**.

pelvis Latin a basin.

pemmican Native American *pemikkan* fat meat, from *pimiy* fat.

pen[1] (writing tool) French *penne,* from Latin *penna* feather, because the earliest pens were made from feathers.

pen[2] (yard) Old English *penn.*

penal Latin *poena* punishment, from Greek *poine* penalty.

penalty Latin *poenalitas* punishment, from *poenalis.*

penance French *peneance,* from Latin *paenitentia* feel sorry for doing wrong.

pence British penny.

penchant French *pencher* lean, from Latin *pendere* hang.

pencil French *pincel* painter's brush, which looked like a little tail, from Latin *penis* tail.

pendant FRENCH *pendre* hang, from LATIN *pendere* hang.

pendulum LATIN *pendere* hang.

penetrate LATIN *penetrare* enter.

penguin probably from WELSH *pen gwyn* white head.

penicillin LATIN *penicillus* painter's brush, because the mold looks like that. See **pencil**.

peninsula LATIN *paeninsula,* from *paene* almost + *insula* island.

penis LATIN tail.

penitence FRENCH, from LATIN *paenitentia.* See **penance**.

pennant FRENCH *penne,* from LATIN *penna* a feather and FRENCH *penon* flag.

penny OLD ENGLISH *pening.*

pension FRENCH payment, from LATIN *pensio.*

pensive FRENCH *pensif,* from *penser* think, from LATIN *pensare* think about.

pent MIDDLE ENGLISH, from *penned.* See **pen**[2].

penta- GREEK, from *pente* five.

pentaprism See **penta-** + **prism**.

penteconter GREEK *penthkonthr*, from *pentekonta* fifty.

penthouse MIDDLE ENGLISH *pendize*, from FRENCH *pentiz*, from *apentis* attached building, from LATIN *appendicium*, from *appendere* hang.

penult LATIN *paenultima syllaba* last syllable but one, from *paene* almost + *ultimus* last.

penumbra LATIN *paene* almost + *umbra* shadow.

penury LATIN *penuria* want.

peon SPANISH foot soldier, from LATIN *pedo,* from *pes* foot.

peony OLD ENGLISH *peonie,* from LATIN *poenia,* from GREEK *palon* name given to Apollo, god of medicine, because of the flower's former medicinal use.

people FRENCH *pueple,* from LATIN *popularis.*

pep See **pepper**.

peplos GREEK.

pepper OLD ENGLISH *pipor,* from LATIN *piper,* from GREEK *peperi.*

per LATIN *per-* through, by.

per- LATIN *per-* through, by.

per capita LATIN *per capita* by heads.

perambulate LATIN *perambulare,* from *per-* through + *ambulare* walk.

percale FRENCH.

perceive FRENCH *percevoir,* from LATIN *percipere,* from *per-* through + *capere* take.

percent LATIN *per centum* for every hundred.

perception See **perceive**.

perch[1] (bird rest) from FRENCH *perche*, from LATIN *pertica* measuring rod.

perch[2] (fish) FRENCH *perche*, from LATIN *perca*, from GREEK *perke.*

perchloride See **per-** + **chlorine**.

percolate LATIN *percolare,* from *per-* through + *colare* strain.

percussion LATIN *percutere* strike.

perdition MIDDLE ENGLISH, from FRENCH *perdiciun,* from LATIN *perdere,* from *per-* thoroughly + *dare* give.

peregrinate LATIN *peregrinari,* from *peregrinus* traveling.

peregrine LATIN *peregrinus* traveling.

peremptory LATIN *peremptorius,* from *per-* thoroughly + *emere* take.

perennial LATIN *perennis,* from *per-* through + *annus* year.

perfect MIDDLE ENGLISH *parfit,* from FRENCH, from LATIN *perficere,* from *per-* completely + *facere* do, make.

perfidy FRENCH *perfidie,* from LATIN *perfidia,* from *per-* through + *fides* faith.

perforate LATIN *perforare,* from *per-* through + *forare* bore (make a hole by drilling).

perforce FRENCH *par force* by force, from LATIN *per-* by + **force**.

perform FRENCH *parformer* do, from *parfournir,* from LATIN *per-* through + *fournir* get done.

perfume FRENCH *parfumer,* from ITALIAN, from LATIN *per-* through + *funare* smoke.

perfunctory LATIN *perfunctorius,* from *per-* thoroughly + *fungi* perform.

pergola ITALIAN arbor, from LATIN *pergula* protecting cover.

perhaps See **per** + **hap**.

peri PERSIAN *pari* a beautiful female being descended from bad angels.

peridot FRENCH.

perihelion GREEK *peri* near + *helios* sun.

peril FRENCH danger, from LATIN *periculum.*

period FRENCH, from LATIN *periodus* sentence, from GREEK *periodos.*

periodontal GREEK *peri-* around + *odon* (*odontos*) tooth.

periphery FRENCH, from LATIN *peripheria,* from GREEK *periphereia,* from *peri-* around + *pherein* carry.

periscope GREEK *peri-* around + *skopein* examine.

perish FRENCH *perir* die, from LATIN *perire.*

peristyle FRENCH, from LATIN, from GREEK *peri-* around + *stylos* a column.

peritoneum GREEK *peritonaion* abdominal membrane, from *peri-* around + *teinein* stretch.

periwinkle[1] (plant) MIDDLE ENGLISH *parvink,* from OLD ENGLISH *perwince,* from LATIN *pervinca,* from *pervincire* entwine, bind, from *per-* thoroughly + *vincire* bind, fetter.

periwinkle[2] (snail) OLD ENGLISH *pinewincle,* from *pine* mussel, probably from LATIN *pina,* from GREEK *pine* + OLD ENGLISH *wincel* corner.

perjure FRENCH *parjurer,* from LATIN *perjurare,* from *per-* through + *jurare* swear.

perk FRENCH *perquer,* from LATIN *pertica* pole.

permanent FRENCH, from LATIN *permanere,* from *per-* through + *manere* remain.

permeate LATIN *permeare,* from *per-* through + *meare* glide.

permit LATIN *permittere,* from *per-* through + *mittere* send.

permutate LATIN *permutare,* from *per-* through + *mutare* change.

pernicious FRENCH *pernicieux,* from LATIN *pernicies,* from *per-* thoroughly + *necare* kill, from *nex* death.

peronall FRENCH *perron,* from LATIN *petra* stone.

peroxide See **per-** + **oxide**.

perpendicular FRENCH, from LATIN *perpendicularis* vertical, from *perpendere* balance carefully, from *per-* thoroughly + *pendere* hang.

perpetrate LATIN *perpetrare,* from *per-* thoroughly + *patrare* bring about.

perpetual FRENCH *perpetuel,* from LATIN *perpetuus* constant.

perplex FRENCH, from LATIN *perplexus* confused, from *per-* through + *plectere* twist.

perquisite LATIN *perquisitum,* from *perquirere,* from *per-* thoroughly + *quaerere* try to get.

persecute FRENCH *persecuter,* from LATIN *persequi,* from *per-* through + *sequi* follow.

persevere FRENCH *perseverer,* from LATIN *perseverare,* from *per-* thoroughly + *severus* severe.

persiflage FRENCH *persifler* make fun of.

persimmon NATIVE AMERICAN.

persist FRENCH, from LATIN *persistere,* from *per-* through + *sistere* make stand, from *stare* stand.

person FRENCH *persone* human being, from LATIN *persona,* from actor's mask.

personate LATIN *personatus,* from *persona* actor's mask.

personnel FRENCH.

perspective LATIN *perspicere,* from *per-* through + *specere* look.

Perspex LATIN *perspicere* look through, from *per* through + *specere* look (at).

perspicacious LATIN *perspicax,* from *perspicere,* from *per* through + *specere* look.

perspicacity FRENCH *perspicacité,* from LATIN *perspicacitas* discernment, from *perspicax* sharp-sighted, from *perspicere* look through.

perspire FRENCH, from LATIN *perspirare,* from *per-* through + *spirare* breathe.

persuade LATIN *persuadere,* from *per-* thoroughly + *suadere* urge.

pert FRENCH *aspert* able, from LATIN *expertus* experienced.

pertain FRENCH *partenir* belong, from LATIN *pertinere,* from *per-* thoroughly + *tenere* hold.

pertinent FRENCH, from LATIN *pertinere* belong.

perturb FRENCH, from LATIN *perturbare,* from *per-* thoroughly + *turbare* disturb.

peruse MIDDLE ENGLISH *perusen* use up, from LATIN *per-* thoroughly + MIDDLE ENGLISH *usen* use.

pervade LATIN *pervadere,* from *per-* through + *vadere* to go.

perverse FRENCH, from LATIN *pervertere* turn about.

pervert See **perverse**.

peso SPANISH, from LATIN *pendere* weigh.

pessary MIDDLE ENGLISH *pessarie,* from LATIN *pessarium,* from GREEK *pessarion,* from *pessos* oval stone.

pessimism FRENCH, from LATIN *pessimus* worst.

pest FRENCH *peste,* from LATIN *pestis* plague (deadly disease that spreads quickly).

pester FRENCH *empestrer* hobble (tie a horse's legs to keep it in one place), from LATIN *pastorum,* from *pastus* pasture.

pestilent LATIN *pestis* plague.

pestle FRENCH *pestel,* from LATIN *pistillum,* from *pinsere* pound.

pet SCOTTISH, of uncertain origin.

petal LATIN, from GREEK *petalos* spread out.

peter (dwindle) AMERICAN miners' slang, origin uncertain.

petiole LATIN *petiolus,* from *pes* foot.

petit FRENCH.

petition FRENCH *peticiun,* from LATIN *petitio,* from *petere* ask.

petrel possibly from LATIN *petrus.*

petrify FRENCH *pétrifier* turn into stone, from LATIN *petra* rock, from GREEK *petra* + LATIN *facere* do, make.

petro- GREEK *petra* a rock, or *petros* a stone.

petroglyph See **petro-** + GREEK *glyphe* carving.

petroleum LATIN rock oil, from *petra* rock, from GREEK *petra* + *oleum* oil.

petticoat FRENCH *petit* (small) + *cote* (coat), because it was originally a short coat for men worn under armor.

pettifogger MODERN ENGLISH *pettifactor*, from **petty** + **factor**.

petty FRENCH *petit* small.

petulant LATIN *petulans,* from *petere* attack.

pew FRENCH *pule,* from LATIN *podium* balcony, from GREEK *podion,* from *pous* foot.

pewter FRENCH *peutre* tin.

phaeton Greek myth of *Phaeton,* son of Helios (god of the sun) who tried to drive the chariot of the sun across the sky.

phalanx LATIN, from GREEK line of battle.

phantasm FRENCH, from LATIN, from GREEK *phantasma,* from *phantazein* show.

phantom FRENCH *fanto(s)me* ghost, from LATIN *phantasma,* from GREEK *phantazein* show.

pharaoh EGYPTIAN *pr-ʿo* great house.

pharmacy FRENCH *pharmacie,* from LATIN, from GREEK *pharmakon* drug.

pharyngeal See **pharynx** + **-al**.

pharyngitis See **pharynx** + **-itis**.

pharynx GREEK, from *pharyngos* windpipe, throat.

phase LATIN *phasis,* from GREEK *phainesthai* appear.

pheasant FRENCH *fesaunt,* from LATIN *phasiana,* from GREEK *phasianos,* from *Phasis* a river in eastern Asia where the bird was observed.

phenomenon LATIN *phaenomenon* appearance, from GREEK *phainesthai* appear.

philander GREEK *philos* loving + *andros,* from *aner* man.

philanthropy LATIN, from GREEK *philein* love + *anthropos* man.

philharmonic FRENCH *philharmonique* loving music, from ITALIAN, from GREEK *philos* loving + *harmonia* harmony.

philodendron GREEK, from *philodendros*, from *philo-* loving + *dendron* tree.

philology FRENCH, from LATIN, from GREEK *philologia* love of literature, from *philein* love + *logos* word, thought.

philomath GREEK *filos* friend, loving + *math* learn

philopena perhaps from GREEK *philo* a friend + LATIN *poena* penalty.

philosophy LATIN *philosphia* study of wisdom, from GREEK *philosophia*, from *philos* loving + *sophos* wise.

philter FRENCH *philtre*, from LATIN *philtrum*, from GREEK *philtron* love-charm, from *philein* love.

phlegm FRENCH *flemme,* from LATIN *phlegma* swelling, from GREEK *phlegein* burn.

phloem GERMAN, from GREEK *phloos* bark.

phobia LATIN, from GREEK *phobos* fear.

phoenix OLD ENGLISH *fenix,* from LATIN *phoenix,* from GREEK *phoinix.*

phoneme GREEK *phonema*, from *phonein*, from *phone* sound, voice.

phonetic LATIN *phoneticus,* from GREEK *phonetikos,* from *phone* sound.

phonic GREEK *phone* sound.

phony BRITISH *fawney* a ring said to be gold that wasn't, from IRISH *fainne* ring.

phosphorus LATIN *Phosphorus* morning star, from GREEK, from *phos* light + *pherein* carry.

photo- GREEK *phos* light.

photography See **photo-** + **-graphy**.

photovoltaic See **photo-** + **volt** + **-ic**.

phrase LATIN *phrasis,* from GREEK *phrasis* speech.

phrenology GREEK *phren* mind + *-logia,* from *logos* word.

phycology GREEK *phykos* seaweed +*-logia,* from *logos* word.

phylactery LATIN *phylacterium* charm, from GREEK *phylakterion.*

phylum LATIN, from GREEK *phylon* class.

physic MIDDLE ENGLISH art of healing, from FRENCH *fisike,* from LATIN *physica* study of nature, from GREEK *physis* nature, from *phyein* bring forth, produce, make grow.

physical MIDDLE ENGLISH, from LATIN *physicalis* of nature, natural, from *physica.* See **physic**.

physiology GREEK *physis* nature + *-logia,* from *logos* word.

pianoforte ITALIAN *piano* soft + *forte* loud, from LATIN *fortis* strong, because the piano can play loud and soft.

piazza ITALIAN, from LATIN *platea* courtyard, broad street, from GREEK *plateia* broad.

pick FRENCH *piquer* pierce.

picket FRENCH *piquet* pointed stake.

pickle DUTCH *pekel.*

picnic probably from FRENCH *pique* pick + *nique* a little bit.

pictograph LATIN *pictus* painted + GREEK *graphos.*

picture LATIN *pingere* paint.

picturesque FRENCH *pittoresque,* from ITALIAN *pittoresco* pictorial, from *pittore* painter, from LATIN *pictorem.*

picul MALAY *pikul* the heaviest load a man can carry on his back.

piddle MIDDLE ENGLISH *peddle,* work in a trifling way, origin uncertain.

pie OLD ENGLISH *pye.*

piece FRENCH, from LATIN *pecia* broken part.

pied MIDDLE ENGLISH *pie* magpie (bird), from LATIN *pica,* from *picus* woodpecker (in reference to the bird's black and white plumage).

piedmont ITALIAN *Piemonte* region in northern Italy, from *piede* foot + *monte* mountain.

pier LATIN *pera,* from *peira* stone.

pierce FRENCH *perc(i)er* make a hole, from LATIN *pertundere,* from *per-* through + *tundere* strike.

piety FRENCH *piete* good conduct, from LATIN *pietas.*

pig MIDDLE ENGLISH *pigge.*

pigeon FRENCH *pijon* young bird, from LATIN *pipio,* from *pipire* chirp.

piggin perhaps from MIDDLE ENGLISH *pig,* earthenware pot, origin uncertain.

pigment LATIN *pigmentum,* from *pingere* paint.

pike[1] (pick) OLD ENGLISH *pic* a pickax.

pike[2] (spear) FRENCH *pique,* from *pic* sharp point or spike.

pike[3] (highway) See **turnpike**.

pike[4] (fish) from **pike**[2], from its long, pointed jaw.

pilau Persian *pilaw.*

pile[1] (heap) Latin *pila* stone barrier.

pile[2] (cloth nap) French *pyle*, from Latin *pilus* hair.

pile[3] (big stake) Old English *pil*, from Latin *pilum* heavy javelin.

pileate Latin *pileus* cap.

pilfer French *pelfrer,* from *pelfre* booty (things taken in a robbery).

pilgrim French *pelerin,* from Latin *peregrinus* foreign.

pillage French *piller* rob.

pillar French *piler*, from Latin *pilare*, from *pila.*

pillion Latin *pellis* a skin.

pillory French *pilori.*

pillow Old English *pyle.*

pilot French *pilote,* from Italian *pilota,* from Greek *pedon* rudder for steering a boat.

pimpernel French, from Latin *piper* pepper.

pimple Old English *pypel.*

pin Old English *pinn.*

pinafore Modern English *pin* + *afore* on the front (it was originally pinned to a dress front).

pince-nez French nose-pincher.

pincers French *pinecure*, from *pincier* pinch.

pinch French *pincier.*

pindar Dutch *piendel,* from African *mpinda* peanut.

pindling American, perhaps from *piddling.* See **piddle**.

pine[1] (tree) Old English *pin,* from Latin *pinus.*

pine[2] (want) Old English *pinian* torment, from Latin *poena,* from Greek *poine.*

pineal French *pinéal,* from Latin *pinea* pine cone, from *pinus* pine tree.

pinion[1] (feather) French *pignon*, from Latin *penna* wing.

pinion[2] (small gear) French *pignon*, from crenellation, battlement, from Latin *pinna.*

pink[1] (color) Middle English *pink* plant name, possibly from Dutch *pink* small.

pink[2] (cut) Middle English *pink* pierce, stab, make holes in.

pinnace French, from Spanish, from Latin *pinus* pine.

pinnacle Middle English *pinacle,* from French, from Latin *pinnaculum,* from *pinna* feather.

piñon Spanish, from Latin *pinus* pine.

pint French, from Latin *pinta,* probably originally a painted spot marking the level in a measure.

pinto Spanish, from Latin *pingere* paint.

pioneer French *pionnier,* from *peon* foot soldier, from Latin *pedo,* from *pes* foot.

pious Latin *pius.*

pip Middle English *pipin* seed of a fleshy fruit, from French *pepin.*

pipe Old English, from Old Norse *pipa*, from Latin *pipare* chirp.

piquant See **pique**.

pique French *piquer* prick.

piranha Portuguese *piranah*, from Native American *pira nya,* from *pira'ya* scissors.

pirate LATIN, from GREEK *peirates,* from *peiran* attack.

pirogue FRENCH, from SPANISH *piragua.*

pirouette FRENCH spinning top.

Pisces LATIN *piscis* fish.

pistachio ITALIAN *pistacchio,* from LATIN *pistacium* pistachio nut, from GREEK *pistakion,* from *pistake* pistachio tree, from PERSIAN *pista.*

pistil FRENCH, from LATIN *pistillum.*

pistol FRENCH *pistole* short firearm, of uncertain origin.

piston FRENCH, from ITALIAN *pistare* pound, from LATIN *pinsere.*

pit OLD ENGLISH *pytt,* from LATIN *puteus* a well.

pita Modern GREEK *petta* bread.

pitch[1] (throw) MIDDLE ENGLISH *picchen.*

pitch[2] (tar) OLD ENGLISH *pic,* from LATIN *pix.*

pith OLD ENGLISH *pitha* necessary part.

piton FRENCH a spike.

pittance FRENCH *pitance* allowance of food, from LATIN *pietas* religious works and duties.

pituitary LATIN *pituitarius* mucous, from *pituita* phlegm, mucus.

pity FRENCH *pite,* from LATIN *pietas* good conduct, kindness.

pivot FRENCH hinge.

pizza ITALIAN pie.

placard FRENCH poster, from *plaquer* stick on, from DUTCH *placken* a piece.

placate LATIN *placare.*

place MIDDLE ENGLISH, from OLD ENGLISH place, open space, from LATIN *platea* wide street, from GREEK *plateia hodos* flat, level road.

placebo LATIN I shall please.

placenta LATIN a cake, from GREEK *plax* a flat object.

placid LATIN *placidus.*

placket[1] (plan, map) probably from FRENCH *plaquette* tablet, from *plaque* thin plate.

placket[2] (clothing) probably from MIDDLE ENGLISH *placard,* armor breastplate, perhaps related to **pocket**.

plagiarism LATIN *plagiarius* kidnapper.

plague FRENCH, from LATIN *plaga,* from GREEK *plege* bad fortune.

plaid SCOTTISH *plaide* blanket.

plain FRENCH flat, from LATIN *planus.*

plaintiff FRENCH *plaintif.* See **plaintive**.

plaintive FRENCH *plaintif* complaining, from LATIN *planctus.*

plait FRENCH *pleit,* from LATIN *plicare* fold.

plan FRENCH ground plan, from LATIN *planus* flat.

planchette FRENCH small board, from *planche* plank.

plane LATIN *planum* level surface.

planet MIDDLE ENGLISH, from FRENCH *planete,* from LATIN *planeta,* from GREEK *planetes* wanderer.

planetarium See **planet** + LATIN *-arium* a place for.

plank FRENCH *planke* board, from LATIN *planca.*

plankton GERMAN, from GREEK *planktos* wandering, from *plazesthai* wander.

plant OLD ENGLISH *plante,* from LATIN *planta.*

plantain SPANISH *pla(n)tano* plane tree, from LATIN *platanus* plane.

plantation LATIN *plantare* plant.

plaque FRENCH, from DUTCH *plake* disk (something thin, flat and round).

plash OLD ENGLISH *plæsc* pool of water, puddle.

plasma LATIN image, from GREEK. See **plastic**.

plaster OLD ENGLISH, from LATIN *implastrum*, from GREEK *emplastron*, from *emplassein* cover with something sticky.

plastic LATIN *plasticus* forming, from GREEK *plastikos*, from *plassein* form.

plasticine See **plastic** + **-ine**[1].

plastron FRENCH, from ITALIAN *piastra* thin plate of metal.

plate FRENCH *plat* flat, from GREEK *platys*.

plateau FRENCH *plat* flat. See **plate**.

platen MIDDLE ENGLISH *plateine*, from FRENCH *platine* metal plate, from *plat* flat.

platform FRENCH *plateforme*, from *plat* flat + *forme* form.

platinum SPANISH *plata* silver, from FRENCH *plate* something flat. See **plate**.

platitude FRENCH *plat* flat. See **plate**.

Platonic MIDDLE ENGLISH, from LATIN *Platonicus*, from GREEK *Platonikos*, from *Platon* Plato (429-347 B.C.), Greek philosopher.

platoon FRENCH *peloton* a ball, group, from *pelote* small ball, from LATIN *pila* ball.

platter FRENCH *plater* dish, from *plat* flat. See **plate**.

platypus LATIN, from GREEK *platypous* flat-footed, from *platys* broad, flat + *pous* foot.

plaudit LATIN *plaudere* applaud.

plausible LATIN *plausibilis* deserving applause, from *plaudere* applaud.

play OLD ENGLISH *pleg(i)an*.

plaza SPANISH, town square or gathering place, from LATIN *platea*, wide street.

plea FRENCH *plaid* discussion, from LATIN *placitum* opinion, from *placere* be pleasing.

pleasant FRENCH *plaisir* be agreeable. See **please**.

please FRENCH *plaisir* be agreeable, from LATIN *placere* be pleasing.

plebian LATIN *plebs* common people.

plebiscite FRENCH *plébiscite*, from LATIN *plebiscitum* a decree or resolution of the people, from *plebis* the common people + *scitum* decree, from *scire* know.

plectrum LATIN, from GREEK *plektron* thing to strike with, from *plek-*, from *plessein* strike.

pledge MIDDLE ENGLISH *plegge* bail, a guarantee, from FRENCH *plege*, from Latin *plebere*, from *pleo* fulfill.

pledget origin uncertain, possibly from MIDDLE ENGLISH *plug*, from DUTCH *plagge* patch of cloth.

plenitude FRENCH, from LATIN *plenus* full.

plenty FRENCH *plente*, from LATIN *plentas*, from *plenus* full.

plenum LATIN *plenum spatium* full space, from *plenus* complete, full.

plethora LATIN, from GREEK *plethos* fullness.

plew FRENCH *poil* hair.

pliable FRENCH *plier* bend, from LATIN *plicare* fold.

plight FRENCH *pleit* a fold, condition.

plinth FRENCH *plinthe*, from LATIN *plinthus*, from GREEK *plinthos* brick, squared stone.

plod imitative.

plop imitative.

plot OLD ENGLISH piece of ground.

plouter SCOTTISH, origin uncertain.

plover FRENCH *plover,* from *plovier*, from LATIN *plovarius*, from *pluvia* rain.

plow MIDDLE ENGLISH *ploh,* from OLD ENGLISH *plog,* from OLD NORSE *plogr.*

pluck OLD ENGLISH *pluccian* pull off.

plug DUTCH *plugge* wooden peg.

plum OLD ENGLISH *plume.*

plumage FRENCH, from LATIN *pluma* feather.

plumb FRENCH *plomb,* from LATIN *plumbum* lead (heavy, soft metal).

plume FRENCH, from LATIN *pluma* feather.

plummet FRENCH *plommet.* See **plumb.**

plump[1] (rounded) DUTCH *plomp* not pointed.

plump[2] (drop) imitative.

plunder GERMAN baggage.

plunge FRENCH *plongier* sink, from LATIN *plumbum.* See **plumb.**

plunk imitative.

plural LATIN *pluralis,* from *plus* more.

plus LATIN *plus* more.

plush FRENCH *peluche,* from LATIN *pilus* hair.

plutocracy GREEK *ploutokratia*, from *ploutos* wealth + *-kratia* rule, from *kratos* rule, power.

plutonic GREEK *Pluto* Greek god of the underworld.

ply See **apply.**

pneumatic LATIN, from GREEK *pneuma* breath.

pneumonia LATIN, from GREEK *pneumon* lung, from *pnein* breathe.

poach[1] (cook egg) FRENCH *pochier* put in a bag, from *poche* pocket.

poach[2] (steal) FRENCH *pocher,* from *pochier* walk on.

pocket FRENCH *pokete* little bag, from *poke* bag.

pod MIDDLE ENGLISH *podware, codware,* from OLD ENGLISH *cod* husk of seeded plants.

podiatry GREEK *pous* foot + *iatreia* art of healing.

podium LATIN, from GREEK *podion,* from *pous* foot.

poem FRENCH, from LATIN *poema,* from GREEK *poiema,* from *poiein* make.

poesimeter apparently an invented word.

pogrom RUSSIAN destruction.

poignant FRENCH *poindre* prick, from LATIN *pungere.*

poinsettia Joel R. *Poinsett* U.S. ambassador to Mexico, who brought the plant to the attention of botanists.

point FRENCH mark, from LATIN *pungere* prick.

poise FRENCH *poiser* weigh, from LATIN *pensare.*

poison FRENCH, from LATIN *potio.*

poke[1] (action) DUTCH *poken.*

poke[2] (sack) FRENCH *poke,* from *poche* pocket, purse.

poke[3] (tobacco) NATIVE AMERICAN *puck* smoke.

poker[1] (card game) possibly from GERMAN *poche*, from *pochen* brag.

poker[2] (metal rod) See **poke**[1].

Polaris LATIN *stella polaris* pole star.

pole[1] (long stick) OLD ENGLISH *pal* stake (stick for putting in the ground), from LATIN *pallus.*

pole[2] (earth axis) LATIN *polus* end of an axis, from GREEK *polos* axis.

polemic FRENCH, from GREEK *polemos* war.

police FRENCH, from LATIN *politia* government, the state, from GREEK *politeia,* from *polis* city.

policy FRENCH *policie* government, from LATIN *politia.* See **police**.

polio LATIN *poliomyelitis,* from GREEK *polios* gray + *myelos* marrow (the soft tissue inside bones).

polish FRENCH *polir* make smooth, from LATIN *polire.*

polite LATIN *polire* make smooth.

politic FRENCH *politique* political, from LATIN *politicus* state, from GREEK *politikos,* from *polis* city.

polka SLAVIC *Polka,* name for the dance, literal meaning "Polish woman."

poll MIDDLE ENGLISH *pol(le)* head, from the idea of counting heads, from DUTCH.

pollard See **poll** + *-ard* in reference to the coin having a head on it.

pollen LATIN dust.

polliwog MIDDLE ENGLISH *polwygle,* from *pol* head + *wiglen* wiggle.

pollock SCOTTISH *podlok.*

pollute LATIN *polluere.*

polo CHINESE *pulu* ball.

polonaise FRENCH *danse polonais* a Polish dance, from *Pologne* Poland, from LATIN Polonia.

polonium LATIN *Polonia* Poland, by the Polish scientist Marie Curie who co-discovered it.

poltergeist GERMAN *poltern* make a noise + *Geist* ghost.

poltroon FRENCH *poultron* rascal, coward, from ITALIAN *poltrone* lazy fellow, coward.

poly- GREEK *polys* much, many.

polychrome FRENCH of many colors, from GREEK *polys* many + *chroma* color.

polyethylene See **poly-** + GREEK *aithein* burn + LATIN *-enus,* from GREEK *-enos.*

polygamy GREEK *polygamia,* from *polys* many + *gamos* marriage.

polymer GREEK *polymeres,* from *polys* many + *meros* part.

polyp FRENCH *polype,* from LATIN *polypus* octopus, from GREEK *polypous* many-footed, from *polys* many + *pous* foot.

polyphony GREEK *polyphonia,* from *polys* many + *phone* sound.

pomade FRENCH, from ITALIAN *pomata,* from LATIN *pomum* fruit.

pome FRENCH *pome* apple.

pomegranate See **pome** + FRENCH *granade,* from LATIN *granatum* having seeds.

pomelé See **pomely**.

pomelo See **pome**.

pomely FRENCH *pomelé* marked with round spots, from *pomel* little apple.

pommel FRENCH *pomel* rounded part on the handle of a sword, from LATIN *pomum* apple.

pomp LATIN *pompa,* from GREEK *pompe.*

pompadour Madame *Pompadour* (1721–1764), a friend of one of the kings of France, she made the style popular.

pompous LATIN *pomposus,* from *pompa.* See **pomp**.

poncho SPANISH *pontho* woolen cloth.

pond MIDDLE ENGLISH, from OLD ENGLISH *pund.*

ponder FRENCH, from LATIN *ponderare* weigh, from *pondus* a weight.

ponderous LATIN *ponderosus* heavy, from *pondus* a weight.

pone NATIVE AMERICAN.

pontiff FRENCH *pontif* high priest in ancient Rome, from LATIN *pontifex,* from *pons* bridge + *facere* do, make.

pontificate LATIN *pontifex,* from *pons* bridge + *facere* do, make.

pontoon FRENCH *ponton* low flat boat, from LATIN *pons* bridge.

pony FRENCH *poulenet,* from LATIN *pullus* young animal.

poodle GERMAN *Pudel,* from *pudeln* splash in water. The dogs were originally used to find and bring back water birds shot by hunters.

pooka IRISH *puca,* from OLD ENGLISH *puki.*

pool[1] (water) OLD ENGLISH *pol* small body of water.

pool[2] (game) FRENCH *poule* stake (money or something that can be won as part of a bet), hen (possible stake in early times), from LATIN *pullus* young bird.

poop deck FRENCH, from LATIN *puppis.*

poor FRENCH *povre,* from LATIN *pauper.*

pop imitative.

pope OLD ENGLISH *papa* father, from GREEK *papas.*

popinjay FRENCH *papagal,* from ARABIC *babagha* parrot.

poplar FRENCH *poplier,* from LATIN *popularius.*

poppy OLD ENGLISH *popæg,* from LATIN *papaver.*

populace FRENCH, from LATIN *populus* the people.

popular LATIN *populus* the people.

population LATIN *populare* live in.

porcelain FRENCH *porcelaine* china, from ITALIAN *porcellana,* from LATIN *porcus* pig, because the china was thought to look a bit like a pig's back.

porch FRENCH, from LATIN *porticus,* from *porta* a gate.

porcupine FRENCH *porc espin* thorny pig, from LATIN *porcus* pig + *spina* thorn.

pore[1] (small opening) FRENCH, from LATIN *porus,* from GREEK *poros.*

pore[2] (read over) MIDDLE ENGLISH *pouren.*

porgy AMERICAN, probably from earlier *pargo,* from SPANISH *pargo,* from LATIN *phagrum,* from GREEK *phagros* sea bream.

pork FRENCH *porc* pig, from LATIN *porcus.*

porpoise FRENCH *porpeis,* from LATIN *porcus* pig + *piscis* fish.

porridge MIDDLE ENGLISH *porrey,* from LATIN *porrata* vegetable soup, from *porrum* vegetable.

porringer FRENCH *potager,* from *potage,* from *pot* pot.

port OLD ENGLISH, from LATIN *portus* harbor.

portable LATIN *portabilis,* from *portare* carry.

portage FRENCH *potager,* from *potage,* from *pot* pot.

portal FRENCH, from LATIN *portale* like a gate, from *porta* door, gate.

portcullis FRENCH *porte colice* sliding gate, from LATIN *porta* gate + *colare* filter (something with spaces in it for things to go through).

portend LATIN *portendere* predict.

portent LATIN *portentum* sign.

porter[1] (baggage carrier) FRENCH *porteur* bearer, from LATIN *portator,* from *portare* carry.

porter[2] (doorkeeper) FRENCH *portier* gatekeeper, from LATIN *portarius* doorkeeper, from *porta* gate, door.

portfolio ITALIAN *portafoglio* wallet, from LATIN *portare* carry + *folium* sheet of paper.

portico ITALIAN, from LATIN *porticus.* See **porch**.

portion FRENCH share, from LATIN *portio.*

portmanteau FRENCH suitcase, cloak carrier (person who carried the king's cloak), from *porter* carry + *manteau* cloak.

portrait FRENCH *portraire* draw. See **portray**.

portray FRENCH *portraire,* from LATIN *protrahere,* from *pro-* forth + *trahere* draw.

pose[1] (position) FRENCH *poser,* from LATIN *pausare* halt.

pose[2] (confuse) FRENCH *aposer* set beside, from LATIN *apponer* place to.

posh probably from BRITISH *posh* dandy (a man who is very particular about his clothes).

position FRENCH, from LATIN *positio* placing.

positive FRENCH, from LATIN *positivus* settled by agreement, from *ponere* place.

posse LATIN from *posse comitatus,* literally "the power of the country," in medieval England the body of men a sheriff could call into service to help carry out the law, from *posse* have power.

possess FRENCH, from LATIN *possidere.*

posset MIDDLE ENGLISH *possot,* origin uncertain.

possible LATIN *possibilis,* from *posse* be able.

post- LATIN after.

post[1] (wood) OLD ENGLISH *post,* from LATIN *postis.*

post[2] (soldier's place of duty) FRENCH *poste* station, from ITALIAN *posto,* from LATIN *ponere* place.

post[3] (mail) FRENCH *poste,* from ITALIAN *ponere* place, from the early custom of mail being moved by carriers from one relay place to another.

posterior LATIN *posterus* following, from *post* after.

posterity MIDDLE ENGLISH *posterite*, from LATIN *posterus* following, from *post* after.

postern FRENCH *posterne* back door to a fort, from LATIN *posterus* coming after.

posthumous LATIN *postumus* lastborn (after the death of the father), from *post-* after + *humare* bury.

postilion FRENCH *postillon*, from ITALIAN *postiglione*, from *posta* mail + LATIN *-ilio.*

post-mortem LATIN after death.

postpone LATIN *postponere,* from *post-* after + *ponere* put.

postscript LATIN *postscribere,* from *post-* after + *scribere* write.

postulate LATIN *postulare* demand.

posture FRENCH situation, from ITALIAN *postura,* from LATIN *positura* position, from *ponere* put.

pot OLD ENGLISH *pott* deep container.

potable LATIN *potabilis,* from *potare* drink.

potash DUTCH *pot* pot + *asch* ash.

potassium LATIN *potassa* potash.

potent LATIN *potentis,* from *posse* be able, from *potis* able.

potentate LATIN *potentatus*, from *potentem* powerful.

potential MIDDLE ENGLISH *potenciall,* from LATIN *potentia*. See **potent**.

pother Middle English *pudder,* origin unknown.

potpourri French *pot pourri* stew, translation from Spanish *olla podrida,* from Latin *olla* pot + *putridus* rotten, probably from food being cooked until it looked "rotten."

potsy origin uncertain, possibly from **pot**.

pottage French *potage,* from *pot* pot.

pottery French *poterie,* from *potier* potter, from Latin *potaria* pottery.

pouch French *po(u)che* bag.

poultice Latin *pultes* thick, soft food, from *puls.*

poultry French *poulet* young chicken, from Latin *pullus* young animal.

pounce Middle English *ponson* sharp tool, from French *poinçon,* from Latin *punctio* pierce.

pound[1] (beat) Old English *punian* beat.

pound[2] (money) Old English *pund* English money, from Latin *pondo* by weight.

pound[3] (stray animals) Old English *pund* place fenced in.

pour Middle English *pouren.*

pout Middle English *pouten.*

poverty French *poverte,* from Latin *pauper* poor.

powder French *poudre,* from Latin *pulvis* dust.

power French *pöer* ability to act, from Latin *potis* able.

power net See **power** + **network**.

powerful See **power** + **-ful**.

powwow Native American shaman, medicine man, from a word meaning to dream.

practical Latin *practicus.* See **practice**.

practice French *pratiquer,* from Latin, from Greek *practikos* practical, from *prassein* do.

pragmatic Latin *pragmaticus* skilled in business, from Greek *pragmatikos,* from *pragma* business, from *prassein* do.

prairie French meadow, from Latin *pratum.*

praise French *preisier* value, from Latin *pretium* worth.

prance Middle English, originally of horses, origin uncertain, perhaps related to Middle English *pranken* show off, from Dutch *pronken* strut, parade.

prank Middle English, origin uncertain.

prate Dutch *praten* chatter.

pratfall Middle English *prat* buttocks + Old English *feallan* drop.

prattle German *prateien.*

pray French *prier,* from Latin *precari* call upon, from *prex* prayer.

pre- Latin *prae-* before.

preach French *prechier,* from Latin *praedicare,* from *prae-* before + *dicare* say out loud.

preamble French *preambule,* from Latin *praembulus* walking in front, from *prae-* before + *ambulare* walk.

precarious Latin *precarius* doubtful, from *prex* prayer.

precaution French, from Latin *praecautio,* from *praecavere,* from *prae-* before + *cavere* take care.

precede French, from Latin *praecedere,* from *prae-* before + *cedere* go.

precedent Latin *praecedere* go before. See **precede**.

precept Latin *praecipere* teach, from *prae-* before + *capere* take.

precinct LATIN *praecinctum* boundary, from *praecingere,* from *prae-* before + *cingere* be around.

precious FRENCH *precios,* from LATIN *pretiosus,* from *pretium* a price.

precipice FRENCH, from LATIN *praeceps,* from *prae-* before + *caput* a head.

precipitance See **precipitate.**

precipitate LATIN *praecipitare* throw down, from *praeceps,* from *prae-* before + *caput* a head.

précis FRENCH, from LATIN *praecidere.* See **precise.**

precise FRENCH *precis,* from LATIN *praecidere* cut off, from *prae-* before + *caedere* cut.

preclude LATIN *praecludere,* from *prae-* before + *claudere* close.

precocious LATIN *praecox* ripen early, from *prae-* before + *coquere* cook, ripen.

precursor LATIN *praecurrere* run ahead.

predatory LATIN *praedari* a prey.

predecessor FRENCH, from LATIN *prae-* before + *decessor* officer who is retiring, from *decedere,* from *de-* from + *cedere* go.

predicament LATIN *praedicamentum,* from *praedicare* say out loud. See **preach.**

predicate LATIN *praedicare* say out loud. See **preach.**

predict LATIN *praedicere,* from *prae-* before + *dicere* tell.

preemption LATIN *preemere,* from *prae-* before + *emere* buy.

preen OLD ENGLISH *proinen.*

preface FRENCH introduction to a book, from LATIN *praefatio,* from *prae-* before + *fari* speak.

prefect LATIN *praefectus* commander, from *prae-* before + *facere* do, make.

prefer FRENCH, from LATIN *praeferre,* from *prae-* before + *ferre* bring.

prefix LATIN *praefixum,* from *praefigere* fix in front, from *prae-* before + *figere* fix.

pregnant LATIN *praegnans,* from *prae-* before + *gnasci* be born.

prejudice FRENCH, from LATIN *praejudicium,* from *prae-* before + *judicium* judgment.

preliminary FRENCH *préliminaire,* from LATIN *prae-* before + *limen* threshold (piece of wood underneath the door).

prelude FRENCH introduction, from *prae-* before + *ludere* play.

premier FRENCH, from LATIN *primarius* chief, from *primus* first.

premise LATIN *praemissa,* from *praemittere,* from *prae-* before + *mittere* send.

premium LATIN *prae-* before + *emere* take.

premonition LATIN *praemonitio* warn in advance, from *praemonere,* from *prae-* before + *monere* warn.

preordain See **pre-** + **ordain.**

prepare LATIN *praeparare,* from *prae-* before + *parare* prepare.

preposition LATIN *praepositio,* from *prae-* before + *ponere* place.

preposterous LATIN *praeposterus,* from *prae-* before + *posterus* coming after.

prerogative LATIN *praerogativus,* from *prae-* before + *rogare* ask.

presage LATIN *praesagium,* from *prae-* before + *sagire* become aware of.

prescribe LATIN *praescribere,* from *prae-* before + *scribere* write.

present FRENCH *presence,* from LATIN *praesentia,* from *prae-* before + *esse* be.

preserve Middle English keep safe, from French *preserver,* from Latin *praeservare* observe beforehand, from *prae* before + *servare* observe, guard.

preside Latin *praesidere,* from *prae-* before + *sedere* sit.

president Latin *praesidens* ruler, from *praesidere.* See **preside.**

press French *presser* crush, from Latin *premere* press.

pressure French, from Latin *pressura,* from *premere* press.

prestige Latin *praestigium* trick.

presume Latin *praesumere,* from *prae-* before + *sumere* take.

pretend Latin *praetendere,* from *prae-* before + *tendere* stretch.

pretense French, from Latin *praetendere.* See **pretend.**

pretentious French *prétentieux,* from Latin *praetendere.* See **pretend.**

pretext Latin *praetexere* pretend. See **pretend.**

pretty Old English *prætt* a trick.

pretzel German *brizilla.*

prevail Latin *praevalere* have greater power, from *prae-* before + *valere* be strong.

prevalent Latin *praevalere.* See **prevail.**

prevent Latin *praevenire,* from *prae-* before + *venire* come.

previous Latin *praevius,* from *prae-* before + *via* a way.

prey French *preie,* from Latin *praeda* take by force.

price French *pris* value, from Latin *pretium* value.

prick Old English *prica* point.

pride Old English *pryte.*

priest Old English *preost,* from Greek *presbyteros,* from *presbys* old, from respect to the elders.

prig Middle English *prigger* thief, origin uncertain.

prim French, from Latin *primus* first.

prima donna Latin first lady.

Primacord See **primer** + **cord.**

primal Latin *primalis,* from *primus* first.

primary Latin *primarius,* from *primus* first.

prime French, from Latin *primus* first.

primer Latin *primarius liber* basic book, from *primarius* first in order.

primeval Latin *primaevus,* from *primus* first + *aevum* an age + French, from Latin *alis.*

primitive French *primitif,* from Latin *primitivus* earliest of that kind, from *primus* first.

primogeniture Latin *primus* first + *geniture* produce.

prince French, from Latin *princeps* leader, from *primus* first + *capere* take.

principal French, from Latin *principalis* chief, from *princeps.* See **prince.**

principle French, from Latin *principium,* from *princeps.* See **prince.**

prink apparently a variation of **prank.**

print French *preinte* stamp, from *preindre,* from Latin *premere* bear down on.

prior Latin sooner.

prism Latin *prisma,* from Greek something sawed, from *priein* saw.

prison French, from Latin *prensio,* from *prehendere* take.

prissy blend of **prim** and **sissy**.

pristine LATIN *pristinus* former.

prithee obsolete form of "I pray thee".

private LATIN *privatus* belonging to the person and not the state.

privet[1] (plant) MIDDLE ENGLISH *primet, primprint*, origin unknown.

privet[2] (surgical tool) FRENCH *esprouvette*, from *esprouver* try, search out.

privilege LATIN *privilegium* law for or against a person, from *privus* one's own + *lex* law.

prize[1] (reward) MIDDLE ENGLISH *prise*. See **price**.

prize[2] (pry loose) MIDDLE ENGLISH *prise*, from FRENCH *prise* take hold, grasp.

pro LATIN in favor of.

pro- LATIN in favor of, for, before, instead of, forward.

probable FRENCH, from LATIN *probare* prove.

probang MODERN ENGLISH *provang*, the name given by the inventor, later changed to *probang* to be like the word **probe**.

probate LATIN *probare*. See **probe**.

probe LATIN *proba* proof, from *probare* test, from *probus* proper.

problem FRENCH *probleme*, from LATIN *problema*, from GREEK *pro-* forward + *ballein* throw.

proboscis LATIN *proboscis*, from GREEK *proboskis* elephant's trunk, from *pro* forward + *boskein* feed, from *boskesthai* graze, be fed.

proceed LATIN *procedure*, from *pro-* forward + *cedere* go.

process FRENCH *proces*, from LATIN *procedere*. See **proceed**.

proclaim FRENCH, from LATIN *proclamare*, from *pro-* before + *clamare* cry out.

procrastinate LATIN *procrastinare*, from *pro-* forward + *cras* tomorrow.

procreate LATIN *procreare*, from *pro-* before + *creare* create.

proctor MIDDLE ENGLISH *procuratour*, from LATIN *procurare*, from *pro-* for + *curare* attend to, from *cura* a care.

procure FRENCH, from LATIN *procurare*, from *pro-* for + *curare* attend to, from *cura* a care.

prod MIDDLE ENGLISH poke with a stick, possibly from *brod*, from *brodden* goad, from OLD NORSE *broddr* shaft, spike.

prodigal FRENCH, from LATIN *prodigalis* wasteful, from *prodigus*, from *pro-* before + *agere* drive.

prodigious See **prodigy**.

prodigy LATIN *prodigium* omen.

produce LATIN *producere*, from *pro-* forward + *ducere* lead.

product LATIN *producere*. See **produce**.

profane FRENCH, from LATIN *profanus* not holy, from *pro-* before + *fanum* temple (place to pray).

profess LATIN *profiteri*, from *pro-* before + *fateri* say openly.

proficient LATIN *proficere*, from *pro-* forward + *facere* do, make.

profile ITALIAN *profilo* side view, from LATIN *pro-* before + *filum* thread (like a thin line).

profit FRENCH advantage, from LATIN *profectus*, from *pro-* forward + *facere* do, make.

profligate LATIN *profligare*, from *pro-* forward + *fligere* drive.

profound FRENCH *profond* deep, from LATIN *profundus*, from *pro-* forward + *fundus* bottom.

profuse LATIN *profundere,* from *pro-* forth + *fundere* pour.

prog[1] (knife) MODERN ENGLISH, origin uncertain, but see **prod.**

prog[2] (food) BRITISH, origin unknown (that which is got by progging). See **prog**[3].

prog[3] (forage) BRITTISH, origin unknown (to poke about or search for food, etc.). See **prog**[1].

progenitor FRENCH *progeniteur,* from LATIN *progenitor,* from *pro-* forth + *gignere* produce.

prognosis LATIN, from GREEK *pro-* before + *gignoskein* know.

program LATIN *programma,* from GREEK public notice, from *pro-* before + *graphein* write.

progress LATIN *progressus,* from *pro-* before + *gradi* step.

prohibit LATIN *prohibere* prevent, from *pro-* before + *habere* have.

project LATIN *proicere,* from *pro-* before + *jacere* throw.

prokaryote FRENCH *procaryote,* from GREEK, from *pro-* before + *karyotos* having nuts, from *karyon* nut.

proletariat FRENCH *prolétariat,* from LATIN *proletarius* citizen of the lowest class, from *proles* offspring, progeny.

proliferate See **profile.**

prolific LATIN *prolifer,* from *proles* children + *ferre* bring.

prolong FRENCH, from LATIN *pro-* forth + *longus* long.

promenade FRENCH *promener* walk, from LATIN *prominare,* from *pro-* forward + *minare* herd.

prominent LATIN *prominere* project, from *pro-* forward + *minere* cause to stick out.

promise LATIN *promissum,* from *pro-* before + *mittere* send.

promontory LATIN *promonturium,* probably from *prominere* project (throw forward).

promote LATIN *promovere,* from *pro-* before + *movere* move.

prompt FRENCH, from LATIN *promere,* from *pro-* forth + *emere* take.

promulgate LATIN *promulgare,* from *pro-* before + *vulgus* the people.

prone MIDDLE ENGLISH, from LATIN *pronus* bent forward, inclined to.

prong MIDDLE ENGLISH, from LATIN *pronga* prong, pointed tool.

pronoun FRENCH, from LATIN *pronomine* instead of a noun.

pronounce FRENCH *prononcier,* from LATIN *pronuntiare* announce, from *nuntius* messenger.

proof FRENCH *prueve,* from LATIN *proba,* from *probare* test.

prop DUTCH *proppe* a support.

propaganda LATIN *propaganda fide prospagate* "tell the people about the faith," from early religious efforts to get more people to come to church.

propel LATIN *propellere* push forward, from pro- forward + *pellere* drive.

propensity LATIN *propendere* hang forward, from *pro-* forward + *pendere* hang.

proper FRENCH *propre,* from LATIN *proprius* one's own.

property FRENCH *propriete,* from LATIN *proprietas* owner.

prophecy FRENCH *profecie,* from LATIN, from GREEK *prophetes.* See **prophet.**

prophet LATIN *propheta,* from GREEK *prophetes,* from *pro-* before + *phanai* speak.

prophylactic GREEK *prophylaktikos* precautionary, from *prophylassein* keep guard before, from *pro-* before + *phylassein* guard.

propitiate LATIN *propitius,* from *pro-* before + *petere* seek.

propitious FRENCH *propicius,* from LATIN *propitius,* from *pro-* before + *petere* seek.

proponent LATIN *proponere,* from *pro-* before + *ponere* place.

proportion FRENCH, from LATIN *proportone,* from *pro-* for + *portio* a part.

propose FRENCH *proposer* put forth, from LATIN *proponere.* See **proponent**.

proprietary LATIN *proprietas.* See **property**.

propriety LATIN *proprietas.* See **property**.

propulsion LATIN *propellere.* See **propel**.

prosaic LATIN *prosaicus,* from *prosa.* See **prose**.

proscenium LATIN *proscaenium*, from GREEK *proskenion* in front of the scenery, from *pro* in front + *skene* stage, tent.

proscribe LATIN *proscribere* publish in writing, from *pro-* before + *scribere* write.

prose FRENCH, from LATIN *prosaoratio* direct speech.

prosecute LATIN *prosequi* go after, from *pro-* before + *sequi* follow.

prospect LATIN *prospectus* view, from *pro-* before + *specere* look.

prosper LATIN *prosperare* make happy.

prosthesis LATIN, from GREEK *pros* to + *tithenai* place.

prostrate LATIN *prosternere,* from *pro-* before + *sternere* stretch out.

protect LATIN *protegere*, from *pro-* before + *tegere* cover.

protégé FRENCH *protéger,* from LATIN. See **protect**.

protein GERMAN, from FRENCH, from GREEK *proteios* primary, from *protos* first.

protest FRENCH *protester* say in public, from LATIN *protestari,* from *pro-* before + *testari,* from *testis* a witness.

protocol FRENCH *protocole* first writing of an important paper, from LATIN, from GREEK *protokollon,* from *protos* first + *kolla* glue, from an early practice of gluing the first sheet (which stated the date and the author's name) to an important piece of writing.

protoplasm GERMAN *Protoplasma*, from GREEK *proto-* first + *plasma* something molded.

protozoa LATIN, from GREEK *protos* first + *zoia,* from *zoion* animal.

protract LATIN *protrahere,* from *pro-* before + *trahere* draw.

protrude LATIN *protrudere,* from *pro-* before + *trudere* push forward.

protuberant LATIN *protuberantem*, from *protuberare* swell, bulge, from *pro-* forward + *tuber* lump, swelling.

proud OLD ENGLISH *prud* value oneself, from FRENCH *prod,* from LATIN *prode,* from *prodesse,* from *pro-* forward + *esse* be.

prove FRENCH *prover,* from LATIN *probare* test.

provender FRENCH, from LATIN *praebenda* state support to a private person, from *praebere* give.

proverb FRENCH, from LATIN *proverbium,* from *pro-* before + *verbum* a word.

provide LATIN *providere* look after, from *pro-* before + *videre* see.

province FRENCH, from LATIN *provincia* Roman territory.

provision French, from Latin *provisio.* See **provide**.

provoke French, from Latin *provocare,* from *pro-* before + *vocare* call, from *vox* voice.

provost Old English and French, from Latin *propositus,* from *praepositus* chief, from *prae-* before + *ponere* place.

prow French *proue,* from Latin *prora,* from Greek *proira.*

prowess French *prouesse,* from *prou* brave. See **proud**.

prowl Middle English *prollen.*

proximate Latin *proximare* come near, from *proximus* nearest.

proxy Middle English *procuracle* office of a procurator (in the Roman Empire, an administrator for a district).

prude French *prudefemme* woman who is respected, from Latin *prode* useful + *femina* woman.

prudent French, from Latin *prudens* skilled.

prune[1] (cut) Middle English *prouyne*, from French *proignier* cut back (vines).

prune[2] (fruit) French *pronne* plum, from Latin *pruna,* from Greek *proumnon.*

pry Middle English *prien.*

psalm Old English, from Latin *psalmus,* from Greek *psalmodia* song sung to a harp.

pseudonym French, from Greek *pseudonymon,* from *pseudes* false + *onyma* name.

pshaw imitative.

psychedelic Greek *psyche* soul + *delein* make clear to the senses.

psychiatry Greek *psyche* soul + *iatreia* art of healing.

psycho- Greek *psyche* soul.

psychology See **psycho-** + **-logy**.

psychometer See **psycho-** + **meter**.

ptarmigan Scottish *tarmachan.*

pterodactyl Latin, from Greek *pteron* wing + *daktylos* a finger.

puberty Middle English, from French *puberté*, from Latin *pubertas,* from *pubes* adult.

pubescent Latin *pubescentia*, from *pubescentem*, from *pubescere* reach puberty, from *pubes* adult.

public Latin *publicus,* from *populus* the people.

publish French *publier* make public, from Latin *publicare.*

puce French a flea, from the color, from Latin *pulex* flea.

pucker French *poque.*

pudding Middle English *puddyng* sausage, from Old English *puduc* swelling.

puddle Old English *pudd* a ditch.

pudgy British from *pudge* something that is short and thick.

pueblo Spanish, from Latin *populus* people.

puff Old English *pyff.*

pug Middle English, origin uncertain.

pugilism Latin *pugil* boxer.

pugnacious Latin *pugnax,* from *pugnare* fight.

pule French *piaule* cheep, chirp, whine.

pull Old English *pullian* pluck.

pulley French *po(u)lie,* from Greek *polos* axis.

pulmonary Latin *pulmo* a lung.

pulp Latin *pulpa* fleshy part.

pulpit Latin *pulpitum* platform.

pulsate Latin *pulsare* beat.

pulse FRENCH, from LATIN *pellere* beat.

pulverize LATIN *pulverizare* make into dust, from *pulvis* dust.

pulvino ITALIAN *pulvino.*

pummel See **pommel**.

pump DUTCH *pompe* pipe of wood, from SPANISH *bomba.*

pumpernickel GERMAN *Pumpernickel* a word for people who aren't agreeable (the bread has a slightly sour taste).

pumpkin FRENCH, from LATIN, from GREEK *pepon* ripe.

pun MODERN ENGLISH, origin uncertain, perhaps from ITALIAN *puntiglio* trivial objection, from LATIN *punctum* point.

punch[1] (hit) MIDDLE ENGLISH *punchen.*

punch[2] (drink) HINDI *pac* five, it originally had five ingredients.

puncheon FRENCH, from LATIN *pungere* pierce.

punctilious ITALIAN *puntiglio* fine point, from LATIN *punctum.*

punctual LATIN *punctualis,* from *punctum* point.

punctuate LATIN *punctuare,* from *punctum* point.

puncture LATIN *pungere* pierce.

pungent See **puncture**.

pungle SPANISH *póngale* put down, from *poner* put, give.

punish FRENCH *punis,* from LATIN *punire.*

punt[1] (kick) Rugby football rules, from *punt* strike, from *bunt* butt with the head.

punt[2] (boat) OLD ENGLISH, from LATIN *ponto.*

puny FRENCH *puîné,* from *puisné* younger, from *puis* afterward + *né* born.

pupa LATIN doll.

pupil LATIN *pupillus,* from *pupus* boy and *pupa* girl.

puppet MIDDLE ENGLISH *popet,* from LATIN *pupa* girl, doll.

purchase FRENCH *purchacer,* from LATIN *pro-* before + *captare* try to catch.

pure FRENCH *pur,* from LATIN *purus* clean.

purfle MIDDLE ENGLISH *purfilen,* from FRENCH *porfiler,* from LATIN *profilare,* from *pro-* forth + *filum* thread.

purge FRENCH *purg(i)er* make pure, from LATIN *purgare.*

Puritan See **purity**.

purity FRENCH *purte,* from LATIN *purus* pure.

purl MIDDLE ENGLISH *pirl* twist threads into a cord.

purloin FRENCH *purloigner* delay, from LATIN *pur-* for + *loin* far.

purple OLD ENGLISH, from LATIN *purpura,* from GREEK *porphyra* shellfish that produces purple dye.

purpose FRENCH *purpos,* from LATIN *proponere,* from *pro-* before + *ponere* place.

purse OLD ENGLISH *purs,* from LATIN *bursa,* from GREEK *byrsa* skin used to make purses.

purslane FRENCH, from LATIN *porcilaca,* from *portulaca.*

pursue FRENCH *pursuer,* from LATIN *prosequi,* from *pro-* forth + *sequi* follow.

pursuivant FRENCH *poursuir.* See **pursue**.

purview FRENCH *purveu,* from LATIN *providere.* See **provide**.

push FRENCH *pousser,* from LATIN *pulsare.*

putrescent LATIN *putrescere* become rotten, from *putris* rotten.

putrid Latin *putridus,* from *putirere* be rotten.

putty French *potée* potful, from *pot* pot.

puzzle Middle English *pusle* bewilder, confound; possibly from **pose**[2].

pylon Greek gateway.

pyogenesis Greek *pyon* pus + **genesis**.

pyometra Greek *pyon* pus + *metra* womb.

pyracantha Latin, from Greek *pyrakantha*, from *pyr-* fire + *akantha* thorn, thorny plant.

pyramid Middle English, from Latin *pyramis,* from Greek *puramis,* origin unknown.

pyre Latin *pyra,* from Greek *pyra* fire.

pyrites Latin, from Greek. See **pyre**.

pyro- See **pyre**.

pyrometer See **pyro-** + **meter**.

q.v. Latin *quod vide.*

quack[1] (duck sound) imitative.

quack[2] (faker) Dutch *quacksalver* one who brags about his medicines, from *quacken* brag + *zalf* salve (greasy medicine for burns, etc.).

quadrant Latin *quadrans* fourth part.

quadri- Latin *quattuor* four.

quadrilateral Latin *quadrilaterus,* from *quottuor* four + *lateralis* from *latus* side.

quaff possibly from German *quassen* eat or drink too much.

quagmire earlier *quag* marsh + Old Norse *myrr* swamp.

quail[1] (bird) Middle English *quayle*, from French *quaille*, from German *quahtala.*

quail[2] (cower) Middle English *quail* curdle, from French *coailler*, from Latin *coagulare* coagulate.

quaint French *queinte* neat, from Latin *cognitus* known.

quake Old English *cwacian* shake.

qualify Latin *qualificare,* from *qualis* of what kind + *facere* do, make.

quality French *qualité,* from Latin *qualis* of what kind.

qualm Old English *cwealm* disaster.

quandary possibly from Latin *quando* when.

quantity French, from Latin *quantitas* amount.

quarantine Italian *quarantina,* from *quaranta* forty (the number of days some foreign ships had to wait before unloading), from Latin *quadraginta.*

quarrel French *querele* argument, from Latin *querela.*

quarry[1] (stone) French *quarriere,* from Latin *quadraria,* from *quadrus* square.

quarry[2] (in hunting) French *cuiree* parts of a dead animal given to dogs after the hunt, from *cuir* skin, from Latin *covium.*

quart French *quarte,* from Latin *quartus* fourth.

quartan Middle English *quartaine*, from French, from Latin *quartus* fourth (fever supposedly occurring every fourth day).

quarter French *quartier,* from Latin *quartus* fourth.

quartet French, from Italian *quarto,* from Latin *quartus* fourth.

quartic Latin *quartus* fourth + French *-ique,* from Latin *-icus,* from Greek *-ikos.*

quash French, from Latin *quassare* shatter, from *quatere* break.

quaver Middle English *cwafien.*

quay French *cai.*

queasy Middle English *coysy,* perhaps influenced by French *queisier*, from *coisier* make uneasy.

queen Old English *cwen.*

queer Middle English, from Scottish, perhaps from German *queer* oblique, off-center.

quell French *cwellan* kill.

quench Old English *acwencan* go out.

quern Old English *cweorn.*

querulous Latin *queri* complain.

query Latin *quaerere* look for.

quest French *queste* search, from Latin *quesita,* from *quaerere* look for.

question French, from Latin *quaestio* looking for, from *quaerere* ask.

queue French *coue,* from Latin *cauda* tail.

quibble Latin *quibus* who, which (formerly common in legal papers).

quiche French, from German *Küche*, from *Kuchen* cake.

quick Old English *cwic* alive.

quiet French, from Latin *quietus* keep quiet, from *quies* rest.

quill probably from German.

quillon French cross-guard of a sword.

quince Middle English *quyn,* from French, from Latin, from Greek *kydonion.*

quinine Spanish *quina*, bark of the cinchona tree, from Quechua *kina* bark.

quinsy Latin *quin(e)sie,* from *quinacia,* from *cynache*, from Greek *knyanche* sore throat.

quintal French, from Arabic *quintar,* from Latin *centenarius* amounting to 100.

quintic Latin *quintus* fifth + French *-ique,* from Latin *-icus,* from Greek *-ikos.*

quip possibly from Latin *quippe* indeed (used to make fun).

quirk Middle English evasion, perhaps from German *quer* odd. See **queer**.

quirl See **curl**.

quit French *quite,* from Latin *quietus* at rest.

quite Middle English completely, from French freed. See **quit**.

quittor Middle English *quiture*, from French *cuiture* act of boiling, from Latin *coctura* boiling liquid, from *coctus*, from *coquere* cook.

quiver[1] (shake) imitative.

quiver[2] (for arrows) French *quivre.*

quiz possibly from Latin *quis* what.

quoit Middle English *coyte* flat stone, quoit, from French *coilte, coite*, from Latin *culcita* cushion.

quonset *Quonset* Point, Rhode Island, where it was first made.

quorum Latin.

quota Latin share, from *quota pars* how great a part.

quote Latin *quotare,* from *quot* how many.

quotidian Latin *quotidianus* daily, from *quotus* how many, as many as + *dies* day.

quotient Latin *quoties* how often, from *quot* how many.

R

rabbi LATIN, from GREEK, from HEBREW my master.

rabble MIDDLE ENGLISH pack of animals.

rabid LATIN *rabere* rage.

rabies LATIN madness.

raccoon NATIVE AMERICAN *arakun* scratcher.

race[1] (run) OLD NORSE *ras* running.

race[2] (people) FRENCH, from ITALIAN *razza* kind, possibly from ARABIC *ra's* origin.

raceme LATIN *racemes* cluster of grapes.

rack possibly from DUTCH *rek,* from *recken* stretch.

racket[1] (noise) imitative.

racket[2] (frame) FRENCH *raquette* frame, from *rachette* palm of the hand, from ARABIC *raha.*

raconteur FRENCH *raconter* recount, from *re-* + *aconter*, from *a-* to + *conter* tell.

racquet See **racket**[2].

radar *ra*(dio) *d*(etection) *a*(nd) *r*(anging).

raddle FRENCH *reddalle,* origin uncertain.

radiant LATIN *radiare* send out light, from *radius* a spoke (as of a wheel), or a beam (as of light).

radiate See **radius.**

radical LATIN *radicalis* having roots, from *radix* root.

radicle LATIN *radicula,* from *radix* root.

radio short for **radiotelegraphy**.

radio- LATIN *radius* ray.

radiotelegraphy See **radio-** + **tele-** + **-grapy.**

radish OLD ENGLISH *rædic,* from LATIN *radix* root.

radium LATIN. See **radius.**

radius LATIN measuring rod, ray.

raffle FRENCH *rafle* game of dice, from GERMAN *raffel* a rake.

raft OLD NORSE *raptr.*

rafter OLD ENGLISH *ræfter.*

rag[1] (cloth) MIDDLE ENGLISH *ragge,* from OLD NORSE *rögg* bit of fur.

rag[2] (scold, tease) slang, of unknown origin.

ragamuffin MIDDLE ENGLISH *raggi* ragged + possibly DUTCH *muffe* mitten.

rage FRENCH, from LATIN *rabies.*

raglan Lord *Raglan*, the British commander in the Crimean war.

ragwort See **rag**[1] + OLD ENGLISH *wyrt* a root.

raid Middle English *ra(i)de,* from Old English *rad* journey.

rail French, from Latin *regula* a rule.

raillery French *raillerie,* from *railler,* from Latin *ragere* yell + French *-erie,* from Latin *-aria.*

raiment French *araiement,* from *arayer* array (put in order).

rain Old English *regn.*

raise Old Norse *reisa.*

rajah Hindi, from Sanskrit *rajan* king.

rake Old English *raca* tool.

rale French *raler* rattling sound in the throat.

rally French *rallier* put together, from Latin *re-* again + *alier* join.

Ramadan Arabic *ramadan* the hot month, from *ramada* be hot.

ramble Middle English *romblen,* from *romen* roam.

rambunctious origin uncertain.

ramekin French *ramequin.*

ramify French *ramifier,* from Latin *ramus* branch + *facere* do, make.

ramp French *rampe* slope, from *ramper* climb.

rampage See **ramp** + **age**.

rampant French *ramper* climb.

rampart French *re-* again + *emparer* defend, from Latin *ante-* before + *parare* prepare.

ramshackle See **ransack**.

ranch: Spanish *rancho* small farm, originally group of people eating together.

rancid Latin *rancere* stinking.

rancor French, from Latin *rancere* stinking.

random French *randon* speed, from *randir* run with force.

range French *ranger* rank, from *renc* a row.

rank[1] (order) French *reng* row.

rank[2] (bad smell) Old English *ranc* strong.

rankle French *draoncle,* from Latin *dracunculus* a sore, from *draco* dragon.

ransack Old Norse *rann* a house + *sækja* search.

ransom French *raençon,* from Latin *redemptio,* from *redimere,* from *re-* back + *emere* get.

rant Dutch *ranten.*

rantipole possibly from **rant**.

rap imitative.

rapacious Modern English *rapacity*, from French *rapacité,* from Latin *rapacitatem* greediness, from *rapax* grasping, plundering, from *rapere* seize.

rape Middle English, from Latin *rapere* take with force.

rapid Latin *rapidus*, from *rapere*. See **rape**.

rapier French *rapière.*

rapport French *rapprocher* bring together, from Latin *re-* back + *ad-* to + *portare* carry.

rapscallion possibly from **rascal**.

rapt Latin *rapere* take with force.

rapture See **rapt** + **-ure**.

rare[1] (uncommon) Latin *rarus.*

rare[2] (in cooking) Old English *hrer* under-cooked.

rascal Middle English *rascaile* low class people, from French *rascaille* outcast, rabble.

rash[1] (careless) Middle English *rasch.*

rash[2] (skin spots) FRENCH *rasche,* from LATIN *rader* scrape.

rasher possibly from MIDDLE ENGLISH *rash* cut.

rasp FRENCH *rasper,* from GERMAN *raspon* scrape together.

ratchet FRENCH *rochet* bobbin, spindle, from ITALIAN *rocchetto* spool, ratchet, from *rocca* distaff.

rate[1] (amount) FRENCH price, from LATIN *rata,* from *reri* think.

rate[2] (scold) MIDDLE ENGLISH *raten.*

rather OLD ENGLISH *hrathor,* from *hræthe* quickly.

ratify FRENCH, from LATIN *ratus* rate + *facere* do, make.

ratio FRENCH *ration,* from LATIN *ratio* relation.

ration FRENCH, from LATIN *ratio.* See **reason.**

rational LATIN *rationalis* relating to reason, from *ratio.* See **reason.**

rattle MIDDLE ENGLISH *ratelen,* probably imitative.

rattlepated See **rattle** + **pate.**

rattling See **rattle.**

raucous LATIN *raucus.*

ravage FRENCH *ravir* carry away, from LATIN *rapere.*

rave FRENCH *raver.*

ravel DUTCH *ravelen* tangle up.

ravelin FRENCH, from ITALIAN *revellino.*

raven OLD ENGLISH *hræfn.*

ravenous FRENCH *ravineux* violent, from *raviner* destroy.

ravine FRENCH, from LATIN *rapina* forceful action.

ravish FRENCH *ravir,* from LATIN *rapere* seize.

raw OLD ENGLISH *hreaw* not cooked.

ray[1] (beam) See **radius.**

ray[2] (fish) FRENCH *raie,* from LATIN *raia.*

raye FRENCH *rayé.*

rayon probably from FRENCH *rayon* beam of light. See **ray**[1].

raze FRENCH *raser* shave, from LATIN *radere* scrape.

razor FRENCH *rasour,* from *raser.* See **raze.**

razzle-dazzle AMERICAN slang.

re- LATIN again, back.

reach OLD ENGLISH *ræcan* stretch out.

read OLD ENGLISH *rædan* understand writing.

ready OLD ENGLISH *ræde* prepared.

real FRENCH, from LATIN *realis* actual, from *res* thing.

realm FRENCH *realme* kingdom, from LATIN *regimen* rule, from *regalis* regal. See **regal.**

reap OLD ENGLISH *repan* cut grain.

rear[1] (back part) FRENCH *arere* backward, from *ad-* to + Germanic *retro* behind.

rear[2] (raise) OLD ENGLISH *ræran* raise.

reason FRENCH *raison,* from LATIN *reri* think.

reaver OLD ENGLISH *reafere.*

rebate FRENCH *rebattre* beat down again, from *re-* again + *abattre* beat down.

rebel FRENCH *rebeller* revolt (rise up against the government), from LATIN *rebellare,* from *re-* again + *bellare* make war.

rebound FRENCH *rebondir* leap back, from *re-* again + *bondir* leap.

rebuff ITALIAN *ribuffo* scolding, from LATIN *re-* back + *buffo* puff (sudden blow of air).

rebuke FRENCH *rebuker* turn back, from *re-* again + *buschier* cut wood, from *busche* log.

recalcitrant LATIN *recalcitrare* kick back, from *re-* back + *calx* heel.

recamier Madame *Récamier* who was portrayed reclining in one in a painting.

recant LATIN *recantare* sing again, from *re-* again + *cantare* sing.

recede LATIN *recedere,* from *re-* back + *cedere* go.

receipt FRENCH *receite* money paid, from LATIN *recepta*, from *recipere,* from *re-* back + *capere* take.

receive FRENCH *receivre* accept, from LATIN *recipere,* from *re-* back + *capere* take.

recent LATIN *recens* new.

receptacle LATIN *receptaculum.* See **receive**.

reception FRENCH, from LATIN *recipere.* See **receive**.

recess LATIN *recessus* going back.

recipe LATIN *recipere.* See **receive**.

reciprocal LATIN *reciprocus* returning.

recite LATIN *recitare* repeat from memory, from *re-* back + *ciere* wake up.

reckless OLD ENGLISH *reccan* care + *-leas.*

reckon OLD ENGLISH *(ge)recenian* explain.

reclaim FRENCH *reclamer* call back, from LATIN *re-* back + *clamare* call.

recluse FRENCH *reclure*, from LATIN *recludere,* from *re-* back + *claudere* shut.

recognize LATIN *recogoscere*, from *re-* again + *cognoscere* know.

recoil FRENCH *reculer* go back, from LATIN *re-* back + *culus* rump (hind part of an animal).

recommend LATIN *recommendare* trust with, from *re-* again + *commendare* trust with.

recompense LATIN *recompensare* reward, from *re-* back + *compensare* weigh together.

reconcile LATIN *reconciliare,* from *re-* back + *concillium* council.

reconnoiter FRENCH *reconnoitre*, from *re-* again + *cognoscere* know.

record FRENCH *recorder* remember, from LATIN *recordari,* from *re-* back + *cor* mind.

recoup FRENCH *recouper* cut back, from *re-* back + *couper* cut.

recourse FRENCH *recours,* from LATIN *recursus* running back. See **re-** + **course**.

recover FRENCH *recovrer* get again, from LATIN *recuperare.*

recreate LATIN *recreare* restore. See **re-** + **create**.

recriminate LATIN *reciminare* accuse someone, from *re-* again + *criminari* accuse.

recruit FRENCH *recruter,* from *recroître,* from LATIN *recrescere,* from *re-* again + *crescere* grow.

rectangle LATIN *rectangulus,* from *rectus* right + *angulus* angle.

rectify LATIN *rectificare*, from *rectus* right + *facere* do, make.

rectitude FRENCH, from LATIN *rectus* straight.

recumbent LATIN *recumbere,* from *re-* back + *cumbere* lie down.

recuperate LATIN *recuperare* recover.

recur LATIN *recurrere,* from *re-* back + *currere* run.

red OLD ENGLISH *read.*

reddy See **red** + **-y**[3].

redeem LATIN *redimere*, from *re-* back + *emere* get.

redolent LATIN *redolere,* from *re(d)-* thoroughly + *olere* smell.

redoubt FRENCH, from ITALIAN *ridotto,* from LATIN *reductus,* from *reducere,* from *re-* back + *ducere* lead.

redoubtable FRENCH *redouter* dread, fear, from *re-* an intensifying prefix + *douter* doubt, fear.

reduce LATIN *reducere,* from *re-* back + *ducere* lead.

redundant LATIN *redundare* flow over, from *re(d)-* thoroughly + *undare* rise.

reed OLD ENGLISH *hroed.*

reef DUTCH *rif,* from OLD NORSE *rif* ridge (upper part of something).

reel OLD ENGLISH *hreol* something used for winding silk or thread.

reeve OLD ENGLISH *gerefa.*

refer LATIN *referre,* from *re-* back + *ferre* bring.

refine LATIN *re-* back + *fine* make fine.

reflect LATIN *reflectere,* from *re-* back + *flectere* bend.

reflex LATIN *reflectere.* See **reflect**.

reform LATIN *reformare.* See **re-** + **form**.

refract LATIN *refringere,* from *re-* back + *frangere* break.

refrain[1] (hold back) FRENCH *refrener* bridle, from LATIN *refrenare,* from *re-* back + *frenum* bridle.

refrain[2] (verse) FRENCH *refraindre* repeat, from LATIN *refringere.* See **refract**.

refrigerate LATIN *refrigerare,* from *re(d)-* thoroughly + *frigerare* cool, from *frigus* cold.

refugee FRENCH *réfugié,* from LATIN *refugim* refuge (shelter).

refund LATIN *refundere,* from *re-* back + *fundere* pour.

refuse FRENCH *refuser* push back, from LATIN *refundere.* See **refund**.

refute LATIN *refutare* repel.

regal LATIN *regalis* royal, from *rex* king.

regale FRENCH *régaler* entertain, from FRENCH *gale* something that pleases, from DUTCH *wale* wealth.

regalia See **regal**.

regard FRENCH *regarder,* from *re-* back + *garder* watch over.

regenerate LATIN *regenerare* bring forth. See **re-** + **generate**.

regent LATIN *regens* ruler, from *regere* keep straight.

regimen FRENCH, from LATIN, from *regere* rule.

regiment LATIN *regimentus* rule, from *regere.* See **regimen**.

region LATIN *regio,* from *regere* rule. See **regal**.

register LATIN *regestum,* from *regerere* record.

regress LATIN *regredi,* from *re-* back + *gradi* go.

regret FRENCH *regreter* mourn.

regular LATIN *regularis* usual, from *regula* rule.

regulate LATIN *regulare* direct. See **regular**.

rehabilitate LATIN *rehabilitare,* from *re-* again + *habilis* fit.

rehearse FRENCH *rehercier* harrow (plow ground for raising crops) over and over, from *re-* again + *hercer* harrow, from LATIN *hirpex* rake, from *hirpus* wolf, from the way the metal teeth of the harrow look like wolf's teeth.

reign FRENCH *regne* kingdom, from LATIN *regnum.*

rein FRENCH *rene,* from LATIN *retinere,* from *re-* back + *tenere* hold.

reindeer OLD NORSE *hreinn* reindeer.

reinforce See **enforce**.

reiver See **reaver**.

reject LATIN *rejecere,* from *re-* again + *jacere* throw.

rejoice FRENCH *rejoir,* from *re-* again + *joir,* from LATIN *gaudere* joy.

relapse LATIN *relabi,* from *re-* back + *lapsus* fall.

relate LATIN *referre,* from *re-* back + *ferre* bring.

relative LATIN *relativus,* from *referre.* See **relate.**

relax LATIN *relaxare,* from *re-* back + *laxare* loosen, from *laxus* loose.

relay FRENCH *relais* set of fresh horses and dogs for a hunt, from *re-* back + *laier* leave, from LATIN *laxare* loosen.

release FRENCH *relaissier* leave behind, from LATIN *relaxare.* See **relax.**

relegate LATIN *relegare,* from *re-* back + *legare* send.

relevant FRENCH *relever* raise up, from LATIN *relevare.* See **relieve.**

relic FRENCH *reliques,* from LATIN *reliquiae* remains.

relief FRENCH restore, from *relever.* See **relieve.**

relieve FRENCH *relever,* from LATIN *relevare,* from *re-* again + *levare* raise, from *levis* light (not heavy).

religion FRENCH, from LATIN *religio,* from *re-* back + *ligare* bind.

relinquish FRENCH *relinquir* leave, from LATIN *relinquere,* from *re-* back + *quere* leave.

relish FRENCH *reles* remainder, from *relaissier.*

reluctant LATIN *reluctari,* from *re-* back + *luctari* struggle.

rely FRENCH *relier* bind together, from LATIN *religare,* from *re-* back + *ligare* bind.

remain FRENCH *remaindre,* from LATIN *remanere,* from *re-* back + *manere* stay.

remand LATIN *remandare,* from *re-* back + *mandare* order.

remark FRENCH *remarquer,* from *re-* again + *marquer* mark.

remedy LATIN *remedium* medicine.

remember FRENCH *remembrer,* from LATIN *rememorari,* from *re-* again + *memor* mindful (keeping something in mind).

reminiscence LATIN *reminiscentia,* from *reminisci,* from *re-* again + *memini* remember.

remiss See **remit.**

remit LATIN *remittere,* from *re-* back + *mittere* send.

remnant FRENCH *remanant,* from *remanoir,* from LATIN *remanere.* See **remain.**

remonstrate LATIN *remonstrare,* from *re-* again + *monstrare* show.

remorse LATIN *remordere,* from *re-* again + *mordere* bite, as if chewing over something in your mind that is worrying you.

remote LATIN *removere.* See **re-** + **move.**

remoulade FRENCH *rémoulade.*

remove FRENCH *remouvoir,* from LATIN *removere* move back. See **re-** + **move.**

remuda SPANISH *remudar* change, from LATIN *mutare.*

remunerate LATIN *remunerare* repay, from *re-* again + *munus* a gift.

renaissance FRENCH rebirth, from *re-* again + *naître,* from LATIN *nasci* be born.

render FRENCH *rendre,* from LATIN *reddere,* from *re-* back + *dare* give.

rendezvous French *se rendre* take yourself to.

rendition French *rendre.* See **render**.

renegade Spanish *renegado* one who denies, from Latin *re-* again + *negare* deny.

renege Latin *renegare* deny. See **renegade**.

renounce French *renoncer,* from *re-* back + *nuntiare* tell, from *nuntius* messenger.

renovate Latin *renovare,* from *re-* again + *novare* make new, from *novus* new.

renown French *renoun,* from Latin *re-* again + *nomen* name.

rent[1] (money) French *rente,* from Latin *rendere* render.

rent[2] (torn) Middle English *renten* tear, rend.

repair[1] (mend) Latin *reparare,* from *re-* again + *parare* prepare.

repair[2] (go) Middle English, from French *repairer*, from *repadrer*, from Latin *repatriare* return to one's own country.

reparation Latin *reparationem*, from *reparatus*, from *reparare* restore.

repeat Latin *repetere,* from *re-* again + *petere* seek.

repent French *repentir,* from Latin *re-* again + *paenitere* cause to be sorry.

repercussion See **re-** + **percussion**.

repertoire French list, from Latin *repertorium,* from *reperire* discover.

replenish French, from Latin *replenir*, from *re-* again + *plenus* full.

replete French, from Latin *replere,* from *re-* again + *plere* fill.

reply French *replier* fold back, from Latin *replicare,* from *re-* back + *placere* fold.

report French, from Latin *reportare,* from *re-* back + *portare* carry.

repose French *reposer* rest, from Latin *re-* again + *pausare* cause to rest.

represent Latin *repraesentare.* See **re-** + **present**.

repress Latin *reprimere,* from *re-* back + *premere* press.

reprieve Middle English *reproven* test again. See **reprove**.

reprimand French *réprimande,* from Latin *reprimere*, from *re-* back + *premere* press.

reprise French, from Latin *reprendre* take back.

reproach French *reprochier* blame, from Latin *re-* again + *prope* near.

reprobate Latin *reprobare,* from *re-* again + *probare* test.

reproduce See **re-** + **produce**.

reprove Middle English, from French *reprover* blame, from Latin *reprobare* disapprove, condemn, from *re-* reversal or opposite of + *probare* prove worthy.

reptile Latin *reptilis* creeping, from *repere* creep.

republic Latin *respublica* state, public thing.

repudiate Latin *repudiare* put away.

repugnance French, from Latin *repugnare,* from *re-* back + *pugnare* fight.

repulse Latin *repellere,* from *re-* back + *pellere* drive.

reputation See **repute**.

repute French, from Latin *reputatio,* from *reputare,* from *re-* again + *putare* think.

request French *requerre* ask, from Latin *requirere.* See **require**.

require Latin *requirere* ask for, from *re-* again + *quaerere* ask.

requisite See **require.**

requite See **re-** + **quit.**

rerebrace French *rerebras,* from *rere-* back + *bras* arm.

rescind Latin *rescindere,* from *re-* back + *scindere* cut.

rescue French *rescourre* save, from Latin *re-* back + *excutere* drive away.

research French *recerche,* from *re-* again + *cerchier* seek.

resemble French *re-* again + *sembler,* from Latin *simulare,* from *simul* same.

resent French *ressentir,* from Latin *re-* back + *sentire* feel.

reserve Latin *reservare,* from *re-* back + *servare* hold.

reservoir French, from Latin *reservare.* See **reserve.**

reside Latin *residere,* from *re-* back + *sedere* sit.

residue French, from Latin *residere,* from *re-* back + *sedere* sit.

resign French *resigner,* from Latin *resignare,* from *re-* back + *signare* sign.

resilient Latin *resilire,* from *re-* back + *salire* jump.

resin Latin *resina* sap from trees, from Greek *rhetine.*

resist Latin *resistere,* from *re-* back + *sistere* set, from *stare* stand.

resolute Latin *resolvere* separate. See **re-** + **solve.**

resolve See **re-** + **solve.**

resonant Latin *resonare* sound again.

resort French *resortir,* from *re-* again + *sortir* go out.

resource French *ressource,* from *resourdre,* from *re-* again + *sourdre* spring up, from Latin *surgere* rise.

respect Latin *respicere,* from *re-* back + *specere* look at.

respite French *respit,* from Latin *respicere.* See **respect.**

respond Latin *respondere,* from *re-* back + *spondere* pledge.

responsible Latin *respondere.* See **respond.**

rest[1] (quiet) Old English *rest* quiet.

rest[2] (remainder) French *reste,* from *rester* remain, from Latin *restare,* from *re-* back + *stare* stand.

restaurant French *restaurer* restore. See **restore.**

restitution French, from Latin *restituere* restore, from *re-* again + *statuere* set up.

restive French *restif* stubborn, from *rester* remain. See **rest**[2].

restore French *restorer,* from Latin *restaurare,* from *re-* again + *staurare* place.

restrain French *restraindre,* from Latin *restringere,* from *re-* back + *stringere* draw tight.

restrict Latin *restringere.* See **restrain.**

result Latin *resultare* spring back, from *resilire,* from *re-* back + *salire* jump.

resume Latin *resumere,* from *re-* again + *sumere* take.

résumé French *résumer,* from Latin *resumere.* See **resume.**

resurrection Latin *resurrectio,* from *resurgere* rise again.

resuscitate Latin *rescuscitare,* from *re-* again + *suscitare* revive (bring back to life).

retail French *retaille* cut up, from *re-* again + *tailler* cut, from the idea of selling things in small amounts.

retain French *retenir,* from Latin *retinere,* from *re-* back + *tenere* hold.

retaliate Latin *retaliare,* from *re-* back + *talio* punishment of the same kind.

retch Old English *hræcan* clear the throat.

reticent Latin *reticere,* from *re-* again + *tacere* be silent.

reticulate Latin *reticulatus* having a net-like pattern, from **reticulum.**

reticule French, from Latin **reticulum.**

reticulum Latin, from *rete* net.

retinue French *retenir.* See **retain.**

retire French *retirer,* from *re-* back + *tirer* draw, pull.

retort Latin *retorquere,* from *re-* back + *torquere* twist back.

retreat French *retraite,* from *retaire,* from Latin *retrahere,* from *re-* back + *trahere* draw.

retrieve French *retrover,* from *re-* again + *trover* find.

retrospect Latin *retrospicere,* from *retro-* back + *specere* look.

return French *retourner.* See **re-** + **turn.**

reveal Latin *revelare* draw back the veil, from *re-* back + *velum* a veil.

revel French *reveler* make merry, from Latin *rebellare.* See **rebel.**

revenge French *revengier,* from Latin *re-* again + *vindicare* avenge (get even for a wrong).

revenue French *revenir* return, from Latin *revenire,* from *re-* back + *venire* come.

reverberate Latin *re-* again + *verberare* beat, from *verber* a whip.

revere Latin *revereri* respect.

reverie French *rever* wander.

reverse French *revers,* from Latin *reversus,* from *revertere.* See **revert.**

revert French *revertir,* from Latin *revertere* turn back, from *re-* back + *vertere* turn.

review French *revue,* from *revoir,* from Latin *re-* again + *videre* see.

revise Latin *revisere,* from *re-* again + *videre* see.

revive Latin *revivere,* from *re-* again + *vivere* live.

revoke Latin *revocare,* from *re-* back + *vocare* call.

revolt French *révolter,* from Italian *rivoltare,* from Latin *revolvere.* See **revolve.**

revolve Latin *revolvere,* from *re-* back + *volvere* roll.

revue French.

reward French *rewarder,* from *regarder* look at. See **regard.**

rhapsody Latin *rhapsodia* part of epic (long serious poem), from Greek *rhapsodia* epic poem, from *rhaptein* stitch together + *oide* song.

rhetoric Latin *rhetorica* art of oratory (formal public speech), from Greek *rhetorike techne* rhetorical art, from *rhetor* orator.

rheumatism Latin *rheumatismus,* from Greek *rheumatismos.*

rhinestone French *caillou de Rhin* pebble of the Rhine (a river in Germany), because the gems were first cut and made into stones there.

rhinoceros Latin, from Greek *rhis* nose + *keras* horn.

rhizome LATIN, from GREEK *rhiza* a root.

rhizopod See **rhizome** + GREEK *-pod* foot.

rhododendron LATIN, from GREEK *rhodon* a rose + *dendron* a tree.

rhombus LATIN, from GREEK *rhombos*, from *rhembesthai* spin, whirl.

rhubarb FRENCH *rubarbe,* from LATIN *reubarbum*, from GREEK *rheon* rhubarb + *barbaron* foreign.

rhyme FRENCH *rime.*

rhythm LATIN *rhythmus,* from GREEK *rhythmos* measured time, from *rhein* flow.

ribbon FRENCH *riban.*

rich MIDDLE ENGLISH, from OLD ENGLISH *rice* wealthy. See **regal**.

rick OLD ENGLISH *hreac.*

rickets MIDDLE ENGLISH, origin uncertain.

rickety See **rickets**.

rickshaw See **jinrikisha**.

rictus LATIN open mouth or jaws.

riddle OLD ENGLISH *rædels* puzzle.

ride OLD ENGLISH *ridan.*

ridge OLD ENGLISH *hrycg* back of a man or animal.

ridicule FRENCH *riducule,* from LATIN *ridiculum,* from *ridere* laugh.

rife OLD ENGLISH *ryfe* more than enough.

riffle AMERICAN make choppy water, perhaps from *ruffle* make rough.

riff-raff FRENCH *rit et raf* one and all.

rifle[1] (gun) FRENCH *rifler* scrape, from GERMAN *riffeln* scratch.

rifle[2] (search) FRENCH *rif(f)ler* rob.

rift DANISH *rive* tear.

rig MIDDLE ENGLISH *riggen,* from SCANDINAVIAN.

right OLD ENGLISH *riht* straight.

righteous OLD ENGLISH *rihtwis,* from *riht* good + *wis(e)* manner.

rigid LATIN *rigidus* stiff.

rigmarole MIDDLE ENGLISH *rageman rolle* a long list.

rigor FRENCH, from LATIN *rigere* be rigid.

riksha See **jinrikisha**.

rile AMERICAN *roil.*

rim OLD ENGLISH *rima* border.

rime OLD ENGLISH *hrim.*

rind OLD ENGLISH.

ring[1] (circle) OLD ENGLISH *hring* circle.

ring[2] (bell sound) OLD ENGLISH *hringan* clear sound.

rink FRENCH *renc* range.

rinse FRENCH *raincier* clean with water, from LATIN *recens* fresh.

riot FRENCH *riote* argument, from *rihoter.*

rip possibly from DUTCH *rippen* tear.

ripe OLD ENGLISH ready to be gathered.

ripple MODERN ENGLISH ruffle a surface, unknown origin, perhaps from **rip**.

rise OLD ENGLISH *risan* go up.

risible LATIN *risibilis,* from *ridere* laugh.

risk FRENCH *risque* danger, from ITALIAN *risico,* from *riscare* go out where there might be danger.

risqué FRENCH *risquer* risk.

rite LATIN *ritus* custom.

ritual LATIN *ritualis,* from *ritus* religious ceremony.

rival LATIN *rivalis* neighbor, using the same stream as another, from *rivus* a brook.

rive[1] (stab) OLD NORSE *rifa.*

rive[2] (arrive) FRENCH *river.* See **arrive**.

river FRENCH *riverre,* from LATIN *riparius,* from *ripa* bank of a stream.

rivet FRENCH small rod, from *river* attach.

rivulet ITALIAN *rivolo* brook, from LATIN *rivus.*

roam MIDDLE ENGLISH *romen.*

roan FRENCH, from early Spanish *roano.*

roar OLD ENGLISH *rarian.*

roast FRENCH *rostir* cook with a fire.

rob FRENCH *rob(b)er* steal.

robe FRENCH things taken in a robbery. In early times robbers often stole clothes.

robin FRENCH diminutive of *Robert.*

robot central European *robota* forced labor, from *rabu* servant.

robust LATIN *robustus,* from *robur* oak.

rock[1] (stone) MIDDLE ENGLISH *rokke*, from FRENCH *roche,* from LATIN *rocca.*

rock[2] (move back and forth) MIDDLE ENGLISH *rocken*, from OLD ENGLISH *roccian.*

rocket ITALIAN *rocchetta* a spool, from *rocca* a staff for spinning, from GERMAN.

rococo FRENCH *rococo*, from *rocaille* shellwork (referring to the use of shell designs).

rod OLD ENGLISH *rodd.*

rodent LATIN *rodere* chew to pieces.

rodeo SPANISH *rodear* surround, from LATIN *rotare* rotate.

rogue MIDDLE ENGLISH beggar, likely from LATIN *rogare* ask or beg

roil origin uncertain, probably from FRENCH *rouiller*, from *rouil* mud, rust, from LATIN *robigo* rust.

roister FRENCH *rustre* one who brags or cheats, from LATIN *rusticus*, from *rus* the country.

role FRENCH *rôle* actor's part, from LATIN *rotula* little wheel. See **roll**.

roll FRENCH *roller,* from LATIN *rotula* little wheel, from *rota* wheel.

romance FRENCH *romanz* work written in a Romance language (one that came from Latin, such as French, Italian, Spanish) from LATIN *Romanus* relating to Rome.

romany GYPSY *romani, romano*, from *rom* man, Gypsy.

romp probably from FRENCH *ramper* climb.

rondo ITALIAN, from FRENCH *rondeau,* from *rondel* little round.

rondure FRENCH *rondeur.*

ronin JAPANESE.

rook[1] (crow) OLD ENGLISH *hroc.*

rook[2] (chess piece) FRENCH *roc,* from ARABIC *rukh.*

roost OLD ENGLISH *hrost.*

root OLD NORSE *rot.*

root[1] (plant part) OLD NORSE *rot.*

root[2] (dig) MIDDLE ENGLISH *wroot*, from OLD ENGLISH *wrot, wrotan.*

rootle See **root**[2]

rope OLD ENGLISH *rap.*

rosary LATIN *rosarium* rose garden.

rose OLD ENGLISH, from LATIN *rosa*, from GREEK *rhodon* rose.

rosemary LATIN *rosmarinus* dew of the sea, from *ros* dew + *marinus.*

rosette FRENCH, from *rose* rose.

roster DUTCH *rooster* a list.

rostrum LATIN beak, from the ancient Roman custom of decorating speaker platforms with the *beaks,* front parts, of captured ships.

rotary LATIN *rota* wheel.

rotate LATIN *rotare* rotate.

rote MIDDLE ENGLISH *bi rote* by heart, origin uncertain.

rotifer LATIN *rotifera,* from *rota* wheel + *-fer* bearing.

rotogravure LATIN *rota* wheel + FRENCH *gravure* engraving.

rotor See **rotate.**

rotten OLD NORSE *rotinn.*

rotund LATIN *rotundus* in a circle.

rotunda ITALIAN, from LATIN. See **rotund.**

rough OLD ENGLISH *ruh* not smooth.

roulette FRENCH *roele* a small wheel, from LATIN *rota* wheel.

round FRENCH *roont,* from LATIN *rotundus.*

rouse FRENCH, a term used with hawks.

rout FRENCH *route* defeat, from LATIN *rumpere* break (an army).

route FRENCH path, from LATIN *rumpere* break (a path in the forest).

rove possibly from SCOTTISH *rave* wander, stray, from MIDDLE ENGLISH *raven*, probably from OLD NORSE *rafa* wander.

row[1] (line) OLD ENGLISH *raw* line.

row[2] (boating) OLD ENGLISH *rowan* a boat.

row[3] (quarrel) slang, origin unknown.

rowan SCOTTISH *rowan-tree, rountree,* from the root of *red,* in reference to the berries.

rowdy AMERICAN, origin uncertain, probably from **row**[3].

royal FRENCH *roial* regal, from LATIN *regalis,* from *rex* king.

rubbage See **rubbish.**

rubbish MIDDLE ENGLISH, from FRENCH *rubouses*, origin uncertain.

rubble MIDDLE ENGLISH related to **rubbish.**

rubric FRENCH *rubrique*, from LATIN *rubrica* red coloring, from *ruber* red.

ruche FRENCH *ruche* bee hive.

ruching FRENCH *ruche* bee hive, because ruched material resembles it, from LATIN *rusca* bark of a tree (used for making hives.).

rucksack GERMAN *Rucksack* back sack.

ruddy OLD ENGLISH *rudig* reddish.

rude FRENCH, from LATIN *rudis* rough.

rudiment LATIN *rudimentium,* from *rudis* rude.

rueful OLD ENGLISH *hreowan* + *-ful* complete.

ruff See **ruffle.**

ruffian FRENCH *rufyen,* origin uncertain.

ruffle OLD NORSE or GERMAN.

ruga LATIN.

rugby *Rugby*, a boys' school in Britain where the game was first played.

rugged SCANDINAVIAN.

rugger See **rugby.**

ruin FRENCH *ruine,* from LATIN *ruina.*

rule FRENCH *riule* ruler, from LATIN *regula,* from *rugere* lead straight.

rum (liquor) MODERN ENGLISH *rumbullion, rombostion,* origin uncertain.

rumble probably from DUTCH *rommelen.*

rumbustious See **rambunctious.**

rumen Latin esophagus.

rumenotomy See **rumen** + **-tomy**.

ruminate Latin *ruminari* chew, from *rumen* from the mouth to the stomach.

rummage French *arrumage* place (hold) where goods (cargo) are put for transport in a ship, from *a* to + *run* ship's hold, from the lack of order in it.

rumor American spelling. See **rumour**.

rumour French, from Latin *rumorem, rumor* noise, din, common talk.

rump Old Norse *rumpr.*

run Old English *rinnan.*

rune Old English *run* mystery, because writing was a mystery to those who couldn't read and write.

rung Old English *hrung* a stick used for walking.

runt Middle English old or decayed tree stump, origin uncertain.

rupee Hindi *rapya* silver jewelry.

rupture French, from Latin *ruptura* break.

rural French, from Latin *ruralis,* from *rus* the country.

ruse French *ruser* use tricks, from *reüser* escape (by using tricks), from Latin *recusare* refuse.

rush French *reüser* escape. See **ruse**.

russet French, from Latin *russus* reddish.

rust Old English.

rustic Latin *rusticus,* from *rus* country.

rustle imitative.

rut French *route* way.

ruthless Old English *hreowan* rue (regret) + *-leas.*

-ry See **-ery**.

rye[1] (grain) Old English *ryge.*

rye[2] (gypsy) Gypsy *rai* gentleman.

S

Sabbath LATIN *sabbatum,* from GREEK *sabbaton,* from HEBREW *sabbath* rest.

Sabbatical FRENCH *sabbatique,* from LATIN *sabbaticus,* from GREEK *sabbatikos.* See **Sabbath**.

sabe See **savvy**.

saber FRENCH, from GERMAN *sabel.*

sable FRENCH, from RUSSIAN *sobol.*

sabotage FRENCH to destroy property, from *saboter* damage, from *sabot* wooden shoe, from the early practice of throwing a wooden shoe at an employer's machines to break them.

saccharin LATIN *saccharum* sugar, from GREEK *sakcharon.*

sachem NATIVE AMERICAN holy man.

sachet FRENCH *sac,* from LATIN *saccus* bag.

sack[1] (bag) OLD ENGLISH *sacc,* from LATIN *saccus,* from GREEK *sakkos.*

sack[2] (rob) FRENCH, from ITALIAN *sacco,* from LATIN *saccus* bag, from GREEK *sakkos.*

sacque imitation of French.

sacrament FRENCH *sacrement,* from LATIN *sacramentum,* from *sacer* sacred.

sacred MIDDLE ENGLISH *sacren* make holy, from LATIN *sacer.*

sacrifice FRENCH, from LATIN *sacrificium,* from *sacer* sacred + *facere* do, make.

sacrilege FRENCH, from LATIN *sacrilegus* temple robber, from *sacer* sacred + *legere* take away.

sacrosanct LATIN *sacer* sacred + *sanctus* holy.

sad OLD ENGLISH *sæd* weary.

saddle OLD ENGLISH *sadol.*

sadism FRENCH *sadisme* after the marquis de *Sade,* an evil French nobleman in the 18th century.

safari ARABIC *safar* journey.

safe FRENCH *sauf,* from LATIN *salvus* unharmed.

saffron FRENCH *safran,* from ARABIC *za'fardin.*

sag MIDDLE ENGLISH *saggen,* probably from SCANDINAVIAN *sagga* move slowly.

saga OLD NORSE.

sagaciate See **sagacious**.

sagacious LATIN *sagacis,* from *sagax* wise.

sage[1] (wise) FRENCH, from LATIN *sapere* be wise.

sage[2] (plant) MIDDLE ENGLISH *sauge,* from FRENCH *sauge,* from LATIN *salvia.*

saguaro Spanish, from Native American name.

sahib Hindi, from Arabic *sahib* master.

said See **say**.

sail Old English *seg(e)l.*

saint French holy, from Latin *sanctus.*

sake Old English *sacru* conflict.

sal Latin salt.

sal volatile Latin volatile (changes to vapor easily) salt.

salaam Arabic *salam* peace.

salad French *salade* cold vegetable dish, from *sal* salt, from Latin.

salamander Latin *salamandra*, from Greek *salamandra.*

salami Italian, from Latin *sal* salt.

salammoniac See **sal** + **ammonia**.

salary Latin *salarium* pay, from *sal* salt, from money given to soldiers to buy salt, which at that time was not easy to get.

sale Old English, from Old Norse *sala.*

saleratus Latin *sal aeratus* salt with air in it.

salicylate French *salicyl*, from Latin *salic-*, *salix* willow + *-atus.*

salient Latin *salire* leap.

saline French *salin* salty, from Latin *sal* salt.

saliva Latin.

sallender French *solandre*, origin uncertain.

sallow Old English *salu.*

sally French *saillie,* from Latin *salire* leap.

salmon French *saumon,* from Latin *salmo.*

salmonella Daniel E. *Salmon,* veterinary surgeon who discovered the bacteria in 1885.

salon French, from Italian *salone* hall, from *sala* hall.

saloon French *salon,* from Italian *sala* a hall.

salsify French *salsifis,* origin uncertain.

salt Old English *sealt* the food seasoning.

saltire French *sauteur,* from Latin *saltatorium.*

salubrious Latin *salubris,* from *salus* health.

salute Latin *salutare* greet, from *salus* health.

salvage French *salver*, from Latin. See **save**.

salvation French *sauvacion, salvatiun,* from Latin *salvationem,* from *salvare.* See **save**.

salve Old English *sealf.*

salver French *salva* tray, from Spanish *salva* test food (placed on a tray) for poison, from Latin *salvare.* See **save**.

salvia Latin.

salvo Italian, from Latin *salve* hail!

sambur Hindi *sambar.*

same Old Norse *samr.*

sampan Chinese *san-pan,* possibly from *san* three + *pan* a plank.

samphire French *herbe de Saint Pierre* St. Peter's herb.

sample French *essample* pattern. See **example**.

samurai Japanese.

sanatorium Latin *sanatorius* giving health, from *sanus* healthy.

sanctify Latin *santificare* make holy, from *sanctus* holy + *facere* do, make.

sanctimony French, from Latin *sanctimonia,* from *sanctus* holy.

sanction French, from Latin *sanctus* holy.

sanctuary FRENCH, from LATIN *sanctuarium* holy place.

sand OLD ENGLISH.

sandal FRENCH *sandale,* from LATIN *sandalium,* from GREEK *sandalion,* from *sandalon* sandal.

sandwich a nobleman in 18th century England named *Sandwich* who ate meat between two pieces of bread at the gambling table so he wouldn't have to leave the table for a meal.

sane LATIN *sanus* healthy.

sang-froid FRENCH *sang froid* cool blood, from *sang* blood + *froid* cold.

sanguine FRENCH, from LATIN *sanguineus,* from *sanguis* blood.

sanitarium LATIN *sanitas* health.

sanitary FRENCH *sanitaire,* from LATIN *sanitas* health.

sannup NATIVE AMERICAN *sannop.*

Sanskrit SANSKRIT *samskrta* made together.

Santa Claus DUTCH *Sant Nikolass.*

sap OLD ENGLISH *sæp.*

sapphire FRENCH *safir,* from LATIN *sappir,* from GREEK *sappheiros,* from HEBREW *sappir.*

saprophyte GREEK *sapros* rotten + *phyton* a plant.

sarcasm LATIN *sarcasmos* tease, from GREEK *sarkasmos,* from *sarkazein* tear flesh like dogs, from *sarx* flesh.

sarcoma LATIN, from GREEK *sarx* flesh.

sarcophagus LATIN special stone (limestone) used for coffins, from GREEK *sarkophagos* flesh-eating stone, from *sarx* flesh + *phagein* eat. The ancient Greeks thought the limestone could eat the flesh of the dead.

sardine FRENCH, from LATIN *sarda* kind of fish, probably from GREEK *Sardo* Sardinia.

sardonic FRENCH *sardonique,* from LATIN *Sardonicus risus* Sardinian laughter, from GREEK *Sardonios gelos.* A poisonous plant of Sardinia which, when eaten, causes the face muscles to pull in a way that make it look like the person is laughing.

sarong MALAY *sarung* sheath, covering.

sarsaparilla SPANISH *zarzaparrilla* the plant, from *zarza* bramble + *parra* vine.

sartorial LATIN *sartor* tailor.

sash ARABIC *shash* muslin.

sashay FRENCH *chassé* a gliding dance step.

sass See **sassy.**

sassy saucy. See **sauce.**

sastruga GERMAN, from RUSSIAN *zastrúga* small ridge, furrow, from *zastrugát* plane, smooth, from *strug* plane.

Satan LATIN, from GREEK, from HEBREW enemy.

satchel FRENCH little bag, from LATIN *saccus* bag. See **sack**[1].

sateen See **satin.**

satellite FRENCH, from LATIN *satelles* an attendant.

satiate LATIN *satiare* satisfy, from *satis* enough.

satin FRENCH, from ARABIC *zaituni,* from *Zaitun,* a port in southeastern China where satin was made.

satire FRENCH, from LATIN *satira* poem on different subjects.

satisfaction LATIN *satisfactio* amends.

satisfy FRENCH *satisfier,* from LATIN *satis* enough + *facere* do, make.

saturate LATIN *saturare* fill.

Saturday OLD ENGLISH *Sæterdæg,* from LATIN *Saturni dies* day of Saturn.

Saturn Old English *Sætern*, from Latin *Saturnus* god of agriculture.

satyr Latin *satyrus* a woodland god, from Greek *satyros*, origin unknown.

sauce French, from Latin *salsus* salted.

saucer French *saussier*, from *sause*. See **sauce**.

sauerkraut German *sauer* sour + *kraut* cabbage.

sauna Finnish bath house.

saunter possibly from Middle English *santren* muse, be in reverie; origin uncertain.

sausage French *saussiche*, from Latin *salsicia* seasoned with salt, from *salsus* salted.

sauté French, from Latin *saltare* dance.

savage French *salvage*, from Latin *silvaticus* wild, from *silva* wood.

savanna Spanish *zavana*, from Native American *zabana*.

save French *sauver*, from Latin *salvare* make safe, from *salvus* safe.

savior French *sauveor*, from Latin *salvator*, from *salvus* safe.

savoir-faire French know how to do.

savor French *savour* flavor, from Latin *sapor* taste.

savvy Spanish *sabe usted* do you know, from *saber* know, from Latin *sapere* be wise.

saw Old English *saga* cutting tool.

sawyer See **saw**.

saxaphone French, from Antoine Joseph *Sax*, Belgian instrument maker who developed it.

saxicolous Latin *saxum* a rock + *colere* live.

saxifrage French, from Latin *saxum* a rock + *frangere* break (the plant grows in rock crevices).

say Old English *secgan*.

scab Old Norse *skabb*.

scabbard French *excaubers* case for a sword.

scads American large amounts, earlier meant dollars, origin uncertain.

scaffold French *eschaufaud* pieces of wood supporting a platform, from Latin *ex-* out of + *cata* by, from Greek *kata* down + *fala* wooden platform.

scalawag (scallywag) American, perhaps from Scottish *scallag* farm servant, rustic.

scald French *escalder* burn with hot water, from *ex-* out + *calidus* hot.

scale[1] (for weight) Old Norse *skal*.

scale[2] (on skin) French *escale* shell.

scale[3] (music) Latin *scala* ladder.

scallop French *escalope* shell.

scalp Middle English, from Scandinavian.

scamp French *escamper* run away, from Latin *ex-* out of + *campus* battlefield.

scampi Italian *scampo* prawn.

scan Latin *scandere* relating to lines of poetry, from *scandere* climb.

scandal Latin *scandalum* stumbling block, from Greek *skandalon* trap.

scant Old Norse *skammr* short.

scape[1] (get away) from **escape.**

scape[2] (scene) from **landscape**.

scapula Latin *scapulae* shoulders.

scar French *escare* scab, from Latin *eschara* scab, from Greek *eschara* scab.

scarab French *scarabeé*, from Latin *scarabaeus*, from Greek *karabos* beetle, crayfish.

scarabae See **scarab**.

scarce FRENCH *escars* not many, from LATIN *excerpere* select.

scare OLD NORSE *skirra* frighten.

scarf FRENCH *escarpe* a purse hung from the neck, from LATIN *scirpa* pouch, from *scirpus* a water plant used in making baskets.

scarlet FRENCH *escarlet,* from LATIN *scarlatum* scarlet cloth, from ARABIC *säqirlat* red dress.

scarp ITALIAN *scarpa.*

scathe OLD NORSE *skathi* harm.

scatter MIDDLE ENGLISH *skateran.*

scavenger FRENCH *scawage* a tax collected from foreign merchants, from *escauwer* inspect.

scenario ITALIAN, from LATIN *scaena* stage, scene.

scene FRENCH, from LATIN *scena* stage, from GREEK *skene* stage.

scent MIDDLE ENGLISH *senten,* from FRENCH *sentir* feel, smell, taste, perceive, from LATIN *sentire* feel, sense, perceive.

scepter FRENCH *sceptre* royal staff, from LATIN *sceptrum,* from GREEK *skeptron.*

schedule FRENCH, from LATIN *schedula* small sheet of paper, from *scheda* strip of papyrus.

scheme LATIN *schema* shape, from GREEK *schema.*

schism FRENCH *scisme,* from LATIN *schisma* split, from GREEK *schisma.*

schizophrenia LATIN, from GREEK *schizein* separate + *phren* the mind.

schmaltz YIDDISH *shmalts* melted fat, from GERMAN *smalz,* related to *smelzan* melt.

schnapps a kind of Holland gin, from GERMAN *Schnaps* a mouthful, gulp.

scholar LATIN *scholaris* about a school, from *schola.* See **school**.

school OLD ENGLISH *scol* place of learning, from LATIN *schola,* from GREEK *schole.*

schooner MODERN ENGLISH (colonial New England), perhaps from SCOTTISH *scon* send over water, skip stones.

sciatic LATIN *sciaticus,* from *ischiadicus,* from GREEK *iskhiadikos,* from *iskhias* pain in the hips, from *iskhion* hip joint.

science FRENCH knowledge, from LATIN *scientia.*

scimitar ITALIAN *scimitara,* origin uncertain.

scion FRENCH *scion.*

scissors FRENCH *cisoires* shears, from LATIN *cisorium* cutting tool, from *caedere* cut.

scoff possibly from OLD NORSE *skopa.*

scold OLD NORSE *skald.*

scolia GREEK bent or curved.

scone SCOTTISH, from DUTCH *schoonbrot* fine bread.

scoop DUTCH *schope* bucket and *schoppe* shovel.

scope ITALIAN *scopo* target, from GREEK *skopos.*

-scope LATIN *-scopium,* from GREEK *-skopion,* from *skopein* view, examine.

scorch MIDDLE ENGLISH, perhaps from OLD NORSE *skorpna* shriveled.

score OLD NORSE *skor* count by using marks.

scorn MIDDLE ENGLISH, from FRENCH *escarn* make fun of.

scorpion FRENCH, from LATIN, from GREEK *skorpios.*

scoter origin uncertain.

scoundrel MIDDLE ENGLISH *skowndrell,* probably from FRENCH *escoundre,* from LATIN *condere* hide.

scour[1] (scrub) DUTCH *schuren* clean, from FRENCH *escurer,* from LATIN *ex-* entirely + *curare* take care of.

scour[2] (search) OLD NORSE *skyra* rush in.

scourge FRENCH *escorgiee,* from LATIN *excoriare* strip off the hide, from *ex-* from + *corrium* hide.

scout FRENCH *escoute* spy, from *escouter* listen, from LATIN *auscultare* listen to.

scowl MIDDLE ENGLISH *scoulen,* probably from SCANDINAVIAN.

scrabble DUTCH *schrabbelen,* from *schrabben* scrape.

scramble possible combination of **scamp(er)** + **scrabble**.

scrap OLD NORSE *skrap* scrapings.

scrape OLD NORSE *skrapa* scratch.

scrapple See **scrap**.

scratch probably from MIDDLE ENGLISH *scracche.*

scrawny probably from SCANDINAVIAN.

scream MIDDLE ENGLISH *screamen,* from OLD ENGLISH *scrœman.*

screech OLD NORSE *skrækja.*

screed OLD ENGLISH *screade.*

screen DUTCH *scherm.*

screw FRENCH *escroue* the hole in which a screw turns, from LATIN *scrofa* sow, from the threads of a screw looking like the curl of a sow's tail.

scribble LATIN *scribillare* write quickly, from *scribere* write.

scribe LATIN *scriba* secretary, from *scribere* write.

scrimp SCOTTISH, also *skrimp*, origin uncertain.

scrimshaw AMERICAN nautical *scrimshander, scrimshonting*, origin uncertain.

scringe unknown origin.

script FRENCH, from LATIN *scriptum* something written.

scripture LATIN *scriptura* writing.

scrivener FRENCH, from LATIN *scriba* a writer.

scroll FRENCH *eschrowe* strip of parchment.

scrotum LATIN.

scrounge AMERICAN *scrunge* rummage, perhaps from *scringe* pry about.

scrub DUTCH *schrobben* rub.

scrumple GERMAN *krumpel.*

scruple FRENCH *scrupule,* from LATIN *scrupulus* small sharp stone, from *scrupus,* from being uncomfortable by having a small stone in the shoe.

scrutiny LATIN *scrutinium* search, from *scrutari.*

scry See **descry**.

scuba s(elf) c(ontained) u(nderwater) b(reathing) a(pparatus).

scud perhaps from MIDDLE ENGLISH *scut* rabbit, rabbit's tail; origin uncertain.

scuff OLD NORSE *skufa* shove.

scuffle See **scuff** + **-le**.

scull MIDDLE ENGLISH a kind of oar, origin uncertain.

scullery FRENCH *escuelerie,* from *escuelle* dish, from LATIN *scutella* tray.

scullion See **scullery**.

sculpture LATIN *sculptura* a carving.

scum DUTCH *scume* foam, froth.

scupper MIDDLE ENGLISH, origin uncertain.

scuppernong AMERICAN, from a river in North Carolina.

scurrilous LATIN *scurrilis* like a buffoon (clown).

scurry See **hurry**.

scurvy probably from SCANDINAVIAN.

scutage MIDDLE ENGLISH from LATIN *scutagium*, from *scutum* shield.

scutcheon See **escutcheon**.

scuttle[1] (sink a ship) MIDDLE ENGLISH *skottell* opening in a ship's deck, from FRENCH *escoutille*, from SPANISH *escotilla* hatchway.

scuttle[2] (run quickly) probably from OLD NORSE *scud*.

scythe OLD ENGLISH *sithe*, from LATIN *scindere* cut.

sea OLD ENGLISH *sæ*.

seal[1] (pledge) FRENCH *seel* formal way to stamp documents to prove they were real, from LATIN *signum* sign.

seal[2] (animal) OLD ENGLISH *seolh*.

seam OLD ENGLISH.

sear OLD ENGLISH *searian*, from *sear* dry.

search FRENCH *cenchier*, from LATIN *circare* explore, from *circum* around.

season FRENCH *saison* time of the year, from LATIN *satio* time to plant, from *satio* planting.

seat OLD NORSE *sæti* chair.

seaton LATIN *setonem*, from *seta* silk.

Seccotine probably from ITALIAN *secco* dry.

secede LATIN *secedere* go away.

secesh See **secede**.

seclude LATIN *secludere* shut off.

second FRENCH, from LATIN *secundus*, from *sequito* follow.

secret FRENCH *secre*, from LATIN *secernere* put apart, from *se-* apart + *cernere* separate.

secretary LATIN *secretarius* confidential officer, from *secretus*. See **secret**.

secrete LATIN *secernere*. See **secret**.

sect FRENCH *secte*, from LATIN *secta* school of philosophy (the study of right and wrong).

section LATIN *secare* cut.

sector LATIN the geometric figure, from *secare* cut.

secular FRENCH *seculer*, from LATIN *saecularis* worldly, from *saeculum* age.

secunda LATIN *secundus*.

secure LATIN *securus*, from *se-* free from + *cura* care.

sedan possibly from LATIN *sedere* sit.

sedate LATIN *sedare* quiet.

sedentary FRENCH *sedentaire*, from LATIN *sedentarius*, from *sedere* sit.

sedge OLD ENGLISH *secg*.

sediment FRENCH, from LATIN *sedimentus*, from *sedere* sit.

sedition FRENCH, from LATIN *seditio*, from *sed* apart + *itio*, from *ire* go.

seduce LATIN *seducere*, from *se-* apart + *ducere* lead.

sedulous LATIN *se-* apart + *dolo* trickery.

seed OLD ENGLISH *sæd*.

seek OLD ENGLISH *secan*.

seethe OLD ENGLISH *seothan* boil.

segashuate See **sagacious**.

segment LATIN *segmentum* a piece cut off, from *secare* cut.

segregate LATIN *segregare*, from *se* apart + *grex* flock.

segue ITALIAN, from LATIN *sequi* follow.

seine OLD ENGLISH *segne,* from LATIN, from GREEK *segene.*

seismic GREEK *seismos* earthquake, from *seiein* shake.

seize FRENCH *seisir*, from LATIN *sacire.*

seldom OLD ENGLISH *seldan.*

select LATIN *seligere* choose.

self OLD ENGLISH *self* own.

sell OLD ENGLISH *sellan* hand over for money.

seltzer GERMAN *Selters,* the name of the village in Germany where it was first made.

selvedge See **self** + **edge**.

semantics FRENCH *sémantique*, from GREEK *semantikos,* from *sema* sign.

semaphore GREEK *sema* a sign + *phoros,* from *pherein* produce.

semblance FRENCH appearance, from *sembler* seem, from LATIN *simulare* make like.

semi- LATIN half, partly.

seminal FRENCH, from LATIN *seminalis* relating to seed, from *semen* seed.

seminar See **seminary**.

seminary LATIN *seminarius* of seed, from *semen* a seed.

Semitic GERMAN, from LATIN *Semiticus,* from GREEK *Sem,* from HEBREW *Shem* the oldest of Noah's three sons.

senate FRENCH *senat*, from LATIN *senatus* the ruling body of ancient Rome, from *senex* old man.

send OLD ENGLISH *sendan* cause to go.

seneschal FRENCH.

senile LATIN *selilis,* from *senex* old.

senior LATIN *senex* old.

sennight OLD ENGLISH *seofon* seven + *niht* night.

sense FRENCH *sens*, from LATIN *sensus* feeling, from *sentire* perceive, feel.

sensitive FRENCH, from LATIN *sensitivus,* from *sensus.* See **sense**.

sensor See **sensory**.

sensory LATIN *sensorium*, from *sensus.* See **sense**.

sensual LATIN *sensualis,* from *sensus.* See **sense**.

sentence FRENCH opinion, from LATIN *sententia,* from *sentire* feel.

sententious LATIN *sententiosus* full of meaning, from *sententia,* from *sentire* feel.

sentient LATIN *sentire.* See **sentiment**.

sentiment FRENCH *sentement,* from LATIN *sentimentus* opinion, from *sentire* feel.

sentinel FRENCH *sentinelle* sentry, from LATIN *sentire* feel.

sentry See **sentinel**.

sepal FRENCH *sépale,* from LATIN *sepalum.*

separate LATIN *separare,* from *se-* apart + *parare* arrange.

sepia LATIN kind of fish, from GREEK cause to rot. The liquid from the fish is used in the process of making the color.

seppuku JAPANESE, from *setsu fuku*, from CHINESE *qie* cut (with a sword or knife) + *fù* belly.

September LATIN *September* seventh month in the early Roman calendar in which March was the first month, from *septem* seven.

septum LATIN *saeptum* a fence, from *saepire* hedge in, from *saepes* hedge, fence.

sepulcher FRENCH *sepulcre* tomb, from LATIN *sepulcrum,* from *sepelire* bury.

sequel French *sequelle,* from Latin *sequela* result, from *sequi* follow.

sequence Latin *sequentia* that which follows, from *sequi* follow.

sequester Latin *sequiestrare* remove, from *sequester* trustee (person put in charge of another's property).

sequin French, from Italian *zecchino,* from *zecca* a mint, from Arabic *sikkah* a stamp.

sequoia Native American *Sequoya.*

seraglio Italian *serraglio* enclosure.

serape Spanish.

sere See **sear.**

serenade French, from Italian *serenata,* from Latin *seremus* clear.

serene Latin *serenus.*

serf French, from Latin *servus* slave.

serge French, from Latin *sericus* silken, probably from Chinese *se* silk.

sergeant French *sergent* officer, from Latin *servire* be a servant.

series Latin *serere* join together.

serious Latin *seriosus* earnest, from *serius* earnest.

sermon Latin *sermo* speech, serve.

serpent Latin *serpens* creeping thing, from *serpere* creep.

serrate Latin *serratus,* from *serra* a saw.

serried French *serrer* crowd, from Latin *serare.*

serum Latin watery part of something.

servant French *servir* serve, from Latin *servire.* See **serve.**

serve Latin *servire* be a slave or servant.

serviette French *servir* serve.

servile Latin *servilis,* from *servus* a slave.

servitor French, from Latin *servitor,* from *servire* serve.

servitude French, from Latin *servus* a slave.

session Latin *sessio* meeting, from *sedere* sit.

set Old English *settan* place.

settle Old English *setl* a seat.

several French separate, from Latin *separ* different.

severe Latin *severus* strict.

sew Old English *siw(i)an* fasten together with thread.

sewer French *esseweur,* from Latin *ex-* out + *aqua* water.

sex Latin *sexus* either male or female.

sextant Latin *sextans* sixth part, because it has the shape of a sixth of a circle.

sexton French *segrestein,* from Latin *sacrista,* from *sacer* sacred.

shabby Old English *sceabb* itch.

shack Origin uncertain, possibly from US slang *shackly* rickety, shaky.

shackle Old English *seceacul* fetter (chain put on the feet to slow movement).

shad Old English *sceadd.*

shade Old English *sceadu* shadow.

shadow See **shade.**

shaft Old English *scealf.*

shah Persian *kshayathiya* king.

shake Old English *sceacan* move quickly.

shale Old English *sceulu* a shell.

shall Old English *sceal.*

shallop French *chaloupe,* from Dutch *sloep* sloop (ship).

shallot FRENCH *eschalotte.*

sham probably from **shame**.

shaman RUSSIAN, from TUNGUS *saman* one who knows, probably from SANSKRIT *cramana* monk.

shamble MIDDLE ENGLISH *shamel,* from OLD ENGLISH *sc(e)amel* stool, from LATIN *scamnum* bench.

shame OLD ENGLISH *sceamu.*

shampoo HINDI *champo* press.

shamrock IRISH *seamar* clover.

shank OLD ENGLISH *sceanca* leg.

shantung *Shantung* province in China where the fabric was made.

shanty possibly from IRISH *sean toigh* old house.

shape OLD ENGLISH *(ge)sceap* a form.

shard OLD ENGLISH *sceard.*

share OLD ENGLISH *scearu* cutting.

shark MIDDLE ENGLISH, origin uncertain.

sharp OLD ENGLISH *scearp* fine cutting edge.

shatter MIDDLE ENGLISH *schateren* scatter.

shave OLD ENGLISH *sceafan* scrape away.

shawl PERSIAN *shal.*

she OLD ENGLISH *seo.*

sheaf OLD ENGLISH *sceaf.*

shear OLD ENGLISH *sceran* cut.

sheath OLD ENGLISH *sceath, scœth.*

shed OLD ENGLISH *sced* shelter.

sheen OLD ENGLISH *scene* bright.

sheer[1] (thin) OLD NORSE *skærr* shine.

sheer[2] (turn away) DUTCH *scheren* move aside, cut.

sheet OLD ENGLISH *sceat.*

sheik ARABIC *shaikh* old man.

sheldrake probably from MIDDLE ENGLISH, from DUTCH *schillede* marked with different colors + *drake* drake.

shelf OLD ENGLISH *scylfe* ledge.

shellac FRENCH *laque en écialles* lac (substance made from tree sap) in thin plates.

shelter OLD ENGLISH *scildtruma* shield soldiers.

shenanigan possibly from SPANISH *chanada, charranada* trick, deceit.

shepherd OLD ENGLISH *sceaphyrde,* from *sceap* sheep + *hyrde* herdsman.

sheriff OLD ENGLISH *scirgerefa* person working for the king in a local area, from *scir* county in Great Britain + *gerefa* officer.

sherry MIDDLE ENGLISH *sherris,* from SPANISH *vino de Xeres* wine from Xeres.

shield OLD ENGLISH *sceld* piece of armor.

shift OLD ENGLISH *sciftan* divide.

shilling OLD ENGLISH *scilling.*

shim MODERN ENGLISH, origin uncertain.

shimmer OLD ENGLISH *scimrian* shine a bit.

shin OLD ENGLISH *scinu.*

shine OLD ENGLISH *scinan* give out light.

shingle[1] (wood) LATIN *scindula* split pieces of wood.

shingle[2] (stones) OLD ENGLISH *chyngell,* origin unknown.

shinny See **shine**.

ship OLD ENGLISH *scip.*

shirk possibly from GERMAN *schurke* dishonest person.

shirr American *shirred*, from *shirr* elastic webbing, origin uncertain.

shoal Old English *sceald* shallow.

shoat Middle English *schote.*

shock French *choc* clash, from *choquer* strike, from Dutch *schokken* crash.

shoe Old English *scoh.*

shoot Old English *sceotan* send forth.

shop Old English *sceoppa* booth.

shore Dutch *schore* coast.

short Old English *sceort* brief.

should Old English *sceolde.*

shoulder Old English *sculdor.*

shove Old English *scufan.*

shovel Old English *scofl.*

show Old English *sceawian* look.

shower Old English *scur.*

shrew Old English *screawa.*

shrewd Middle English *schrewen* curse, from *schrewe* shrew (the animal).

shriek Old Norse *skrækja* screech.

shrill Middle English *schrille.*

shrimp Old English *scrimman* shrink.

shrine Old English *scrin,* from Latin *scrinium* box.

shrink Old English *scrincan.*

shrive Old English *scrifan,* from Latin *scribere* write.

shrivel possibly from Scandinavian.

shroud Old English *scrud* clothing.

shrub Old English *scrybb.*

shuck American husk, pod, origin uncertain.

shudder Middle English *shoddren* tremble with fear, from Old English *scudan* shake.

shuffle German *schuffeln* walk awkwardly.

shun Old English *scunian.*

shut Old English *scyttan* lock a door.

shutter See **shut** + **-er.**

shuttle Old English *scytel* arrow.

shy[1] (afraid) Old English *sceoh.*

shy[2] (throw) origin unknown.

sibilant Latin *sibilare* hiss.

sibling Old English.

sibyl French *sibile*, from Latin *Sibylla*, from Greek name for a prophetess meaning "divine wish."

sick Old English *seoc.*

sickle Old English *sicol,* from Latin *secula,* from *secare* cut.

side Old English *side.*

sidle See **side** + **-ling.**

siege French *sege* seat, throne, from Latin *sedere* sit.

sierra Spanish, from Latin *serra* a saw.

siesta Spanish, from Latin *sexta hora* sixth hour, noon.

sieve Old English *sife.*

sift Old English *siftan.*

sigh Middle English *sighen*, from Old English *sican.*

sight Old English *(ge)siht* something seen.

sign French *signe* mark, from Latin *signum.*

signal French, from Latin *signale* sign, from *signum* mark.

signature Latin signing, from *signum* mark.

signet French *signe* a sign.

significant Latin *significantia.* See **signify**.

signify French *signifier*, from Latin *significare* show by signs, from *signum* mark + *facere* make.

signor Italian.

silent Latin *silere* still.

silesia German *Schlesien,* east German province the cloth came from.

silhouette Étienne de *Silhouette* (1709–1767), said to be in reference to his unpopular efforts to economize, as silhouettes were less expensive than painted portraits.

silica Latin *silex.*

silk Old English *seolc* the material, from Greek *serikon* the material, from *Seres* the Chinese, who were famous for their silks.

sill Old English *syll.*

silly Old English *(ge)sælig* happy.

silo Spanish, from Latin *sirus,* from Greek *siros.*

silt probably from Scandinavian.

silver Old English *seolfer.*

simian Latin *simia* an ape, probably from *simus* flat-nosed, from Greek.

similar French *similaire* like, from Latin *similis.*

simile Latin *similis* similar.

simper perhaps from Scandinavian, origin uncertain.

simple French plain, from Latin *simplex.*

simulacra See **simulate**.

simulacrum See **simulate**.

simulate Latin *simulare* imitate.

simultaneous Latin *simultas,* from competition, from *simul* at the same time.

sin Old English *synn.*

since Middle English *sinnes,* from Old English *siththan* after.

sincere French, from Latin *sincerus* clean.

sinecure Latin *beneficium sine cura* benefice (room and board provided to a priest) without also having religious duties, such as the care of souls.

sinew Old English *sinu.*

sing Old English *singan.*

singe French *sengan.*

single French, from Latin *singulus* separate, from *singuli* one to each.

singlet See **single**.

singletree Middle English *swingle* a rod + *tre* a tree.

sinister Middle English, from French *sinistre,* from Latin *sinister* left, from the early belief that omens seen on the left side were unlucky.

sink Old English *sincan.*

sinus Latin a bent surface.

sip Old English *sypian.*

siphon French, from Latin, from Greek a tube.

sir See **sire**.

sire French a master, from Latin *senior* older.

siren French, from Latin *Siren* a sea goddess, from Greek *Seiren* a sea goddess, part bird and part woman, who sang to sailors to get them to join her in the sea.

sisal *Sisal,* port in Yucatan from which the fiber was exported.

siskin German *sisschen,* from *zisec.*

sissy AMERICAN *sis* sister.

sister OLD NORSE *systir.*

sit OLD ENGLISH *sittan.*

site LATIN *situs* position.

situate LATIN *situare* place, from *situs* position.

size MIDDLE ENGLISH *syse* limit, from FRENCH *sise* a set amount.

sizzle imitative.

skate[1] (ice blade) DUTCH *schaats* a skate, from FRENCH *eschace* stilt.

skate[2] (fish) OLD NORSE *skata.*

skedaddle AMERICAN Civil War military slang.

skeet MODERN ENGLISH, supposed to be an old form of *shoot*, perhaps from OLD NORSE *skotja.*

skeeter See **mosquito**.

skein FRENCH *escaigne* yarn.

skeleton LATIN, from GREEK mummy *skeletas* dried up.

skelter See **helter-skelter**.

skep OLD NORSE *skeppa.*

skeptic GREEK *skeptikos* thoughtful.

sketch DUTCH *schets* model, from LATIN *schedium* poem, from GREEK *schedios* done on the spur of the moment.

skew FRENCH *eskiuwer* avoid.

skewer OLD NORSE *skifa* a slice.

ski OLD NORSE *skith* snowshoe.

skid probably from OLD NORSE *skith.*

skidoo possibly from **skedaddle**.

skiff FRENCH *esquif*, from ITALIAN *schifo.*

skill OLD NORSE *skil* knowledge.

skilligalee origin uncertain.

skim FRENCH *escumer* get floating things off a liquid, from *escume* foam.

skin OLD NORSE *skinn.*

skink FRENCH *scinc*, from LATIN *scincus*, from GREEK *skinkos* lizard.

skip probably from SCANDINAVIAN.

skipple DUTCH *schepel.*

skirl probably from Norwegian *skrylla* scream.

skirmish FRENCH *eskimer* fight with a sword.

skirt OLD NORSE *skyrta* shirt.

skit probably from OLD NORSE *skjota* shoot.

skive OLD NORSE *skifa.*

skivvy nautical slang, origin unknown.

skoal DANISH *skaal* a toast, from OLD NORSE bowl, cup.

skrike probably from SCANDINAVIAN.

skulk probably from GERMAN *schulken.*

sky OLD NORSE cloud.

slab MIDDLE ENGLISH *sclabbe.*

slack OLD ENGLISH *slæc* lazy.

slag GERMAN *slagge.*

slake OLD ENGLISH *slacian.*

slam probably from SCANDINAVIAN.

slander FRENCH *esclandre* disgrace, from LATIN *scandalum* cause of disgrace, from GREEK *skandalon* trap.

slang origin unknown.

slap GERMAN *slapp.*

slash FRENCH *esclachier* break.

slat FRENCH *esclat* piece.

slate FRENCH *esclat* splinter, from *esclater* split.

slather origin uncertain.

slattern Middle English *slatter* spill or splash awkwardly, waste, origin uncertain.

slaughter Old Norse *slatr* butcher's seat.

slave Middle English *Sclavus* one of the Slavic (eastern Europe) people, from Greek *Sklabos*, which refers to a time in the Middle Ages when a German people made many Slavic people their slaves.

slay Old English *slean.*

sledge Dutch *sleedse* sled.

sleek See **slick**.

sleep Old English *slæpan* be numb (have no feeling).

sleet possibly from Old English *slet.*

sleigh Dutch *slee,* from *slede* sled.

sleight Old Norse *slægth* sly.

slender Middle English *slendre,* origin unknown.

slew[1] (swamp) American, from **slough**.

slew[2] (swing) nautical *slue,* origin unknown.

slew[3] (many) Irish *sluagh* a host, crowd, multitude.

slice French *esclicier* split.

slick Old English *slician* make smooth.

slide Old English *slidan* glide.

slight Dutch *slicht* simple.

slim Dutch bad.

slime Old English *slim.*

sling Middle English *slinge(n),* probably from Old Norse *slyngva* throw.

slip[1] (slide) German *slippen* glide, from Old English *slupan.*

slip[2] (strip) Dutch *slippe* cut, slit.

slip[3] (clay) Old English *slyppe* slime.

slippery Old English *slipur.*

slit Old English *slitan.*

slither Old English *sliderian* slip.

sliver Old English *slifan* slice off.

slob Irish *slab* mud, of Scandinavian origin.

slobber Middle English, origin uncertain.

slog[1] (work) Middle English *sluggen.*

slog[2] (hit) See **slug**[2].

slogan Scottish *sluagh-ghairm* cry for battle, from *sluagh* army + *gairm* shout.

sloop Dutch *sloep.*

slop Middle English mudhole, from Old English *slypa* a paste.

slope Old English *aslupan* slip away.

slosh probably from a blend of **slush** and **slop**, origin uncertain.

sloth Old English *slaw* slow.

slouch Old Norse *sllokr* lazy person, from *sloka* droop.

slough Old English *sloh* piece of muddy ground.

sloven possibly from Dutch *slof* careless.

slow Old English *slaw* dull.

sludge Middle English *slich* slime.

slue See **slew**[2].

slug[1] (snail) Middle English *slugge* clumsy one, origin uncertain.

slug[2] (hit) Old Norse *slag.*

sluggard Middle English *sluggen* be lazy.

sluice French *escluse* floodgate, from Latin *escludera* shut out.

slum American *back slum* back alley, from slang for back room, origin unknown.

slumgullion AMERICAN slang, probably a made up word.

slump probably from GERMAN *slumpen* happen by accident.

slur possibly from DUTCH *sleuren* walk in mud.

slush origin uncertain, perhaps from SCANDINAVIAN.

sly OLD NORSE *slægr* deceiving.

smack imitative.

small OLD ENGLISH *smæl* narrow.

smart OLD ENGLISH *smeortan* be painful.

smash See **mash**.

smear OLD ENGLISH *smerian*.

smell MIDDLE ENGLISH *smellen*.

smelt[1] (fish) OLD ENGLISH *smelt* small salmon-like sea fish.

smelt[2] (melt) DUTCH *smelten* melt.

smile MIDDLE ENGLISH *smilen*, possibly from GERMAN *smilan*.

smirk OLD ENGLISH *smearcian* smile.

smite OLD ENGLISH *smitan* smear.

smithereens IRISH *smiodar* piece.

smock OLD ENGLISH *smoc* woman's underclothes.

smoke OLD ENGLISH *smoca*.

smolder MIDDLE ENGLISH *smoldren*.

smolt See **smelt**[1].

smooch possibly from German *schmutzen* kiss, smile.

smooth OLD ENGLISH *smoth* rough.

smorgasbord SWEDISH *smorgasbord* open sandwich table, literally butter-goose table, from *smorgas* bread and butter, from *smor* butter + *gas* goose + *bord* table.

smother MIDDLE ENGLISH *smorithren*, from *smorther* thick smoke.

smouch See **smooch**.

smudge probably from MIDDLE ENGLISH *smogen*.

smug probably from GERMAN *smuck* neat.

smuggle GERMAN *smuggein*.

snack MIDDLE ENGLISH bite or snap (of a dog), probably from DUTCH *snacken* snatch, chatter.

snaffle probably from early Dutch *snabbe* bill of a bird.

snag possibly from SCANDINAVIAN.

snail OLD ENGLISH *snægl*.

snake OLD ENGLISH *snaca*.

snap DUTCH *snappen* speak quickly.

snare OLD ENGLISH *sneare* noose.

snarl probably from GERMAN *snarren* rattle.

snatch probably from MIDDLE ENGLISH *snakken* take.

sneak MIDDLE ENGLISH *sniken* creep, from OLD ENGLISH *snican*.

sneer MIDDLE ENGLISH *sneren*.

sneeze MIDDLE ENGLISH *finesen*, from OLD ENGLISH *fneosan*.

snell[1] (quick) MIDDLE ENGLISH, from OLD ENGLISH, from GERMAN *snel*.

snell[2] (fish line) AMERICAN, origin uncertain.

snib SCOTTISH.

snick imitative.

snicker imitative.

snide origin unknown, possibly from thieves' slang meaning bad or fake.

sniff imitative.

snifter imitative

snig MIDDLE ENGLISH small eel, origin uncertain.

snip DUTCH *snippen* clip.

snit AMERICAN, origin uncertain.

snivel possibly from OLD ENGLISH *snofl* liquid from the nose.

snob OLD NORSE *snapr* lower class person. In the 1800s the word changed to its current meaning.

snood OLD ENGLISH *snod.*

snore imitative.

snorkle GERMAN *Schnorchel*, from navy slang *Schnorchel* nose.

snort MIDDLE ENGLISH *snorten.*

snout GERMAN and DUTCH *snute.*

snow OLD ENGLISH *snaw.*

snub OLD NORSE *snubba* scold.

snuff DUTCH *snuffen.*

snuffle DUTCH *snuffelen* smell out.

snug MIDDLE ENGLISH compact, trim (of a ship), perhaps from SCANDINAVIAN.

so OLD ENGLISH *swa.*

soak OLD ENGLISH *socian.*

soap OLD ENGLISH *sape.*

soar FRENCH *essorer* throw up in the air, from LATIN *ex-* out of + *aura* breeze, from GREEK *aura.*

sob MIDDLE ENGLISH *sobben.*

sober FRENCH *sobre* moderate, from LATIN *sobrius* not drunk.

sobriquet FRENCH *soubriquet* a chuck under the chin.

social FRENCH, from LATIN *socius* companion.

society FRENCH *socite,* from LATIN *societas,* from *socius* companion.

sock OLD ENGLISH *socc,* from LATIN *soccus* a light, low-heeled shoe.

sockdolager AMERICAN *sock* hit hard + made-up ending.

socket MIDDLE ENGLISH, from FRENCH *soket* spearhead shaped like a blade for cutting soil.

sod probably from DUTCH *sode.*

soda MIDDLE ENGLISH alkaline substance, from LATIN for saltwort, a plant from which soda was obtained, probably from ARABIC *suwwad* a saltwort plant.

sodden See **seethe**.

sodium See **soda**. The element was isolated, from caustic soda.

sofa ARABIC *suffah.*

soft OLD ENGLISH *softe* gentle.

soggy probably from OLD NORSE *sog* sucking.

soil[1] (dirt) FRENCH, from LATIN *solum.*

soil[2] (stain) FRENCH *sollier* get dirty, from LATIN *suculus* little pig.

soiree FRENCH *soir* evening.

sojourn FRENCH *sojorner* rest, from LATIN *sub-* under + *diurnus* daily.

solace FRENCH *solaz* console (make less sad), from LATIN *solacium.*

solar LATIN *solaris* having to do with the sun, from *sol* sun.

solder FRENCH *soldure,* from *sou(l)der* fasten together, from LATIN *solidus* firm.

soldier French someone who fights for pay, from *soulde* pay, from Latin *solidus* a Roman gold coin.

sole[1] (bottom) Old English *sole* sandal, from Latin *solea* sole of a sandal, from *solum* soil.

sole[2] (only) Latin *solus* alone.

solemn Latin *sollemnis* yearly, from *sollus* all + *annus* year.

soleus Latin *solea*. See **sole**.

solicitous Latin *sollicitus,* from *sollus* whole + *ciere* put in motion.

solid Latin *solidus* firm.

soliloquy Latin *soliloquim* talking to oneself, from *solus* alone + *loqui* speak.

solitary Latin *solitarius* alone.

solo Italian alone, from Latin *solus.*

solstice French, from Latin *solstitium*, from *sol* sun + *sistere* cause to stand.

soluble French, from Latin *solubilis,* from *solvere* loosen, dissolve. See **solve**.

solution French *solucion,* from Latin *solutio* explanation.

solve Latin *solvere* loosen, from *se-* apart + *luere* let go.

solvent See **solve**.

somatic Greek *somatikos* of the body, from *soma* body.

somber French *sombre* gloomy, dark, from Latin *sub-* under + *umbra* shade.

sombrero Spanish *sombra* shade.

some Old English *sum.*

somersault French *sombresault* leap, from Latin *supra* above + *saltus* leap.

somnolent French, from Latin *somnolentus,* from *somnus* sleep.

son Old English *sunu.*

sonar so(und) n(avigation) a(nd) r(anging).

sonata Italian, from Latin *sonare* sound.

song Old English *sang.*

sonic Latin *sonus* noise.

sonnet Italian *suono* sound, from Latin *sonus* noise.

sonse Irish *sonas* good fortune.

soon Old English *sona.*

soot Old English *sot.*

sooth Old English *soth.*

soothe Old English *sothian* prove to be true.

sophism Latin *sophisma* false belief, from Greek *sophos* clever or wise.

sophisticate Latin *sophisticare* disguise, from Greek *sophistikos* clever, from Sophists, early Greek teachers of philosophy (the study of right and wrong) and ethics.

sorcery French *sorcerie* magic, taking a chance by drawing lots (things like pieces of pottery used in games of chance), from Latin *sors* lot.

sordid French, from Latin *sordes* filth.

sore Old English *sar* painful.

sorghum Italian *sorgo.*

sorority Latin *sororitas* sisterhood, from *soror* sister.

sorrel[1] (color) French *sor* light brown, from Latin *saurus.*

sorrel[2] (plant) French *surele*, from *sur* sour, from the taste of its leaves.

sorrow Old English *sorg.*

sort French *sortie* manner, from Latin *sors* kind, from *sortem, sors* lot, condition.

sortie FRENCH *sortie* a going out, from *sortir.* See **sort.**

sot OLD ENGLISH *sott* stupid person, from FRENCH *sot*, origin uncertain.

souffle FRENCH *souffler* blow.

sough OLD ENGLISH *swogan* sound.

soul OLD ENGLISH *sawol* spiritual part of people.

sound[1] (hearing) FRENCH *son,* from LATIN *sonus.*

sound[2] (healthy) OLD ENGLISH *(ge)sund.*

sound[3] (water channel) OLD ENGLISH *sund.*

sound[4] (depth) FRENCH *sonder,* from LATIN *sub-* under + *unda* a wave.

soup FRENCH *soupe.*

sour OLD ENGLISH *sur.*

source FRENCH *sourse* point where a river or stream starts, from *sourdre* rise, from LATIN *surgere.*

soutache FRENCH, from HUNGARIAN *szuszak* curl of hair.

south OLD ENGLISH *suth.*

souvenir FRENCH remember, from LATIN *subvenire* come to mind.

sovereign FRENCH *soverain* supreme ruler, from LATIN *super* above.

soviet RUSSIAN *sovet* council.

sow[1] (pig) OLD ENGLISH *sugu.*

sow[2] (plant seed) OLD ENGLISH *sawan.*

soy DUTCH *soya*, from JAPANESE *soyu*, from *shoyu*, from CHINESE *shi-yu*, from *shi* fermented soy beans + *yu* oil.

space FRENCH *espace* length of place or time, from LATIN *spatium* room.

spade OLD ENGLISH *spadu.*

spaghetti ITALIAN *spago* small cord.

spalpeen IRISH *spailpin.*

span OLD ENGLISH *spannen* clasp, fasten, stretch.

spang[1] (action) SCOTTISH, with a leap.

spang[2] (buckle) See **spangle.**

spangle MIDDLE ENGLISH *spang* a clasp, from OLD ENGLISH.

spaniel FRENCH *espagnol,* from LATIN *Hispania* Spain.

spank imitative.

spanker See **spank** + **-er.**

spanner GERMAN.

spar OLD NORSE *sperra* beam.

spar[1] (pole) MIDDLE ENGLISH *sparre*, from DUTCH.

spar[2] (to box) FRENCH *esparer* kick, from ITALIAN *sparare*, from LATIN *ex-* + *parare* ward off, parry.

spar[3] (mineral) GERMAN *spar, sper.*

spare OLD ENGLISH *sparian* leave unhurt.

spark OLD ENGLISH *spearca.*

sparrow OLD ENGLISH *spearwa.*

sparse LATIN *spargere* scatter.

spasm FRENCH *spasme,* from LATIN *spasmus*, from GREEK *spaein* tear.

spat imitative.

spate MIDDLE ENGLISH, from SCOTTISH sudden flood, origin unknown.

spatial LATIN *spatium.*

spatter possibly from DUTCH *spatt(en)* splash.

spatula LATIN broad piece, from GREEK *spathe.*

spavin FRENCH *esparvain.*

spawn FRENCH *espandre* get rid of.

speak OLD ENGLISH *specan* say words.

spear OLD ENGLISH *spere.*

special FRENCH *especial,* from LATIN *specialis* particular, from *species* kind.

species LATIN kind.

specific LATIN *spectifucus,* from *species.* See species.

specimen LATIN *specere* see.

specious LATIN *speciosus* beautiful, from *species* kind.

speck OLD ENGLISH *specca.*

spectacle FRENCH, from LATIN *spectaculum* show.

spectator LATIN see.

specter (spectre) FRENCH, from LATIN *spectrum* appearance, from *spectare* behold.

spectroscope See **spectrum** + **-scope**.

spectrum LATIN appear.

speculate LATIN *speculari* view, from *specula* watch tower, from *specere* see.

speculum LATIN *specere* look.

speech OLD ENGLISH *spæc* talk.

speed OLD ENGLISH *sped* success.

spell[1] (write words) FRENCH *espeller* explain.

spell[2] (magic) OLD ENGLISH *spell* story.

spell[3] (relieve) OLD ENGLISH *spellan.*

spelunker MIDDLE ENGLISH *spelunk* cave, cavern, from FRENCH *spelunque*, from LATIN *spelunca*, from GREEK *spelynx.*

spencer[1] (butler) FRENCH *espenser, despenser*, from *despencier* dispenser.

spencer[2] (in product names) the name *Spencer.*

spend OLD ENGLISH *spendan* pay out, from LATIN *expendare* pay.

sperm FRENCH *esperme*, from LATIN *sperma*, from GREEK seed, from *speirein* sow.

spew OLD ENGLISH *speowan.*

sphagnum LATIN *sphagnos,* a kind of lichen, from GREEK *sphagnos* a spiny shrub.

sphere FRENCH, from LATIN *sphera* ball, from GREEK *sphaira.*

sphinx LATIN, from GREEK strangler.

sphygmo- GREEK *sphygmos* the pulse.

sphygmomanometer See **sphygmo-** + **manometer**.

spice FRENCH *espice,* from LATIN *species* kind.

spicule LATIN *speculum*, from *spicule* point.

spider MIDDLE ENGLISH *spithre,* from OLD ENGLISH *spinnan* spin.

spigot MIDDLE ENGLISH, origin uncertain.

spike possibly from DUTCH nail.

spill OLD ENGLISH *spillan* waste.

spiller[1] (fish line) IRISH, origin uncertain.

spiller[2] (fire stick) MIDDLE ENGLISH *spill* splinter, origin uncertain.

spin OLD ENGLISH *spinnan* twist into thread.

spinach FRENCH *espinache*, from Spanish *espinac,* from ARABIC *isbanakh*, from PERSIAN *aspanakh.*

spindle OLD ENGLISH *spinnan* spin.

spine FRENCH *espine,* from LATIN *spina* a thorn.

spinet FRENCH, from ITALIAN *spinetta,* from Giovanni *Spinetti,* inventor of the instrument in the early 1500s.

spinney MIDDLE ENGLISH *spenne* thorn hedge, from FRENCH *espinei*, from LATIN *spinetum*, from *spina* thorn.

spinster MIDDLE ENGLISH *spinnestere,* woman who spins thread (as an occupation), from *spinnen* spin. In earlier times the *-ster* was added to show a woman's occupation.

spiracle MIDDLE ENGLISH, from LATIN *spiraculum,* from *spirare* breathe.

spiral LATIN *spiralis* winding, from *spira* coil, from GREEK *speira.*

spire OLD ENGLISH *spir* stalk of a plant.

spirillum LATIN *spira.* See **spiral.**

spirit FRENCH *esprit,* from LATIN *spiritus* breath, life, soul.

spirochete LATIN *spirochaeta,* from GREEK *speira* spiral + *chaite* hair.

spirometer LATIN *spirare* breathe + GREEK *metron* measure.

spit OLD ENGLISH *spitu.*

spite See **despite.**

spittoon See **spit.**

splay MIDDLE ENGLISH *displaten* display.

spleen LATIN *splen,* from GREEK.

splendid LATIN *splendidus* bright.

splendor FRENCH, from LATIN *splendere* shine.

splice DUTCH *splissen* join ropes together.

spline OLD NORSE *splindra* splinter.

splint GERMAN *splinte* metal pin.

split DUTCH *splitten.*

splotch MODERN ENGLISH, origin uncertain (perhaps a blend of **spot, blot,** and **botch**).

spoil FRENCH *espoillier* take by robbing, from LATIN *spolium* things taken by robbing.

spondulick GREEK *spondylikos,* from *spondylos* a seashell used as money.

sponge OLD ENGLISH, from LATIN, from GREEK *spongia.*

sponsor LATIN surety (person who pays the bills of another).

spontaneous LATIN *spontaneus* voluntary, from *sponte.*

spoof A card game called *Spoof* that includes tricks. It was invented by an English comedian in the late 19th century.

spook DUTCH ghost.

spool DUTCH *spoele.*

spoon OLD ENGLISH *spon* a chip.

spoor AFRIKAANS *spor,* from DUTCH.

spore LATIN *spora,* from GREEK *spora* seed.

sport FRENCH *disporter,* from LATIN *dis-* opposite + *porter* carry, from the idea of leading the attention away from serious things.

spot possibly from DUTCH *spotte* stain.

spouse FRENCH *espous* bridegroom and *espouse* bride, from LATIN *sponsus* engaged man and *sponsa* engaged woman.

spout DUTCH *spouten* spurt.

sprain MODERN ENGLISH, origin uncertain.

sprawl OLD ENGLISH *sprewlian.*

spray possibly from DUTCH *spra(e)yen* sprinkle.

spread OLD ENGLISH *sprædan* extend.

spree AMERICAN slang, origin uncertain, perhaps from FRENCH *esprit* spirit.

sprig MIDDLE ENGLISH *sprigge.*

sprightly See **sprite.**

spring OLD ENGLISH *springan* grow.

sprinkle possibly from DUTCH *sprenkelen,* from *sprenkel* small spot.

sprint MIDDLE ENGLISH spring, leap, from OLD NORSE *spretta* jump up.

sprite FRENCH *esprit,* from LATIN *spiritus* breath, life, soul.

sprocket MODERN ENGLISH, origin uncertain.

sprout OLD ENGLISH *sprutan* shoot forth.

spruce MIDDLE ENGLISH *Spruce,* Russia, a place where the tree can be found.

spry SWEDISH *sprygg* lively.

spume FRENCH, from LATIN *spuma* foam.

spunk IRISH *sponc* tinder, from LATIN *spongia* sponge.

spur OLD ENGLISH *spura.*

spurious LATIN *spurius.*

spurn OLD ENGLISH *spurnan* kick off, reject, despise.

spurt MIDDLE ENGLISH *spirt*, origin uncertain.

sputter DUTCH *sputteren.*

spy FRENCH *espier* watch with attention.

squab MODERN ENGLISH, origin uncertain.

squad FRENCH *esquades* small party of soldiers, from LATIN *ex-* out + *quadra* square, referring to the arranging of soldiers into squares.

squalid LATIN *squalidus* extremely dirty.

squall[1] (storm) MIDDLE ENGLISH, related to SWEDISH *skval,* rushing water.

squall[2] (cry) OLD NORSE *skvala,* cry out.

squalor LATIN. See **squalid**.

squamous LATIN *squamosus* scaly, from *squama* scale.

squander MIDDLE ENGLISH, origin uncertain.

square FRENCH *esquarrer*, from LATIN *ex-* out + *quadrare* square, from *quadrus* a square, from *quattuor* four.

squash[1] (crush) FRENCH *esquasser* break in pieces, from LATIN *ex-* thoroughly + *quatere* shake.

squash[2] (vegetable) NATIVE AMERICAN.

squat FRENCH *esquatir,* from LATIN *ex-* out + *cogere* force.

squaw NATIVE AMERICAN.

squawk imitative.

squeak OLD NORSE *skvakka* gurgle.

squeamish FRENCH *escoimous* shy.

squeeze OLD ENGLISH *cwysan* crush.

squelch imitative.

squib MIDDLE ENGLISH, origin uncertain.

squid perhaps from a sailors' variation of squirt.

squiggle See **squirm** + **wiggle**.

squint possibly from MIDDLE ENGLISH *skwyn.*

squire FRENCH *esquier.* See **esquire**.

squirm imitative.

squirt probably from GERMAN and DUTCH *swirtjen.*

St. Elmo ITALIAN *Sant'Ermo* St. Erasmus, patron saint of Mediterranean sailors, possibly influenced by GREEK *elene* torch.

stab MIDDLE ENGLISH *stabbe.*

stable FRENCH *(e)stable* firm, from LATIN *stabilis*, from *stare* stand.

staccato ITALIAN separated.

stack OLD NORSE *stakkr* haystack.

stadium LATIN measure of length about 607 ft (the length of ancient Greek and Roman tracks for athletic events), from GREEK *stadion.*

staff OLD ENGLISH *stæf* pole.

stag OLD ENGLISH *stagga.*

stage FRENCH *estage* floor, from LATIN *stare* stand.

stagger OLD NORSE *stakra* push.

stagnant LATIN *stagnare,* from *stagnum* swamp.

staid See **stay**.

stain FRENCH, from LATIN *dis-* from + *tingere* color.

stair OLD ENGLISH *stæger.*

stake OLD ENGLISH *staca* strong stick.

stalactite LATIN *stalactites,* from GREEK *stalaktos* dripping, from *stalassein* trickle.

stalagmite LATIN *stalagmites,* from GREEK *stalagmos* a dropping, from *stalagma* a drop, drip, from *stalassein* trickle.

stale probably from DUTCH *stel.*

stalk[1] (pursue) OLD ENGLISH *bestealcian* go secretly.

stalk[2] (stem) OLD ENGLISH *stela* a stalk.

stall OLD ENGLISH *steall* place in a stable.

stalwart OLD ENGLISH *stælwierthe,* from *stathol* foundation + *wierthe* worth.

stamen LATIN, a thread on an upright loom. See **stamina**.

stamina LATIN *stamen* thread, from the idea that the warp threads on a loom were the foundation of the fabric. Also, from the idea in mythology that threads spun by the Fates determined the length of the person's life.

stammel probably from FRENCH *estamel,* from *estame* woolen thread, from LATIN *stamen* thread.

stance FRENCH, from LATIN *stare* stand.

stanchion FRENCH *estanchon,* from *estance,* from LATIN *stare* stand.

stand OLD ENGLISH *standan* be upright.

standard FRENCH *estandart* flag.

stang OLD NORSE *stong.*

stanza ITALIAN room, from LATIN *stare* stand.

staple[1] (produce) FRENCH *estaple* market, from DUTCH *stapel.*

staple[2] (metal) OLD ENGLISH *stapol* a post.

star OLD ENGLISH *steorra.*

starboard OLD ENGLISH. See **steer** + **board** (boats were steered using a paddle on the right side).

starch OLD ENGLISH *stearc* stiff.

stare OLD ENGLISH *starian.*

stark OLD ENGLISH *stearc* severe.

start OLD ENGLISH *styrtan.*

startle OLD ENGLISH *steartlian* struggle.

starve OLD ENGLISH *steorfan* die.

-stat GREEK *-states.*

state FRENCH *estat,* from LATIN *status* condition, from *stare* stand.

static LATIN *staticus,* from GREEK *statikos* causing to stand.

station FRENCH, from LATIN *stare* stand.

statistics GERMAN *Statistik* science of collecting numerical data, from LATIN *statisticus* having to do with state affairs, from *status* condition, from *stare* stand.

stator LATIN, from *stare* stand.

statue FRENCH, from LATIN *statua* image, from *stare* stand.

statuesque See **statue** + **-esque**.

status LATIN condition, from *stare* stand.

staunch FRENCH *estanche* watertight, from *estanchier,* from LATIN *stans.* See **stance**.

stave MIDDLE ENGLISH plural of **staff**.

stay FRENCH *estai,* from *ester* stand, from LATIN *stare.*

stead OLD ENGLISH *stede* place.

steak Old Norse *steik* slice of meat roasted over a fire.

steal Old English *stæfan.*

stealth Middle English *steithe,* from *stelen* steal.

steam Old English smoke.

steed Old English *steda* stallion.

steel Old English *stiele.*

steep Old English *steap* high.

steer Old English *stieran.*

stellar Latin *stellaris,* from *stella* star.

stem Old Norse *stemma* dam up.

stench Old English *stenc.*

stencil French *estenceler* sparkle, from *stencelle* spark, from Latin *scintilla.*

stenography Greek *stenos* narrow + *graphia* writing.

step Old English *steppan* go on foot.

stephanotis Greek fit for a crown or wreath, from *stephanos* crown.

steppe Russian *step.*

stereo Greek *stereos* hard, firm, solid.

stereophonic See **stereo** + **phonic**.

stereopticon See **stereo** + **optic**.

sterile Latin *sterilis.*

stern[1] (strict) Old English *stirne* severe.

stern[2] (ship end) Old Norse *stjorn,* from *styra* steer.

sternal Latin *sternalis,* from **sternum**.

sternum Latin, from Greek *sternon* chest.

stet Latin let it stand.

stethoscope Greek *stethos* chest + Latin *-scopium,* from Greek *-skopion,* from *skopein* view, examine.

stevedore Spanish *estivar* put away, from Latin *stipare* cram.

stew French *estuver* bathe in hot water, from Latin *ex-* out + Greek *typhos* steam.

steward Old English *stigweard,* from *stig* house + *weard* keeper.

stick Old English *sticca.*

stiff Old English *stif* rigid.

stifle[1] (smother) French *estouffer.*

stifle[2] (leg joint) Middle English.

stigma Latin brand (mark with a hot iron), from Greek.

stile Old English *stigan* climb.

stiletto Italian *stilo* dagger, from Latin *stilus.*

still Old English *stille.*

stilt probably from German or Dutch *stelte.*

stimulate Latin *stimulare* prick with a stick.

sting Old English *stingan* cut with something pointed.

stink Old English *stincan* have an odor.

stint Old English *styntan* make dull.

stipend Latin *stipendium* tax, from *stips* wages + *pendere* pay.

stipulate Latin *stipulare* bargain.

stir Old English *styrian* move.

stirrup Old English *stigrap.*

stitch Old English *stice* a puncture.

stoat Middle English *stote.*

stock Old English *stocc* tree trunk.

stockade French *estacade,* from Spanish *estacada,* from *estaca* stake.

stoic LATIN *stoicus,* from GREEK *stoikos,* from *stoa* (roof supported by pillars). The followers of the Greek philosopher Zeno were called Stoics, after the great hall in Athens where he taught.

stole LATIN *stola,* from GREEK a garment.

stolid LATIN *stolidus* dull.

stomach FRENCH *stomeque,* from LATIN *stomachus*, from GREEK *stomachos,* from *stoma* mouth.

stomacker See **stomach.**

stone OLD ENGLISH *stan.*

stool OLD ENGLISH *stol* seat.

stoop OLD ENGLISH *stupian.*

stop OLD ENGLISH.

store FRENCH *estorer* establish, from LATIN *instaurare* build.

stork OLD ENGLISH *storc* stiff, from its stiff-legged walk.

storm OLD ENGLISH disturbance.

story FRENCH *storie* history, from LATIN *historiea* story of past events, from GREEK *historia* information.

stoup MIDDLE ENGLISH *stowpe* bucket, from OLD NORSE *staup.*

stout FRENCH *estout* bold.

stow OLD ENGLISH a place.

straddle OLD ENGLISH *stridan.*

straggle probably from MIDDLE ENGLISH *straken* roam.

straight MIDDLE ENGLISH *strecchen* stretch out.

strail OLD ENGLISH *stræl* blanket, from LATIN *stragula*, from *sternere* lay down, spread.

strain FRENCH *estraindre* press tightly, from LATIN *stringere* pull tight.

strait FRENCH *estreit* narrow, from LATIN *stringere* pull tight.

strake MIDDLE ENGLISH, a line of planking on a boat hull.

strand origin uncertain.

strange FRENCH *estrange* foreign, from LATIN *extra* outside.

strangle FRENCH *estrangler* choke, from LATIN *strangulare,* from GREEK *strangalan* halter.

stratagem LATIN, from GREEK *strategema* act of a general, from *stratos* army + *agein* lead.

strategy FRENCH, from GREEK *strategia* command, from *strategos* general, from *stratos* army + *agein* lead.

stratosphere FRENCH *stratosphère*, from LATIN *stratus* spreading out, from *sternere* spread out + FRENCH, from LATIN *sphera* ball, from GREEK *sphaira.*

stratum LATIN something spread out, from *sternere* spread out.

straw OLD ENGLISH *streaw.*

stray FRENCH *estraier,* from LATIN *estra* beyond + *vagari* wander.

streak OLD ENGLISH *strica* mark.

street OLD ENGLISH *stræt,* from LATIN *strata via* paved way, from *sternere* spread out.

strength OLD ENGLISH *strengthu* power.

strenuous LATIN *strenuus* active.

stress FRENCH *estrece* narrowness, from LATIN *stringere* draw tight.

stretch OLD ENGLISH *streccan.*

strew OLD ENGLISH *streowian* scatter.

strict LATIN *stringere* draw tight.

stricture See **strict.**

stride OLD ENGLISH *stridan.*

strident LATIN *stridere* say in a rough tone.

strife FRENCH *estrif.*

strike OLD ENGLISH *strican* go.

string OLD ENGLISH *streng.*

stringent LATIN *stringere* draw tight.

strip[1] (take away) OLD ENGLISH *bestriepan* rob.

strip[2] (narrow band) DUTCH *stripe* streak.

stripe DUTCH.

stroboscope GREEK *strobos* whirl around + LATIN *-scopium,* from GREEK *-skopion,* from *skopein* view, examine.

stroke OLD ENGLISH *stracian* strike.

stroll probably from GERMAN *strollen*, from *strolchen*, from *Strolch* fortuneteller, vagabond.

strong OLD ENGLISH *strang* able.

structure LATIN *structura.*

struggle MIDDLE ENGLISH *strogelen*, origin uncertain.

strut OLD ENGLISH *strutian* stand in a stiff way.

stubble FRENCH *estuble* stubble, from LATIN *stupla*, from *stipula* stalk, straw.

stubborn origin uncertain.

stucco ITALIAN.

stud[1] (post) OLD ENGLISH *studu.*

stud[2] (breed) OLD ENGLISH *stod.*

student FRENCH *estudiant,* from LATIN *studere* study.

studio ITALIAN workroom, from LATIN *studium* a study.

study FRENCH *estudier,* from LATIN *studere* study.

stuff FRENCH *estoffe* material, from LATIN *stup(p)a,* from GREEK *styppe.*

stultify LATIN *stultificare* make foolish, from *stultus* foolish + *facere* make.

stumble OLD NORSE *stumla.*

stump DUTCH *stomp.*

stun FRENCH *estoner,* from LATIN *ex-* out + *tonare* thunder.

stunt[1] (slow the growth) OLD ENGLISH *stunt* foolish, stupid.

stunt[2] (trick) AMERICAN, origin unknown.

stupefy LATIN *stupefacere* stun, from *stupere* be amazed + *facere* do, make.

stupendous LATIN *stupere.*

stupid LATIN *stupidus* dull.

stupor LATIN.

sturdy FRENCH *estourdir* stunned.

sturgeon FRENCH *esturfon.*

stutter MIDDLE ENGLISH *stutten.*

sty OLD ENGLISH *sti.*

style FRENCH pointed writing tool, from LATIN *stilus.*

stylus LATIN *stilus* pointed writing tool.

suave FRENCH, from LATIN *suavis* agreeable.

sub- FRENCH, from LATIN under.

subdue FRENCH, from LATIN *subducere* remove.

subject FRENCH, from LATIN *subjicere*, from *sub-* under + *jacere* throw.

subjugate LATIN *subjugare* make under one's rule, from *sub-* under + *jugum* yoke (wooden collar for a pair of oxen to join them), from an early Roman custom that made defeated soldiers crawl under a yoke to show their defeat.

subjunctive LATIN *subjunctivus* serving to join, connecting, from *sub-* under + *jungere* join.

sublime LATIN *sublimis*, from *sub-* under + *limen* lintel (horizontal top part of a doorway).

submarine See **sub-** + **marine**.

submerge LATIN *sub-* under + *mergere* jump into.

submerse LATIN *submersus*, from *submergere*. See **submerge**.

submit LATIN *submittere*, from *sub-* under + *mittere* send.

subordinate LATIN *subordinare* place in a lower order, from *sub-* under + *ordo* order.

subscribe LATIN *subscribere*, from *sub-* under + *scribere* write.

subscript See **subscribe**.

subsequent LATIN *subsequi*, from *sub-* under + *sequi* follow.

subside LATIN *subsidere*, from *sub-* under + *sidere* settle.

subsist LATIN *subsistere* stand still, from *sub-* under + *sistere* stand up, from *stare* stand.

substance FRENCH, from LATIN *substantia*, from *sub-* under + *stare* stand.

substantive LATIN *substantia*. See **substance**.

substitute LATIN *substituere*, from *sub-* under + *statuere* put.

subsume LATIN *subsumere* take under, from *sub-* under + *sumere* take.

subterfuge FRENCH *subterfuge*, from LATIN *subterfugium* evasion, from *subterfugere* flee by stealth, from *subter* beneath, secretly + *fugere* flee.

subtle FRENCH *soutil* thin, from LATIN *subtilis* thin, from *sub-* under + *tela* web.

subtract LATIN *subtrahere*, from *sub-* under + *trahere* draw.

suburb LATIN *suburbium*, from *sub-* under + *urbs* city.

subvert FRENCH, from LATIN *subversio*, from *subvertere*, from *sub-* under + *vertere* turn.

succeed FRENCH *succeder*, from LATIN *succedere* come after, go near to, from *sub-* next to, after + *cedere* go, move.

success See **succeed**.

succinct LATIN *succingere*, from *sub-* under + *cingere* gird (get ready for action).

succor FRENCH, from LATIN *succurrere*, from *sub-* under + *currere* run.

succulent LATIN *succulentus*, from *sucus* juice.

succumb LATIN *succumbere*, from *sub-* under + *cumbere* lie.

such OLD ENGLISH *swelc*.

suck OLD ENGLISH *sucan*.

sucrose FRENCH *sucre* sugar + chemical suffix *-ose*.

suction LATIN *sugere* suck.

sudden FRENCH *soudian* quick, from LATIN *subitaneus* hasty, from *sub-* under + *ire* go.

suds probably from DUTCH *sudse* marsh water.

sue FRENCH *sivre* follow, from LATIN *sequi*.

suede FRENCH *Suéde* Sweden, from *gants de Suéde* SWEDISH gloves.

suet LATIN *sebum*.

suffer FRENCH, from LATIN *sufferre* endure, from *sub-* under + *ferre* bring.

suffice FRENCH, from LATIN *sufficere*, from *sub-* under + *facere* do, make.

sufficient See **suffice**.

suffix LATIN *suffigere*, from *sub-* under + *figere* fix.

suffocate LATIN *suffocare* choke, from *sub-* under + *fauces* throat.

suffrage LATIN *suffragium,* from *sub-* under + *fragor* loud applause.

suffuse LATIN *suffundere* fill, from *sub-* under + *fundere* pour.

sugar MIDDLE ENGLISH, from FRENCH *sucre,* from LATIN *succarum,* from ARABIC *sukkar,* from PERSIAN *shakar,* from SANSKRIT *sharkara* candied sugar, originally grit, gravel.

suggest LATIN *suggerere* advise.

suicide LATIN *sui* self + *caedere* kill.

suit FRENCH *suite,* from LATIN *sequi* follow.

suite FRENCH.

sukiyaki JAPANESE.

sulfur LATIN *sulphur.*

sulky probably from OLD ENGLISH *solcen* idle.

sullen FRENCH *solain* only one, from LATIN *solus* alone.

sully FRENCH *souiller* make dirty, soil.

sulphonamide LATIN *sulphon,* from *sulphur* + *amide,* from *ammonia* + *-ide.*

sultry OLD ENGLISH *sweltan* die.

sum LATIN *summa* top, from the early Roman practice of figuring out the problem from the bottom and going upward and placing the sum at the top.

summary LATIN *summa* a sum.

summer OLD ENGLISH *sumor.*

summit FRENCH *somete,* from LATIN *summum* highest.

summon FRENCH, from LATIN *summonere* remind secretly, from *sub-* secretly + *monere* warn.

summons FRENCH *sononse.*

sumpter FRENCH *som(m)etier,* from LATIN *sagma* packsaddle.

sumptuous FRENCH *somptueux,* from LATIN *sumptus* expense, from *sumere* take.

sun OLD ENGLISH *sunne.*

sundae AMERICAN, probably from Sunday, possibly because it was originally a special treat sold on that day.

Sunday MIDDLE ENGLISH *sunnenday,* from OLD ENGLISH *sunnandæg,* from LATIN *solis dies* sun's day.

sundry OLD ENGLISH *syndrig* separate.

super- LATIN beyond, over, above.

superb LATIN *superbus* superior, from *super-* above.

supercilious LATIN *supercilium* eyebrow, from *super-* above + *cilium* eyelid, from raising the eyebrows to show pride.

superficial LATIN *superficialis* surface, from *superficies,* from *super-* above + *facies* face.

superfluous LATIN *superfluere,* from *super-* above + *fluere* flow.

superintendent See **super-** + **intend.**

superior FRENCH, from LATIN higher, from *super-* above.

superlative FRENCH, from LATIN *superlativus,* from *super-* above + *ferre* bring.

supernal FRENCH, from LATIN *supernus,* from *super-* above.

superscript LATIN *superscribere,* from *super-* above + *scribere* write.

supersede FRENCH *superceder,* from LATIN *supersedere,* from *super-* above + *sedere* sit.

superstition FRENCH, from LATIN *superstitio,* from *super-* over + *stare* stand.

supervise LATIN *supervidere* look over, from *super-* over + *videre* see.

supine LATIN *supinus.*

supper FRENCH *souper,* from *soupe* soup.

supplant LATIN *supplantare* trip one's feet, from *sub-* under + *planta* bottom of the foot.

supple FRENCH *agile*, from LATIN *supplex* bending under.

supplement LATIN *supplementum* supply.

suppliant FRENCH *supplier,* from LATIN *supplicare.* See **supplicate**.

supplicate LATIN *supplicare* kneel down, from *sub-* under + *plicare* fold.

supply FRENCH *soupleier* fill up, from LATIN *supplere,* from *sub-* under + *plere* fill.

support FRENCH *supporter* endure, from LATIN *supportare* bring to, from *sub-* under + *portare* carry.

suppose FRENCH *supposere* set under, from LATIN *supponere,* from *sub-* under + *ponere* place.

suppress LATIN *supprimere* press under, from *sub-* under + *premere* press.

supreme LATIN *superus* upper, from *super* above.

sur- FRENCH *sur, sour* over, above, beyond, from LATIN *super.*

surcease FRENCH *surseoir* stop, from LATIN *supersedere,* from *super-* above + *sedere* sit.

surcingle FRENCH *surcengle*, from *sur-* over + *cengle* a girdle, from LATIN *cingulum* girth.

sure FRENCH *sur* certain, from LATIN *securus* free from care.

surf origin uncertain.

surface FRENCH *sur-* above + *face* a face.

surfeit FRENCH *sorfaire* overdo, from LATIN *super-* above + *facere* do, make.

surge FRENCH *sorgir* rise, from LATIN *surgere.*

surgery FRENCH *surgerie*, from LATIN, from GREEK *cheirourgia*, from *cheir* hand + *ergon* work.

surly MIDDLE ENGLISH *sirly* lordly, majestic.

surmise FRENCH *surmettre* accuse, from LATIN *supermittere,* from *super-* above + *mittere* send.

surmount FRENCH *surmonter* rise above, from LATIN *super-* above + *mons* mountain.

surplus FRENCH, from LATIN *super-* over + *plus* more.

surprise FRENCH, from LATIN *super-* over + *prehendere* take.

surreal FRENCH *surréalisme*, from *sur-* beyond + *réalisme* realism.

surrender FRENCH *surrendre*, from *sur-* over + *rendre* give back.

surreptitious LATIN *surripere,* from *sub-* under + *rapere* take by force.

surrey *Surrey,* the county in England where it was first built.

surrogate LATIN *surrogare,* from *sub-* in place of + *rogare* elect.

surround FRENCH *soronder,* from LATIN *super-* over + *undare* rise, from *unda* a wave.

surtout FRENCH *sur* above + *tout* everything.

survey FRENCH *surveier* look over, from LATIN *super-* over + *videre* see.

survive LATIN *survivre,* from *supervivere,* from *super-* above + *vivere* live.

susceptible LATIN *susceptibilis* able to receive, from *suscipere,* from *sub-* under + *capere* take.

suspect LATIN *suspicere*, from *sub-* under + *spicere* look.

suspend FRENCH *suspendre,* from LATIN *suspendere,* from *sub-* under + *pendere* hang.

suspense FRENCH *suspens,* from LATIN *suspendere.* See **suspend**.

suspicion French *sospecon,* from Latin *suspicere.* See **suspect**.

sustain Middle English, from French *sustenir* hold up, from Latin *sustinere,* from *sub-* under + *tenere* hold.

susurrant Middle English, from Latin *susurrare*, from *susurrus* murmur, whisper; imitative origin.

sutler Dutch *soetelen* do dirty work.

suttee Hindi *satl* virtuous wife.

suture Latin *suere* sew.

svelte French, from Italian, from Latin *evellere* pluck out.

swab Dutch *zwabben* splash in water.

swaddle Old English *swethel.*

swagger probably from Scandinavian.

swain Old Norse *sveinn* boy.

swale probably from Old Norse *svalr* cool.

swallow[1] (throat action) Old English *swelgan.*

swallow[2] (bird) Old English *swealwe.*

swamp Middle English *sompe.*

swan Old English.

swank probably from German *swanken* sway.

swarm Old English *swearm.*

swarthy Old English *sweard* a skin.

swastika Sanskrit *svastika*, from *svasti* well-being, luck, from *su-* well + *as-*, from *asti* he is. Originally an ancient cosmic or religious symbol thought to bring good luck.

swat possibly from Middle English *swap* strike, smite.

sway Old Norse *sveigja* bend.

swear Old English *swerian.*

sweat Old English *swætan.*

sweep possibly from Old English *swapan.*

sweet Old English *swete* pleasing.

swell Old English *swellan* increase in size.

swelter Old English *sweltan* die.

swerve Old English *sweorfan* rub.

swift Old English rapid.

swig origin unknown.

swindle German *schwindeln* cheat.

swing Old English *swingan* rush.

swish imitative.

switch Dutch *swijch* branch.

switchel origin uncertain.

swivel Middle English *swyvel,* from Old English *swifan* revolve.

swoon Middle English *swownen,* from Old English *geswogen.*

sword Old English something that destroys.

sycamore French *sicamor,* from Latin *sycomorus,* from Greek *sykomoros.*

sycophant Latin, from Greek *sykophantes,* from *sykon* a fig + *phainein* show.

syllable French *sillabe*, from Latin *syllaba,* from Greek *syllabe* that which holds together.

syllabub origin uncertain.

sylvan Latin *silva* a woods.

symbiosis Latin, from Greek *sumbioun,* from *syn-* together + *bioun* live.

symbol Latin *symbolum* sign, from Greek *symbolon,* from *syn-* together + *ballein* throw.

symmetry French *symmetrie,* from Latin *symmetria* proportion, from Greek *symmetria,* from *syn-* together + *metron* a measure.

sympathy LATIN *sympathia* feeling in common, from GREEK *sympatheia,* from *syn-* together + *pathos* feeling.

symphony FRENCH *simphonie,* from LATIN *symphonia* agreement of sounds, from GREEK *sympatheia*, from *syn-* together + *phone* sound.

symposium LATIN, from GREEK *syn-* together + *posis* drinking.

symptom LATIN *symptoma*, from GREEK *symptoma*, from *syn-* together + *piptein* fall.

synagogue FRENCH *sinagoge,* from LATIN *synagoga,* from GREEK *synagoge,* from *syn-* together + *agein* bring.

synapsis LATIN, from GREEK *syn-* together + *apsis* a joining, from *haptein* join.

synchronize GREEK *synchronos,* from *syn-* together + *chronos* time.

syncopate LATIN *syncopare* cut short, from *suncope,* from GREEK *syn-* together + *koptein* cut.

syndicate FRENCH *syndicat,* from *syndic,* from *syn-* together + *dike* justice.

syndrome LATIN, from GREEK *syn-* with + *dramein* run.

syne MIDDLE ENGLISH, possibly from OLD NORSE *sioan.*

synonym LATIN *synonymum* word having the same meaning as another word, from GREEK *synonymon,* from *syn-* together + *onyma* a name.

synopsis LATIN plan, from GREEK *synopsis,* from *syn-* together + *opsis* a seeing.

synovia LATIN.

syntax FRENCH *syntaxe,* from LATIN, from GREEK *syn-* together + *tassein* arrange.

synthesis GREEK *syn-* together + *tihenai* place.

syphilis LATIN.

syringe LATIN, from GREEK *syringos,* from *syrinx* thin pipe.

syrup FRENCH *sirop,* from LATIN, from ARABIC *sharab* a drink.

system LATIN *systema* a whole that has several parts, from GREEK *systema,* from *syn-* together + *histanai* set.

systolic GREEK *systole* contraction, from *syn-* together + *stellein* put, send.

T

tab from tablet. See **table.**

tabard French *tabart.*

tabernacle Latin *tabernaculum* a tent, from *taberna* a hut.

table Old English *tabule* board, from Latin *tabula.*

tableau French picture.

tablet See **table.**

tabloid French *tablete* table + Greek *eidos* form, shape.

taboo Tongan *tabu* forbidden, not allowed.

tabulate See **table** + **-ate.**

tachometer Greek *tachos* speed + *metron* measure.

tacit Latin *tacere* be silent.

taciturn Latin *tacere* be silent.

tack[1] (fastener) Middle English *tak,* from French *taque* nail, pin, peg.

tack[2] (gear, food) See **tackle.**

tackle Dutch *takel* ship rigging, rope.

tact French, from Latin *tangere* touch.

tactics Latin *tacticus,* from Greek *takikos,* from *tassein* arrange.

tactile French, from Latin *tangere* touch.

taffeta French *taftan* weave.

taffrail Dutch *taffereel,* from *tafel* table, from Latin *tabula* tablet.

taffy origin uncertain, perhaps from *tafia* a liquor distilled from molasses.

tag Middle English, origin uncertain, related to **tack**[1].

tail Old English *tægel.*

tailor French *tailleur* cut, from Latin *tailiare* split, from *talea* a twig.

taint French *teindre* dye, from Latin *tingere* wet.

take Old Norse *taka* grasp.

talc French, from Arabic *talq.*

tale Old English *talu* story.

talent Old English *talente,* from Latin *talentum* sum of money, from Greek *talanton.*

talisman French *talisman,* from Arabic *tilsam,* from Greek *telesma,* from *telein* perform religious rites, from *telos* end.

talk Middle English *talken* speak, from Old English *talian* account.

tall Old English *(ge)tæl* prompt.

tallow probably from German *talg.*

tally FRENCH *tallie* score kept on a piece of wood, from LATIN *talea* rod.

Talmud HEBREW *talmudh* learning.

talon FRENCH, from LATIN *talus* an ankle.

tamale SPANISH *tamales,* from NATIVE AMERICAN *tamalli* steamed cornmeal.

tamarack NATIVE AMERICAN.

tambour FRENCH drum.

tame OLD ENGLISH *tam.*

tam-o-shanter the title character in a poem by Scottish poet Robert Burns (1759–1796).

tamper See **temper**.

tampion FRENCH *tampon* stopper.

tan FRENCH, from LATIN *tannum.*

tanager LATIN *tanagra* named 1758 by the naturalist Linnaeus, from PORTUGUESE, from NATIVE AMERICAN *tangara.*

tandem LATIN length.

tang OLD NORSE *tangi* spit of land, pointed metal tool.

tangent LATIN *tangere* touch.

tangible LATIN *tangibilis,* from *tangere* touch.

tangle MIDDLE ENGLISH *tagilen* involve in a difficult situation, from SCANDINAVIAN source.

tank MODERN ENGLISH, from HINDI *tankh* a reservoir of water, influenced by PORTUGUESE *tanque*, from *estanque* pool.

tankard MIDDLE ENGLISH, origin unknown.

tantalize LATIN *Tantalus*, from GREEK *Tantalos,* in mythology, a son of Zeus. In the afterlife, as a punishment, he had to stand in water up to his chin under branches full of fruit; both fruit and water withdrew from his reach when he tried to eat or drink.

tantamount FRENCH *tant amunter* amount to as much, from *tant* so much, from LATIN *tantus* + *amounter* amount to. See **amount**.

tantrum origin uncertain.

tap[1] (light hit) FRENCH *taper* hit.

tap[2] (faucet) OLD ENGLISH *tæppa.*

tape OLD ENGLISH *tæpe* strip of cloth.

taper MIDDLE ENGLISH, from OLD ENGLISH *tapor* wax candle (because a candle is generally narrower at one end).

tapestry FRENCH *tapisserie* heavy fabric that is decorated, from *tapis* carpet, from GREEK *tapes.*

tapioca PORTUGUESE *tapioca*, from NATIVE AMERICAN *tipioca*, from *tipi* residue + *ok* squeeze out (from roots of the cassava plant).

tapir NATIVE AMERICAN *tapira.*

tar OLD ENGLISH *teoru.*

tardy FRENCH *tardif*, from LATIN *tardus* slow.

target FRENCH *targuete* small shield, from OLD NORSE *targa* shield.

tariff FRENCH *tarif* list of prices, from ARABIC *ta'rir* information.

tarlatan FRENCH *tarlatane*, from *tarnatane* thin, stiffly starched muslin from India.

tarnal AMERICAN slang. See **eternal**.

tarnation AMERICAN *darnation*, from *damnation* influenced by **tarnal**.

tarnish FRENCH *ternir* stain.

taro MAORI.

tarot FRENCH, from ITALIAN *tarocchi,* from ARABIC *taraha* remove.

tarpaulin OLD ENGLISH *teru* tar + *pæll* cover.

tarpon DUTCH *tarpoen.*

tarry probably from French *targer* delay, from Latin *tardus* slow.

tarsier French *tarse* ankle, from Latin *tarsus* ankle (animal so named because of its long ankle bones). See **tarsus**.

tarsus Latin, from Greek *tarsos,* ankle, flat part (sole) of the foot, originally a flat surface.

tart[1] (sour) Old English *teart.*

tart[2] (pastry) Middle English *tarte.*

tarweed Old English *teoru weod.*

task Latin *tasca* tax, from *taxare* put a tax on. See **tax**.

tassel French knob.

taste French *taster* touch, taste.

tatter probably from Old Norse *töturr* rags.

tatting possibly from shortening of German *frivolitäten* knotted lace used for edging, etc.

tattle Dutch *telen* chatter.

tattoo Tongan *tatau* mark twice.

taunt Middle English, possibly from French *tanter* tempt.

Taurus Middle English, from Latin bull, the constellation Taurus.

taut Middle English *toght* tense.

tavern French *taverne,* from Latin *taberna* hut.

taw[1] (marble) origin uncertain, possibly from **tawny**.

taw[2] (leather) Old English *tawian* do, make.

tawdry fancy laces sold at a fair in Norwich, England called *St. Audrey* laces.

tawny French *tan(n)er* tan, from Latin *tannare.*

tax Latin *taxare* put a tax on, from *taxare* value.

taxi cab abbreviation for *taxi(meter) cab,* from French *taximéter,* from German, from Latin *taxa* a tax + *-meter,* from Greek *metron* measure + French *cabriolet* one-horse carriage, from Italian *capriola* leap like a goat, from Latin *caper* goat, because the carriage bounced like a goat leaping.

taxidermy Greek *taxis* arrangement + *derma* a skin.

tea Chinese *t'e.*

teach Old English *tæcan* show.

teak Portuguese *teca*, from Malay *tekka.*

team Old English two or more animals harnessed together for work.

tear[1] (pull apart) Old English *teran.*

tear[2] (from crying) Old English *tear.*

tease Old English *tsan* pull.

teat French *tete.*

technique French, from Greek *technikos* having to do with art and skill, from *techne* art, skill, craft.

technology Greek *technologia* systematic treatment, from *techne* art, skill, craft.

teddy bear American president Theodore "*Teddy*" Roosevelt.

tedium Latin *taediosus* weary, from *taedium.*

teepee Native American.

teeter possibly from Old Norse *titra* tremble.

teetotal repeating the first letter of **total**.

tele- Greek *tele-* far off.

telepathy See **tele-** + Greek *-pathia* suffering.

telephone See **tele-** + Greek *-phone* sound.

telescope See **tele-** + Greek *-skopion* examine.

television See **tele-** + **vision**.

temenos Greek *temew* cut off.

temper Old English *temprian* regulate, from Latin *temperare* regulate, from *tempus* a period.

temperance See **temper**.

temperate Latin *temperatus* restrained, regulated, from *temperare* moderate, regulate. See **temper**.

temperature Latin *temperatura* measure.

tempest French *tempest(e)* storm, from Latin *tempestas,* from *tempus* time.

temple[1] (building) Old English, from Latin *templum* space marked out.

temple[2] (head) French, from Latin *tempora* side of forehead.

tempo Italian, from Latin *tempus* time.

temporal Latin *temporalis* worldly, from *tempus* time.

temporary Latin *tempus* time.

temporize French *temporiser,* from Latin *tempus* time.

tempt French, from Latin *temptare* try.

tenable French *tenir* hold, from Latin *tenere.* See **tenet**.

tenacious Latin *tenax* hold fast, from *tenere.* See **tenet**.

tenant French *tenir* hold, from Latin *tenere.* See **tenet**.

tend French *tendre* offer, from Latin *tendere* direct.

tendency Latin *tendere* stretch.

tender French *tendre* gentle, from Latin *tener* soft.

tendon Latin *tendo,* from Greek *teinein* stretch.

tendril French *tendrum,* from Latin *tener* soft.

tenement Latin *tenementum,* from *tenere.*

tenet Latin, from *tenere* hold.

tennis probably from French *tenetz,* from *tenir* hold, from Latin *tenere.*

tenon Middle English, from French *tenir* hold, from French *tenant,* from Latin *tenere* hold.

tense[1] (tight) Latin *tendere* stretch.

tense[2] (verb form) French, from Latin *tempus* time.

tensile See **tense**[1] + **-ile**.

tent French *tente,* from Latin *tendere* stretch.

tentacle Latin *tentare* touch.

tentative Latin *tentativus,* from *tentare* try.

tenterhook Middle English *tenter,* from French *tente,* from Latin *tendere* stretch + Old English *hoc* bent piece of metal.

tenure French, from Latin *tenere* hold.

tepid Latin *tepidus.*

term French *terme* limit, from Latin *terminus.*

termagant French *Tervagant* an imaginary Muslim deity appearing in medieval Christian morality plays.

terminal Latin *terminalis* boundary, from *terminus* limit.

terminate Latin *terminare* end, from *terminus* limit.

tern Old Norse *therna.*

terra Latin earth.

terra cotta Italian baked earth, from Latin.

terrace French platform, from Latin *terra* earth.

terrain French, from Latin *terra* earth.

terrapin Native American.

terrarium LATIN *terra* earth + suffix *-arium.*

terremote FRENCH, from LATIN *terre motus* earthquake.

terrestrial LATIN *terrestris,* from *terra* earth.

terret FRENCH *tour* a turn.

terrible FRENCH, from LATIN *terribilis* frightful, from *terrere* frighten.

terrific LATIN *terrificus* causing terror, from *terrere* frighten + *ficus,* from *facere* make.

territory LATIN *territorium* area, from *terra* land.

terror LATIN *terrere* frighten.

terse LATIN *tergere* wipe.

tesseract GREEK *tesser(es)* four + *aktis* ray.

test[1] (exam) MIDDLE ENGLISH small vessel used in testing precious metals, from FRENCH, from LATIN *testum* earthen pot.

test[2] (shell) LATIN *testa* piece of burned clay, earthen pot, shell.

testament FRENCH, from LATIN *testamentum* last will, from *testari* make a will.

tester[1] (one who tests) See **test**[1] + **-er.**

tester[2] (bed covering) MIDDLE ENGLISH *testere,* from FRENCH *testiere* headpiece, from *teste* head, from LATIN *testa.* See **test**[2].

tester[3] (head armor) See **tester**[2].

testicle MIDDLE ENGLISH *testicule,* from LATIN *testiculus,* from *testis.*

testify LATIN *testificari,* from *testis* witness + *facere* do, make.

testimony LATIN *testis* witness.

tetanus LATIN quick tightening of a muscle in the neck, from GREEK *tetanos.*

tête-à-tête FRENCH head-to-head.

tether OLD NORSE *tjothr.*

tetrarch LATIN *tetrarcha,* from GREEK *tetraches,* from *tetra* four + *archos* ruler.

text FRENCH *tixte,* from LATIN *textus* wording, from *textus* style, from *texere* weave.

textile LATIN *textillis,* from *textus* style, from *texere* weave.

texture LATIN *textura* web, from *texere* weave.

thallophytic LATIN *Thallophyta,* from GREEK *thallos* green twig + *phyte* plant.

than OLD ENGLISH *thanne.*

thane OLD ENGLISH *thegen.*

thank OLD ENGLISH *thancian* give thanks.

that OLD ENGLISH *thæt.*

thatch OLD ENGLISH *theccan* cover.

thaw OLD ENGLISH *thawian.*

the OLD ENGLISH.

theatre FRENCH, from LATIN *theatrum* stage, from GREEK *theatron* place for seeing plays.

theft OLD ENGLISH *theofth.*

their OLD ENGLISH, from OLD NORSE *theirra.*

theism GREEK *theos* god + *-ismos.*

them OLD ENGLISH, from OLD NORSE *theim.*

theme FRENCH, from LATIN *thema* topic, from GREEK *thema* subject, something laid down.

then OLD ENGLISH *thænne.*

thence MIDDLE ENGLISH *thannes,* from that place, from OLD ENGLISH *thanon.*

theodolite LATIN *theodelitus* an instrument for measuring horizontal angles.

theology LATIN *theologia* science of religious things, from GREEK *theologia,* from *theos* a god + *-logia* study of.

theorbo FRENCH *teorbe.*

theorem FRENCH *théorème*, from LATIN *theorema*, from GREEK spectacle, speculation.

theory LATIN *theoria*, from GREEK, from *theorein* consider, speculate, look at, from *theoros* spectator, from *thea* a view + *horan* see.

therapy LATIN *therapia*, from GREEK *therapeuein* nurse.

there OLD ENGLISH *thær.*

thermo- GREEK *therme* heat.

thermogenesis See **thermo-** + **genesis.**

thermometer See **thermo-** + **meter**[1].

thermos GREEK hot.

thermosphere See **thermo-** + **sphere.**

thesis LATIN, from GREEK a placing, from *tithenai* put.

thespian ancient Greek dramatic writer *Thespis,* considered the creator of ancient Greek tragedy.

thews MIDDLE ENGLISH *theawes* good qualities, from OLD ENGLISH *theaw* custom.

they OLD NORSE *their.*

thick OLD ENGLISH *thicce.*

thicket MIDDLE ENGLISH, from OLD ENGLISH *thiccet*, from *thicce.*

thief OLD ENGLISH *theof.*

thigh OLD ENGLISH *theoh.*

thilke MIDDLE ENGLISH. See **the** + **ilk.**

thimble OLD ENGLISH *thuma* a thumb.

thin OLD ENGLISH *thynne.*

thing MIDDLE ENGLISH, from OLD ENGLISH *thing.*

think OLD ENGLISH *thencan.*

thiopentone GREEK *theion* brimstone (sulfur) + *pente* five + *-one* chemical compound.

this OLD ENGLISH *thes* (male), *theos* (female), *this* (neither male nor female).

thistle OLD ENGLISH *thistle.*

thole OLD ENGLISH *tholl.*

thong OLD ENGLISH *thwang* narrow strip of leather.

thorax LATIN *thorax*, from GREEK *thorax* breastplate, chest.

thorough OLD ENGLISH *thuruh.* See **through.**

thou OLD ENGLISH *thu.*

though OLD ENGLISH *thea* + OLD NORSE *tho.*

thought OLD ENGLISH *thoht* idea.

thow MIDDLE ENGLISH form of thou.

thrall OLD NORSE *thræll* slave.

thrash OLD ENGLISH *therscan* beat.

thread OLD ENGLISH *thræd* thin long cord.

threaten OLD ENGLISH *threatnian* force.

thresh See **thrash.**

threshold OLD ENGLISH *threscold.*

thrice MIDDLE ENGLISH *thries.*

thrift OLD NORSE having wealth and success.

thrill OLD ENGLISH *thyr(e)lian* pass through, from *thyrel* hole, from *thurh* through.

thrive OLD NORSE *thrifask,* from *thrifa* take with the hand.

throat OLD ENGLISH *throte.*

throb MIDDLE ENGLISH *throbben.*

throe probably from OLD ENGLISH *thrawu* pain.

throne FRENCH, from LATIN, from GREEK *thronos* a seat.

throng OLD ENGLISH *(ge)thrang,* from *thringan* crowd.

throttle probably from Old English *throte.*

through Old English *thurh.*

throw Old English *thrawan* twist.

thrush Old English *thrysce.*

thrust Old Norse *thrysta* press.

thug Hindi *thag,* perhaps from Sanskrit *sthaga* cunning, fraudulent.

thumb Old English *thuma.*

thunder Old English *thunor.*

Thursday Old English *Thuresdæg* Thor's (the Old Norse god of thunder) day.

thus Old English.

thwart Old Norse *thvert* across.

thyme French, from Latin, from Greek *threin* offer sacrifice.

tiara Latin, from Greek.

tibia Latin.

tick[1] (sound) Middle English *tic.*

tick[2] (parasite) Middle English *teke,* from Old English *ticia.*

tick[3] (cover) Middle English *tykke,* from Latin *theca* cover, sheath.

ticket French *etiquet* a little note, from *estiquier* attach. See **etiquette**.

tickle Middle English *tikelen.*

tiddlywinks probably from Modern English *tiddly-wink* small beer shop where such games were played, from *tiddly* a drink.

tide Old English *tid* time.

tidings Old English *tidung.*

tidy Middle English in good condition, from *tid* time, from Old English *tid.*

tie Old English *tigan.*

tier French *tire* order.

tierce French *terce,* from Latin *tertiam* third.

tig tag See **tag** (the game).

tiger Middle English *tygre,* from Old English *tiger* from French *tigre,* from Latin *tigris,* from Greek.

tight Old Norse *thettr* close.

till[1] (plow) Old English *tilian.*

till[2] (drawer) possibly from Middle English *tillen* draw.

tiller French, from Latin *telarium* roller in a loom, from *tela* a web.

tilt Middle English *tilten* cause to fall, from Old English *tealt* not steady.

timber Old English.

timbre French bell hit with a hammer, from Greek *tympanon* tympani (large horizontal drum that can be tuned to different sounds).

time Old English *tima.*

timid Latin *timidus.*

timothy *Timothy* Hanson, who took the seed to the Carolinas around 1720.

tin Old English.

tincture Latin *tintura* using dye, from *tinctus* dye.

tinder Old English *tynder.*

tine Old English *tind.*

tinge Latin *tingere* dye.

tingle Middle English *tinklen* make light sounds.

tinker Middle English, possibly from *tink* ring, from the sound tinkers made when mending pots and pans.

tinkle imitative.

tinsel French *estincelle,* from *estencele,* from Latin *scintilla* a spark.

tint Modern English *tinct*, from Latin *tinctus* dying, from *tingere* dye.

tiny Middle English *tine* a little something.

-tion French, from Latin *-tionis.*

tip Middle English *tippe.*

tippet Middle English, origin uncertain.

tipple probably from Middle English *tipelar* bar keeper.

tirade French, from Italian *tirata,* from *tirare* fire.

tire[1] (needing rest) Old English *tiorian.*

tire[2] (rubber) probably from Middle English *atir* equipment.

tissue French cloth, from *tistre* weave, from Latin *texere.*

titanic Greek *Titanikos* Titan, from the Greek myth.

titanium Latin, from Greek *Titan* a Titan.

tithe Old English *teothe* a tenth.

titillate Latin *titillare* tickle.

title Middle English inscription, heading, from French, from Latin *titulus.*

titter imitative.

titular Latin *titulus* inscription.

to Old English.

toad Old English *tade.*

toady Modern English *toadeater,* a fake doctor's assistant who pretended to eat poisonous toads and then drank the doctor's cure.

toast[1] (heated bread) French *toster* roast, from Latin *torrere* make dry using heat.

toast[2] (drink) **toast**[1], from flavoring liquor by putting spiced toast in it.

tobacco Spanish *tobaco* the plant.

toboggan French *tabaganne,* from Native American *tepaqan* a type of sled for moving things.

today Old English *todæg(e)* on this day.

toe Old English *ta.*

toff French, probably from Latin *tufa* helmet decoration.

toga Latin *toga* man's outer clothes worn in ancient Rome.

together Old English *togædere* into one gathering.

toggle Modern English, nautical, probably from *tog* tug.

toil French *toiller,* from *toeillier* make dirty, from Latin *tudiculare* stir up, from *tundere* beat.

toilet French *toilette* dressing table, from *toile* cloth, from Latin *tela* web.

token Old English *tac(e)n* symbol.

tolerate Latin *tolerare* put up with.

toll Old English tax, from Latin *telonium* place where taxes were collected, from Greek *telos* tax.

tom the name *Thomas.*

tomb French *tombe* grave, from Latin *tumba,* from Greek *tymbos.*

tome French volume, from Latin *tomus,* from Greek *tomos.*

tomorrow Middle English *to morwe*, from Old English *to* to + *morgen* morning.

tompion French *tampon* stopper.

-tomy Greek *temnein* cut.

ton Old English *tunne* barrel, its weight when full.

tone Latin *tonus* stretching, from Greek *tonos* thing stretched.

tong Old English *tange, tang.*

tongue Old English *tunge.*

tonic Greek *tonikos* of stretching. See **tone**.

tonight Old English *toniht* on the night of this day.

tonneau French *tonneau* cask.

tonsil Latin *tonsillae* (plural) tonsils.

tool Old English *tol* something to help do work.

toot imitative.

tooth Old English *toth.*

top Old English.

topgallant See **top** + **gallant**.

topic Latin, from Greek *Ta Topika* title of a book about common things, written by the Greek philosopher Aristotle, from *topos* a place.

topography Latin *topographia* description of a place, from Greek *topographia.* See **topic** + **-graphy**.

toque French cap, from Spanish *toca,* from Basque *tauka* kind of cap.

tor Middle English, from Old English *torr.*

Torah Hebrew instruction.

torch French *torche* light, made with a bundle of straw that was covered with wax so it would burn, from Latin *torques* twisted neck chain.

toreador Spanish *toro* bull, from Latin *taurus.*

torment French torture, from Latin *tormentum,* from *torquere* twist.

tornado Spanish *tronada* thunderstorm, from Latin *tornare* thunder.

torpedo Latin numbness, from *torpere* stiff.

torpid Latin *torpidus* numb.

torque Latin *torques* a twisted metal necklace.

torrent Latin *torrens.*

torrid Latin *torridus* needing water.

torsion French *torsion,* from Latin *torsionem,* from *tortionem* torture, torment, from *tortus,* from *torquere* twist.

torso Italian, from Latin, from Greek *thyrsos* a stem.

tortilla Spanish *torta* cake.

tortoise Latin *tortuca,* from *torquere* twist, because of the crooked look of a turtle's feet.

tortuous Latin *tortuosus* full of turns, from *torquere* twist.

torture French, from Latin *tortura,* from *torquere* twist.

tosh British slang, origin uncertain.

toss Middle English.

total French, from Latin *totalis* whole, from *totus.*

tote unknown origin.

totem Native American *ototeman* family.

totter possibly from Dutch *touteren* swing.

touch French *touchier* strike.

tough Old English *toh* hard to break.

tour French *to(u)r* a turn, from Latin *tornus* lathe (tool that cuts wood as it turns), from Greek *tornos.*

tourmaline French.

tournament French *torneiement,* from *torneier* turn around. See **turn**.

tourniquet French *tourner* turn, from Latin *tornare* turn in a lathe. See **turn**.

tousle Middle English *tusen* pull.

tout Old English *titian* look out.

tow[1] (pull) Old English *togian* pull.

tow[2] (unspun flax) OLD ENGLISH *tow.*

toward OLD ENGLISH *toweard.*

towel FRENCH *toaille.*

tower FRENCH *tour,* from LATIN *turris* high building, from GREEK *tyrsis.*

town OLD ENGLISH *tun* village.

toxaemia See **toxic** + **anemia.**

toxic LATIN *toxicus* poisonous, from *toxicum* poison, from GREEK *toxikon* poison for arrows.

toxoid See **toxic** + **-oid.**

toyon SPANISH *tollon* the name of the holly.

trace FRENCH *tracier* follow a trail, from LATIN *trahere* drag.

trachea LATIN, from GREEK *tracheia arteria* rough windpipe.

track FRENCH *trac* path.

tract LATIN *trahere* draw.

traction LATIN *tractio* pull, from *trahere* drag.

tractor LATIN that which drags, from *trahere* drag.

trade MIDDLE ENGLISH, from GERMAN *trade* track, course, way of life.

tradition FRENCH, from LATIN *traditio* handing over.

traffic FRENCH *trafique* trade, from ITALIAN *traffico.*

tragedy FRENCH *tragedie* serious play with unhappy ending, from LATIN *tradoedia,* from GREEK *tragodia,* from *tragos* goat + *oide* song. The goat may have been the prize for winning a dramatic competition in ancient Greece.

trail FRENCH *trailler* tow a boat, from LATIN *tragula* drag with a net.

train FRENCH *trainer* drag, from LATIN *trahere* pull.

traipse perhaps from FRENCH *trepasser* pass over or beyond, from *trespasser*. See **trespass.**

trait FRENCH, from LATIN *trahere* draw.

traitor FRENCH, from LATIN *tradere* betray.

trajectory LATIN *trajicere,* from *trans-* across + *jacere* throw.

tram SCOTTISH iron trucks used in coal mines.

tramp GERMAN *trampen* stamp.

trample GERMAN *trampen,* stamp, but implying doing such repetitively.

trance FRENCH *transe,* from LATIN *transire* die, from *trans-* over + *ire* go.

tranquil LATIN *tranquillus.*

trans- LATIN across, beyond, over.

transact LATIN *transigere,* from *trans-* across + *agere* drive.

transcend LATIN *transcendere*, from *trans-* over + *scandere* climb.

transcribe LATIN *transcribere*, from *trans-* over + *scribere* write.

transfer LATIN *transferre*, from *trans-* across + *ferre* bring.

transform LATIN *transformare*, from *trans-* over + *forma* a shape.

transfuse LATIN *transundere,* from *trans-* across + *fundere* pour.

transgress FRENCH, from LATIN *transgredi,* from *trans-* over + *gradi* step.

transient LATIN *transire,* from *trans-* over + *ire* go.

transistor LATIN *trans-* across + *sistere* set, from *stare* stand.

transit LATIN *transitis*, from *trans-* over + *ire* go.

translate See **transfer.**

translucent LATIN *translucere,* from *trans-* through + *lucere* shine.

transmit LATIN *transmittere*, from *trans-* over + *mittere* send.

transmute LATIN *trans-* over + *mutare* change.

transom probably from LATIN *transtrum* crossbeam.

transparent LATIN *transparere,* from *trans-* across + *parere* appear.

transpire FRENCH *transpirer*, from LATIN *trans-* through + *spirare* breathe.

transport FRENCH, from LATIN *trans-* over + *portare* carry.

transpose FRENCH *transposer*, from LATIN *transponere*, from *trans-* across + *ponere* place.

transverse LATIN *transversus*, from *transvertere*, from *trans-* across + *vertere* turn.

trap OLD ENGLISH *træppe* something to catch animals.

trapezium LATIN *trapezium*, from GREEK *trapezion* small table, from *trapeza* table, from *tra-* four + *peza* foot, edge.

trapezius LATIN. See **trapezium**.

trapezoid LATIN *trapezoides*, from GREEK *trapezoeides* trapezium-shaped, from *trapeza* table + *-oeides* shaped.

trash probably from OLD NORSE *tros.*

trauma LATIN, from GREEK.

travail FRENCH labor, from LATIN *trepalium* something used to torture, from *tres* three + *palus* stake.

travel MIDDLE ENGLISH *travailen* make a journey, originally to labor. See **travail**. The usage probably comes from the difficulty of travel in earlier times.

traverse FRENCH *traverser* cross, from LATIN *transversare,* from *transversus,* from *trans-* over + *vertere* turn.

travesty FRENCH *travestir* disguise, from LATIN *trans-* across + *vestire* dress.

travois See **travail**.

tray OLD ENGLISH *treg* wood board.

treachery FRENCH *trichier* cheat.

treacle FRENCH, from LATIN, from GREEK *theriake* remedy for poisonous bites, from *ther* wild beast.

tread OLD ENGLISH *tredan* walk on.

treadle OLD ENGLISH *trede* step.

treason FRENCH *traison,* from LATIN *tradere* deliver up, from *trans-* over + *dare* give.

treasure FRENCH *tresor* precious things, from LATIN *thesaurus* storehouse, from GREEK *thesauros.*

treat FRENCH *traitier* drag, from LATIN *trahere* drag.

treaty FRENCH *trait(i)e*, from LATIN *tractary* manage.

treble FRENCH, from LATIN *triplus.* See **triple**.

tree OLD ENGLISH *treow.*

trek DUTCH *trekken* draw.

trellis FRENCH, from LATIN *trilix* wound three times.

tremble FRENCH *trembler* shiver, from LATIN *tremulus* quaking.

tremendous LATIN *tremendus*, from *tremere* tremble (shake).

tremolo ITALIAN shaking, from LATIN *tremulus.*

tremor FRENCH, from LATIN trembling.

tremulous LATIN *tremere* tremble.

trench FRENCH *trenche,* from LATIN *truncare.*

trenchant FRENCH *trenchier* cut.

trencher FRENCH *trencheor* tool used for cutting, origin uncertain.

trend Old English *trendan* roll.

trepidation Latin *trepidatio* alarm.

trespass French *trespasser* go across, from Latin *trans-* across + *passus* step.

tress Middle English, from French *tresse*, perhaps from Latin *trichia* braid, rope, from Greek *trikhia* rope, from *thrix* hair.

trestle French *trestel* beam of wood, from Latin *transtrum* beam that goes across.

tri- Latin *tres* three, from Greek *treis.*

triad Latin *triadis*, from Greek *triados*, from *treis* three.

trial French judge in court, from *trier* try.

triangle French, from Latin *triangulum*, from *tri-* three + *angulus* corner or angle.

tribe Latin *tribus* one of the three divisions of the Roman state, perhaps from *tri-* three.

tribulation French *tribulacion*, from Latin *tribulationem* affliction, from *tribulare* thresh out grain, from *terere* rub + *-bulum* tool.

tribune Latin *tribunus* ancient Roman official, from *tribus.* See **tribe**.

tributary Latin *tributarius* liable to tax or tribute, from *tributum.* See **tribute**.

tribute Latin *tributum* payment, from *tribuere* allot to a tribe, from *tribus.* See **tribe**.

trice Middle English, from Dutch *trisen* hoist, from *trise* pulley.

triceps Latin *triceps* three-headed, from **tri-** + *-ceps*, from *caput* head. So called because the muscle has three origins.

trick French *trichier* cheat.

tricorn French *tricorne*, from Latin *tricornis*, from **tri-** + *cornu* from horn.

tricot French, from *tricoter* knit, from *trique* a stick, from French *estriquer* strike.

trident Latin *tres* three, from Greek *treis* + *dens* tooth.

trifle French *trufle* trickery.

triglyph Latin *triglyphus*, from Greek *triglyphos,* from **tri-** + *glyphe* carving.

trigonometry Latin *trigonometria*, from Greek *trigonon* triangle + *metron* measure.

trill Italian *trillare,* imitative.

trillion French *tri-* third power + Italian *millione,* from *mille* thousand, from Latin.

trilogy Greek *trilogia* group of three sad dramas, from *tri-* three + *logos* story.

trim Old English *trymman* strengthen.

trinity French *trinite,* from Latin *trinus* triple.

trinket Modern English, possibly from *trink*, *trick* style of adornment, ornament.

trio Latin *tres* three.

trip French *trip(p)er* dance, from Dutch *trippen* skip.

tripartite Latin *tripartitus* divided into three parts, from *tri-* three + *partitus*, from *partiri* divide.

tripe Arabic *tharb* intestines.

triple Latin *triplus* having three parts, from Greek *triplous.*

trireme Latin *triremis*, from *tri-* three + *remus* oar.

trite Latin *terere* wear away.

triumph French, from Latin *triumphus* victory, possibly from Greek *thriambos* song to the Greek god Bacchus in his honor.

trivial Latin *trivalis* common, from *trivum* place where three roads meet, from *tri-* three + *via* way.

trocar French *troquart,* from *trois* three + *carre* side, from its triangular shape.

trocharise See **trocar**.

troll[1] (monster) Old Norse.

troll[2] (roll) Middle English *trollen* wander.

trolley See **troll**[2].

trombone Italian *tromba* a trumpet, from German *trumba.*

tromp See **tramp**.

troop French *troup* group of persons, from *troupeau* herd, from Latin *troppus* a flock.

trophy French *trophee* sign of victory, from Latin, from Greek *tropaion* stone showing an enemy's defeat, from *trope* defeat.

-trophy Greek *trophia*, from *trephein* feed.

tropic Latin *tropicus* turning of the sun, from Greek *trope* turning.

troposphere French *troposphère*, from Greek *tropos* turn, change + *sphaira* sphere.

troth Old English *treowth* truth.

troubadour French, from earlier *trobar* compose in verse.

trouble French *trubler* disturb, from Latin *turba* thick.

trough Old English *trog.*

trounce Middle English harass, origin uncertain.

trousers Irish *triubhas,* possibly from French *trebus* pants that stop at the knee.

trousseau French *trousse* a bundle.

trout Old English *truht*, from French *truite*, from Latin *tructa*, from Greek *troktes* a kind of fish.

trowel French *truele,* from Latin *truella,* from *trua* ladle.

truant Middle English shiftless beggar, from French, related to Scottish *truaghan,* wretched.

truce Middle English *trewes* temporary peace, from Old English *treow* promise.

truck Latin *trochus* iron hoop, from Greek *trochos* wheel.

truculent Latin *truculentus* cruel.

trudge Modern English, origin uncertain.

true Old English *treowe* faithful.

truffle French *trufle*, from *truffe*, from Latin *tufera*.

trump See **triumph**.

trumpet French *trombe.*

truncate Latin *truncatus* cut off, from *truncus* trunk.

truncheon Middle English *tronchoun*, from French *tronchon*, from Latin *truncus* stem, trunk.

trundle Old English *trendel* circle, from *trendan* roll.

trunk Middle English *tronke*, from French *tronc*, from Latin *truncus.*

truss French *trousser.*

trust Old Norse *traust* help.

truth Old English *treowth.*

try French *trier* choose.

tryst French *triste* hunting station.

tub Dutch *tubbe.*

tuba French, from Latin *tuba* trumpet.

tube Latin *tubus* pipe.

tuber Latin a swelling.

tuberculosis Latin *tuberculum,* from *tuber* a swelling.

Tuesday OLD ENGLISH *Tiwesdæg* day of *Tiw* (ancient German god of war), from LATIN *dies* day.

tuft FRENCH *tufe,* probably from LATIN *tufa* top of helmet.

tug MIDDLE ENGLISH *toggen* pull, from OLD ENGLISH *teo(ha)n* pull.

tuition FRENCH, from LATIN *tuitio* protection, from *tueri* protect.

tulip DUTCH *tulipa*, from FRENCH *tulipe*, from TURKISH *tülbent* turban, from PERSIAN *dulband* turban, from resemblance of the flower to a turban.

tulle *Tulle,* the city in France where it was first made.

tumble MIDDLE ENGLISH *tumblen* perform as an acrobat, fall, from *tumben* dance, jump, from OLD ENGLISH *tumbian.*

tumbrel FRENCH *tomber* fall.

tumor LATIN *tumere* swell.

tump[1] (mound) BRITISH, origin uncertain.

tump[2] (carry) AMERICAN, probably NATIVE AMERICAN origin.

tumult LATIN *tumultus.*

tundra RUSSIAN.

tune See **tone.**

tungsten SWEDISH *tungsten,* from *tung* heavy + *sten* stone.

tunic FRENCH *tunique,* from LATIN *tunica.*

tunnel FRENCH *tonele* shaped like a funnel (tube with a wide mouth).

turban FRENCH, from ITALIAN, from TURKISH *tülbent,* from PERSIAN *dulband.*

turbine FRENCH, from LATIN *turbo* a whirl.

turbulent FRENCH, from LATIN *turbulentus* anxious or disturbed, from *turba* something disturbed.

tureen FRENCH *terrine,* from LATIN *terra* earth.

turf OLD ENGLISH.

turkey from an African bird imported into Europe by way of *Turkey.* The wild American turkey looked similar and came to be called this as well.

turmoil perhaps from FRENCH *tremouille* mill hopper, from the hopper's constant motion. (The name *tremouille* for the hopper comes from LATIN *trimodia* vessel containing three measures, from *modius* a Roman dry measure.)

turn OLD ENGLISH *turnian* turn around, from LATIN *tornare,* from *tornus* lathe (tool that cuts wood as it turns), from GREEK *tornos.*

turnip possibly from **turn**, because of rounded shape.

turnpike See **turn** + **pike**[2], from the barriers used to stop travellers for tolls.

turpitude FRENCH, from LATIN *turpis* bad.

turret FRENCH *tour.* See **tower.**

turtle OLD ENGLISH *turtla.*

tusche GERMAN, from *tuschen*, from FRENCH *toucher* touch.

tush[1] (backside) AMERICAN slang *tochus*, from YIDDISH *tokhes*, from HEBREW *tahat* beneath.

tush[2] (tooth) MIDDLE ENGLISH *tusch.* See **tusk.**

tusk OLD ENGLISH *tusc.*

tussle MIDDLE ENGLISH *tusen* pull.

tussock possibly from MIDDLE ENGLISH *tusen* rumple + *ock* little.

tutelage LATIN *tutela* protection.

tutor LATIN protector.

tuxedo *Tuxedo* Park, New York, a vacation place for wealthy families, where the suit first was worn.

twang imitative of the sound of a plucked string.

tweed See **twill**.

tweet imitative.

tweezers Modern English, from *tweeze* case for tweezers, from *etwee* a small case, from French *étui*, from *estuier* keep.

twig Old English *twigge*, from *twi-* two, forked.

twilight Middle English *twi-* two + Old English *leht*, from *leoht*.

twill Old English *twilic* woven of double thread, from Latin *bilix* with a double thread.

twin Old English *twinn* double.

twine Old English *twin* twisted thread.

twinge Old English *twengan* pinch.

twinkle Old English *twinclian* sparkle.

twirl origin uncertain.

twist Old English rope.

twitch Old English *twiccian* pluck.

twitter imitative.

tycoon Japanese *taikun* shogun (name of the rulers of Japan during the 11th and 19th centuries), from Chinese *ta* great + *chün* ruler.

tyke Old Norse *tik* female dog.

tympani Latin, from Greek *tympanon* drum.

tympanites See **tympani**.

tympanum See **tympani**.

type Latin *typus* image, from Greek *typos* form.

typhoid See **typhus** + **-oid**.

typhoon Chinese *tai fung* great wind, from Greek *typhon* whirlwind.

typhus Latin, from Greek *typhos* fever.

typical Latin *typicalis,* from *typicus,* from Greek *tupos* type.

tyrant French, from Latin, from Greek *tyrannos*.

ubiquity FRENCH *ubiquité,* from LATIN *ubique* everywhere.

udder OLD ENGLISH *udr.*

ugly OLD NORSE *uggligr* terrible.

ulcer FRENCH *ulcere,* from LATIN *ulcus,* from *ulcerare* make sore.

ulcerate See **ulcer** + **-ate.**

ulna LATIN elbow.

ulterior LATIN.

ultimate LATIN *ultimatus* final, from *ultimus* last.

ultra- LATIN *ultra* beyond.

umbel LATIN *umbella* sun shade, from *umbra* shade.

umbilical LATIN *umbilicalis* of the navel, from *umbilicus* navel.

umbilicus LATIN.

umbra LATIN shade, shadow.

umbrage FRENCH shade, from LATIN **umbra.**

umbrella ITALIAN *ombrella,* from *onbra,* from LATIN **umbra.**

umpire FRENCH *nomper* not even, from LATIN *non* not + *par* even, from the job of the umpire as the odd or third man (someone not on either team) to settle an argument.

un- OLD ENGLISH not, opposite or negative of.

unanimous LATIN *unanimus,* from *unus* one + *animus* the mind.

uncle FRENCH, from LATIN *avunculus* a mother's brother.

uncouth OLD ENGLISH *uncuth* strange, from *un-* not + *cuth* known.

unctuous LATIN *unctuosus* oily, from *unctus* anoint (put oil on during a ceremony to make holy).

under OLD ENGLISH.

under- OLD ENGLISH.

underneath OLD ENGLISH *underneothan.*

understand OLD ENGLISH *understandan* stand under, get the meaning of.

undine LATIN *unda* wave.

undulate LATIN *undulatus* wavy, from *unda* wave.

ungulate LATIN *unguia* a hoof.

unicorn LATIN *unicornus,* from *unis* one + *cornu* horn.

uniform LATIN *uniformis* having one form, from *unus* one + *forma* form.

union FRENCH, from LATIN *unio* unity, from *unus* one.

unique FRENCH single, from LATIN *unicus.*

unison LATIN *unisonus* having the same sound, from *unus* one + *sonus* sound.

unit LATIN *unus* one.

unite LATIN *unire* join together, from *unus* one.

universe LATIN *universum* the whole world, from *universus* whole, from *unus* one + *versus* turn.

university FRENCH, from LATIN *univeritas* the whole, from *universus.* See **universe**.

until OLD NORSE *unz.*

up OLD ENGLISH *uppe.*

upbraid OLD ENGLISH *upbregdan*, from *up-* up + *bregdan* pull.

upholster MIDDLE ENGLISH *upholdster* dealer in used goods, from *upholden* repair.

upright OLD ENGLISH *upriht* straight up.

uproar DUTCH *oproer.*

uranium LATIN *Uranus* the planet.

Uranus LATIN *Uranus*, from GREEK *Ouranos* heaven. In Greek cosmology, the god who represents the heavens.

urban LATIN *urbanus* having to do with a city, from *urbs* city.

urbane FRENCH *urbain*, from LATIN *urbanus.* See **urban**.

urchin FRENCH *herichon* hedgehog, from LATIN *(h)ericius.*

-ure FRENCH, from LATIN *-ura.*

urea LATIN, from FRENCH *urée*, from GREEK *ouron* urine.

uremia LATIN *uraemia,* from GREEK *ouron* urine + *haima* blood.

urge LATIN *urgere* press hard.

urgent See **urge**.

urine FRENCH, from LATIN *urina.*

urn LATIN *urna* pot for holding the ashes of the dead.

use FRENCH *user* practice, from LATIN *uti* make use of.

usher FRENCH *usser* doorkeeper, from LATIN *ostiarius*, from *ostium* door, from *os* mouth.

usual LATIN *usualis* ordinary, from *usus* use.

usurp FRENCH, from LATIN *usurpare* get, from *usu* use + *rapere* take by force.

usury LATIN *usura,* from *usus* use.

uterus LATIN womb, belly.

utility LATIN *utilitas*, from *uti* use.

utmost OLD ENGLISH *ut(e)mest* most distant, from *ut(e)* out + *-mest* most.

utopia LATIN no place, from GREEK *ou* not + *topos* place, from a book written in 1516 by Sir Thomas More called *Utopia,* which was about an imaginary, ideal place.

utter DUTCH *uteren* speak.

uvula LATIN *uva* a grape.

uxorious LATIN *uxor* wife.

V

vacant French, from Latin *vacare.* See **vacate.**

vacate Latin *vacare* be empty.

vacation Latin *vacatio* being free from a duty.

vaccine Latin *vaccinus* having to do with cows, from *vacca* cow, from the use of the cowpox virus for vaccination.

vacillate Latin *vacillare* waver.

vacuole French *vacuole,* from Latin *vacuus* empty.

vacuous Latin *vacuus* empty.

vacuum Latin empty space.

vagabond French, from Latin *vagabundus* walking about, from *vagari* wander.

vagary Latin *vagari* wander, from *vagus* roving, wandering.

vagina Latin *vagina* sheath, scabbard.

vagrant French *vagarant* wanderer, from Latin *vagari* wander.

vague French, from Latin *vagus* wandering.

vain French *vein* worthless, from Latin *vanus* idle, empty.

valance probably from *Valence,* a city in France famous for its fabrics.

vale French, from Latin *vallis.*

valediction Latin *valedicere,* from *vale* farewell + *dicere* say.

valence Latin *valentia* power, from *valere* be strong.

valet French groom, from *vaslet* young man.

valiant French *vaillant* have worth, from Latin *valere* be strong.

valid French *valide,* from Latin *validus* strong.

valise French, from Italian *valigia.*

valley French *valey,* from Latin *valles.*

valor French *valour,* from Latin *valor* courage, from *valere* be strong.

value French worth, from Latin *valere* be strong.

valve Latin *valva* folding door.

vamp[1] (of a shoe) Middle English *vampe,* from French *avampié,* from *avant* before + *pié* a foot.

vamp[2] (woman) See **vampire.**

vampire French *vampyre,* from German *Vampir,* from Slavic *vampir.*

vandal Latin *Vandalus,* from the name of the early Germanic tribe called Vandals, who invaded and robbed Rome in 455 A.D.

vane Old English *fana* a flag.

vang DUTCH a catch, from *vangen* catch. Nautical, rope used for steadying a sail.

vanguard FRENCH *avant* guard, from LATIN *ante-* before + *garde* guard.

vanilla SPANISH *vaina* a pod, from LATIN *vagina* a tube shape.

vanish FRENCH *esvanis* disappear, from LATIN *evanexcere*, from *ex-* out of + *vanus* empty.

vantage FRENCH *advantage* head start. See **advantage**.

vapid LATIN *vapidus.*

vapor LATIN steam.

vaquero SPANISH *vaca* cow, from LATIN *vacca* cow.

variable FRENCH, from LATIN *variabilis* changeable, from *variare* vary.

varicose LATIN *varicis,* from *varix.*

variety LATIN *varietas* different.

various LATIN *varius* changing.

varlet FRENCH *vaslet* male servant, attendant for a knight.

varnish FRENCH *vernis* the liquid, from LATIN *veronix,* probably from GREEK *Bereniki,* ancient Eastern town where varnish was supposedly first used.

varsity from **university**.

varvel FRENCH *vervelle,* from LATIN *vertibulum* joint.

vary LATIN *variare* change.

vascular LATIN *vascularis* pertaining to vessels or tubes, from *vasculum*, from *vas* vessel.

vase FRENCH, from LATIN *vas* dish.

vassal FRENCH subject, from LATIN *vassallus* servant, from *vassus* servant.

vast LATIN *vastus.*

vat OLD ENGLISH *fæt.*

vaudeville FRENCH comedy, from *Vau de Vire,* a place in Normandy famous for light, merry songs.

vault FRENCH *vaute* arch, from LATIN *volvere* roll.

veal FRENCH *veel* a calf, from *vedel,* from LATIN *vitellus*, from *vitulus* calf.

vector LATIN traveler.

veer FRENCH *virer* turn.

vegetable LATIN *vegetabilis* able to grow, from *vegetare,* from *vegetus* full of energy.

vehement LATIN *vehemens* violent.

vehicle LATIN *vehiculum* carriage.

veil FRENCH *veil(l)e* cloth covering that hides, from LATIN *velum* cloth.

vein FRENCH *veine,* from LATIN *vena* blood vessel.

velcro from *Velcro,* a British trademark, the name having been created by the Swiss inventor of the fastener, from FRENCH ***velours*** *croché* hooked velvet.

vellum MIDDLE ENGLISH *velim*, from FRENCH *velin* parchment made from calfskin, from FRENCH *vel, veel* calf. See **veal**.

velocipede FRENCH, from LATIN *velocis,* from *velox* swift + *pes* foot.

velocity LATIN *velocitas* quickness.

velvet FRENCH *velu,* from LATIN *villus* shaggy hair.

venal LATIN *venalis* for sale, from *venum* sale.

vendue DUTCH, from FRENCH *vendre* sell.

veneer GERMAN *furnieren,* from FRENCH *fournir* provide.

venerate LATIN *venerari* worship.

vengeance FRENCH *vengeance* revenge, from *venger* avenge (get even for a wrong done), from LATIN *vindicare.*

venial FRENCH, from LATIN *venialis,* from *venia* grace.

venison FRENCH *veneisum,* from LATIN *venatio* hunting.

venom FRENCH *venin* poison, from LATIN *venenum.*

vent FRENCH wind, from LATIN *ventus.*

ventilate LATIN *ventilare* set in motion, from *ventus* wind.

ventral FRENCH *ventral,* from LATIN *ventralis* pertaining to the belly or stomach, from *venter* belly, paunch.

venture MIDDLE ENGLISH *aventure.* See **adventure**.

venue FRENCH *venir* come, from LATIN *venire.*

Venus LATIN.

veracity LATIN *veracitas* truthfulness, from *verax* truthful.

veranda HINDI *varanda,* probably from PORTUGUESE *veranda* railing.

verb FRENCH *verbe,* from LATIN *verbum* word.

verbatim LATIN *verbum* word.

verbena LATIN.

verbose LATIN *verbosus* full of words, from *verbum* word.

verdant FRENCH *verdioer,* from LATIN *viridis* green.

verderer FRENCH *verd,* from LATIN *viridis* green.

verdict FRENCH *verdit* true saying, from LATIN *verus* true + *dictum* saying.

verdigris FRENCH *vertegrez,* from *vert de Grece* green of Greece, from LATIN *viridis* green + *de-* of + *Graecia* Greece.

verge FRENCH rod, from LATIN *virga.*

verify FRENCH *verifier* examine to make sure it is correct, from LATIN *verus* true + *facere* do, make.

veritable FRENCH, from LATIN *veritas* truth.

vermillion FRENCH *vermeil* bright-red.

vermin FRENCH *vermine* insects, from LATIN *vermis* worm.

vermis LATIN worm.

vernacular LATIN *vernaculus* native, from *verna* slave born in the master's house.

vernal LATIN *vervus,* from *ver* spring.

vernier Paul *Vernier,* a 17th century French mathematician.

verrucos LATIN *verruca* wart.

versatile LATIN turning round, from *vertere* turn.

verse OLD ENGLISH *fers* line of poetry, from LATIN *vertere* turn.

versificator LATIN, from *versificare* versify.

version LATIN *versio* translation, from *vertere* turn.

versus LATIN *vertere* turn.

vertebra LATIN a joint, from *vertere* turn.

vertex LATIN top of the head.

vertical LATIN *verticalis* upright, from *vertex* highest point.

vertiginous FRENCH *vertigineux,* from LATIN *vertiginosus* suffering from dizziness. See **vertigo**.

vertigo LATIN, from *vertere* turn.

very FRENCH *vrai,* from LATIN *verus* true.

vespers French *vespres*, from Latin *vespera* evening.

vessel French, from Latin *vas*.

vest French *veste* short jacket, from Italian, from Latin *vestis*.

vestibule Latin *vestibulum* entrance hall.

vestige French footprint, from Latin *vestigium*.

vestment French, from Latin *vestimentum*, from *vestire* clothe.

vestry probably from French *vestairie* place for keeping clothes for religious ceremonies, from Latin *vestiarium* wardrobe (clothing for a person or situation), from *vestis* clothing.

vetch French, from Latin *vicia*.

veteran Latin *veteranus* experienced soldier, from *vetus* old.

veterinary Latin *veterinarius* relating to beasts of burden (animals used for carrying things).

veto Latin "I forbid", from the officials of ancient Rome when they disagreed with a suggestion brought before the ruling body.

vex French, from Latin *vexare* stir up.

via Latin a way.

viable French *vie* life, from Latin *vita*.

viaduct Latin *via* road + *-duct*, from *ductus*, from *ducere* lead.

vial French, from Greek *phiale* shallow cup.

vibrant Latin *vibrare* shake.

vicar Latin *vicarius* substituted, from *vicis* change.

vicarious Latin *vicis* change.

vice French fault, from Latin *vitium*.

vice versa Latin *vice* in place of, from *vicis* change + *versa* turn about.

viceroy French *vice-* in the place of another + *roy* king, from Latin *rex*.

vicinity Latin *vicinus* of the same village, from *vicus* village.

vicious Latin *vitiosus* full of faults, from *vitium*. See **vice**.

vicissitude French, from Latin *vicissitudo*, from *vicis* a turn.

victim Latin *victima* animal offered for sacrifice.

victor Latin *victere* conquer.

victual French *vitaille* supply of food, from Latin *victualia*, from *victus* food.

video Latin I see.

vie French *envier* challenge, from Latin *invitare*.

view French *vewe* eyes, from *veoir* see, from Latin *videre*.

viga Spanish beam.

vigil French *vigile* staying awake on the night before a holy day, from Latin *vigilia* watching.

vigilant Latin *vigilare* watch.

vigilante Spanish *vigilante* watchful, from Latin *vigilans*. See **vigilant**.

vignette French little vine, ornamental border that has vines. See **vine**.

vigor French *vigour* strength, from Latin *vigor* activity.

viking Old Norse *vikingr*.

vile French *vil* cheap, from Latin *vilis*.

vilify Latin *vilificare* make have little value, from *vilis* cheap + *facere* do, make.

village French small group of houses of peasants, from Latin *villa* farm.

villain French *vilain* peasant, from Latin *villanus* farm servant, from *villa* farm.

villein See **villain**.

vim LATIN, from *vis* energy.

vindicate LATIN *vindicare* avenge (get even for a wrong done).

vindictive LATIN *vindicta* revenge. See **vindicate** + **-ive**.

vine FRENCH, from LATIN *vinum* wine.

vinegar FRENCH *vinaigre* sour wine, from LATIN *vinum* wine + *acer* sharp.

vintage MIDDLE ENGLISH *vendage* gathering grapes, from LATIN *vindemia*, from *vinum* wine + *demere* take away.

vinyl MODERN ENGLISH *polyvinyl*, from *vinyl* as a chemical derived from alcohol, from LATIN *vinum* wine.

viol FRENCH *viole,* from *viula*, from LATIN *vitula.*

violate LATIN *violare* injure, dishonor.

violence FRENCH, from LATIN *violentia* much force.

violin ITALIAN *viola* viol (early stringed instrument, usually played with a bow).

viper LATIN *vipera* snake.

virago OLD ENGLISH, from LATIN a manlike or heroic woman, from *vir* a man.

vireo LATIN *vireo* green bird, from *virere* be green.

virgin FRENCH *virgine* maiden (girl who is not married), from LATIN *virgo.*

viridian LATIN *viridis* green.

virtual See **virtue**.

virtue MIDDLE ENGLISH *vertu*, from FRENCH, from LATIN *virtus* manliness, from *vir* man.

virus LATIN poison.

visage FRENCH *vis,* from LATIN *visus* look.

viscount FRENCH *visconte,* from LATIN *vice* in place of + *comes* companion.

vise FRENCH *vis* screw, from LATIN *vitis* vine, which tends to wind around things.

visible LATIN *visibilis* can be seen, from *videre* see.

vision LATIN *visio* sight.

visit LATIN *visitare* go to see.

visor FRENCH *viser* visor of a helmet, from *vis* face. See **visage**.

vista ITALIAN, from LATIN *videre* see.

vital LATIN *vitalis* having to do with life, from *vita* life.

vitamin LATIN *vita* life + *amine*, because they were thought to contain amino acids.

vitiate LATIN *vitiare* spoil.

vituperate LATIN *vitrium* a fault + *parare* prepare.

vivacious LATIN *viviax* lively.

vivandier FRENCH, from LATIN *vivenda,* from *vivere* live.

vivid LATIN *vividus* full of life, from *vivus* alive.

vivisection LATIN *vivus* alive + *secare* cut.

vixen MIDDLE ENGLISH *fixen,* from OLD ENGLISH *fyxe* a female fox.

vocabulary LATIN *vocabularium* list of words, from *vocabulum.*

vocal LATIN *vocalis,* from *vox* sound.

vocation LATIN *vocatio* invitation.

vociferate LATIN *vociferari* cry out, from *vox* sound + *ferre* bring.

vogue FRENCH fashion, from *voguer* move along, row, from GERMAN.

voice FRENCH *vois* sound, from LATIN *vox.*

void French *voide* imply, from Latin *vacare* be empty.

volatile Latin *volare* fly.

volcano Italian, from Latin *Vulcanus* Vulcan, the Roman god of fire.

vole Modern English *volemouse*, probably from Old Norse *völlr* field.

volition French, from Latin *volitio,* from *velle* will.

volley French *volee,* from Latin *volare* fly.

volly French *volee* flight, from *voler* fly, from Latin *volare.*

volt Allessandro *Volta* (1745–1827), Italian scientist and inventor.

voluble French, from Latin *volubilis,* from *volere* roll.

volume French book, from Latin *volumen* roll of writing, from *volvere* roll.

voluntary Latin *voluntarius* willing, from *volantas* will.

volunteer French *volontaire* one who offers to do something on his own, from Latin *voluntarius* willing.

voluptuous Latin *voluptas* pleasure.

voodoo French *voudou,* from African *vodu* spirit.

voracious Latin *voracis,* from *vorare* devour (eat up hungrily).

vortex Latin *vertere* turn.

votary Latin *vovere* vow + *-arius, -aria, -arium.*

vote Latin *votum* wish.

vouch French *voucher* claim, from Latin *vocare* call.

vow French *veu* promise made to a god, from Latin *votum.*

vowel French, from Latin *vocalis littera* vocal letter, from *vox* voice.

voyage French *voiage* way, from Latin *viaticum* money or food for a journey.

vulgar Latin *vulgaris* common, having to do with large numbers (masses) of people, from *vulgus* the masses.

vulnerable Latin *vulnerabilis* a wounding, from *vulnus* wound.

vulture Latin *vultur.*

wad LATIN *wadda,* from ARABIC *bata'in* lining inside clothes.

waddle See **wade.**

wade OLD ENGLISH *waden* go.

wadi ARABIC.

wafer FRENCH *waufre*, from DUTCH *wafel.*

waft GERMAN, from DUTCH *wachten* guard, the original sense meaning "carried by water," the way an escort ship would accompany another.

wag MIDDLE ENGLISH *waggen* shake, from OLD ENGLISH *wagian* sway.

wage FRENCH pledge.

wagon DUTCH *wagen* cart with wheels used for carrying heavy loads.

waif FRENCH *gayf,* of SCANDINAVIAN origin.

wail OLD NORSE *væla,* from *væ* woe.

wain OLD ENGLISH *wægn* wheeled vehicle.

waist OLD ENGLISH *weaxan* grow.

wait FRENCH *waiter* watch.

waive FRENCH *wehver*, from OLD NORSE *veifa* keep changing.

wake OLD ENGLISH *wacian.*

walk OLD ENGLISH *wealcan* move about.

wall OLD ENGLISH *weall*, from LATIN *valum* side of a building built for protection, from *vallus* a stake.

wallet MIDDLE ENGLISH *walet,* origin uncertain.

wallop OLD NORSE *waloper* gallop.

wallow OLD ENGLISH *wealwian* roll about.

walnut OLD ENGLISH *wealh* foreign + *hnutu* a nut.

waltz GERMAN *walzen* dance about.

wan OLD ENGLISH *wann* dark.

wander OLD ENGLISH *wandrian.*

wane OLD ENGLISH *wanian* fade.

wang[1] (plow part) See **wing.**

wang[2] (tooth) OLD ENGLISH cheek.

want OLD NORSE *vanta.*

wanton MIDDLE ENGLISH *wantowen* not having discipline, from OLD ENGLISH *wan* not having + *teon* educate.

wapatoo NATIVE AMERICAN *wapatowa* white mushroom.

war FRENCH *werre* fighting, from GERMAN *werra* disagreement.

warble OLD NORSE *werbler.*

ward OLD ENGLISH *weard* keep guard.

warden Middle English guard, from French *wardein.*

wardrobe French *warderobe* place to keep clothes, from *warder* guard + *robe* clothing.

ware Old English *waru* goods.

warm Old English *wearm.*

warn Old English *warnian* take notice of.

warp Old English *weorpan* throw.

warrant French *warant* protection.

warren French *warir* keep safe.

wary Old English *wær* aware.

was Old English *wæs.*

wash Old English *wæscan.*

waste French *waster* destroy totally, from Latin *vastare* make empty.

wastel French, from Latin *wastellum.*

watch Old English *wæccan* be awake.

water Old English *wæter.*

watt James *Watt* (1736–1819), Scottish inventor.

wattle Old English *watel* twigs woven in.

wave Old English *wafian.*

waver Middle English *waven* wave.

wax[1] (beeswax) Old English *weax.*

wax[2] (increase) Old English *weaxan* increase.

wax-chandler Middle English *chaundeler,* from French *chandelier,* from Latin *candella* a candle.

way Old English *weg* path.

weak Old Norse *veikr.*

weal Old English *walu.*

wealth Old English *wela.*

wean Old English *wenian.*

weapon Old English *wæpen.*

wear Old English *wearian.*

weary Old English *werig.*

weasel Old English *wesle.*

weather Old English *weder* wind.

weave Old English *wefan* make cloth by threading.

web Old English *webb* woven cloth.

wedding Old English *weddung.*

wedge Old English *wecg.*

wedlock Old English *wedlac* marriage vow, from *wedd* promise + *lac* activity.

Wednesday Old English *Wodnesdæg* Woden's Day. Woden was the chief god of the ancient Germanic people.

weed Old English *weod.*

week Old English *wice.*

weep Old English *wepan.*

weevil Old English *wifel.*

weft Old English *wefta*, from *wefan* weave.

weigh Old English *wegan* carry.

weir Old English *wer.*

weird Middle English *wyrde* fate, from Old English *wyrd.*

welcome Old Norse *velkominn,* from *vel* well + *koma* come.

weld Old English *wellan* boil.

welfare Middle English good fortune, from *wel faren* fare well, from Old English *wel faran.*

well[1] (good) Old English *wel* properly.

well[2] (hole) Old English *wella.*

wellington Arthur, first duke of *Wellington* in England (1769–1852), who first wore the boots.

welt MIDDLE ENGLISH *welte.*

welter DUTCH *welteren.*

wench MIDDLE ENGLISH *wenche* female servant, from OLD ENGLISH *wencel.*

wend OLD ENGLISH *wendan* go.

wentletrap DUTCH *wenteltrap* winding stair, spiral shell, from GERMAN *wendeltreppe.*

were OLD ENGLISH *wæron.*

werewolf OLD ENGLISH *werewulf*, from *wer* man + *wulf* wolf.

wergeld OLD ENGLISH, from *wer* man + *geld* yield.

west OLD ENGLISH.

wester OLD ENGLISH *westra* west, from OLD NORSE *verstri.*

wet OLD ENGLISH *moist.*

whack imitative.

wharf OLD ENGLISH *hwearf.*

what OLD ENGLISH *hwæt.*

wheedle possibly from GERMAN *wedeln* wag the tail.

wheel OLD ENGLISH *hweol* circle turning around a rod.

wheeze OLD NORSE *hvæsa* hiss.

whelk OLD ENGLISH *weoloc,* origin uncertain.

whelm MIDDLE ENGLISH *whelmen* turn upside down, from OLD ENGLISH *-hwelfan* cover over.

whelp OLD ENGLISH *hwelp.*

when OLD ENGLISH *hwienne.*

whence OLD ENGLISH *hwanan.*

where OLD ENGLISH *hwær.*

whet OLD ENGLISH *hwettan* sharpen.

whether OLD ENGLISH *hwæther.*

which OLD ENGLISH *hwilc.*

whicker imitative.

whiff imitative.

Whig *Whiggamore,* Scottish Presbyterians who marched on a city in Scotland in 1648, from *whig,* from a sound to get horses to move, from *mare* a horse.

whim MIDDLE ENGLISH *whim-wham* fanciful object, origin unknown.

whimper MIDDLE ENGLISH, possibly from GERMAN *wimmern.*

whimsey probably from *whim-wham.* See **whim**.

whine OLD ENGLISH *hwinan.*

whinny See **whine**.

whip DUTCH *wippen* swing.

whippoorwill imitative.

whir MIDDLE ENGLISH *quirre,* of SCANDINAVIAN origin.

whirl OLD NORSE *hvirfla* turn about.

whisk MIDDLE ENGLISH *wysk* fast sweeping movement, of SCANDINAVIAN origin.

whiskey[1] (liquor) IRISH *usquebaugh,* from *uisce* water + *beathadh* life.

whiskey[2] (carriage) GERMAN *wisken* move quickly.

whisper OLD ENGLISH *hwisprian.*

whist MIDDLE ENGLISH *whisk*, perhaps influenced by MIDDLE ENGLISH *whist* silent. See **whisk**.

whistle OLD ENGLISH *hwistlian* make a hissing sound.

whittle OLD ENGLISH *thwitan* cut.

who OLD ENGLISH *hwa.*

whole OLD ENGLISH *hal* not divided into parts.

whoop imitative.

whopper MIDDLE ENGLISH *whop* beat, origin uncertain.

whorl probably from **whirl**.

whortleberry BRITISH *hurtleberry,* from OLD ENGLISH *horte.*

wick OLD ENGLISH *weoce.*

wicked MIDDLE ENGLISH *wikke* evil, from OLD ENGLISH *wicce* witch.

wicker DANISH *vigger* branch of willow.

wicket FRENCH *wiket.*

wide OLD ENGLISH *wid.*

widow OLD ENGLISH *widuwe.*

wield OLD ENGLISH *wieldan* control.

wiener GERMAN *Wiener Wurst* Viennese sausage.

wife OLD ENGLISH *wif.*

wig MODERN ENGLISH, from *periwig,* from *perwyke,* from FRENCH *perruque.*

wiggle MIDDLE ENGLISH *wegelen*, from GERMAN *wiggelen.*

wight MIDDLE ENGLISH, from OLD ENGLISH *wiht* creature, being, thing.

wig-wag BRITISH *wig* move + *wag,* from OLD ENGLISH *wegan* move.

wild OLD ENGLISH *wilde.*

wildebeest AFRIKAANS wild beast.

wilderness OLD ENGLISH *wildeoren* wild, from *wilde* wild + *deor* animal.

wile OLD ENGLISH *wigle* magic.

will[1] (going to) OLD ENGLISH *willan* be willing.

will[2] (choice) OLD ENGLISH *willa* desire.

willow OLD ENGLISH *welig.*

willy-nilly MODERN ENGLISH *will I, nill I* I am willing, I am unwilling, from OLD ENGLISH *nyllan.*

wilt MODERN ENGLISH, probably from MIDDLE ENGLISH *welk* dry up.

wimple OLD ENGLISH *wimpel.*

win OLD ENGLISH *winnan* fight.

wince FRENCH *guenchir* turn aside.

winch OLD ENGLISH *wince.*

wind[1] (air) OLD ENGLISH.

wind[2] (turn) OLD ENGLISH *windan* turn.

windle See **wind**[2] + **-le**.

window OLD NORSE *vindauga*, from *viondr* wind + *auga* eye.

wing OLD NORSE *vægr* bird's wing.

wink OLD ENGLISH *wincian* close one's eyes.

winker See **wink**.

winnow OLD ENGLISH *wind-wian* let air go through grain to separate it from its dry covering, from *wind.*

winsome OLD ENGLISH *wynsum* pleasant, from *wynn* pleasure + *-sum* -like.

winter OLD ENGLISH.

winze See **wind**[2].

wipe OLD ENGLISH *wipian.*

wire OLD ENGLISH *wir.*

wise OLD ENGLISH *wis.*

wish OLD ENGLISH *wyscan* want.

wisp MIDDLE ENGLISH.

wistful OLD ENGLISH *wyscan* want.

wit OLD ENGLISH mind.

witch Old English *wicce,* feminine form of *wicca* sorcerer.

witch hazel Middle English *wyche hazel,* from *wyche,* from Old English *wice* having pliant branches.

with Old English.

withe Old English *withthe.*

wither Middle English *widderal* get smaller, from *wederan* let out in the weather, from Old English *weder.* See **weather**.

withers Middle English *wither* resistance, from Old English *withre,* from *wither* against.

withy Old English.

witness Old English *witnes* evidence. See **wit**.

wizard Middle English *ywsard* wise person, from Old English *wis.* See **wise**.

wizen Old English *wisnian, weosnian* shrivel.

wobble German *wabblen* move without being steady.

woe Old English *wa.*

wok Chinese.

wolf Old English *wulf.*

wolfsbane English translation of Latin *lycoctonum,* from Greek *lykotonon,* from *lykos* wolf + *kteinein* kill.

woman Old English *wifman.*

womb Middle English *wombe,* from Old English *wamb* belly.

wonder Old English *wundor* miracle.

wont Middle English *wonen,* from Old English *wunian.*

woo Old English *wogian.*

woodbine Old English *wudubinde.*

woof[1] (cloth) Old English *owef,* from *o-* on + *wefan* weave.

woof[2] (dog bark) echoic.

woosle See **ousel**.

woozy See **ooze**.

word Old English news.

work Old English *weorc.*

world Old English *weorold.*

worry Old English *wyrgan* strangle.

worse Old English *wyrsa.*

worship Old English *weorthscipe* respect.

worsted Middle English *Worstead,* from Old English *Wurthestede* town in England where the cloth was originally made.

worth Old English *weorth.*

would See **will**[1].

wound Old English *wund.*

wrack Old English *wræc* misery.

wraith Old Norse *vartha* guard.

wrangle Middle English *wringen* squeeze.

wrap Middle English *wrappen.*

wrath Old English *wræththu.*

wreak Old English *wrecan* avenge.

wreath Old English *writha.*

wreathe Old English *writhan* wrap around.

wreck French *wrec* shipwreck, from Scandinavian.

wren Old English *wrenna.*

wrench Old English *wrencan* twist.

wrest Old English *wræsten* turn.

wretch Old English *wrecca.*

wriggle German *wriggeln.*

wright Old English *wyrcan* work.

wring OLD ENGLISH *wringan* squeeze.

wrinkle MIDDLE ENGLISH *wringled* twisted, from OLD ENGLISH *gewrinclod* crooked.

writ See **write.**

write OLD ENGLISH *writan.*

writhe OLD ENGLISH *writhan* wrap around.

wrong OLD ENGLISH *wrang* not just, from OLD NORSE *rangr* crooked.

wroth OLD ENGLISH *wrath.*

wrought See **work.**

wry MIDDLE ENGLISH *wrien* twist, from OLD ENGLISH *wrigian* move.

wurst GERMAN *Wurst* sausage.

wych-elm OLD ENGLISH *wice* tree with branches that bend easily + *elm.*

xanthophyll FRENCH *xanthophylle,* from GREEK *canqos* yellow + *phyllon* leaf.

xebec FRENCH *chébec*, from ITALIAN *sciabecco*, from ARABIC *shabbak* a small warship.

xylophone GREEK *xylon* wood + *phone* voice, sound.

-y[1] (little) MIDDLE ENGLISH *-y, -i, -ie.*

-y[2] (full of) MIDDLE ENGLISH *-y, -ie*, from OLD ENGLISH *-ig.*

-y[3] (kind) MIDDLE ENGLISH *-ie*, from FRENCH, from LATIN *-ia.*

-y[4] (action) MIDDLE ENGLISH *-ie*, from FRENCH, from LATIN *-ium.*

yacht DUTCH *jachtschip* ship that chases.

yam SPANISH *igname.*

yammer OLD ENGLISH *geomerian*, from lament, from *geomor* sorrowful.

yank SCOTTISH, origin uncertain.

Yankee DUTCH, possibly from *Janke* Little John, from *Jan* John. Used by the early settlers in New York to refer to English settlers in Connecticut.

yap imitative.

yard[1] (ground enclosed) OLD ENGLISH *geard* something enclosed.

yard[2] (measure) OLD ENGLISH *gierd* staff (stick).

yarn OLD ENGLISH *gearn.*

yaw OLD NORSE *jaga* move or swing back and forth.

yawn OLD ENGLISH *geonian* open the mouth wide.

yawp MIDDLE ENGLISH *yolpen.*

year OLD ENGLISH *gear.*

yearn OLD ENGLISH *giernan.*

yellow OLD ENGLISH *geolu.*

yeoman MIDDLE ENGLISH *yeman,* probably from contraction of *yengman* young man.

yes OLD ENGLISH *gese.*

yet OLD ENGLISH *giet(a)* still.

yew OLD ENGLISH *iw.*

yield OLD ENGLISH *gieldan* give in return.

yodel GERMAN *jodeln.*

yoga SANSKRIT union.

yogurt TURKISH *yoghurt,* from *yog* intensify.

yoke OLD ENGLISH *geoc.*

yokel perhaps from GERMAN *Jokel,* "little Jakob" a derogatory name for a farmer.

yolk OLD ENGLISH *geolca.*

yon OLD ENGLISH *geon* that.

yonder MIDDLE ENGLISH *yond,* from OLD ENGLISH *geond.*

yore OLD ENGLISH *geara* of years.

you Old English *eow.*

young Old English *geong* fresh.

your Old English *eower.*

youth Old English *geoguth* being young.

yowl Old Norse *gaula.*

yo-yo a trademark name, originally probably from the name of the toy in the language of the Phillippines, where it originated.

yucca Spanish *yuca.*

yule Old English *geol.*

yurt Russian *yurta.*

Z

zaftig GERMAN *saftig* juicy.

zany ITALIAN *zanni* clown.

zeal LATIN *zelus* strong feeling, from GREEK *zelos.*

zenith LATIN *cenith* highest point of the sky, from ARABIC *sami* way.

zephyr LATIN, from GREEK *zephyros.*

zero ITALIAN nothing, from ARABIC *çifr* empty.

zest FRENCH *zeste* orange or lemon peel used as a flavoring, from GREEK *zesti* warm, hot.

zester See **zest.**

zetetic GREEK *zhthtikos,* from *zhtew* inquire.

zig-zag FRENCH having sharp turns in alternating directions.

zinc GERMAN *Zink*, from *Zinke* prong, point, from *zint* a point, jag.

zip imitative.

zither GERMAN, from LATIN, from GREEK *kithara* a stringed instrument.

zodiac LATIN *zoidion*, from GREEK *zoidiakos* circle of figures.

zoetrope GREEK *zoe* life + *trope* turn.

zombie AFRICAN.

zone LATIN *zona* belt, from GREEK *zone.*

zoo *Zoological Gardens* (of the London Zoological Society).

zoology GREEK *zoion* animal + *-logia* study of.

zoom imitative.

zucchini ITALIAN *zucca* a gourd (vegetable).

APPENDIX

List of Languages

Here is a list of the languages referenced in the derivations in this dictionary. Below some are sub-category languages that are not used in this dictionary, but which you may run into in other dictionaries.

Explanations of all these languages can be found in the following glossary.

African

Afrikaans

American English (American)

Amharic

Arabic

Australian Aboriginal

British English (British)

Chinese

Danish
- Old Danish

Dutch
- Middle Dutch

Egyptian

Eskimo
- Greenland Eskimo

Finnish

Frankish

French
- Old French
- Anglo-French
- Norman French
- Middle French
- Canadian French
- Louisiana French
- Swiss French

German
- Old High German
- Middle High German
- High German
- Middle Low German
- Low German
- Old Saxon

Greek

Gypsy

Hebrew

Hindi

Hungarian

Icelandic

Irish (Gaelic)
- Old Irish
- Irish English (Anglo-Irish)

Italian
- Old Italian

Japanese

Latin
- Vulgar Latin
- Late Latin
- Medieval Latin
- Modern Latin

Malay

Maori

Middle English

Modern English

Native American
- North American Indian
- Arawakan
- Aztec Indian
- Brazilian Indian
- Canadian Indian
- Nahuatl
- Taino

Norwegian

Old English

Old Norse

Pashto

Persian
- Old Persian

Portuguese

Quechua

Romanian

Russian

Sanskrit

Scandinavian

Scottish
- Scots
- Scottish Gaelic
- Scottish English

Slavic

Spanish
- American Spanish
- Mexican Spanish

Swedish

Tamil

Thai

Tongan

Tungus

Turkish

Welsh

Yiddish

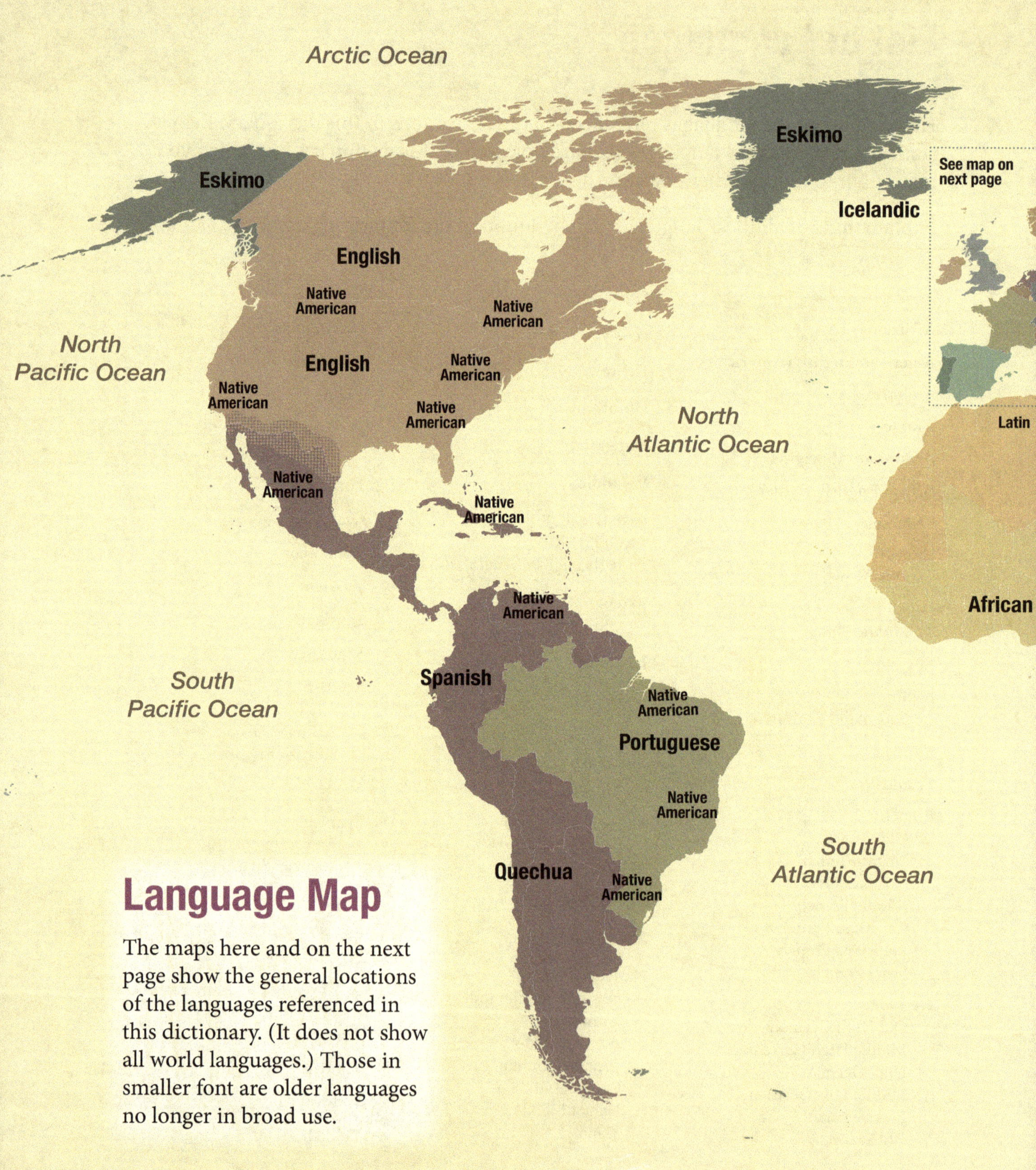

Language Map

The maps here and on the next page show the general locations of the languages referenced in this dictionary. (It does not show all world languages.) Those in smaller font are older languages no longer in broad use.

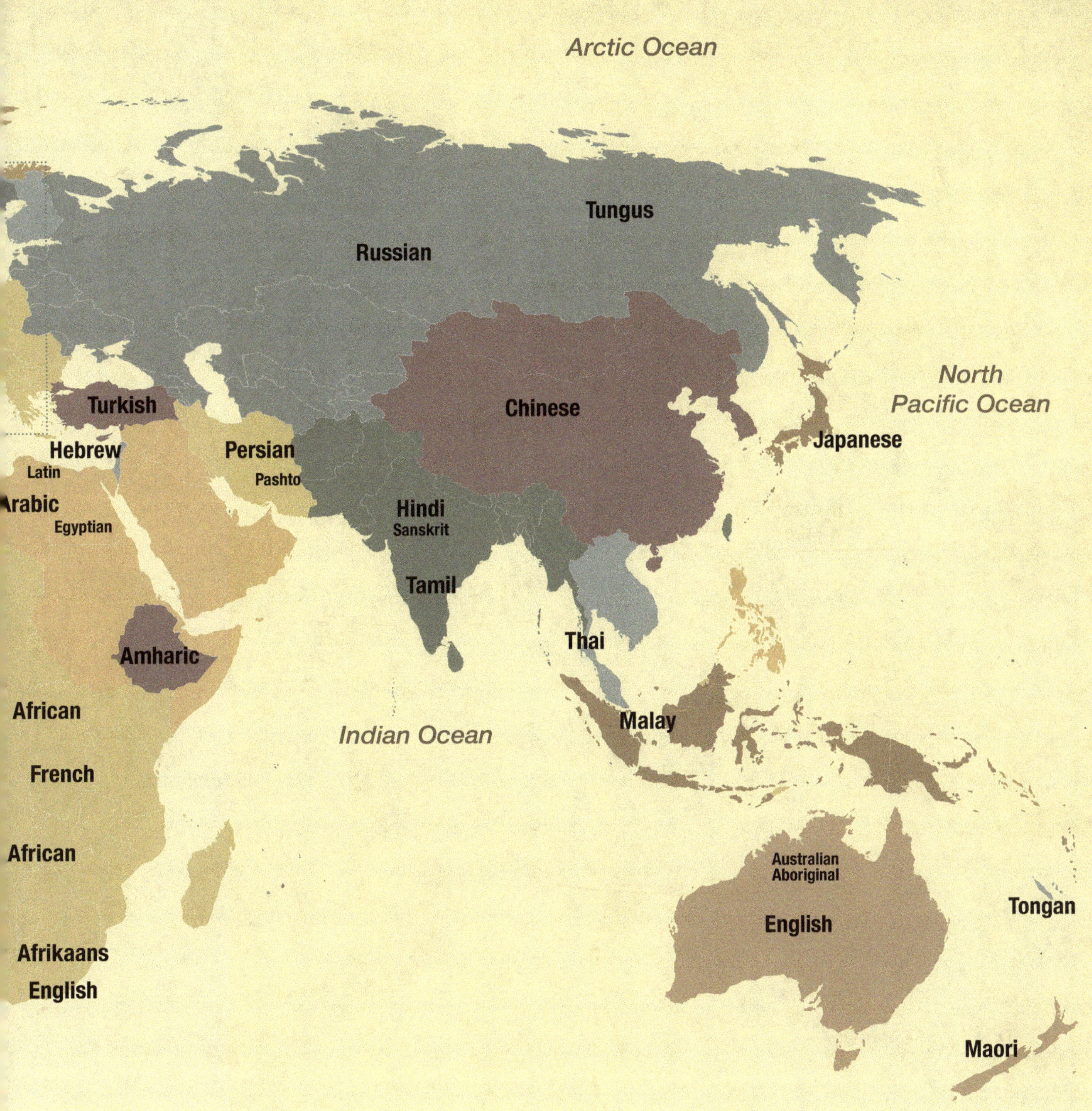
Arctic Ocean
Tungus
Russian
North
Pacific Ocean
Turkish
Chinese
Japanese
Hebrew
Latin
Persian
Pashto
rabic
Egyptian
Hindi
Sanskrit
Tamil
Thai
Amharic
African
Malay
Indian Ocean
French
African
Australian
Aboriginal
English
Tongan
Afrikaans
English
Maori
Southern Ocean

Norwegian
Old Norse
Finnish
Swedish
Old Norse
Scottish
Danish
Old Norse
Irish
British English
Welsh
Old English
Middle English
Dutch
German
S l a v i c
Y i d d i s h
Frankish
G y p s y
French
Hungarian
Romanian
Latin
Latin
Latin
S l a v i c
Italian
Latin
Spanish
Portuguese
Greek

Glossary

African a group of native languages, a number of which remain the primary language spoken in large parts of the continent.

Afrikaans one of 11 official languages of South Africa, developed by 17th century Dutch settlers to the area. Today it is spoken by about 7 million South Africans, the majority of them people of color. While it borrowed quite a few African words, it is primarily a form of Dutch.

American (or **American English**) the English spoken and written in the United States. *French fries* is an American English term while the British call these *chips*. An American parks a car in a *parking lot* while the British term is *car park*. American English is part of Modern English, but it is distinctly American.

American Indian See **North American Indian.**

American Spanish the Spanish spoken in North America. It includes, for example, Mexican Spanish, Puerto Rican Spanish and the Spanish spoken in parts of the United States like California, New Mexico, Arizona and Texas.

Amharic the language of the African country of Ethiopia.

Ancient Greek the language spoken by the people of Greece starting around 3000 BCE. Between 700 BCE and 500 CE it spread and was widely spoken throughout the Mediterranean area. Today it is the world's oldest recorded language still in use. Many words in English and other languages have their roots in Ancient Greek. Examples of words acquired from Greek are *democracy* (from *demos* people + *kratos* power) and *planet* (meaning "wanderer," as the Greeks saw planets as wandering stars.)

Angles (AN GULZ) a people from parts of what we now call Denmark and Germany who invaded Britain about 450 CE. Their spoken language, mixed with Saxon, became Anglo-Saxon, the earliest version of English. The name "England" comes from Old English *Engla land*, meaning "land of the Angles."

Anglo-French same as **Anglo-Norman.**

Anglo-Irish the version of English spoken in Ireland. It is also known as Irish English.

Anglo-Norman a version of Norman French spoken by the ruling class in England from 1066 to about 1450 CE. This ruling class consisted of Normans, people from other areas of France and some Anglo-Saxons. Anglo-Norman was the language used in the king's court, in courts of law, literature, schools and universities, and trade. Many Anglo-Norman words became part of English. *Apprentisse* (apprentice), *grammeire* (book learning) and *were* (war) are examples of Anglo-Norman words.

Anglo-Saxon See **Old English.**

Arabic the language spoken throughout the Arab world, which includes the Middle East and most of northern Africa. Spoken by more than 200 million people, it is the official language of more than 20 countries. Arabic was first written down in the 4th century CE. It is written and read from right to left.

Arawakan (AR UH WOK UN) a large family of native languages of South and Central America, including the Caribbean.

Australian Aboriginal a group of over 250 languages spoken by the native (aboriginal) people of Australia before English was established there during the 1800s. Only a few of these native languages survive today.

Examples of Native Australian words are *wallawani* (hello), *billabong* (lake), and *yakka* (hard work).

Aztec, Aztec Indian, Aztecan See **Nahuatl.**

BCE an abbreviation for *Before Common Era*. BCE following a date means it was that many years before the Common Era which starts in year 1 with the birth of Christ.

back-formation forming a new word by removing things that look like prefixes or suffixes. So the word *looks like* it is the base of another word, but it was really formed *from* that word. For example, *peddle* is a back-formation of the word *peddler* because the word *peddler* came into existence before *peddle.*

blend a word formed by combining parts of other words. *Smog* is a blend made by combining *smoke* and *fog*. *Brunch* is a blend made from *breakfast* and *lunch.*

Brazilian Indian Tupinambá (TOO PIN NAM BAH), an extinct Native American language of Brazil's Tupinambá or Tupi people.

Britons the ancient inhabitants of Britain.

Canadian Indian a group of about 70 Native American languages of Canada. In Canada, Native Americans are generally referred to as First People or Native Canadians.

British (or **British English**) the English spoken and written in the United Kingdom. Some of its vocabulary is different from the English spoken in other places. Americans, for example, open the *hood* of their cars while in Britain they open the *bonnet*. British English is part of Modern English, but it is distinctly British.

CE an abbreviation for *Common Era,* it begins with the birth of Christ, which is designated as Year 1.

Celtic (KEL TIC) a group of mostly extinct languages named for the Celtic people who controlled much of Europe from about 800 to 50 BCE. Celtic is still spoken in a few places, mainly Wales, Ireland and Scotland.

cf. short for Latin *confer*, which means "compare." In a derivation, cf. directs one to consider other information as well and points to where it can be found.

Chinese a group of similar languages spoken by the people of China. While somewhat different from one another, they share a common system of writing, one in which each word has its own symbol. About 1.2 billion people speak a variety of Chinese. Some examples of Chinese words are *shu* (book), *mao* (cat) and *shengri* (birthday.) Note that these are written using the English alphabet and would look very different written in Chinese.

colloquial found in informal, conversational speech or writing. From Latin *colloquium* conversation.

Danish (or **Modern Danish)** the language spoken today by the people of Denmark. It is descended from *Old Norse.* Examples of Danish words are *dansk* (Danish), *tak* (thank you) and *posthus* (post office.)

derivation a brief explanation of where a word comes from. In addition to a word's origin, a derivation may also give some history that shows how it evolved into its current form.

dialect a form of a particular language used by a specific area or group. It can differ in pronunciation, grammar, or vocabulary from the regular language. An example would be a Southern dialect where people might say "you all" or "y'all" instead of "you," or "hold your horses!" instead of "stop!"

diminutive (dim.) a word or name with an added beginning or ending that indicates smallness or, occasionally, affection or familiarity. The words *droplet*, *minivan, kitty, duckling* and *kitchenette* are all diminutives.

Dutch the language of the Netherlands where it is spoken by about 30 million people. Dutch is closely related to both English and German. All three are descended from the same parent language. Examples of Dutch words are *goedenmorgan* (good morning), *honderd* (one hundred) and *bedankt* (thank you.)

echoic See **imitative.**

Egyptian (or **ancient Egyptian**) an extinct language that was spoken in Egypt throughout several different periods, from roughly 3000 BCE to 1600 CE. It was one of the first written languages. Around 640 CE, Egypt was conquered by the Arabs and the use of Arabic spread. Around 1600 Arabic became its official language, so today Egyptians speak a variety of Arabic.

Englisc (ANG LISH) the Old English (Anglo-Saxon) name for the culture and language brought to Britain by the invading Angles and Saxons. The earliest form of English, Englisc developed and changed over a period of several hundred years, from about 450 to 1100 CE, gradually becoming what we now refer to as Middle English.

Eskimo a family of Native American languages spoken in Alaska, parts of Canada and Greenland. The two main Eskimo languages are Yupik and Inuit. Examples of Eskimo words are *akiak* (brave), *denilgi* (moose) and *qimmig* (dog.)

Finnish one of two official languages of Finland (the other being Swedish.) It is related to Hungarian. Although sometimes Finland is thought of as a Scandinavian country, its language is very different from the Scandinavian languages used in Denmark, Norway and Sweden. Some examples of Finnish words are *kiitos* (thank you), *hyvää huomenta* (good morning), *anteeksi* (sorry) and *kyllä* (yes.)

Frankish language of the Franks, one of the Germanic tribes who conquered the Roman territory of Gaul (now France) about 400 CE. France gets its name from the Franks.

French the language spoken in France and 28 other countries around the world. It originated around 700 CE and is mostly based on Latin. Nearly half the words in the French vocabulary are identical or similar to English words, for example *chef, salade* and *omelette.* Other examples of French words are *adieu* (good-bye), *avoir* (have), *autre* (other) and *faire* (make or do.)

Gaelic See **Irish.**

German the language spoken today in Germany, Austria and parts of Switzerland. It originated around 750 CE and is closely related to English and Dutch, as they all share the same parent language. Examples of German words are *Deutsch* (the German language), *Jahr* (yar) meaning year and *Morgen* (morning). (Nouns are always capitalized in written German.)

Germanic a group of languages widely spoken around Europe starting at the beginning of the Common Era by tribes we now refer to as Germanic. The Angles and the Saxons were Germanic tribes, and their languages were from the Germanic group. English, German, Dutch and the Scandinavian languages of Norwegian, Danish and Swedish are all descended from Germanic languages.

Greenland Eskimo (more commonly called **Greenlandic**) the native Eskimo language spoken by about 60,000 people in Greenland. (See **Eskimo.**) Examples of Greenlandic are the words *qanik* (snow in the air), *unnugu* (tonight) and *immuk* (milk.)

Greek See **Ancient Greek.**

Gypsy (or **Romani**) a group of languages spoken by the Romani or Gypsy people. Originally from India, the Romani mostly live in Europe. They are unique in that they have a culture and a history, but no country. Examples of Romani words are *chauv* (child), *mush* (man), *shav* (run) and *yog* (fire.) (Note: the term Gypsy is sometimes considered derogatory but is usually the most commonly recognized name for the Romani people.)

Hebrew Modern Hebrew is the official language of the country of Israel in the Middle East. The name *Hebrew* derives from the name for the people of ancient Israel. Ancient Hebrew was spoken from about 1000 BCE until 400 CE and is the language of the Old Testament (the first section of *The Bible*). It is a Semitic language, which means it is one of several related languages spoken throughout the Middle East and parts of Africa. Arabic is probably the best-known Semitic language. Some examples of Hebrew words are *shalom* (peace), *imma* (mommy) and *ivrit* (the modern Hebrew language.)

High German the standard version of spoken and written German. It is the language used in central and southern Germany, Austria and parts of Switzerland. The term "high" comes from the fact that the central and southern parts of Germany are covered with hills and mountains, so they are "higher" than the northern part of the country. (compare Low German)

Hindi the language spoken in the northern part of India. It is one of the most commonly spoken languages in the world. Much of Hindi comes from Sanskrit. Some examples of Hindi words are *namaste* (good-bye), *danyavāda* (thank you) and *hān* (yes).

Hungarian called *Magyar* in Hungarian, is the national language of Hungary in Eastern Europe. It is related to Finnish, and has borrowed a number of words from German, Slavic and Turkish. Examples of Hungarian words are *ma* (today), *holnap* (tomorrow), *kicsi* (small) and *nevet* (laugh.)

imitative words that are created in imitation of a sound. The word *hiss,* for example, is a close imitation of the sound a snake makes. The word *clang* imitates the sound of metal hitting metal, as in a ringing bell.

Icelandic the national language of Iceland. Descended from Old Norse, written Icelandic has not changed much in the last thousand years. Some examples of Icelandic words are *epli* (apple), *steinn* (stone), *bók* (book) and *hús* (house).

Indo-European a language spoken by ancient settlers of the eastern part of Europe about 3000 BCE. About 2500 BCE these settlers began spreading out into other parts of the world. Some went towards what is now India, some into what is now Greece and Turkey, and some into Europe. The name that has been given to these people, and their language, is Indo-European. This is because they settled in areas from India to Europe. In places where they settled, the Indo-European language became a foundation for a number of modern languages, such as German, English, Italian, French, Spanish and Russian. Now, about half the world's people speak a language descended from Indo-European.

Irish (also known as **Gaelic**) the traditional language of Ireland, spoken by most Irish until the 1700s when English began to take over. Some examples of Irish words are *im* (butter), *uisce* (water), *bui* (yellow) and *feoil* (meat).

Irish English the English language as it is spoken in Ireland today. It is also called Anglo-Irish.

Italian the language spoken in Italy. It is the language still the most like Latin, from which it is descended. Some examples of Italian words are *caio* (hello or goodbye), *felicita* (happiness) and *amore* (love).

Jamaican a language spoken by the people of Jamaica, which they call Patois. It is based in English with some African words mixed in. Even though English is the official language of Jamaica, most Jamaicans speak Patois. Example words are *bredda* (brother), *fren'* (friend) and *cyar* (car.)

Japanese the national language of Japan, spoken by roughly 130 million people. An Asian language that has been around since roughly 700 CE, it has a number of words borrowed from Chinese. Some examples of Japanese words are *Nihon* (Japan), *ashita* (tomorrow), *gakkou* (school) and *susshin* (hometown).

Late Latin a form of Latin spoken and written by administrators and educated citizens during the last part of the Roman Empire from about 200 to 600 CE.

Latin a language that was spoken, beginning about 700 BCE, by an ancient people who lived in Italy. They inhabited an area they called Latium, close to what we now know as Rome. Gradually their tongue, Latin, became the main language of Italy. As the Roman Empire expanded, Latin spread. The Latin spoken before the days of the Roman Empire is called "Old Latin." Latin as it was spoken and written by the literate class (educated writers, poets, historians and so on) in the days of the Roman Empire is called "Classical Latin" and this is what is usually referred to as simply Latin. The everyday speech of the same period is often called "Vulgar Latin."

Louisiana French versions of French that are mainly spoken in southern parts of the state of Louisiana. It has words from French as well as English, Native American, Spanish and African. *Padna* (friend), *beaucoup* (a lot), and *Tante* (aunt).

Low German the version of German spoken in the lower, flatter coastal lands found in the northern part of Germany. (compare High German)

Malay a language spoken by roughly 300 million people across Indonesia and Malaysia, Singapore and parts of Thailand and the Philippines. English has a number of words that have come from Malay, words like *gong, gecko* and *ketchup.* Some common Malay words are *membaca* (read), *gambar* (picture), *haiwan* (animal) and *kerja* (work).

Maori (MAO REE) a native language of New Zealand and one of three official languages of the country. Examples of Maori words are *haka* (a Maori dance), *moana* (sea), *tamariki* (children) and *aroha* (love).

Medieval (MID EE VUL) **period** (or **Middle Ages**) occurred in Europe from about 470 to 1450 CE, beginning with the defeat of the Roman Empire. Invading tribes from Northern Europe caused great destruction, and much of the learning and art of early Greece and Rome was lost to western Europe for centuries. The term *medieval* comes from Latin *medium* middle and *aevum* age.

Medieval Latin the form of Latin in use during the Middle Ages, from about 600 to 1500 CE. It was the language of the Roman Catholic Church. (In the Middle Ages nearly all inhabitants of western Europe were followers of this religion.) It was also the language of learning, and the first books printed in Europe were in Medieval Latin.

Mexican Spanish the Spanish spoken in Mexico and parts of the United States. Spanish was originally carried to Mexico in the 1500s by the Spanish conquistadores, and there it gradually mixed with words from Native American languages of the area. An example of a Mexican Spanish word is *guacamole* from Native American *ahuacatl* (avocado) + *mōlli* (sauce). Other examples are *macho* (manly), *bronco* (not tamed, wild) and *chicle* (gum, also originally Native American.)

Middle in the history of a language, describes the period between the **Old** or earliest version of the language and its **Modern** or most current version. For example, Middle English was spoken between Old English (450 to 1100 CE) and Modern English (1550 CE forward).

Middle Dutch the version of Dutch spoken in the Netherlands from about 1100 to 1500 CE.

Middle English the language spoken in England from 1100 to 1550 CE.

Middle French the language spoken in France from approximately 1250 to 1500 CE.

Middle High German the version of German used in the mountainous southern area of Germany from about 1100 to 1500 CE.

Middle Low German the version of German used in the lowlands of Germany from about 1100 to 1500 CE.

Modern in the history of a language, refers to its most recent version, the one currently in use.

Modern English English as it has been spoken and written from about 1550 until the present. When books first began to be printed in the 1400s, agreement had to be reached as to what written English should look like. The spelling, writing and grammar that was decided on at that time continues, for the most part, to this day.

Modern Latin (or **New Latin**) the version of Latin in use from about 1500 on. Latin was revived during the Renaissance, and most of the original scientific works written at that time were in Modern (New) Latin. An example is Galileo's 1610 work *Siderius Nuncias* (Starry Message) describing the first scientific observations made with a telescope. Much of our scientific vocabulary is Modern Latin. For example, the names of all the bones of the body, the scientific name for the crow (*corvus),* and the bumblebee (*bombus),* are all Modern Latin.

Nahuatl (NAH WAH TUL) the Native American language of the Aztec people, whose empire flourished from about 1300 to 1500 in what is now Mexico. Versions of Nahuatl are still spoken in about half the Mexican states. Here are some examples of Nahuatl words: *coyotl* (coyote), *āhuacatl* (avocado) and *tomatl* (tomato).

Native American a large group of languages that includes all the native and first people languages of North, Central, and South America, including Canada, the Caribbean, Alaska and Greenland. Before Europeans arrived, there were thousands of native languages spoken throughout the Americas. Several had systems of writing. Sometimes settlers learned native languages. At other times, they ignored or suppressed them in favor of their own. By the 1800s, English, French, Spanish, Dutch and Portuguese had become the main languages of the Americas. Many Native American words have been absorbed into English. (For examples of some Native American languages see **Brazilian Indian, Arawakan, Eskimo, Greenland Eskimo, Nahuatl, Taino, Quechua.**)

nautical from the speech of sailors.

Nordic See **Scandinavia, Scandinavian.**

Norman (or **Norman French**) a variety of French spoken in Normandy, where William the Conqueror came from. When he and his Norman army invaded England, they brought the Norman language. It mixed with some Anglo-Saxon and eventually became the variety of French spoken in England. (See **Anglo-Norman.**) Norman is still spoken in parts of Normandy. Examples of Norman words are *creire* (believe), *feis* (time) and *gaumbe* (leg).

Norman invasion the Normans were from Normandy, a region of France across the channel from Britain. In 1066, under the leadership of William of Normandy (also known as William the Conqueror), they defeated the English army. William became king and the Normans became the ruling class of England.

Norse the Norse people, also called Norsemen, or Vikings. *Norse* meant *north* in their language, which we call Old Norse. Norsemen came from what is now Denmark, Norway and Sweden. They invaded the northern parts of England beginning around 800 CE. See **Old Norse**.

North American Indian the large group of Native American languages of the United States (including Alaska), Canada, Mexico and Greenland. Examples of North American Indian languages are Navajo, Cherokee, Seneca, Oneida, Nahuatl, Eskimo and Greenland Eskimo.

Norwegian a main language spoken and written in Norway where it is an official language, along with Swedish and Danish. Norwegian is descended from Old Norse. Examples of Norwegian words are *vann* (water), *navn* (name), *verdensrommet* (outer space), and *blad* (leaf).

obsolete (obs.) words that are no longer actively used in the spoken and written versions of a language.

Old used to designate the earliest written version of a language. For example, Old English is the name given to the earliest version of English.

Old Danish a version of Old Norse, used from about 800 to 1500 CE. The Danish language used today (Modern Danish) is descended from this particular form of Old Norse.

Old English (or **Anglo-Saxon**) the language spoken in Britain between 450 and 1100 CE. Brought from Europe by the invading Angle and Saxon tribes, it was the first English to be spoken. A fairly simple but lively and descriptive language, it had a lot of short, punchy words, thousands of which we still use. *Bridd* (bird), *fox, cild* (child) and *hamor* (hammer) are examples.

Old French the earliest version of French, spoken from about 1000–1400 CE.

Old High German the earliest version of German in use in the mountainous southern area of Germany from about 700 to 1100 CE.

Old Irish (or **Old Gaelic**) the earliest form of Irish, used from roughly 600 to 900 CE. Examples of Old Irish words are *son* (sound), *long* (ship), *derc* (dierk) *hole* and *marb* (dead),

Old Italian the earliest version of Italian, spoken from about 1000 until the mid-1500s CE.

Old Latin (or **Early Latin**) the earliest version of Latin, spoken until about 75 BCE. See **Latin**.

Old Low German (or **Old Saxon**) the earliest version of German spoken in the low, flat coastal area of northern Germany up to about 1100 CE. Old Low German and Old Saxon are two names used for the same language.

Old Norman French the French language spoken in Normandy around the time of the Norman invasion. See **Norman invasion**.

Old Norse the language spoken by the people of Scandinavia (now Norway, Sweden, Denmark and Iceland) from about 600 to 1400 CE. Old Norse was the language of the Vikings. Modern Norwegian, Swedish, Danish and Icelandic are all descended from it. As the Vikings took over parts of northern England, a number of Old Norse words were borrowed into Old English. Some examples of Old Norse words are *geta* (get), *taka* (take), *vanta* (want) and *hvirfla* (whirl).

Old Persian the earliest version of the Persian language, used up until about 300 BCE. See **Persian**.

Old Saxon See **Old Low German, Saxon**.

Pashto the language of the people of Afghanistan. Examples of Pashto words are *zel* (one hundred), *angresi* (English) and *manana* (thank you).

Persian known to those who speak it as **Fārsī** (FAR SEE), Persian is the official language of Iran, Afghanistan and some other surrounding areas. It gets its name from ancient Persia which we know today as Iran. Some examples of Persian words are *salam* (hello), *parande*

(bird), *bozorg* (big) and *barg* (leaf). Note that these example words are written using the English alphabet, which makes them look very different than they would if written in Persian.

Phoenicians ancient traders who lived across the Mediterranean from the Greeks. They had an early alphabet that the Greeks used as a basis for theirs.

Portuguese the official language of Portugal, Brazil and several African countries. One of the most commonly spoken languages in the world, it has about 340 million speakers. Some examples of Portuguese words are *ano* (year), *rir* (laugh), *minuto* (minute) and *bonito* (beautiful).

Quechua (KETCH WUH) a family of related native languages spoken by about 9 million people in the Andean mountains of Peru, Ecuador, Colombia, Bolivia, Chile and Argentina. Quechua originated in Peru around 500 BCE and today is the most widely spoken surviving native language of the western hemisphere. The words *llama* and *puma* come to English from Quechua. Other Quechuan words are *yaku* (water), *wasi* (home), *pachu* (earth) and *killa* (moon).

Renaissance a period of the 15th and 16th centuries marked by a revival in western Europe of Greek and Latin learning. A person of the Renaissance was considered educated if they knew how to read and write Latin and Greek, resulting in many Greek and Latin words entering English.

Romance languages the languages descended from Vulgar Latin, the everyday language spoken during the days of the Roman Empire. We get the term "romance" from the Vulgar Latin word *romanice,* which meant "in the Roman tongue." The most widely spoken of the Romance languages are Spanish, Portuguese, French, Italian and Romanian.

Romani See **Gypsy**.

Romanian a language spoken by about 25 million people in Romania, a country in the Balkan Peninsula. It is descended from Vulgar Latin. Some examples of Romanian are *Salut* (hello), *la multi ani* (happy birthday) and *unu, doi, trei* (one, two, three.)

root a word or part of a word used as a base for making other words, and which has no added parts. The word "certain" is a root found in the words *uncertain* and *certainly.*

Russian the language spoken in Russia and some of its surrounding areas. One of the most widely spoken languages in Europe, it has its own alphabet. Some words that have traveled from Russian into English are *cosmonaut* and *mammoth.* Some examples of Russian words (written using the English alphabet) are *preevyet* (hello), *zvat* (call) and *peet* (drink).

Sanskrit an ancient language of India, dating back to about 1500 BCE, or even earlier. It is the language of Hinduism and the parent of a number of languages now spoken in India.

Saxon the name given to the language spoken by the ancient Saxon tribes, some of whom invaded Britain and some of whom remained in part of what is now Germany. Those that remained in Germany are sometimes referred to as Old Saxons, while those that invaded Britain came to be known as Anglo-Saxons.

Scandinavia the region of northern Europe that includes Denmark, Norway and Sweden. Because they have cultures similar to those countries, Finland and Iceland are often referred to as part of Scandinavia. The larger group, including Finland and Iceland, are properly referred to as the Nordic countries.

Scandinavian (also called **Nordic**) not to be confused with the Nordic countries, a group of similar languages, all descended from Old Norse, consisting of Danish, Swedish, Norwegian and Icelandic. The languages are similar enough that speakers of Danish,

Swedish and Norwegian can generally understand one another.

Scots the native language of the southern lowland parts of Scotland.

Scottish (or **Scottish English**) is the version of Modern English spoken in Scotland.

Scottish Gaelic a native language spoken in the northern parts of Scotland (the Highlands) starting around 1200 CE. It developed from Irish Gaelic but today it is a distinctly separate language.

Semitic (SUH MIT IK) refers to several related languages spoken throughout the Middle East and parts of Africa. Arabic is the most widely spoken Semitic language.

slang used to describe informal or very informal language, more often spoken than written. Examples of American slang are *no worries, chill out, slay,* and *epic!*

Slavic a group of languages spoken in most of the central and eastern parts of Europe, a number of the Balkan countries, and parts of Asia. They include languages like those spoken in Russia, Ukraine, Poland, Croatia, Bulgaria, Slovakia and the Czech Republic.

Spanish a language that originated in what is now Spain. Descended from Vulgar Latin, it arrived to the Americas in the late 1400s. It is now most widely spoken throughout the Americas. Examples of Spanish words are *chica, chico* (girl, boy), *amigo* (friend), *nuevo* (new) and *feliz* (happy.)

Swedish the Scandinavian language spoken in Sweden. It is descended from Old Norse. Some examples of Swedish words are *tack* (thank you), *komma* (come), *vatten* (water) and *Svenska* (Swedish).

Swiss French a version of French spoken in Switzerland that is quite similar to the French spoken in France. The main languages spoken in Switzerland are Swiss forms of French, German and Italian.

Taino a Native American language spoken by the Taino people who lived throughout much of the Caribbean. When Columbus and the Spanish arrived in the New World, it was the Taino they met first. Some examples of Taino words are *inaru* (woman), *canoa* (canoe), *hamaca* (hammock), *huracan* (hurricane), *guey* (sun) and *ni* (water.)

Tamil: a language spoken by the Tamil people of southern India and Sri Lanka. It is an ancient language over two thousand years old, yet is still spoken by roughly 75 million people. It has its own alphabet. Examples of Tamil words (written using the English alphabet) are *talai* (head), *itayam* (heart), *kai* (hand) and *vitu* (house).

Thai the national language of Thailand. Thai has its own alphabet. Examples of Thai words (written using the English alphabet) are *sawa dee* (hello), *ahan* (food), *hong* (room) and *nam* (water.)

Tongan the national language of the Kingdom of Tonga, a group of islands in the South Pacific partway between Australia and the United States, and part of Oceania. Some examples of Tongan words are *taha* (one), *tohi* (book), *faiako* (teacher) and *liuaki* (goodbye.)

Tungus (or **Tungusic**) a family of native languages still spoken by about 75,000 people in eastern Siberia and Manchuria.

Turkish a language spoken in Turkey, Greece, Cyprus and other nearby countries. Until 1928, Turkish was written with the Arabic alphabet, but it is now written using the same alphabet used for English. Some examples of Turkish words are *türk* (Turkish), *merhaba* (hello), *mutluluk* (happiness), *evet* (yes) and *güle güle* (goodbye.)

ultimately (ult.) means the point beyond which further investigation in a word's origins is not possible.

US a designation used in some dictionaries for variations and additions to English developed in the United States.

variant (var.) a different spelling, pronunciation, or form of the same word.

vernacular the everyday language spoken by a people in a particular region, often considered informal, not broadly accepted or used.

Vikings a seafaring people from what we now call Sweden, Norway and Denmark, the Vikings were excellent craftsmen and traders as well as raiders. From about 800–1000 CE they invaded and settled in northern Britain and other areas of Europe. The language they spoke was Old Norse, and a number of Viking words are still part of the English we speak today.

Vulgar Latin meaning "common speech," Vulgar Latin was the everyday Latin spoken by the various inhabitants of the Roman Empire, which included the common folk of many Roman provinces and members of the Roman Army. Latin *vulgaris* meant "common, everyday." A number of European languages are descended from Vulgar Latin.

Welsh the native language of Wales, descended from the language of the ancient Britons who left Britain after the Angles and Saxons invaded. It is spoken today by about twenty percent of the Welsh people, while a form of English called "Welsh English" is spoken there as well. Some examples of Welsh: *Cymraeg* (the Welsh language), *dyn* (human being), *plentyn* (child), *anifail* (animal), *aderyn* (bird) and *deilen* (leaf.)

word family a group of words with the same root. In some dictionaries a derivation is provided at the root word and is not then repeated for every word in the family.

Yiddish a vernacular language based on German that has been spoken by Jewish people for centuries, most particularly in areas of central and eastern Europe and Russia. The literal meaning of Yiddish is "Jewish," and it was called that for a period. It includes words from Hebrew, Slavic, German and other European languages. It is still spoken in a number of Jewish communities today. Examples of Yiddish words are *klutz* (a clumsy person), *kvetch* (complain), *nosh* (snack), *punim* (face) and *spiel* (a long speech or tale).

If you like the *Derivation Dictionary,* we invite you to explore our wide selection of books and learning materials for students of all ages at heronbooks.com.

Using the Dictionary
Workbooks 1 & 2

Fun exploring dictionaries
Ages 6-8

Animal Kingdom
book & flash cards

The beauty and wonder of animals
Ages 7-9

Working with Grammar
& Workbook

Grammar made simple
Ages 13 and up

Math Essentials
Finding & Filling the Gaps

Math repair through simple algebra
Ages 13 and up

www.ingramcontent.com/pod-product-compliance
Lightning Source LLC
LaVergne TN
LVHW081256100826
845148LV00005B/892

* 9 7 8 0 8 9 7 3 9 2 0 6 8 *